SCHAUM'S OUTLINE OF

THEORY AND PROBLEMS

of

ADVANCED
ACCOUNTING

•

by

JOSEPH A. WISEMAN, Ph.D., CPA

Professor of Accounting
Iona College

and

JAMES A. CASHIN, M.B.A., CPA

Emeritus Professor of Accounting
Hofstra University

•

SCHAUM'S OUTLINE SERIES

McGRAW-HILL BOOK COMPANY

New York   St. Louis   San Francisco   Auckland   Bogotá   Guatemala   Hamburg   Johannesburg
Lisbon   London   Madrid   Mexico   Montreal   New Delhi   Panama   Paris
San Juan   São Paulo   Singapore   Sydney   Tokyo   Toronto

JOSEPH A. WISEMAN is currently Professor of Accounting at Iona College, New Rochelle, New York. Dr. Wiseman has been a Certified Public Accountant for more than forty years and a teacher of accounting for more than thirty years, and is the author of numerous articles on accounting theory and practice. He holds his B.B.A. and M.B.A. from Baruch College, where for many years he taught accounting at both the graduate and undergraduate levels, and his Ph.D. is from the New York University Graduate School of Business Administration.

JAMES A. CASHIN is Emeritus Professor of Accounting at Hofstra University, where he was formerly Chairman of the Accounting Department. He is a coauthor of many accounting textbooks, including several Schaum's Outlines in accounting, and he is Editor-in-Chief of the *Handbook for Auditors*. Professor Cashin is a Certified Public Accountant and a Certified Internal Auditor. He holds a B.S. in Accounting from the University of Georgia and an M.B.A. from New York University, and has taught at the Graduate School of the City University of New York and at New York University.

Schaum's Outline of Theory and Problems of
ADVANCED ACCOUNTING

1 2 3 4 5 6 7 8 9 10 11 12 13 14 15 16 17 18 19 20 SH SH 8 7 6 5 4 3 2

ISBN 0-07-071138-0

Sponsoring Editor, Paul Farrell
Editing Supervisor, Sylvia Warren
Production Manager, Nick Monti

Library of Congress Cataloging in Publication Data

Wiseman, Joseph A.
  Schaum's outline of theory and problems of
advanced accounting.
  (Schaum's outline series)
  Includes index.
  1. Accounting—Problems, exercises, etc.
I. Cashin, James A. II. Title. III. Title: Outline
of theory and problems of advanced accounting.
IV. Series.
HF5661.W66   657'.046'076   81-8305
ISBN 0-07-071138-0   AACR2

Preface

This outline was written primarily for the advanced accountancy student, who is frequently overwhelmed by the extensive detail found in most standard textbooks. The goal of this book is to emphasize and clarify fundamental concepts through a series of progressive solved problems in each chapter. The topics include those which are generally covered in a one-semester advanced course in undergraduate and graduate accounting programs.

The numerous illustrations and solved problems, including extensive journal entries and worksheets, should be helpful to students, CPA candidates, and practitioners who may wish to review advanced topics in accounting. Moreover, three sample examinations have been included for readers who wish to test themselves. These examinations may also be used for review purposes.

We acknowledge an indebtedness to generations of students who frequently served as guinea pigs for much of the material contained herein. We also wish to thank Professor Calvin Engler of Iona College, who made valuable suggestions regarding the material on pooling of interests and foreign transactions. We do, however, take full responsibility for any errors or inadequacies which may remain.

The most recent pronouncements of the Financial Accounting Standards Board and of other authorities have been carefully observed.

Suggestions and constructive comments with respect to the material contained herein will be most welcome.

JOSEPH A. WISEMAN
JAMES A. CASHIN

September, 1981

Contents

CONTENTS

Chapter 7 CONSOLIDATED STATEMENTS—INTERCOMPANY SALES AND SERVICES **184**

Chapter 8 CONSOLIDATED STATEMENTS—INTERCOMPANY TRANSACTIONS: LONG-TERM ASSETS **207**

Chapter 9 CONSOLIDATED STATEMENTS—INTERCOMPANY TRANSACTIONS: LONG-TERM DEBT **234**

CONTENTS

CONTENTS

Part I

Partnerships and Branch Accounting

The two chapters on partnership accounting constitute a topic which is separate and distinct from the other topics in advanced accounting. Thus, they may be studied at any time.

Four or five decades ago, partnership accounting was a topic generally included in elementary accounting courses. As accounting theory expanded over the decades, partnership accounting was gradually pushed upward into intermediate and later into advanced courses.

For everyday transactions a partnership may be regarded as a collection of sole proprietorships. However, a partnership presents special problems when it comes to the division of profits, limitations on drawings, changes in partners' equities, and the dissolution of the partnership.

Branch accounting is considered by many teachers as a good basis for consolidated statements. Others prefer to treat the combination of home office and branch statements as a separate topic. Chapter 3 has been written so that it may be studied in either sequence.

Chapter 1

Partnerships: Organization and Operation

1.1 INTRODUCTION

A *partnership* is a voluntary association of two or more persons to carry on, as co-owners, a business for profit. Until recently only natural persons could be partners; now, however, many states permit a corporation to be a member of a partnership.

A partnership is easily formed. The partnership agreement may be oral, although it is good business practice to have a written contract which spells out, among other things, the investment of each partner, limitations on drawings, and the division of profits. In many states, the only required filing is that of a fictitious name if one is adopted by the firm.

Most states have adopted the *Uniform Partnership Act* (UPA), which holds each partner responsible for the debts of the partnership and thus gives rise to the view that partners have unlimited liability. In general, each partner has the authority to act for the firm. However, the UPA also provides that a partnership may hold real and personal property in its own name and that liabilities may be owed in the partnership name.

Some states permit *limited partnerships*, in which one or more partners have no liability beyond that amount which they originally invested. Such states usually require that the name and investment contribution of each limited partner be advertised at the time of formation of the partnership. However, even in a limited partnership there must be at least one *general*, or *unlimited*, partner, who may be liable for obligations which cannot be met from partnership assets.

When a partner contributes assets to a firm his or her capital account is increased, but the partner does not retain ownership in such assets. The assets belong to the partnership, and each partner has an undivided equity in all of the assets of the firm. Therefore, if property is contributed by a partner, the assets should be recorded at the fair market value at the date of acquisition by the partnership.

1.2 PARTNERSHIP ACCOUNTING: GENERAL

For accounting purposes a partnership is considered as an entity distinct from the partners. The day-to-day record keeping used by partnerships is similar to that used by sole proprietors up to the point of determining the net income or loss. In partnerships, this net amount is divided among the partners in any agreed fashion. (In some cases partners have not agreed on a division of profit or loss, in which case state laws generally provide that it be divided equally.)

There should be a *capital* account and a *drawing* (or *personal*) account for each partner. Each partner's capital is increased by his share of profits or income and is decreased by his drawings and his share of partnership losses. Of course, a partner's capital account would also be increased by additional investments and would be immediately decreased by any withdrawal of capital.

In general, a partner invests property, time, and effort for the purpose of earning a share of the profits of the firm. The partner is not entitled to compensation for his or her time or for interest on an investment of cash or other property, though such factors may be considered in devising a profit-sharing arrangement. There are, however, situations where a partner may make a loan to the partnership. In such cases, the loan should be segregated in the accounts, and that partner will be entitled to interest from the firm. Such interest should be treated as a financial expense of the business. See Section 1.4.

Loans to or from partners should be separately classified in a balance sheet, as there is the general presumption that they are repayable before capital balances may be withdrawn. On the other hand, capital balances are generally invested for indefinite periods.

Any priority of loans over capital realistically applies only to a going, solvent business. In a subsequent chapter it will be demonstrated that during dissolution, when the legal right of *offset* comes into play, only outside creditors have any meaningful priority.

1.3   DIVISION OF PARTNERSHIP EARNINGS

There is no limit to the variety of plans partners may adopt to divide the profits (income) or losses of a business. No matter what the plan, however, the accounting procedure is the same: At year end, in the partners' respective capital accounts, income is recorded as a *credit* and loss as a *debit*. At the same time, the partners' drawing accounts should be closed by debiting their capital accounts.

Assume that A. Jensen and B. Martin are partners and that each one's weekly withdrawals conform to the partnership agreement. Withdrawals in excess of such stipulated weekly amounts, however, are treated as reductions in capital. In the year 19X6, the books indicate a net income of $37,600. A partial trial balance, as of December 31, 19X6, follows:

	Dr.	Cr.
Income Summary		37,600
A. Jensen, Drawing	10,400	
B. Martin, Drawing	15,600	
A. Jensen, Capital		36,000
B. Martin, Capital		38,000

A summary of the capital accounts for the year 19X6 follows:

A. Jensen, Capital

Date		Dr.	Cr.	Balance
Jan. 1	Balance			20,000
Apr. 1	Investment		28,000	48,000
June 1	Reduction of Capital	12,000		36,000

B. Martin, Capital

Date		Dr.	Cr.	Balance
Jan. 1	Balance			52,000
May 1	Reduction of Capital	6,000		46,000
Oct. 1	Reduction of Capital	8,000		38,000

In each of the following illustrations (see Examples 1 through 10), the drawing accounts should be closed at the end of the year by a journal entry such as the one which follows:

A. Jensen, Capital	10,400	
B. Martin, Capital	15,600	
A. Jensen, Drawing		10,400
B. Martin, Drawing		15,600

To transfer drawing accounts to respective capital accounts.

The foregoing entry has no effect on net income or loss, and therefore it has no effect on the division of profits or of losses.

Several of the more common methods of dividing partnership earnings are described in Examples 1 through 10 below. Each example makes use of the data given on Jensen and Martin on the preceding page.

Equal Division of Profit

If the partnership agreement calls for equal division of profits or if it is silent on this matter, the net income is divided equally.

EXAMPLE 1. Divided equally, Jensen and Martin's $37,600 net income results in $18,800 for each partner. The journal entry is as follows:

Income Summary	37,600	
A. Jensen, Capital		18,800
B. Martin, Capital		18,800

    To divide net income equally.

Profit to Be Divided in an Agreed Ratio

EXAMPLE 2. Assume that the partnership contract calls for the profit to be divided between Jensen and Martin in the ratio of 3 to 2 respectively. This may also be expressed as 3/5 to 2/5 or 60:40. The journal entry is as follows:

Income Summary	37,600	
A. Jensen, Capital		22,560
B. Martin, Capital		15,040

    To divide net income in the ratio of 3:2.

Profits to Be Divided in Ratio of Capitals at Beginning of Year

EXAMPLE 3. Jensen and Martin's capital balances as of January 1 were $20,000 and $52,000, respectively. This relationship may be expressed as a ratio of 20:52, or 5:13. In fraction form the foregoing ratio may be expressed as 5/18 to 13/18. The journal entry to record this division of profits follows:

Income Summary	37,600	
A. Jensen, Capital		
($37,600 × 5/18)		10,444
B. Martin, Capital		
($37,600 × 13/18)		27,156

    To divide the net income in the ratio of capitals as of January 1, 19X6: $20,000 to $52,000.

Profit to Be Divided in Ratio of Average Capital Balances

It is rarely equitable to divide net income according to the ratio of capitals as of the beginning of the year or as of any other particular date. If capital is an important factor in achieving net income, it would be better to give appropriate weight to the length of time that the firm had the use of the respective capital balances.

One method of ascertaining average capital balances is simply to list the partners' respective monthly capital balances, total each list, and divide by 12. A more sophisticated and more widely used method is to determine the number of months in which the capital balance remains unchanged and then to use that number as a multiple of the balance. In this way, each balance is given its proper weight.

EXAMPLE 4. Suppose that the capital balances of Jensen and Martin are summarized in the following way:

Date	Balance	Months Unchanged	Dollar-Month Product	Average Monthly Capitals
		A. Jensen		
Jan. 1	$20,000	3	$ 60,000	
Apr. 1	48,000	2	96,000	
June 1	36,000	7	252,000	
Total		12	$408,000	$34,000
		B. Martin		
Jan. 1	$52,000	4	$208,000	
May 1	46,000	5	230,000	
Oct. 1	38,000	3	114,000	
Total		12	$552,000	$46,000

The ratio of 408:552, from the total dollar-month product for each partner, may be used to divide the earnings accordingly. This ratio (or a reduced form such as 17:23) can then be used to show a division of profits as follows:

Income Summary		37,600
A. Jensen, Capital ($37,600 × 17/40)	15,980	
B. Martin, Capital ($37,600 × 23/40)	21,620	

To divide the net income in the ratio of average capital balances during the year 19X6.

Compare this income summary with the one in Example 3. Obviously, the method used for computing the division of partnership earnings can have a considerable impact on how the earnings will be divided.

Interest Allowed on Average Capitals; Balance in Agreed Ratio

Division of the entire amount of net income in accordance with the average capital ratio may give excessive weight to the capital balances. Therefore, a common approach is to divide one portion of the net income in the ratio of the average capitals and the balance in some other ratio. For example, *interest* may be allowed on the average capital of each partner, and the balance divided equally. In this situation, any amount designated as *interest* is not truly interest expense, but merely a method of allocating a portion of the net income in the average capital ratio.

EXAMPLE 5. Assume that Jensen and Martin have agreed to allow 10 percent interest on average capitals, and thereafter the balance is to be divided equally. The following schedule illustrates the method and the results of carrying out this plan for division of net income amounting to $37,600.

	A. Jensen	B. Martin	Total
Interest at 10% on Average Capitals	$ 3,400	$ 4,600	$ 8,000
Balance Divided Equally	14,800	14,800	29,600
Totals	$18,200	$19,400	$37,600

The journal entry to record the division of net income follows:

Income Summary	37,600	
A. Jensen, Capital		18,200
B. Martin, Capital		19,400

To divide net income in accordance with agreement:
(a) 10% interest on average capitals, and
(b) balance equally.

Many accountants would include the foregoing schedule as part of the explanation so that the details of the division of net income will become a part of the permanent journal entry.

Salary Allowed to a Partner; Balance in Agreed Ratio

Since a partner cannot be an employee of a partnership in which he or she is a partner, any *salary* to a partner should be regarded as a plan which aims to allocate a fixed amount of the partnership net income to one partner. Such an arrangement may be based on time, experience, expertise, or any other factor the partners consider relevant.

EXAMPLE 6. Assume that Jensen is to be allowed a salary of $20,000 per year; the balance of the net income to be divided equally. As in the previous illustrations, the net income for the year is $37,600. The division of the net income is summarized in the following schedule.

	A. Jensen	B. Martin	Total
Salary to Jensen	$20,000		$20,000
Balance Divided Equally	$8,800	8,800	17,600
Totals	$28,800	$8,800	$37,600

The journal entry to record the foregoing division of net income is as follows:

Income Summary	37,600	
A. Jensen, Capital		28,800
B. Martin, Capital		8,800

To divide net income in accordance with agreement:
(a) $20,000 salary to Jensen, and
(b) balance equally.

It is worthwhile to add the foregoing schedule as part of the journal explanation so that one can readily ascertain that the details of the agreement have been carried out.

There are situations where it is thought that the *salary* of a working partner should be charged to manufacturing costs, or included in appropriate expense accounts, in order to yield a better picture of costs and expenses.

EXAMPLE 7. Assume that $20,000 of salary to A. Jensen has been charged to operations during the year. Of course, such salary should be segregated in the accounts because it is not subject to payroll taxes, workers' compensation, or other expenses normally related to true salaries. The salaried partner would have to include this $20,000 as income from the partnership along with other shares of profit.

If the $20,000 salary had been included in the partnership expenses then the remaining profit of $17,600 would be divided equally between A. Jensen and B. Martin. Thus the economic result to the partners would be identical with that in Example 6, which treated the salary to A. Jensen as a division of net income. This fact may be verified in the following recapitulation of the earnings of each partner in the situation where Jensen's salary had been included in partnership expenses.

	A. Jensen	B. Martin	Total
Salary to Jensen	$20,000		$20,000
Net Income Divided Equally	8,800	$8,800	17,600
Total Income	$28,800	$8,800	$37,600

Finally, a partnership cannot divide more net income than the firm has earned.

EXAMPLE 8. Assume that Jensen and Martin had planned on salaries of $20,000 each, and that the net income is only $37,600 before the division of profits is effectuated. In this case the salaries are not expenses on the partnership books. Any attempt to enter a debit of $40,000 to income summary in order to assign the designated salaries of $20,000 to each partner would simply leave a debit balance of $2,400 in the income summary account. This *deficit* in the income summary account would have to be treated in a manner similar to a loss and charged one-half to each partner. These steps are summarized in the following schedule.

	A. Jensen	B. Martin	Total
Salaries to Partners	$20,000	$20,000	$40,000
Resultant "Deficit" in Income Summary Divided Equally	(1,200)	(1,200)	(2,400)
Totals	$18,800	$18,800	$37,600

In view of the fact that the *salary* of each partner is identical, and the balance of the net income (or loss) is divided equally, the result is the same as if the partners had arranged a simple equal division of the net income. (You should compare the foregoing result with that in Example 1.) All other things being equal, it is only the excess of one partner's *salary* over the *salary* of the other partner which could result in a larger amount of net income being assigned to the former partner. In case of a net loss the partner with the larger *salary* would end up with a smaller share of the loss.

Bonus to One Partner; Balance in Agreed Ratio

It may be desirable to give one partner a larger share of the net income than the other one is given, provided there are earnings to divide. In such a case a bonus based on net income would be appropriate.

EXAMPLE 9. Assume that B. Martin is to receive a bonus equal to 20 percent of the net income; the balance to be divided equally. The net income before any division of profits is $37,600. The following schedule shows how the net income should be divided.

	A. Jensen	B. Martin	Total
Bonus to Martin		$ 7,520	$ 7,520
Balance Divided Equally	$15,040	15,040	30,080
Totals	$15,040	$22,560	$37,600

The journal entry to record the division of net income is as follows:

Income Summary	37,600	
A. Jensen, Capital		15,040
B. Martin, Capital		22,560

To record division of net income as per agreement:
(a) 20% to Jensen, and
(b) balance equally.

Bonus to Employee; Balance of Earnings in Agreed Ratio

There are situations where a valuable employee is rewarded with a percentage of the business net income in recognition of superior efforts or for some other business reason. Any compensation to an employee is an expense of the firm and thus reduces the net income available for the partners, who are the owners of the business. Thus it is necessary first to compute a tentative net income on which to base the bonus to the employee. Then, after the bonus expense is computed and entered, the final net income is divided between the partners.

EXAMPLE 10. Assume that R. Van is to receive a bonus of 20 percent of the net income of the partnership, after deducting the bonus as an expense. Also assume that the net income, before the employee bonus, is $37,600. Thus, $37,600 equals 120 percent of the basis of the bonus and the net income which will be available to the partners. The basis for the bonus is $31,333.33 ($37,600 ÷ 1.20), and the bonus will amount to $6,266.67 (20 percent of $31,333.33). After the bonus expense has been entered, the net income of $31,333.33 should be divided among the partners in the agreed ratio.

1.4 LOANS TO AND FROM PARTNERS

Loans by a partner to a partnership and those by a partnership to a partner should be clearly labeled as such in the books of account and should be appropriately classified as such in statements. It is advisable for the partners to have a clear understanding with each other: When property is received from a partner, is it an addition to his or her capital or is it a loan that will be repaid within a stipulated, or limited, time? Loans usually bear interest, so the rate of interest should be understood as well. Interest on a loan by a partner is an expense of the business in the same fashion as interest paid or accrued on loans from outsiders. In analogous fashion, interest earned by the partnership on a loan to a partner is treated as income of the firm.

Assume that C, D, and E are partners who divide profits and losses equally. During 19X7, E loaned $20,000 to the partnership at 7 percent interest for one year. The income statement for the year 19X7, showing the interest expense of $1,400, is as follows:

C, D, and E
Income Statement
Year 19X7

Sales	$234,600	
Cost of Goods Sold	145,000	
Gross Profit		$89,600
Less Operating Expenses:		
Selling	$ 28,000	
General	24,000	
Total Operating Expenses		52,000
Net Operating Income		$37,600
Interest Expense		1,400
Net Income		$36,200

1.5 ADMISSION OF A NEW PARTNER—GENERAL

When a person is admitted to a partnership, a new entity is commenced and the old entity is dissolved. As a practical matter, however, formal dissolution is not always necessary or practical. Frequently the business is carried on with a change or changes only in the equity accounts. As a general rule it is advisable for the partners to draw up a new partnership agreement.

Basically there are two ways by which a new partner may be admitted to an existing partnership: either the new partner purchases all or part of an interest from one or more of the existing partners, or the new partner makes an investment in the firm which increases the net assets and the capital of the partnership. When an interest is purchased from one or more partners, the assets of the firm are generally unchanged, since the consideration usually passes outside of the business.

Occasionally a person may be admitted as a partner without any specific investment. Here, too, it is important that the partnership agreement spell out the division of profits, losses, and other arrangements. Such a partner will usually have a capital balance after the first formal division of profits.

If A and B have been partners for any length of time, it is likely that the net assets (assets minus liabilities) per the firm's books may be worth more or less than the current fair value. As long as A and B continue in business, it is generally considered proper to utilize the historical cost basis with appropriate modifications. If C is to be admitted to the partnership, however, the *current* fair value of the net assets will undoubtedly be the basis for the admission of C.

In some situations the real value of the net assets of a going business is equal to the book value but the firm's business has unusually high earning power. The existing partners would undoubtedly insist that this factor be recognized in determining the amount a new partner must invest. When a business is valued at an amount greater than its book value due to exceptionally high earning power, the excess over the book value is generally referred to as *goodwill*. (It is also possible that the new partner may bring in goodwill attributable to herself or himself.)

In some other situations either the new partner or the existing partners may consider that the potential earning power of the combination is so great that one or the others will pay a bonus in order to effectuate the association.

1.6   ADMISSION OF A PARTNER—PURCHASE OF AN INTEREST

Assume that A. Arthur and B. Brown are partners with capital balances of $15,000 and $25,000 respectively. They share profits and losses equally. C. Charles is to be admitted to the partnership by purchasing an interest from Arthur or Brown or from both. Some of the more common situations will be illustrated in Examples 11 through 15. In each case, it is assumed that the same books will be continued.

Purchase of Interest by Payment to One Partner

EXAMPLE 11. Assume that Charles purchases a one-fifth interest in the partnership and pays $8,000. The entire $8,000 may be paid by Charles directly to Brown. The only entry normally required on the books of the firm is as follows:

Brown, Capital	8,000	
Charles, Capital		8,000

To record the transfer of one-fifth interest in the partnership to Charles, the consideration having passed outside of the business.

Many accountants think that it is preferable to mention the amount of the consideration in the explanation. It is thought that doing so minimizes questions that may arise at a later date concerning the payment of consideration by the new partner.

Purchase of an Interest from More than One Partner

EXAMPLE 12. Assume that Charles purchases a one-fifth interest in the partnership by paying $10,000 to the existing partners, Arthur and Brown. The capital account of Charles should be credited with $8,000 ($\frac{1}{5}$ of $40,000). How much should be transferred from Arthur and from Brown? One logical interpretation is that each of the existing partners will transfer one-fifth of his or her capital to Charles. Ideally, all of the parties would spell out their intentions and put the agreement in writing. If the previous interpretation is followed, Arthur will give up $3,000 ($\frac{1}{5}$ of $15,000), and Brown will give up $5,000 ($\frac{1}{5}$ of $25,000). The general journal entry for this situation is as follows:

Arthur, Capital	3,000	
Brown, Capital	5,000	
Charles, Capital		8,000

To record the transfer of one-fifth interest in the partnership to Charles, the consideration having passed outside of the business.

The next question to be resolved is how the $10,000 which Charles pays should be divided between Arthur and Brown. Arthur and Brown should receive $3,000 and $5,000 respectively for the capital balances given up. The additional $2,000 should be divided in their profit and loss ratio, which in this example is equally. Thus, Arthur and Brown should receive an additional $1,000 each. A recapitulation of the division of the cash received from Charles is shown in the following schedule:

	Arthur	Brown	Total
Capital Balances Transferred	$3,000	$5,000	$ 8,000
Gain on Sale of Partial Interest in the Partnership	1,000	1,000	2,000
Totals	$4,000	$6,000	$10,000

Purchase of an Interest in Profits

EXAMPLE 13. Charles purchases a one-fifth interest in the partnership's profits and losses only, paying $5,000. In this case Charles is not to have a capital account, at least not immediately; the partnership contract should be examined to ascertain the intent of the parties. For the present, no formal journal entry need be made. A pro forma notation should be made in the general journal, and the $5,000 should be divided between Arthur and Brown in their profit-sharing ratio.

Purchase of an Interest at More than Book Value—Goodwill

EXAMPLE 14. Assume that Charles is to purchase a one-fifth interest in the partnership; there is implied (or unrecorded) goodwill of $20,000; other assets and the liabilities of the partnership are accepted at book values. Thus, goodwill is an additional asset which should be recognized prior to the admission of Charles. Since the goodwill existed prior to the admission of Charles, it is deemed to have been created by the efforts of Arthur and Brown, and is shared by them in their profit-sharing ratio.

The general journal entry to record the goodwill is as follows:

Goodwill	20,000	
Arthur, Capital		10,000
Brown, Capital		10,000

To recognize goodwill created by Arthur and Brown prior to the admission of Charles.

The effect of the foregoing journal entry is to increase the capital balances of Arthur and Brown to $25,000 and $35,000 respectively. When the goodwill of $20,000 is added to the other net assets of $40,000, the total assets on which Charles should base his payment amounts to $60,000. Therefore, Charles should pay $12,000 ($\frac{1}{5}$ of $60,000). In the following journal entry for the admission of Charles, it is assumed that Arthur and Brown each gives up one-fifth of his or her revised capital balance:

Arthur, Capital ($\frac{1}{5}$ of $25,000)	5,000	
Brown, Capital ($\frac{1}{5}$ of $35,000)	7,000	
Charles, Capital		12,000

To record the admission of Charles to a one-fifth interest, the consideration having passed outside of the business.

Purchase of Interest at More than Book Value—Bonus

EXAMPLE 15.   Assume that Charles is to purchase a one-fifth interest in the partnership; there is implied (or unrecorded) goodwill of $20,000; other assets and the liabilities are agreed to be worth book value. These data are similar to those in the previous case, except that the parties are reluctant to enter goodwill in the accounts. Thus, the cash or other consideration which Charles is required to pay amounts to the same $12,000, and it should be divided as above, $5,000 to Arthur and $7,000 to Brown.   The entry in general journal form for the admission of Charles would be as follows:

Arthur, Capital	3,000	
Brown, Capital	5,000	
Charles, Capital		8,000

To record the admission of Charles to a one-fifth interest in the partnership, the consideration having passed outside of the business.

1.7   ADMISSION OF NEW PARTNER—INVESTMENT IN FIRM

A new partner may be admitted to a partnership by making an investment of assets in the firm; this action will also result in an increase in the capital of the partnership.   It is important to evaluate the new partner's contribution properly; any gain or loss on the subsequent disposition of such assets becomes a gain or loss of the new partnership.   By the same token, the incoming partner will undoubtedly desire that the assets of the firm be realistically valued as of the date of his or her admission.   The incoming partner will also want to see that all of the firm's liabilities are completely recorded.

Assume that A. Arthur and B. Brown are partners with capital balances of $15,000 and $25,000 respectively.   They share profits and losses equally.   C. Charles is to be admitted to the partnership by investing assets in the firm.   Some of the more common situations will be illustrated in the following cases.   If nothing is said about profits and losses, each of the three partners will share equally in future profits and losses.   In each of the following cases (Examples 16 through 22) it is assumed that the books of the existing partnership will be continued.

Investment Equal to Increase in Capital

EXAMPLE 16.   Charles invests an amount sufficient to achieve a one-fifth interest in the capital of the new firm; thus the combined capitals of Arthur and Brown will make up four-fifths of the capital of the new firm.   If $40,000 equals four-fifths of the capital of the new firm, then the entire capital of the new firm will amount to $50,000 ($40,000 ÷ $\frac{4}{5}$).

The entry in general journal form to record the admission of Charles is as follows:

Cash (or other assets)	10,000	
Charles, Capital		10,000

To record the investment by Charles, who will have a one-fifth interest in the new capital of $50,000.

Unrecorded Goodwill Attributable to Existing Partners

EXAMPLE 17. Charles is to invest an amount sufficient to achieve a one-fifth interest in the firm after recognition of $8,000 of goodwill developed by Arthur and Brown prior to the admission of Charles. The general journal entry to record the goodwill is as follows:

Goodwill	8,000	
Arthur, Capital		4,000
Brown, Capital		4,000

> To record goodwill developed by Arthur and Brown prior to the admission of Charles.

The revised capital balances of Arthur and Brown amount to $19,000 and $29,000, respectively. This total of $48,000 represents four-fifths of the capital of the new partnership; thus, the total capital of the new partnership will be $60,000 ($48,000 ÷ $\frac{4}{5}$). Charles will then have to invest $12,000 to achieve a one-fifth interest in the new firm. The entry in general journal form for the admission of Charles is as follows:

Cash	12,000	
Charles, Capital		12,000

> To record the investment by Charles who will have a one-fifth interest in the new capital of $60,000.

Implied Goodwill Attributed to Original Partners

EXAMPLE 18. Charles is to invest $14,000 and is to be credited with the same amount for a one-fifth interest. If $14,000 is equal to one-fifth interest in the new partnership of Arthur, Brown, and Charles, then the entire capital of the new partnership will be $70,000 (5 × $14,000) and the combined capitals of Arthur and Brown in the new partnership should equal $56,000 ($70,000 × $\frac{4}{5}$). However, the combined capitals of Arthur and Brown prior to any adjustment for goodwill amounts to $40,000. Thus, the amount of goodwill attributable to Arthur and Brown works out to $16,000 ($56,000 − $40,000). The general journal entry to enter the goodwill is as follows:

Goodwill	16,000	
Arthur, Capital		8,000
Brown, Capital		8,000

> To record goodwill developed by Arthur and Brown prior to the admission of Charles.

The entry in general journal form for the admission of Charles is as follows:

Cash (or other assets)	14,000	
Charles, Capital		14,000

> To record investment by Charles, who will have a one-fifth interest in the new capital of $70,000.

Goodwill Attributable to Incoming Partner

EXAMPLE 19. Charles is to invest $8,000 and is to be credited with $10,000 for a one-fifth interest. Since Charles is to be credited with $10,000 for a one-fifth interest, the total capital will be $50,000 (5 × $10,000). The difference between the cash of $8,000 which Charles is to invest and the capital credit he will receive indicates that Charles must be bringing in some other asset, such as intangible goodwill. (It cannot be any asset attributable to the original partners.) This fact may be verified by comparing the net assets and capital balances of Arthur and Brown. The net assets of Arthur and Brown, before the admission of Charles, amount to $40,000, and the combined capitals of Arthur and Brown also amount to $40,000, which is equal to four-fifths of the new capital of $50,000.

The entry in general journal form for the admission of Charles is as follows:

Cash	8,000	
Goodwill	2,000	
Charles, Capital		10,000

To record the admission of Charles for a one-fifth interest in a total
capital of $50,000.

Bonus to Original Partners

EXAMPLE 20.   Charles is to invest $15,000 and is to be credited with $11,000 for a one-fifth interest in the new partnership. The combined net assets and the combined capitals of Arthur and Brown amount to $40,000. After Charles invests $15,000, the combined net assets will amount to $55,000. The total capital of the new partnership should also equal $55,000 (5 × $11,000). As no goodwill is involved, the implication is that there is to be a transfer of $4,000 from the capital balances of Arthur and Brown to Charles. Such a transfer is frequently referred to as a bonus. The entry in general journal form for the admission of Charles is as follows:

Cash (or other assets)	15,000	
Arthur, Capital		2,000
Brown, Capital		2,000
Charles, Capital		11,000

To record the admission of Charles for a one-fifth interest in a total
capital of $55,000.

Bonus Allowed to New Partner

EXAMPLE 21.   Charles is to invest $5,000 and is to be credited with $9,000 for a one-fifth interest in the new partnership. If $9,000 is equal to one-fifth of the total capital of the new partnership, then the total capital will be $45,000 (5 × $9,000). Since the combined assets of the new partnership will also amount to $45,000 ($40,000 + $5,000), there must be a transfer of $4,000 from the capital accounts of Arthur and Brown to Charles's capital account—the difference between the amount which Charles is investing and the amount for which he is being credited. The entry in general journal form for the admission of Charles is as follows:

Cash (or other assets)	5,000	
Arthur, Capital	2,000	
Brown, Capital	2,000	
Charles, Capital		9,000

To record the admission of Charles for a one-fifth interest in a total
capital of $45,000.

Revaluation of Assets

EXAMPLE 22.   Charles is to invest $15,000 and is to be credited for the same amount, which will represent a one-fifth interest in a total capital of $75,000. Arthur and Brown own a parcel of land that cost them $17,000 in 1961 and now has a fair market value of $37,000. The three parties to the new partnership agree that this increase in the value of the land is to be recognized prior to the admission of Charles. Such appreciation in value is a holding gain to be shared by Arthur and Brown in their profit-sharing ratio. Accordingly, the following entry should be made in the journal of Arthur and Brown:

Land (or Incremental Value of Land)	20,000	
Arthur, Capital		10,000
Brown, Capital		10,000

To record appreciation in value of land from 1961 to the present.

The entry for the admission of Charles, in general journal form, is as follows:

Cash (or other assets)	15,000	
Charles, Capital		15,000

To record the admission of Charles for one-fifth interest in a total capital of $75,000.

After the admission of Charles, the capital accounts of the three partners will be as follows:

Arthur ($15,000 + $10,000)	$25,000
Brown ($25,000 + $10,000)	35,000
Charles	15,000
Total	$75,000

1.8 RETIREMENT OF A PARTNER

A partner who retires from a firm is entitled to receive cash or other property equivalent to the balance in his capital account after an actual or constructive closing of the partnership books as of the date of the retirement. Although such an action would mean the end of the existing firm, the business is frequently carried on by a new firm consisting of the remaining partners. Often there is no formal dissolution; the remaining partners simply continue the business with a reduced capital and a concurrent reduction in assets.

In those instances where the retired partner is to be paid off over a period of time, any balance due should be removed from the partner's capital account and transferred to a liability account which distinctly describes his or her status as a former partner.

The partnership contract may spell out the method for determining the amount to be paid to the retiring partner, or the partners may agree on an amount and terms. If a revaluation of assets has been agreed upon by the partners, there are three basic methods of recognizing the revaluation: (a) record the entire revaluation; (b) record only a portion of the revaluation equivalent to the fractional interest of the retiring partner; or (c) adjust the capital accounts of the partners who remain in the business.

Assume that Arm, Baker, and Clark are partners with capital balances of $45,000, $30,000 and $25,000, respectively, and Clark wishes to retire. They have been sharing profits and losses equally. The three partners agree that the recorded net asset balances approximate their fair market values, except that goodwill in the amount of $30,000 should also be recognized. The following cases (Examples 23 through 25) illustrate three common approaches to recognizing the increment in the asset goodwill.

The Entire Amount of Goodwill Is Placed on the Books

EXAMPLE 23. Goodwill developed by the three partners should be divided among them in their profit and loss ratio, which is equally. The general journal entry to recognize goodwill is as follows:

Goodwill	30,000	
Arm, Capital		10,000
Baker, Capital		10,000
Clark, Capital		10,000

To record goodwill developed by Arm, Baker, and Clark.

The entry for the settlement with Clark, in general journal form, is as follows:

Clark, Capital ($25,000 + $10,000)	35,000	
Cash		35,000

To record the retirement of Clark and settlement in full.

Frequently the partnership is not in a position to liquidate in one cash distribution the entire amount due to a retiring partner. Any amount due to a retired partner should be removed from his or her capital account and should be transferred to a liability account. Assume that Arm, Baker, and Clark agree on the retirement of Clark as above, except that $12,000 is to be paid immediately, and the balance is in the form of an interest-bearing note due in eight months. The journal entry for the retirement of Clark would be as follows:

Clark, Capital	35,000	
Cash		12,000
Note Payable to Retired Partner		23,000

To record the retirement of Clark, as per agreement. Note payable due in 8 months with interest.

Retiring Partner's Share of Goodwill Placed on Books

EXAMPLE 24. The partners may be reluctant to record goodwill unless it has been specifically bought and paid for. In such a case, only $10,000 ($\frac{1}{3}$ of $30,000), is to be recorded. The journal entry for the retirement of Clark will then be as follows:

Clark, Capital	25,000	
Goodwill	10,000	
Cash		35,000

To record the retirement of Clark, as per agreement, and to recognize his share of goodwill acquired by the remaining partners.

The Capital Balances of Remaining Partners to Be Adjusted in Lieu of Recording Goodwill

EXAMPLE 25. Many accountants feel that goodwill should not be recorded unless it has been acquired in an arm's-length transaction. They may question the objectivity of partners determining the goodwill of a business which they had been operating for some length of time. If Clark is to receive $10,000 more than his capital balance, the only other procedure to be followed would be to charge the remaining partners with a bonus of $10,000 divided between them in their profit- and loss-sharing ratio. The entry for the retirement of Clark, in general journal form, is as follows:

Clark, Capital	25,000	
Arm, Capital	5,000	
Baker, Capital	5,000	
Cash		35,000

To record the retirement of Clark, as per agreement.

1.9 DEATH OF A PARTNER

If a partner dies the firm is automatically terminated. If the surviving partners wish to continue the business and use the same set of books, then the capital balance of the deceased partner should be transferred to another account such as Amount Due to Estate of Deceased Partner, pending final settlement with the executor or administrator of the estate. The partnership contract should spell out the method of valuation and the terms of settlement of the deceased's interest. Otherwise, there may be practical problems in agreeing on the amount due the estate, and once such amount is determined it may have to be completely paid out in a relatively short space of time.

    Once the amount due the estate of a deceased partner is determined, the journal entries are similar to the entries in the previous section relating to the voluntary settlement with a retiring partner.

Summary

(1) A partnership is a contractual association of two or more persons to carry on as co-owners a business for _____.

(2) When the partnership contract is silent, state laws generally require that _____ and _____ be divided equally.

(3) If a partnership contract calls for salaries to partners, such salaries should be considered as part of the _____ sharing arrangement.

(4) When a partnership contract calls for interest on capitals, it means that a portion of the net income will be divided in the _____ ratio.

(5) Interest allowed to a partner, based on a loan by him to the partnership, is to be treated as an _____ of the business.

(6) A partnership has a limited existence. It may be terminated by the _____, _____, _____, or _____ of a partner.

(7) When a new member is admitted to a partnership, the existing firm is _____ and a new one is _____.

(8) When a partnership is organized, the initial entries should indicate the _____ contribution of each partner.

(9) The number of methods of dividing net income or losses among partners is _____.

(10) If the amount of salaries allowed to partners exceeds the net income for the period, the resultant _____ is divided in the ratio for dividing _____.

(11) Goodwill is associated with above-normal _____ power.

(12) When goodwill is placed on the books of a partnership, the resultant credit is divided among the partners in their _____ sharing ratio.

(13) A new partner may acquire an interest in a partnership business by purchasing part or all of the interest of an existing partner, or by making an _____ in the business.

Answers: (1) profit;   (2) profits, losses;   (3) profit;   (4) capital;   (5) expense;   (6) death, withdrawal, incompetency, bankruptcy;   (7) dissolved or terminated, established;   (8) capital;   (9) infinite;   (10) deficit, losses;   (11) earning;   (12) profit;   (13) investment

Solved Problems

1.1   The partnership of Dorr and Slater had the following capital accounts for the year 19X7:

Dorr				Slater			
	Dr.	**Cr.**			**Dr.**	**Cr.**	
Jan. 1		30,000		Jan. 1		20,000	
Apr. 1	400			June 1		5,000	
Sept. 1		5,000		July 1		1,000	
Dec. 1	300			Oct. 1	3,000		

The net income for the year 19X7 was $30,000.

Required:

Indicate how the net income should be divided under each of the following agreements:

(*a*)   Division in average capital ratio

(*b*)   Interest of 5 percent on average capitals and the remainder equally

(*c*)   Interest of 5 percent on the difference between opening and closing balances and the remainder 60 percent and 40 percent respectively

(*d*)   No agreement

(*Note*:   Round answers to nearest whole dollar.)

SOLUTION

(*a*)

Dorr

	Dr.	Cr.	Balance	Months	$ × Months	Average Capital
Jan. 1		$30,000	$30,000	3	$ 90,000	
Apr. 1	$400		29,600	5	148,000	
Sept. 1		5,000	34,600	3	103,800	
Dec. 1	300		34,300	1	34,300	
				12	$376,100	$31,342

Slater

	Dr.	Cr.	Balance	Months	$ × Months	Average Capital
Jan. 1		$20,000	$20,000	5	$100,000	
June 1		5,000	25,000	1	25,000	
July 1		1,000	26,000	3	78,000	
Oct. 1	$3,000		23,000	3	69,000	
				12	$272,000	$22,667

Dorr: $30,000 × $31,342/$54,009 = $17,409

Slater: $30,000 × $22,667/$54,009 =   12,591

$30,000

(b)

	Dorr	Slater	Total
Interest on Average Capital:			
$31,342 × 0.05	$ 1,567		
$22,667 × 0.05		$ 1,133	$ 2,700
Balance Equally	13,650	13,650	27,300
Totals	$15,217	$14,783	$30,000

(c)

	Dorr	Slater	Total
Interest on Excess of Ending Capital over Beginning Capital:			
($34,300 − $30,000) × 0.05	$ 215		
($23,000 − $20,000) × 0.05		$ 150	$ 365
Balance 60:40	17,781	11,854	29,635
Totals	$17,996	$12,004	$30,000

(d) $30,000 ÷ 2 = $15,000 each

1.2 The firm of Burns and Allen allows 5 percent interest on original capital balances and divides the remaining profit 60 percent and 40 percent respectively. On January 1, Burns invested $15,000 and Allen invested $25,000.

Required:

Prepare journal entries to close the revenue and expense accounts on December 31 in each of these situations:

(a) Revenue $35,000; Expense $25,000

(b) Revenue $18,000; Expense $16,500

(c) Revenue $15,000; Expense $20,000

SOLUTION

Calculation of Interest on Capitals:

Burns:	$15,000 × 5% =	$ 750
Allen:	$25,000 × 5% =	1,250
Total Interest		$2,000

	Case (a)	Case (b)	Case (c)
Revenue	$35,000	$18,000	$15,000
Expenses	25,000	16,500	20,000
Net Income	$10,000	$ 1,500	($ 5,000)
Interest on Capital	(2,000)	(2,000)	(2,000)
	$ 8,000	($ 500)	($ 7,000)
Division of Balance			
Burns (60%)	$ 4,800	($ 300)	($ 4,200)
Allen (40%)	$ 3,200	($ 200)	($ 2,800)
Totals	$ 8,000	($ 500)	($ 7,000)

(a)   Revenue   35,000
                            Expenses   25,000
                            Burns, Capital ($750 + $4,800)   5,550
                            Allen, Capital ($1,250 + $3,200)   4,450
                    To divide net income of $10,000.

(b)   Revenue   18,000
                            Expenses   16,500
                            Burns, Capital ($750 − $300)   450
                            Allen, Capital ($1,250 − $200)   1,050
                    To divide net income of $1,500.

(c)   Revenue   15,000
                       Burns, Capital ($750 − $4,200)   3,450
                       Allen, Capital ($1,250 − $2,800)   1,550
                            Expenses   20,000
                    To divide net loss of $5,000.

1.3 Burke and Charles agree that profits shall be divided between them as follows: Both partners get salaries and interest; Burke receives a bonus equal to 10 percent of the profit after deducting salaries, interest, and bonus; the remainder is divided, 60 percent to Burke and 40 percent to Charles.

The profit for the year before any deductions was $63,750. Salaries were: Burke, $13,200; Charles, $10,450. Interest was: Burke, $5,500; Charles, $6,000.

Required:

Prepare a schedule showing the distribution of the profit.

SOLUTION

	Total	Burke	Charles
Net Profit	$63,750		
Less: Salaries	23,650	$13,200	$10,450
	$40,100		
Less: Interest	11,500	5,500	6,000
	$28,600		
Less: Bonus*	2,600	2,600	–0–
	$26,000		
Less: Division of Remainder	26,000	15,600	10,400
Totals	–0–	$36,900	$26,850

* To calculate bonus:

$$1.10 \text{ Base} = \$28,600$$
$$\text{Base} = \$26,000$$
$$\text{Bonus (10\% of } \$26,000) = \$ 2,600$$

1.4 Kramer and Ullman are partners with capital accounts of $40,000 and $20,000; their profit and loss ratio is 40:60 respectively. Dunn is to acquire a one-fourth interest in the firm by making an investment.

(*a*) Dunn contributes $20,000 cash.

(*b*) Dunn contributes $25,000; the total capital is to be $100,000.

(*c*) Dunn contributes $16,000; the total capital is to be $76,000.

(*d*) Dunn contributes $17,000 and is to have a capital account of $20,000.

(*e*) Dunn contributes $26,000 and the total capital is to be $86,000.

Required:

Prepare the appropriate journal entries for the admission of Dunn under each of the five foregoing conditions.

SOLUTION

(*a*)	Cash	20,000	
	Dunn, Capital		20,000
(*b*)	Cash	25,000	
	Goodwill	15,000	
	Kramer, Capital		6,000
	Ullman, Capital		9,000
	Dunn, Capital		25,000
(*c*)	Cash	16,000	
	Kramer, Capital	1,200	
	Ullman, Capital	1,800	
	Dunn, Capital		19,000
(*d*)	Cash	17,000	
	Goodwill	3,000	
	Dunn, Capital		20,000
(*e*)	Cash	26,000	
	Kramer, Capital		1,800
	Ullman, Capital		2,700
	Dunn, Capital		21,500

1.5 Brady, DeLaura, and Scherdel operate a partnership sharing profits and losses in the ratio 50 percent, 30 percent, 20 percent.

On January 1, 19XX, the balance sheet recorded $100,000 in Brady's capital account, $150,000 for DeLaura, and $180,000 in Scherdel's capital account.

It was agreed by the partners to allow Mr. Percio to buy an interest of $100,000 for $120,000 cash from Ms. Scherdel. After Percio acquired his interest, Brady and DeLaura invested additional cash increasing their capital accounts to $170,000 each. After the transactions are completed, the new ratio for profit and loss would be 50 percent for Brady, 30 percent for DeLaura, 10 percent for Scherdel, and 10 percent for Percio.

Required:

(a) Write the journal entries which should be recorded on the partnership books.

(b) Determine how the $120,000 cash paid by Percio should be divided.

SOLUTION

(a)

Cash		90,000	
	Capital, Brady		70,000
	Capital, DeLaura		20,000
Capital, Scherdel		100,000	
	Capital, Percio		100,000

(b) Scherdel would keep the $120,000 in payment for her capital, which she gave away. This transaction was not with the other partners, so they should not receive any portion unless they donate a percentage of their interest.

1.6 Devine contributed $14,000 and LaPointe contributed $56,000 to form a partnership. The partners agreed to share profits and losses in the ratio of their capital contributions. In the first year of operation, the partnership had profits of $18,230, of which Devine withdrew $6,500 and LaPointe withdrew $9,400. At this point the partners agreed to allow Seger to purchase a one-fifth interest for $18,000 cash.

Required:

Prepare a statement showing the distribution of the $18,000 cash between Devine and LaPointe.

SOLUTION

	Devine	LaPointe	Seger	Total
Original Contribution	$14,000.00	$56,000.00		$70,000.00
Division of Profit (1:4)	3,646.00	14,584.00		18,230.00
Subtotal	$17,646.00	$70,584.00		$88,230.00
Less: Drawings	6,500.00	9,400.00		15,900.00
Subtotal	$11,146.00	$61,184.00		$72,330.00
Transfer of Capital	(2,893.20)	(11,572.80)	$14,466.00	–0–
Capital Balances	$ 8,252.80	$49,611.20	$14,466.00	$72,330.00

Statement of Payment Distribution

	Total	Devine	LaPointe
Paid by Seger	$18,000.00		
Capital Transferred	14,466.00	$2,893.20	$11,572.80
Division of Gain (1:4)	$ 3,534.00	706.80	2,827.20
Amount Received		$3,600.00	$14,400.00

1.7 At June 30, 19XX, the partners of R & S Auto Body had capital accounts as follows: Bradly $31,000, Spahn $24,000, Wendt $25,000. The partners have agreed to share profits and losses equally. At this date Ching enters the partnership, securing a one-fifth interest in the net assets and profits of the partnership by paying $23,000.

Required:

Prepare entries, in general journal form, for the admission of Ching.

SOLUTION   *1. Goodwill to Old Partners*

Goodwill	12,000	
Capital, Bradly		4,000
Capital, Spahn		4,000
Capital, Wendt		4,000

To record goodwill developed by partnership prior to the admission of Ching.

Cash	23,000	
Capital, Ching		23,000

To record the admission of Ching to a one-fifth interest in a total capital of $115,000.

2. Bonus to Old Partners

Cash	23,000	
Capital, Ching		20,600
Capital, Bradly		800
Capital, Spahn		800
Capital, Wendt		800

To record the admission of Ching to a one-fifth interest in a total capital of $103,000.

1.8   Andon, Baker, Clark, and Down are partners sharing profits and losses in the ratio of 40 percent, 30 percent, 15 percent, and 15 percent. Their capital accounts are $95,000, $140,000, $110,500, and $104,500, respectively. Egan acquires a one-fifth interest in the business by paying the partners a total of $95,000, and all become partners with equal interest in both capital and profits.

Required:

(a) Journal entries to record the admission of Egan to the firm, assuming goodwill is recorded on the basis of the valuation implicit in the price paid by Egan.

(b) A schedule showing the distribution of the cash among the partners, assuming that the old partners agree that the cash is to be divided according to the capitals transferred.

SOLUTION

(a) *Journal entries:*

Goodwill	25,000	
Andon, Capital		10,000
Baker, Capital		7,500
Clark, Capital		3,750
Down, Capital		3,750

To recognize goodwill implicit in payment of $95,000 for a one-fifth interest:

$95,000 × 5	$475,000
Existing Capital	450,000
Goodwill	$ 25,000

Andon, Capital	10,000	
Baker, Capital	52,500	
Clark, Capital	19,250	
Down, Capital	13,250	
Egan, Capital		95,000

To record capital transfers to Egan to give him a one-fifth interest.

(b) *Schedule of distribution of Egan's payment:*

	Andon	Baker	Clark	Down
Balances, before Admission of Egan	$ 95,000	$140,000	$110,500	$104,500
Goodwill Recognized, P & L Ratio	10,000	7,500	3,750	3,750
Total	$105,000	$147,500	$114,250	$108,250
Balances, if Partners Are to Have Equal Interests in Capital	95,000	95,000	95,000	95,000
Capital Transfers and Cash Distribution Resulting from Egan's Purchase of a One-fifth Interest for $95,000	$ 10,000	$ 52,500	$ 19,250	$ 13,250

1.9   Hansen, LeVinn, and McCarthy are partners with capital balances maintained as follows: Hansen, $60,000; LeVinn, $40,000; McCarthy, $20,000.

Profits are to be distributed in the capital ratio. LeVinn wants to retire from the partnership, and all agree that he shall be paid $46,400 from the partnership funds.

Required:

Prepare journal entries to record LeVinn's retirement, showing three alternative solutions. (*Suggestion:* Round amounts to the nearest dollar.)

SOLUTION

Partner	Capital Balances	Capital Ratios
Hansen	$ 60,000	50.0%
LeVinn	40,000	$33\frac{1}{3}\%$
McCarthy	20,000	$16\frac{2}{3}\%$
	$120,000	100%

Alternative 1:   Goodwill to all partners

LeVinn's goodwill is $6,400 ($46,400 − $40,000). However, $6,400 is only $33\frac{1}{3}$ percent of the total goodwill. Therefore, the total goodwill is $19,200.

(a)			
	Goodwill	19,200	
	Hansen, Capital		9,600
	LeVinn, Capital		6,400
	McCarthy, Capital		3,200
(b)			
	LeVinn, Capital	46,400	
	Cash		46,400

Alternative 2: Goodwill to the retiring partner only:

(a)	Goodwill	6,400	
	LeVinn, Capital		6,400
(b)	LeVinn, Capital	46,400	
	Cash		46,400

Alternative 3: Goodwill is not recognized:

LeVinn, Capital	40,000	
Hansen, Capital	4,800	
McCarthy, Capital	1,600	
Cash		46,400

Bonus to LeVinn, $6,400, allocated to Hansen and McCarthy in their capital ratio (60:20).

1.10   The adjusted trial balance for the firm of Kelly & Tobin on April 30, 19X8, appears as follows:

Kelly & Tobin
Adjusted Trial Balance
April 30, 19X8

Cash	$ 16,815	
Accounts Receivable	25,533	
Inventories	46,073	
Buildings & Equipment	13,921	
Accumulated Depreciation		$ 3,165
Accounts Payable		16,039
Kelly, Capital		10,206
Kelly, Drawings	3,445	
Tobin, Capital		68,920
Tobin, Drawings	3,903	
Revenue		30,009
Expenses	18,649	
	$128,339	$128,339

The profits and losses are shared in the ratio of 30 percent to Kelly and 70 percent to Tobin. The fiscal year ends December 31. Kelly decides to withdraw from the partnership as of April 30 and to allow Tobin to continue the business as a sole proprietor. The terms of their dissolution agreement also include the following:

(a)   Kelly is to be paid book value of his equity in the business.

(b)   Kelly is to receive an additional $12,000 to cover his interest in goodwill.

(c)   Kelly is to be paid 30 percent cash as of April 30 and the remainder in two equal notes due at the end of each of the next two years, with interest of 6 percent.

(d)   No goodwill is to be placed on the books.

Required:

Prepare the journal entries to be made in connection with the dissolution.

SOLUTION

Revenue	30,009.00	
Expenses		18,649.00
Kelly, Capital		3,408.00
Tobin, Capial		7,952.00

To record income earned and to apportion it to the partners.

Tobin, Capital	12,000.00	
Kelly, Capital		12,000.00

To record Kelly's share of goodwill.

Kelly, Capital	3,445.00	
Kelly, Drawing		3,445.00

To transfer drawings to capital account.

Kelly, Capital		
($10,206 + $3,408 + $12,000 − $3,445)	22,169.00	
Cash		6,650.70
Notes Payable to Retired Partner		15,518.30

To record the retirement of Kelly.

1.11 The capital balances of Tinkers, Evers, and Chance on December 31, 19X3 are $100,000, $60,000, and $35,000, respectively. Chance is to receive a 20 percent bonus of net profits each year for his services as manager. The bonus is *not* considered an expense. The remaining profit is shared 60 percent, 25 percent, and 15 percent, respectively.

On the above date Chance wishes to retire. A CPA has examined the firm's records and has found these items:

(*a*) Profits were:
Year 19X1	$20,000
Year 19X2	$25,000
Year 19X3	$10,000

(*b*) Inventories were understated:
December 31, 19X1	$ 8,000
December 31, 19X2	$ 3,000
December 31, 19X3	$10,000

(*c*) Depreciation was understated $3,000 in each of the first two years.

Required:

A statement showing corrections to the partners' capital accounts and the adjusted balances on December 31, 19X3.

SOLUTION

Correction of Earnings 19X1–19X3

	Year 19X1		Year 19X2		Year 19X3	
	Dr.	Cr.	Dr.	Cr.	Dr.	Cr.
Original Profit		$20,000		$25,000		$10,000
Inventories Understated		8,000	$ 8,000	3,000	$3,000	10,000
Depreciation Understated	$3,000		3,000			
	$3,000	$28,000	$11,000	$28,000	$3,000	$20,000
Corrected Profit		$25,000		$17,000		$17,000
Less: Original Profit		20,000		25,000		10,000
Increase (Decrease)		$ 5,000		($ 8,000)		$ 7,000

Net Increase ($5,000 + $7,000 − $8,000)	$ 4,000	
Less: Bonus (20%)	800	
Balance:	$ 3,200	
Tinkers (60%)		$ 1,920
Evers (25%)		800
Chance (15%)		480
		$ 3,200

Restatement of Capital Balances

	Tinkers	Evers	Chance
Original Balances	$100,000	$60,000	$35,000
Increase Bonus to Chance			800
Increase Net Profits	1,920	800	480
Revised Balances	$101,920	$60,800	$36,280

Chapter 2

Partnerships: Liquidation

2.1 INTRODUCTION

There are many reasons why the existence of a partnership may terminate. Some of them are:

1. expiration of partnership contract
2. agreement by partners to end their association
3. death of a partner
4. violation of partnership contract by a partner
5. improper assignment of interest in the partnership
6. bankruptcy of a partner.

Some of these events are rooted in occurrences over which a particular partner may have some degree of control. Others are not under the influence of a particular partner or group of partners.

This chapter will be concerned with the complete termination of a partnership business. There are situations where a partnership may be terminated in a technical sense while the business is continued by some or all of the partners. This type of situation has been discussed in Chapter 1, and is not included here.

Even when a partnership business terminates prior to the end of its fiscal year, all revenue, cost, and expense accounts should be transferred to the regular income and expense summary account with the resultant net income or net loss distributed to the partners. Any gains and losses during the winding-up process are usually summarized separately, but they are nevertheless distributed to the partners. The sharing of such gains and losses is in the regular ratio unless the partners have provided for some other method of apportionment.

2.2 REALIZATION AND LIQUIDATION

In a narrow sense, *realization* is the process of converting assets to cash, and *liquidation* is the process of discharging liabilities. However, the entire procedure of realization and liquidation is frequently referred to simply as *liquidation*.

When a business is dissolved, the assets are converted to cash and the creditors are paid. Before any assets are distributed to partners, however, all gains and losses during the realization period should be divided among the partners.

If for some reason an outside creditor cannot be paid but the amount due is determinable, it is generally satisfactory to reserve such an amount of cash and pay the partners those monies to which they would in any event be entitled.

2.3 STATUS OF A PARTNER'S LOAN IN LIQUIDATION

It is frequently stated that a loan by a partner to a partnership has priority over repayment of capital to any partner. While this is generally the rule in the case of a going business, it may not pertain under the circumstances of a partnership liquidation. For example, realization losses may cause a partner to have a debit balance in his or her capital account. In such a case, the legal doctrine of the *right of offset* would be invoked, and some or all of the partner's loan may not be paid while another partner may receive cash which reduces the latter's capital balance.

As a practical matter, all of the *equities* of each partner may be grouped for convenience in working out the cash distributable to any one partner. While it is possible that a partner may accept noncash assets, it will be assumed in this chapter that all payments to a partner are in the form of cash.

2.4 ASSETS REALIZED BEFORE DISTRIBUTION: EACH PARTNER'S CAPITAL ACCOUNT SUFFICIENT TO ABSORB LOSS

EXAMPLE 1. Assume that Able and Baker are partners sharing profits and losses in the ratio of two to one (2:1). They decide to dissolve their partnership as of July 1, 19X7, when their condensed balance sheet appears as follows:

ASSETS

Cash	$ 15,000
Other Assets	85,000
Total Assets	$100,000

EQUITIES

Vouchers Payable	$ 15,000
Able, Loan	10,000
Able, Capital	25,000
Baker, Capital	50,000
Total Equities	$100,000

On July 15, a sale of the other assets is made for $55,000, resulting in a loss of $30,000. Journal entries to record the sale and to distribute the loss follow:

Cash	55,000	
Loss or Gain from Realization	30,000	
Other Assets		85,000

To record the sale of assets at a loss.

Able, Capital	20,000	
Baker, Capital	10,000	
Loss or Gain from Realization		30,000

To allocate the loss from realization in the ratio of 2:1.

At this point, a trial balance of Able and Baker appears as follows:

Cash	$70,000	
Vouchers Payable		$15,000
Able, Loan		10,000
Able, Capital ($25,000 − $20,000)		5,000
Baker, Capital ($50,000 − $10,000)		40,000
	$70,000	$70,000

Journal entries for the final distributions of cash are as follows:

Vouchers Payable	15,000	
Cash		15,000

To pay outside creditors.

Able, Loan	10,000	
Able, Capital	5,000	
Baker, Capital	40,000	
Cash		55,000

To distribute remaining cash in accordance with partners' equity balances.

2.5 ASSETS REALIZED BEFORE DISTRIBUTION: ONE PARTNER'S CAPITAL IS EXHAUSTED

EXAMPLE 2.   Assume that the balance sheet of Able and Baker as of July 1, 19X7 is the same as in Example 1. However, the noncash assets ("Other Assets") realize only $35,000 when sold.   Journal entries to record the sale and to distribute the loss follow:

Cash	35,000	
Loss from Realization	50,000	
Other Assets		85,000

To record the sale of assets at a loss.

Able, Capital	33,333	
Baker, Capital	16,667	
Loss from Realization		50,000

To distribute the loss from realization in the ratio of 2:1.

A trial balance of Able and Baker, after realization of its assets and distribution of the loss, follows:

Cash	$50,000	
Vouchers Payable		$15,000
Able, Loan		10,000
Able, Capital	8,333	
Baker, Capital		33,333
	$58,333	$58,333

Able's capital account now has a deficit, and it behooves the partnership to offset this claim of the firm against an equivalent amount of the loan payable to Able.   The following journal entry reflects this action:

Able, Loan	8,333	
Able, Capital		8,333

To transfer an amount from Able's loan sufficient to make up his capital deficit.

The available cash can now be distributed as reflected in the following journal entries:

Vouchers Payable	15,000	
Cash		15,000

To pay outside creditors.

Able, Loan	1,667	
Baker, Capital	33,333	
Cash		35,000

To distribute remaining cash in accordance with partners' equity balances.

2.6   ASSETS REALIZED BEFORE DISTRIBUTION: CAPITAL DEFICIENCY EXCEEDS LOAN

EXAMPLE 3.   Assume that the balance sheet of Able and Baker as of July 1, 19X7 is the same as in Example 1. However, the "Other Assets" realize only $25,000 when sold. This results in a realization loss of $60,000. Journal entries to record the sale and the distribution of the loss follow:

Cash	25,000	
Loss from Realization	60,000	
Other Assets		85,000

To record loss on sale of assets.

Able, Capital	40,000	
Baker, Capital	20,000	
Loss from Realization		60,000

To allocate loss from realization in the ratio of 2:1.

A trial balance of Able and Baker, after realization of its assets and distribution of the loss, follows:

Cash	$40,000	
Vouchers Payable		$15,000
Able, Loan		10,000
Able, Capital	15,000	
Baker, Capital		30,000
	$55,000	$55,000

The deficit in Able's capital account is reduced by transferring the balance of his loan account, as reflected in the following journal entry:

Able, Loan	10,000	
Able, Capital		10,000

To offset loan payable to Able against the deficit in his capital account.

Able still has a deficit in his capital account of $5,000, which he should cover by paying $5,000 to the partnership. Assuming that Able makes the payment, it would be recorded as follows:

Cash	5,000	
Able, Capital		5,000

To record the investment by Able to cover the deficit in his capital account.

After receipt of the additional contribution from Able, the partnership will have $45,000 in cash, which may be distributed in complete liquidation of the firm, as indicated in the following entries:

Vouchers Payable	15,000	
Cash		15,000

To liquidate obligations to outside creditors.

Baker, Capital	30,000	
Cash		30,000

To redeem Baker's capital balance in final liquidation of partnership.

EXAMPLE 4. In Example 3 it was assumed that Able was in a position to cover his deficit. Let us now assume that Able cannot make any contribution to the partnership. Able's deficit will have to be assumed by the remaining partner or partners. The absorption of Able's deficit by Baker is reflected in the following journal entry:

Baker, Capital	5,000	
Able, Capital		5,000

To transfer deficit of Able to Baker.

The remaining $40,000 of available cash is distributed as indicated in the following journal entries:

Vouchers Payable	15,000	
Cash		15,000

To liquidate obligations to outside creditors.

Baker, Capital	25,000	
Cash		25,000

To redeem Baker's capital balance in final liquidation of partnership.

The inability of Able to cover his deficit does not in itself relieve him of his obligation. Should Able become able to pay at a future date, he would then have to pay $5,000 to Baker.

If the deficit of one partner is shared among several partners, it would be divided among them in the ratio in which they share losses.

2.7 LIQUIDATION IN INSTALLMENTS: GENERAL

When the realization and liquidation process extends over a period of several months, the partners may desire the distribution of some cash before all of the assets have been realized. Once all of the outside creditors have been paid, available cash may be distributed as long as no partner receives more than the amount he or she will ultimately be entitled to receive after all realization losses and expenses ultimately become known.

When the liquidation process is lengthy, care should be taken to see that outside creditors are paid first; this payment includes amounts due for expenses that may arise during the liquidation process.

It is not necessary literally to pay creditors first; as long as funds are reserved for the creditors, safe payments to the partners may be distributed. If partial payments are made to partners, they are often made before all losses are known and before it is known whether a deficit of one or more partners will have to be absorbed by another partner. Thus, if assumptions are to be made, the worst possible conditions should be assumed.

In order to safeguard the liquidator and the partners, the following rules should be observed:

1. Do not distribute any assets to a partner until all losses incurred have been divided among the partners.

2. Assume that all noncash assets may become worthless, and that such loss will have to be distributed among the partners.

3. Assume that any partner who has or might have a capital deficiency will be unable to pay anything to the firm; that is, his or her deficiency will have to be absorbed by the other partners.

4. Make payments only to those partners who would have credit balances in their equity (capital plus loan) accounts, and then the payments should not exceed such credit balances.

When installment payments are made following these rules, the partners' equity balances tend to be brought into the loss ratio. Once the partners' equity balances are in the loss sharing ratio, no further calculations are necessary, since division of losses (or profits) maintains the equity balances in the same ratio. Any subsequent cash payments may be safely distributed in the resultant equity ratio.

2.8   LIQUIDATION IN INSTALLMENTS: PARTNERS' CAPITAL SUFFICIENT TO ABSORB LOSSES

EXAMPLE 5.   R, S, and T are partners sharing profits and losses in the ratio of 50:30:20. They decide to dissolve the partnership as of July 31, when their condensed balance sheet appeared as follows:

ASSETS

Cash	$10,000	
Other Assets	90,000	
Total Assets		$100,000

EQUITIES

Accounts Payable	$18,000	
R, Capital	27,000	
S, Capital	24,000	
T, Capital	31,000	
Total Equities		$100,000

During the following August other assets, which had been carried on the books for $48,000, were sold for $36,000. Summary journal entries to record the sale of the assets and the distribution of the loss follow:

Cash	36,000	
Loss on Realization	12,000	
Other Assets		48,000

To record the sale of assets at a loss.

R, Capital	6,000
S, Capital	3,600
T, Capital	2,400
Loss on Realization	12,000

To divide loss in profit and loss ratio of 50:30:20.

Before any money is paid to a partner the outside creditors should be paid, as indicated in the following journal entry:

Accounts Payable	18,000	
Cash		18,000

To discharge obligations to outside creditors.

The August transactions to this point and the resulting account balances are summarized in the following schedule.

	Assets		Liabilities	Partners' Capital		
	Cash	Other		R	S	T
Balances, July 31	$10,000	$90,000	$18,000	$27,000	$24,000	$31,000
Sale of Assets at a Loss	36,000	(48,000)		(6,000)	(3,600)	(2,400)
	$46,000	$42,000	$18,000	$21,000	$20,400	$28,600
Pay Creditors	(18,000)		(18,000)			
Balances after Payment to Creditors	$28,000	$42,000	–0–	$21,000	$20,400	$28,600

How should the available cash of $28,000 be distributed among the partners? A safe technique is to assume the worst: that all remaining noncash assets may be worthless. In such a case, a potential loss of $42,000 would be divided among the partners in the ratio of 50:30:20, or $21,000, $12,600, and $8,400. R's equity would be reduced to zero, since $21,000 would be just enough to absorb the maximum loss on the remaining noncash assets. Partners S and T could receive $7,800 and $20,200, respectively. A schedule indicating the calculation of the safe payments follows:

	Partners' Capital		
	R	S	T
Capital Balances of Partners before First Installment Payment	$21,000	$20,400	$28,600
Possible Future Loss Divided 50:30:20 (remaining noncash assets of $42,000)	21,000	12,600	8,400
Safe Payments to Partners	–0–	$ 7,800	$20,200

Note that the above schedule is primarily for the purpose of determining safe payments to partners, therefore no entries are recorded for possible losses or potential expenses. In preparing a schedule to determine safe payments to partners, estimated expenses should be handled in the same manner as possible future losses. This will frequently result in retaining a cash balance equivalent to the estimated expenses.

An entry in general journal form to summarize payments at the end of August follows:

S, Capital	7,800	
T, Capital	20,200	
Cash		28,000

To record partial payments to partners.

The capital balances of the partners, R, S, and T, after the above payments would be $21,000, 12,600, and 8,400, respectively. Thus, each of the three partners is left with sufficient capital to absorb his or her share of any possible future loss from sale of the remaining assets. To use an extreme example, if all of the remaining noncash assets turned out to be worthless, each partner's share of the loss would equal his or her remaining capital.

During September, the second month of liquidation, the remaining assets of R, S, and T were sold for $27,000, resulting in a loss of $15,000. Journal entries to summarize the sale and distribution of the loss are as follows:

Cash	27,000	
Loss on Realization	15,000	
Other Assets		42,000

To record sale of remaining assets at a loss.

R, Capital	7,500	
S, Capital	4,500	
T, Capital	3,000	
Loss on Realization		15,000

To divide loss in profit and loss ratio—50:30:20.

The cash balance of $27,000 would be distributed to R, S, and T in the resultant capital balances: $13,500, $8,100, and $5,400, respectively. A schedule summarizing the events for the two-month period follows:

R, S, and T
Schedule of Partnership Liquidation
July 31 to September 30, 19XX

	Assets		Liabilities	Partners' Capital		
	Cash	Other		R	S	T
Balances, July 31	$10,000	$90,000	$18,000	$27,000	$24,000	$31,000
August						
Sale of Assets	36,000	(48,000)	–0–	(6,000)	(3,600)	(2,400)
Balances	$46,000	$42,000	$18,000	$21,000	$20,400	$28,600
Pay Liabilities	(18,000)	–0–	(18,000)	–0–	–0–	–0–
Balances	$28,000	$42,000	–0–	$21,000	$20,400	$28,600
Pay Partners	(28,000)	–0–		–0–	(7,800)	(20,200)
Balances, August 31	–0–	$42,000		$21,000	$12,600	$ 8,400
September						
Sale of Assets	$27,000	(42,000)		(7,500)	(4,500)	(3,000)
Balances	$27,000	–0–		$13,500	$ 8,100	$ 5,400
Pay Partners	($27,000)			($13,500)	($ 8,100)	($ 5,400)

Although this schedule is a correct summary of the realization and liquidation of the partnership of R, S, and T from July 31 to the end of September, persons not familiar with liquidation procedures and goals may find the following statement preferable.

R, S, and T
Schedule of Partnership Liquidation
July 31 to September 30, 19XX

	R	S	T	Totals
Balances before Liquidation	$27,000	$24,000	$31,000	$82,000
Losses Due to Realization:				
August $12,000				
September 15,000				
Total Losses $27,000				
Losses Allocated to Partners				
50:30:20	13,500	8,100	5,400	27,000
Balances Due to Partners	$13,500	$15,900	$25,600	$55,000
Payments to Partners:				
August	–0–	$ 7,800	$20,200	$28,000
September	13,500	8,100	5,400	27,000
Totals, as above	$13,500	$15,900	$25,600	$55,000

The alternate statement clearly demonstrates that the sum of the installment payments to each partner equals the correct amount to which each partner is entitled. In other words, if no installments had been paid but the cash had been accumulated to the end of September, the amount each partner would then receive is exactly equal to the sum of the installments received in August and September.

2.9 LIQUIDATION IN INSTALLMENTS: PARTNER'S CAPITAL NOT SUFFICIENT TO ABSORB LOSSES

EXAMPLE 6. D, E, and F were partners sharing profits and losses equally. They decided to dissolve the partnership as of May 31, when their condensed balance sheet appeared as follows:

ASSETS

Cash	$ 10,000	
Other Assets	190,000	
Total Assets		$200,000

EQUITIES

Accounts Payable	$30,000	
Loan Payable to D	20,000	
D, Capital	30,000	
E, Capital	60,000	
F, Capital	60,000	
Total Equities		$200,000

During the following June, other assets, which had been carried on the books for $90,000, were sold for $36,000. Summary journal entries to record the sale of the assets and the distribution of the loss follow:

Cash	36,000	
Loss on Realization	54,000	
Other Assets		90,000

To record the sale of assets at a loss.

D, Capital	18,000	
E, Capital	18,000	
F, Capital	18,000	
Loss on Realization		54,000

To divide loss equally.

The equity account balances to this point are now summarized in the following schedule:

	Liabilities	Partners' Equity D	E	F
Balances, May 31:				
Outside creditors	$30,000			
Loan from Partner		$20,000		
Capital Balances		30,000	$60,000	$60,000
Total Equities	$30,000	$50,000	$60,000	$60,000
Loss on Sale of Assets	–0–	18,000	18,000	18,000
Balances	$30,000	$32,000	$42,000	$42,000

Before any money is paid to a partner, the outside creditors should be paid, as indicated in the following journal entry:

Accounts Payable	30,000	
Cash		30,000

To discharge obligations to outside creditors.

How should the remaining cash of $16,000 ($10,000 + $36,000 − $30,000) be distributed among the partners? A safe technique is to assume the worst: that all remaining noncash assets may be worthless. In such case, a potential loss of $100,000 would be divided equally among the partners.

A schedule showing the calculation of the safe payments follows:

	Partners' Equity D	E	F
Equity of partners before first installment payment	$32,000	$42,000	$42,000
Possible future loss divided equally (remaining noncash assets $100,000)	33,333	33,333	33,334
Balances	($ 1,333)	$ 8,667	$ 8,666
Potential Deficit of D divided between E and F	1,333	667	666
Safe Payments to Partners	–0–	$ 8,000	$ 8,000

The schedule shown is for the purpose of determining safe payments to partners, therefore no entries are recorded for possible losses or potential deficits. Note that D does not receive any payment during June even though she does have a credit balance in her loan account. It is not safe at this time to reduce her loan because possible future losses might require her loan balance to be used to offset a potential deficit in capital.

An entry in general journal form to summarize the payments at the end of June follows:

E, Capital	8,000	
F, Capital	8,000	
Cash		16,000

To record partial payments to partners.

The equity balances of the partners D, E, and F after the above payments would be $32,000, $34,000, and $34,000 respectively. Note that D's equity is equal to the sum of her loan balance, $20,000, plus the balance of her capital, $12,000.

During July, the second month of liquidation, the remaining assets of the partnership were sold for $55,000, resulting in a loss of $45,000. Journal entries to summarize the sale and distribution of the loss are as follows:

Cash	55,000	
Loss on Realization	45,000	
Other Assets		100,000

To record sale of remaining assets at a loss.

D, Capital	15,000	
E, Capital	15,000	
F, Capital	15,000	
Loss on Realization		45,000

To divide loss equally.

The cash balance of $55,000 would be distributed to D, E, and F in accordance with the following tabulation:

	Partners' Equity		
	D	E	F
Balances, July 1:			
Loan	$20,000		
Capitals	12,000	$34,000	$34,000
Totals	$32,000	$34,000	$34,000
Loss on Sale of Assets	15,000	15,000	15,000
Balances	$17,000	$19,000	$19,000
Distribution of Cash	($17,000)	($19,000)	($19,000)

The balance of D's Capital account prior to the July division of the loss on sale of assets was only $12,000. Thus, the allocation of $15,000 as D's share of the loss in July would cause D to have a capital deficit of $3,000. This deficit would be made up by transferring $3,000 from D's loan account.

The additional journal entries for July may be summarized as follows:

D, Loan	3,000	
D, Capital		3,000

To transfer an amount sufficient to offset deficit in D's capital.

D, Loan	17,000	
E, Capital	19,000	
F, Capital	19,000	
Cash		55,000

To record final distribution of partnership.

A schedule summarizing the events for the months of June and July follows:

D, E, and F
Schedule of Partnership Liquidation
June 1 to July 31, 19XX

			Partners' Equity		
	Outside Creditors	D Loan	D Capital	E Capital	F Capital
Balances, May 31	$30,000	$20,000	$30,000	$60,000	$60,000
June					
Loss on Sale of Assets	–0–	–0–	18,000	18,000	18,000
Balances	$30,000	$20,000	$12,000	$42,000	$42,000
Pay Outside Creditors	30,000	–0–	–0–	–0–	–0–
Balances	–0–	$20,000	$12,000	$42,000	$42,000
Payments to Partners		–0–	–0–	8,000	8,000
Balances, June 30		$20,000	$12,000	$34,000	$34,000
July					
Loss on Sale of Assets		–0–	15,000	15,000	15,000
Balances (Deficit)		$20,000	($ 3,000)	$19,000	$19,000
Transfer Portion of D's Loan Equal to Deficit in Her Capital		(3,000)	3,000	–0–	–0–
Final Distribution to Partners		$17,000	–0–	$19,000	$19,000

The following statement is an alternate form of summary of the realization and liquidation for the two-month period ending July 31:

D, E, and F
Schedule of Partnership Liquidation
June 1 to July 31, 19XX

		D Loan	D Capital	E Capital	F Capital	Totals
Balances before Liquidation		$20,000	$30,000	$60,000	$60,000	$170,000
Losses Due to Realization:						
June	$54,000					
July	45,000					
Total Losses	$99,000					
Losses Divided Equally Among Partners			33,000	33,000	33,000	99,000
Balances (Deficit)		$20,000	($ 3,000)	$27,000	$27,000	$ 71,000
Transfer $3,000 of D's Loan to Offset Her Deficit		(3,000)	3,000	–0–	–0–	–0–
Balances Due to Partners		$17,000	–0–	$27,000	$27,000	$ 71,000

(Schedule continued on next page.)

	D Loan	D Capital	E Capital	F Capital	Totals
Payments to Partners:					
June	–0–	–0–	$ 8,000	$ 8,000	$ 16,000
July	$17,000	–0–	19,000	19,000	55,000
Totals, as above	$17,000	–0–	$27,000	$27,000	$ 71,000

Summary

(1) The process of converting assets into _____ is generally referred to as realization.

(2) In a limited sense, liquidation means payment of a _____.

(3) A fundamental rule in a partnership liquidation is that any loss or gain should be divided among the partners before any _____ is made to a partner.

(4) Under the right of _____ a loss may be debited to a partner's loan account if his _____ is not sufficient to absorb his share of the loss.

(5) During liquidation, cash payments to a partner should be made only after all _____ (real and assumed) have been divided.

(6) After all assets have been converted to cash and all liabilities have been paid, the remaining cash should be divided among three partners in the _____ ratio.

(7) After all partnership assets have been realized and all liabilities have been paid, the remaining cash should equal the sum of the balances of the _____ accounts of the partners.

(8) Before completion of the liquidation of the partnership of P and Q, their condensed balance sheet is as follows:

ASSETS		LIABILITIES	
Cash	$10,000	P, Capital	$50,000
Other Assets	80,000	Q, Capital	30,000
		Q, Loan	10,000
	$90,000		$90,000

It is safe to pay the $10,000 of cash to _____.

Answers: (1) cash; (2) liability; (3) payment; (4) offset, capital; (5) losses; (6) capital, or equity; (7) capital, or equity; (8) P (The profit and loss ratio is 50:50 unless otherwise stated. Thus, if other assets become worthless, Q's equity would be wiped out.)

Solved Problems

2.1   Lendon, Moran, and Norton are in partnership, with capital account balances and profit and loss ratios as follows:

Lendon	$60,100	60%
Moran	22,700	30%
Norton	7,200	10%
	$90,000	100%

The partners agree to liquidate the partnership. The assets are sold, the liabilities of $63,650 are paid, and the cash remaining to be distributed to the partners amounts to $44,400.

Required:

Prepare a schedule showing how the $44,400 cash should be divided among the partners. If necessary, assume that any capital deficiency is uncollectible.

SOLUTION

	Assets		Liabilities	Partners' Capitals		
	Noncash	*Cash*		*Lendon*	*Moran*	*Norton*
Balances	$153,650	–0–	$63,650	$60,100	$22,700	$7,200
Realization and Loss ($45,600)	153,650	$108,050	–0–	27,360	13,680	4,560
Balances	–0–	$108,050	$63,650	$32,740	$ 9,020	$2,640
Payment of Liabilities		63,650	63,650			
Cash to Be Distributed		$ 44,400	–0–	$32,740	$ 9,020	$2,640

2.2   Green and Pink are partners who share profits and losses in the ratio of 70 percent and 30 percent, respectively. Their capital balances are: Green, $10,500; Pink, $4,800.

It is decided by the partners that the business should be dissolved. The business has liabilities of $13,400, including $500 owing to Pink and $300 owing to Green on loans.

After realization the cash on hand amounts to $14,600.

Required:

Prepare a statement of liquidation.

SOLUTION

	Assets		Liabilities	Partners' Equity	
	Noncash	*Cash*		*Green*	*Pink*
Balances before Realization	$28,700	–0–	$12,600	$10,800	$5,300
Realization and Loss ($14,100)	(28,700)	$14,600	–0–	9,870	4,230
Balances	–0–	$14,600	$12,600	$ 930	$1,070

(Statement continued on next page.)

Cash Payments:

Liabilities	$12,600	$12,600	–0–	–0–
Partners' Loans	800	–0–	$ 300	$ 500
Partners' Capital	1,200	–0–	630	570
Totals, as above	$14,600	$12,600	$ 930	$1,070

2.3 The balance sheet of Roberto & Kozak as of June 30, 19XX, is shown below.

Roberto & Kozak
Balance Sheet
June 30, 19XX

ASSETS			**EQUITIES**	
Cash		$ 18,000	Accounts Payable	$ 43,500
Receivables		48,000	Notes Payable	30,000
Inventory		69,000	Roberto, Capital	63,000
Plant & Equipment	$102,000		Kozak, Capital	79,500
Less: Accumulated				
Depreciation	21,000	81,000		
		$216,000		$216,000

The partners accept an offer from Peerless Corporation to purchase the firm's assets (except cash) and to assume the firm's liabilities. The Corporation will issue 6000 shares of its unissued capital stock to the partners. (Since it is not stated otherwise, the profit and loss ratio is 50:50.)

Required:

Assuming the sale is carried through and the partnership is dissolved, prepare the journal entries on the partnership books. The stock is selling at $48 per share. Goodwill is to be recognized.

SOLUTION

Goodwill*	163,500	
Roberto, Capital		81,750
Kozak, Capital		81,750

To record goodwill developed by the partnership.

Peerless Corporation Receivable	288,000	
Accumulated Depreciation	21,000	
Accounts Payable	43,500	
Notes Payable:	30,000	
Goodwill		163,500
Accounts Receivable		48,000
Inventory		69,000
Plant and Equipment		102,000

To record the transfer of assets and liabilities to the Peerless Corporation.

*Goodwill is calculated as follows:

$$(6000 \times \$48) - \$63,000 - \$79,500 + \$18,000 = \$163,500$$

Stock of Peerless Corporation	288,000	
Peerless Corporation Receivable		288,000

To record receipt of Peerless Corporation stock.

Roberto, Capital ($63,000 + $81,750)	144,750	
Kozak, Capital ($79,500 + $81,750)	161,250	
Cash		18,000
Stock of Peerless Corporation		288,000

To record distribution of assets upon dissolution of partnership.

2.4 On December 31, 19X4, the balance sheet of Nook and Crook was as follows:

Nook & Crook
Balance Sheet
December 31, 19X4

ASSETS			EQUITIES	
Cash		$ 15,000	Accounts Payable	$ 26,000
Receivables		40,000	Notes Payable	10,500
Inventories		52,500	Nook, Capital	50,000
Plant and Equipment	$60,000		Crook, Capital	75,000
Less: Accumulated				
Depreciation	6,000	54,000		
		$161,500		$161,500

At this time the partners accept an offer from the Hook Corporation to purchase all of the assets of the firm (excluding cash) and to assume the firm's liabilities, for which the corporation will issue 3000 shares of unissued capital stock. (Again, the profit and loss ratio is assumed to be 50:50 unless otherwise stated.)

Required:

(a) Journal entries on the partnership books, assuming that the sale is carried through and the partnership is dissolved. The stock of Hook Corporation is currently selling at $60 per share. Goodwill is not to be recorded in the partnership accounts.

(b) Same as (a), but assume the stock is selling for $25 per share.

SOLUTION

(a)

Hook Corporation Receivable	110,000	
Accumulated Depreciation	6,000	
Accounts Payable	26,000	
Notes Payable	10,500	
Receivables		40,000
Inventories		52,500
Plant and Equipment		60,000

To record sale of partnership business.

Stock of Hook Corporation	180,000	
Hook Corporation Receivable		110,000
Nook, Capital		35,000
Crook, Capital		35,000

To record receipt of consideration from purchaser and to divide gain
on sale equally.

Nook, Capital	85,000	
Crook, Capital	110,000	
Cash		15,000
Stock of Hook Corporation		180,000

To divide assets of the partnership in final capital ratio.

(b) First entry is the same as in part (a) above.

Stock of Hook Corporation	75,000	
Nook, Capital	17,500	
Crook, Capital	17,500	
Hook Corporation Receivable		110,000

To record receipt of consideration from purchaser and to divide loss
on sale equally.

Nook, Capital	32,500	
Crook, Capital	57,500	
Cash		15,000
Stock of Hook Corporation		75,000

To divide assets of partnership in final capital ratio.

2.5 Knife and Fork are partners sharing profits and losses in the ratio of 60 percent and 40 percent, respectively. Knife's capital investment is $2,900 and Fork's is $1,100. When the partners decided to dissolve the business, the firm had liabilities of $4,200, which included $300 owed to Fork and $200 to Knife for loans. After realization the cash on hand amounted to $4,500.

Required:

   Prepare a statement of liquidation, assuming that either partner would be able to cover a capital deficiency with a cash contribution.

SOLUTION

	Assets		Liabilities	Knife		Fork	
	Cash	Noncash		Loan	Capital	Loan	Capital
Balances before Realization	–0–	$8,200	$3,700	$200	$2,900	$300	$1,100
Realization and Division of Loss ($3,700)	$4,500	(8,200)	–0–	–0–	(2,220)	–0–	(1,480)
Balances	$4,500	–0–	$3,700	$200	$ 680	$300	($ 380)

(Statement continued on next page.)

	Assets		Liabilities	Knife		Fork	
	Cash	Noncash		Loan	Capital	Loan	Capital
Balances (from previous page)	$4,500	–0–	$3,700	$200	$ 680	$300	($ 380)
Transfer Fork's Loan Balance to Reduce His Capital Deficiency						(300)	300
Balances	$4,500		$3,700	$200	$ 680	–0–	($ 80)
Contribution by Fork to Make up His Deficiency	80		–0–	–0–	–0–		80
Balances	$4,580		$3,700	$200	$ 680		–0–
Distribution of Cash:	($4,580)						
Outside Creditors			($3,700)				
Knife's Loan				($200)			
Knife's Capital					($ 680)		

2.6 Ulysses, Vernon, and Waldo are in partnership, with capital account balances and profit and loss ratios as follows:

Ulysses	$ 91,000	50%
Vernon	35,000	30%
Waldo	10,500	20%
	$136,500	100%

The partners agree to liquidate the partnership. The assets are sold, the liabilities of $104,800 are paid, and the cash remaining to be distributed to the partners amounts to $63,000.

Required:

Prepare a schedule showing how the $63,000 cash should be distributed among the partners. If necessary, assume that any capital deficiency is uncollectible.

SOLUTION

	Assets		Liabilities	Partners' Capital		
	Cash	Noncash		Ulysses	Vernon	Waldo
Balances before Realization		$241,300	$104,800	$91,000	$35,000	$10,500
Realization and Loss* (5:3:2)	$167,800	(241,300)		(36,750)	(22,050)	(14,700)
Balances	$167,800	–0–	$104,800	$54,250	$12,950	($ 4,200)
Debit Balance of Waldo Absorbed by Other Two Partners (5:3)				(2,625)	(1,575)	4,200
	$167,800		$104,800	$51,625	$11,375	–0–
Distribution of Cash	($167,800)		($104,800)	($51,625)	($11,375)	

*Loss: $241,300 − $104,800 − $63,000 = $73,500

2.7 Prepare schedules showing the first distribution to partners in each of the following cases. The condition at the beginning of liquidation, after payment of liabilities, is as follows:

Partner	Capital	Profit and Loss Ratio		
		Case 1	Case 2	Case 3
A	$25,000	5%	10%	15%
B	7,500	15%	30%	10%
C	18,000	35%	25%	20%
D	30,000	20%	15%	40%
E	13,000	25%	20%	15%
Total	$93,500	100%	100%	100%
Cash for Division	3,500			
Remainder	$90,000			
Cash on Hand Held for Expenses	1,400			
Noncash Assets	$88,600			

Required:

Prepare calculations to determine the safe payment of $3,500 in each of the three cases.

SOLUTION

Case 1

	A, 5%	B, 15%	C, 35%	D, 20%	E, 25%
Balances before Payment	$25,000	$ 7,500	$18,000	$30,000	$13,000
Possible Loss: ($90,000)	(4,500)	(13,500)	(31,500)	(18,000)	(22,500)
	$20,500	($ 6,000)	($13,500)	$12,000	($ 9,500)
Distribution of Possible Deficits	(5,800)	6,000	13,500	23,200	9,500
	$14,700			($11,200)	
Transfer of D's Possible Deficit	(11,200)			$11,200	
Safe Payment	$ 3,500				

Case 2

	A, 10%	B, 30%	C, 25%	D, 15%	E, 20%
Balances before Payment	$25,000	$ 7,500	$18,000	$30,000	$13,000
Possible Loss: ($90,000)	(9,000)	(27,000)	(22,500)	(13,500)	(18,000)
	$16,000	($19,500)	($ 4,500)	$16,500	($ 5,000)
Distribution of Possible Deficits	(11,600)	$19,500	4,500	(17,400)	5,000
	$ 4,400			($ 900)	
Transfer of D's Possible Deficit	(900)			900	
Safe Payment	$ 3,500				

Case 3

	A, 15%	B, 10%	C, 20%	D, 40%	E, 15%
Balances before Payment	$25,000	$7,500	$18,000	$30,000	$13,000
Possible Loss: ($90,000)	(13,500)	(9,000)	(18,000)	(36,000)	(13,500)
	$11,500	($1,500)	–0–	($ 6,000)	($ 500)
Transfer of Possible Deficits	8,000	1,500		6,000	500
Safe Payment	$ 3,500				

2.8   The condensed trial balance of Anton, Beres, and Dent before liquidation was as follows:

Anton, Capital		$ 6,000
Beres, Capital		17,000
Dent, Capital		18,000
Beres, Drawing Account	$ 1,000	
Liabilities		40,000
Assets	80,000	
	$81,000	$81,000

Anton possesses $3,000 of cash which is unencumbered, while the other two partners possess none. The assets of the partnership were sold for $38,000, with profits and losses to be shared equally.

Required:

Prepare a statement of liquidation.

SOLUTION

	Liabilities	Partners' Equity Anton	Beres	Dent	Total
Balances (credit)	$40,000	$ 6,000	$17,000	$18,000	$81,000
Less: Drawing Account	–0–	–0–	1,000	–0–	1,000
Balances Before Realization	$40,000	$ 6,000	$16,000	$18,000	$80,000
Realization Loss Divided Equally	–0–	14,000	14,000	14,000	42,000
Balances	$40,000	($ 8,000)	$ 2,000	$ 4,000	$38,000
Cash from Anton	–0–	3,000	–0–	–0–	3,000
Balances	$40,000	($ 5,000)	$ 2,000	$ 4,000	$41,000
Deficit of Anton to Others	–0–	5,000	(2,500)	(2,500)	–0–
Balances	$40,000	–0–	($ 500)	$ 1,500	$41,000
Deficit of Beres to Dent	–0–		500	(500)	–0–
Balances	$40,000		–0–	$ 1,000	$41,000
Cash Distributed*	$40,000			$ 1,000	$41,000

*Cash: $38,000 + $3,000 = $41,000.

2.9   Michelle and Gary were partners in a retailing business. The adjusted trial balance for the business as of June 30, 19X4, is as follows:

Michelle and Gary
Adjusted Trial Balance
June 30, 19X4

Cash in Bank	$ 22,420	
Accounts Receivable	34,044	
Inventories	61,430	
Buildings & Equipment	18,560	
Accumulated Depreciation		$ 4,220
Accounts Payable		21,386
Michelle, Capital		13,608
Michelle, Drawings	4,594	
Gary, Capital		91,894
Gary, Drawings	5,204	
Revenues		40,010
Expenses	24,866	
	$171,118	$171,118

The fiscal year for the partnership ends on January 31 and the partners share profits: one-fourth to Michelle and three-fourths to Gary. On June 30 the partners agreed to dissolve the partnership as of that date, with the arrangement that Gary was to continue the business as a sole proprietor. The dissolution agreement contained the following terms:

(1) Michelle was to be paid the book value of her equity in the business.

(2) Michelle was to receive an additional $16,000 to cover her interest in the goodwill of the business.

(3) Payment to Michelle was to be made one-fourth in cash on dissolution date and the balance in two notes of equal amount due one and two years from the date of the dissolution with interest at 7 percent.

Gary did *not* want to put any goodwill on the books.

Required:

Prepare journal entries to be made on June 30, 19X4, in connection with the partnership dissolution.

SOLUTION

Michelle, Capital	4,594	
Michelle, Drawings		4,594

To transfer Michelle's drawings to her capital account.

Revenues	40,010	
Expenses		24,866
Michelle, Capital		3,786
Gary, Capital		11,358

To divide net income in the profit and loss ratio.

Michelle, Capital ($13,608 − $4,594 + $3,786)	12,800	
Gary, Capital	16,000	
Cash		7,200
Notes Payable to Retired Partner		21,600

To close Michelle's capital account and to charge Gary for $16,000 of goodwill, since he elected not to place any goodwill on the books.

2.10 Four partners, sharing profits and losses equally, decide to liquidate when their books show the following condensed trial balance:

	Dr.	Cr.
Assets	$90,000	
Morton, Capital		$30,000
Pelham, Capital		25,000
Harlan, Capital		25,000
West, Capital		10,000
	$90,000	$90,000

Month	Assets Sold	Loss	Cash Distributed
January	$30,000	$ 4,000	$26,000
February	20,000	6,000	14,000
March	40,000	10,000	30,000

Required:

(*a*) Prepare a worksheet to determine safe distribution of available cash balances.

(*b*) Prepare a summary statement of the liquidation for the three months ended March 31.

(*Note:* Worksheet amounts should be rounded to nearest dollar.)

SOLUTION

(*a*) *Worksheet for distribution of available cash balances:*

	Morton	Pelham	Harlan	West	Total
Capital Balance per Ledger	30,000	25,000	25,000	10,000	90,000
1st Month—January					
Realization Loss Divided Equally	1,000	1,000	1,000	1,000	4,000
Balances after Realization	29,000	24,000	24,000	9,000	86,000
Cash to Be Divided					26,000
Assumed Loss Divided Equally	15,000	15,000	15,000	15,000	60,000
Potential Debit Balance of West Divided Equally	2,000	2,000	2,000	(6,000)	
Total Assumed Loss	17,000	17,000	17,000	9,000	60,000
Cash Divided	12,000	7,000	7,000	–0–	26,000
Capital Balances after Cash Distribution	17,000	17,000	17,000	9,000	60,000
2nd Month—February					
Realization Loss Divided Equally	1,500	1,500	1,500	1,500	6,000
Balances after Realization	15,500	15,500	15,500	7,500	54,000
Cash to Be Divided					14,000
Assumed Loss Divided Equally	10,000	10,000	10,000	10,000	40,000
Potential Debit Balance of West Divided Equally	834	833	833	(2,500)	
Total Assumed Loss	10,834	10,833	10,833	7,500	40,000
Cash Divided	4,666	4,667	4,667	–0–	14,000
Capital Balances after Cash Distribution	10,834	10,833	10,833	7,500	40,000
3rd Month—March					
Loss Divided Equally	2,500	2,500	2,500	2,500	10,000
Balances after Realization	8,334	8,333	8,333	5,000	30,000
Cash Divided	8,334	8,333	8,333	5,000	30,000

(b)

Morton, Pelham, Harlan and West
Statement of Liquidation
Three Months Ended March 31, 19XX

	Morton	Pelham	Harlan	West	Total
Capital Balances before Realization	$30,000	$25,000	$25,000	$10,000	$90,000
Total Loss Divided	5,000	5,000	5,000	5,000	20,000
Capital Balances	$25,000	$20,000	$20,000	$ 5,000	$70,000
Cash Paid —January	$12,000	$ 7,000	$ 7,000	–0–	$26,000
—February	4,666	4,667	4,667	–0–	14,000
—March	8,334	8,333	8,333	$ 5,000	30,000
Total Cash Paid, as above	$25,000	$20,000	$20,000	$ 5,000	$70,000

2.11 The following schedule shows the facts concerning capital investments in a partnership which is about to be liquidated:

	Profit and Loss Ratio	Capital Balances	Drawing Balances (Debit)	Loan Account Balances
Arden	45%	$ 90,000	–0–	–0–
Glatter	35%	70,000	–0–	$35,000
Witkin	20%	40,000	($6,000)	–0–
	100%	$200,000	($6,000)	$35,000

The total book value of the assets of the firm amounts to $239,400.

Required:

Prepare a schedule showing the distribution of possible losses and how the cash which is received from realization of the firm's assets may be safely distributed.

SOLUTION

	Equity Balances		Ratios		Potential Loss Necessary to Extinguish Capital Balances	Degree of Vulnerability
Arden	$ 90,000	÷	45%	=	$200,000	2
Glatter	$105,000	÷	35%	=	$300,000	3
Witkin	$ 34,000	÷	20%	=	$170,000	1

	Noncash Assets	Liabil-ities	Partner's Equity		
Schedule Showing Distribution of Possible Losses					
			Arden	Glatter	Witkin
Profit and Loss Ratio			45%	35%	20%
Balances before Realization	$239,400	$10,400	$90,000	$105,000	$34,000
Loss Which Would Eliminate Witkin from Participa-tion in Cash Distributions Divided in the Profit and Loss Ratio	(170,000)		(76,500)	(59,500)	(34,000)
Balances	$ 69,400	$10,400	$13,500	$ 45,500	
Additional Loss Which Would Eliminate Arden from Participation in Cash Distribution Divided in the Ratio of 45:35	24,000[c]*		13,500	10,500	
	$ 45,400	$10,400[a]		$ 35,000[b]	

[a] Thus, the first $10,400 goes to outside creditors.
[b] The next $35,000 goes to Glatter.
[c] The next $24,000 goes to Arden and Glatter in ratio of 45:35 respectively.
   Any additional funds should be divided among the three partners in their profit and loss ratio.
* If Witkin had a balance of $6,000 or more, an additional loss of $30,000 could be divided among the three partners. Since Witkin may be eliminated by this time, a loss of only $24,000 would be sufficient to eliminate Arden.

2.12   The following schedule shows data concerning the capital investments in a partnership which is about to be liquidated:

	Profit and Loss Ratio	Capital Balances	Drawing Balances	Loan Balances	Total Equities
Thomas	50%	$36,000	–0–	$15,000	$ 51,000
Dick	30%	21,000	–0–	6,000	27,000
Harry	20%	26,000	($3,000)	–0–	23,000
Total	100%	$83,000	($3,000)	$21,000	$101,000

Total book value of the assets of the firm, including cash of $4,000, amounts to $104,000.

Required:

Prepare a cash distribution plan showing how the cash received from realization of the firm's assets may be safely paid out.

SOLUTION

Computation of relative abilities to absorb losses:

		Degree of Vulnerability
Thomas	$51,000 ÷ 0.50 = $102,000	2
Dick	$27,000 ÷ 0.30 = $90,000	1
Harry	$23,000 ÷ 0.20 = $115,000	3

Distribution of potential losses:

	Assets		Outside Creditors	Partners' Equity		
	Noncash	*Cash*		*Thomas*	*Dick*	*Harry*
Balances, Per Books	$100,000	$4,000	$3,000	$51,000	$27,000	$23,000
Loss Which Would Eliminate Dick	90,000			45,000	27,000	18,000
Balances	$ 10,000	$4,000	$3,000	$ 6,000	–0–	$ 5,000
Loss Which Would Eliminate Thomas	8,400*			6,000		2,400
Balances	$ 1,600	$4,000	$3,000	–0–		$ 2,600

```
* $12,000   ($102,000 − $90,000)
 −$ 3,600   ($ 12,000 × 30%)
  _____
  $ 8,400
```

Cash distribution plan:

	Cash	*Outside Creditors*	*Thomas*	*Dick*	*Harry*
First Installment	$ 5,600	$3,000			$2,600
Second Installment	$ 8,400		5/7		2/7
Third Installment	$90,000		5/10	3/10	2/10
Additional Cash			5/10	3/10	2/10

Chapter 3

Branch Operations

3.1 INTRODUCTION

A *branch* is one of several means a company can use to extend its sales and services into areas which may be a considerable distance from the main locus of operations.

The degree of autonomy granted to a branch is determined by the *home office*. Most branches maintain their own records of sales, accounts receivable, and receipts from customers. Checks received from branch customers are generally deposited in a local bank. Some branches have authority to pay for most expenses, while others are permitted to make disbursements for only small amounts—roughly equivalent to petty cash.

The chief purpose of a branch set of books is to determine the profit or loss of each branch. Thus, the accounting records of a branch frequently resemble a complete set of double entry books. In lieu of a capital account, however, the branch ledger shows the investment of the home office.

A branch usually carries a stock of merchandise and thus is able to make delivery from stock located closer to the customer than the goods located at the main office or warehouse. A branch may acquire merchandise from the home office or may purchase goods from outsiders. If merchandise is purchased from outsiders, the branch manager may be required first to obtain approval from a central purchasing office, or the branch manager may have to place the order through the central purchasing division or office.

Occasionally a branch may have authority to pay vendors for goods purchased by or for the branch. Most businesses, however, prefer to centralize purchasing and accounts payable.

A *sales agency* differs from a branch in that the agency generally carries a line of samples and takes orders from customers that are forwarded to the home office. All other activities are usually centralized in the home office. Accounting for sales agencies depends on the needs and desires of management. It is basically similar to accounting for departmental operations. Some firms merely accumulate sales by agencies; others allocate cost of goods sold and thus are able to determine gross profit by agencies; still others attempt to allocate expenses and determine a selling or operating profit for each agency.

3.2 BRANCH ACCOUNTING

When a branch is established the home office opens an account in its general ledger entitled Branch, or Branch Control, or Investment in Branch, or some other similar name. Frequently, one account will be used to show the long-term investment in a branch while another account (such as Branch Current) will be used for more common events. In the home office ledger, this account or group of accounts is charged for everything sent to the branch or for services rendered to or for the branch, and it is credited for amounts received from the branch.

In a similar fashion, the branch ledger will contain an account entitled Home Office, Home Office Control, Home Office Current, or perhaps a group of similarly named accounts corresponding to the branch accounts in the home office ledger. This account is credited for all assets received by the branch from the home office. It is also credited for all debts incurred for merchandise acquired or for services rendered by the home office for the branch. Such an account would also be credited as a result of expenses incurred by the home office for the benefit of the branch. It is debited for amounts sent by the branch to the home office.

In operation, the branch account on the home office books will be debited when the home office account on the branch books is credited, and vice versa. Thus, the balances of each of such pair of accounts should be equal in dollar amount, but the balances should be on opposite sides of the respective accounts. For example, if the branch account of the home office books has a debit balance of $14,000, then the home office account on branch books should have a credit balance of the same amount. Two accounts that have such a relationship are often described as *reciprocal*.

When there are many remittances between the home office and a branch, it will probably be useful for the home office to maintain a special account for remittances from Branch X, and for Branch X to maintain a reciprocal account entitled Remittances to Home Office. Such specialization of function is particularly useful when the two balances do not initially agree and a reconciliation of the two accounts must be prepared. After reconciliation, errors should be corrected, and items in transit should be entered in the records of the unit which will be receiving them.

The home office may receive many returns from each branch. Reconciliation is simplified if the returns received from Branch A, as well as the returns to the home office by Branch A, can be easily identified. Such a pair of accounts would also be reciprocal in nature. Any difference between the two dollar balances will probably be the result of a return in transit or of an error.

When the books at a branch are closed the balance in its income summary account is transferred to the home office account. Assume that the Branch A accounts indicated a profit of $65,000. The final entry on the branch books would be as follows:

Income Summary	65,000	
Home Office		65,000

To transfer net income for year ended December 31, 19XX.

The home office will be notified of this entry and a comparable entry will be made in the home office journal:

Branch A	65,000	
Income: Branches		65,000

To record net income for year reported by Branch A.

3.3 BILLING PROCEDURES

The shipment of goods by the home office to a branch is an intracompany transfer, not a sale. Nevertheless the change in location of the goods should be recognized and recorded.

In general, there are three bases for charging goods sent to a branch. One procedure is for the home office to bill the merchandise sent to each branch at cost. The strongest argument in favor of this procedure is that no sale has taken place, therefore the cost to the business entity should remain the basis for the goods while they are located at a branch of the company.

Many managements use a second procedure. They hold that the home office performs services—merchandising, purchasing, and so on—and thus they reason that the transfer price should reflect the cost of these services. In such cases the firm usually averages the cost of the services and adds a flat percentage to the cost of all goods transferred from the home office to a branch.

In the third procedure, firms simply charge a branch for the expected *selling* price of the merchandise. One argument in favor of this method is that it facilitates control of the inventory at a branch. Since the goods are charged to the branch at selling price, the cost of goods sold should equal sales for any given period of time. Thus, the branch accounts are bound to show a net loss equivalent to the expenses of the branch during that period.

3.4   SHIPMENTS TO BRANCH BILLED AT COST

EXAMPLE 1.   Assume that the Drexel Corp. established a new branch on June 1, Year 1, and that the following transactions took place during the balance of the calendar year.

(a)   Home office sent a check to Branch A for $10,000.

(b)   Merchandise which cost $30,000 was sent to the branch.

(c)   Branch sales all on credit amounted to $38,000.

(d)   Branch collections from customers amounted to $28,000.

(e)   Branch paid expenses amounting to $3,000.

(f)   Branch transferred $18,000 cash to home office.

(g)   Branch received a memorandum from the home office indicating that $2,000 of the operating expenses recorded on its books were applicable to Branch A.

(h)   Branch inventory at December 31 amounted to $6,000.

(i)   Branch closed its nominal accounts for the year.

(j)   The net income of the branch amounted to $9000.

The following journal entries summarize the transactions relating to Branch A for Year 1.

	Home Office Books			*Branch Books*		
(a)	Branch	10,000		Cash	10,000	
	Cash		10,000	Home Office		10,000
(b)	Branch	30,000		Shipments from		
	Shipments to			Home Office	30,000	
	Branch		30,000	Home Office		30,000
(c)				Accounts Receivable	38,000	
				Sales		38,000
(d)				Cash	28,000	
				Accounts Receivable		28,000
(e)				Expenses	3,000	
				Cash		3,000
(f)	Cash	18,000		Home Office	18,000	
	Branch		18,000	Cash		18,000
(g)	Branch	2,000		Expenses	2,000	
	Expenses		2,000	Home Office		2,000
(h)				Inventory	6,000	
				Income Summary		6,000
(i)				Sales	38,000	
				Shipments from		
				Home Office		30,000
				Expenses		5,000
				Income Summary		3,000
(j)	Branch	9,000		Income Summary	9,000	
	Income: Branches		9,000	Home Office		9,000

In the home office ledger the account entitled Branch will have a debit balance of $33,000 and may be summarized as follows:

Branch

	Dr.	Cr.	Balance
Cash to Branch	10,000		10,000
Shipments to Branch	30,000		40,000
Cash Received from Branch		18,000	22,000
Expense Applicable to Branch	2,000		24,000
Net Income Reported by Branch	9,000		33,000

In the branch ledger, the account entitled Home Office will have a credit balance of $33,000, and is summarized as follows:

Home Office

	Dr.	Cr.	Balance
Cash from Home Office		10,000	10,000
Shipments from Home Office		30,000	40,000
Cash Sent to Home Office	18,000		22,000
Expenses Allocated by Home Office		2,000	24,000
Net Income		9,000	33,000

Although the balances in these two accounts are equal, the Branch account on the home office books has a debit balance. The Home Office account on the Branch books has a credit balance of the same amount. These two accounts are reciprocal to each other.

There is another pair of reciprocal accounts in this example. The account entitled Shipments to Branch on the home office books should have a credit balance equal to the debit balance in the account entitled Shipments from Home Office on the branch books.

3.5 WORKSHEET FOR COMBINED STATEMENTS

A worksheet to prepare combined statements for the home office and its branch or branches should accomplish the following:

1. Combine similar assets and liabilities
2. Eliminate reciprocal amounts
3. Eliminate intracompany profit, if any.

The accompanying worksheet for the Drexel Corp. is based on the branch transactions detailed in the previous section of this chapter, and on assumed data for the home office. It has also been assumed that all adjusting entries have been recorded, including the ending inventories.

The worksheet is used primarily to facilitate the preparation of combined statements. Thus, the following worksheet is divided into two parts. The income section is used to prepare the combined income statement; the balance sheet section is used to prepare a combined statement of retained earnings for the period involved, and also to prepare a combined balance sheet at the end of the period. Some accountants prepare a worksheet divided into three parts; they group separately the items which make up the retained earnings. However, these items usually consist of only a few lines, so most accountants feel it is not worth the additional effort required for a third section.

The elimination entries in this type of worksheet are not recorded in the company's books—neither in those of the home office nor those of a branch. A two-column sheet detailing these journal entries should be prepared and preserved along with the worksheet itself, as these papers will generally be the only connecting links between the trial balances and the statements. The explanations to worksheet entries are given as footnotes at the bottom of the worksheets.

Drexel Corp.
Worksheet to Combine Income Statements
Year Ended December 31, Year 1

	Home Office		Branch		Eliminations		Combined
	Dr.	Cr.	Dr.	Cr.	Dr.	Cr.	Statements
Sales		100,000		38,000			138,000
Inventory—Jan. 1	18,000						18,000
Purchases	93,000						93,000
Shipments to Branch		30,000			[a]30,000		
Shipments from Home Office			30,000			[a]30,000	
Inventory—Dec. 31		10,000		6,000			16,000
Expenses	11,000		5,000				16,000
Income: Branch		9,000			[b] 9,000		
Totals	122,000	149,000	35,000	44,000			127,000	154,000
Net Income	27,000			9,000		[b] 9,000	27,000
	149,000	149,000	44,000	44,000			154,000	154,000

[a] To eliminate intracompany shipments.
[b] To eliminate net income of branch previously recorded by home office.

Drexel Corp.
Worksheet to Combine Balance Sheets
December 31, Year 1

	Home Office		Branch		Eliminations		Combined
	Dr.	Cr.	Dr.	Cr.	Dr.	Cr.	Statements
Cash	49,000		17,000				66,000
Accounts Receivable	19,000		10,000				29,000
Inventory	10,000		6,000				16,000
Branch	33,000					[1]33,000	
Accounts Payable		20,000					20,000
Home Office				33,000	[1]33,000		
Capital Stock		50,000					50,000
Retained Earnings—Jan. 1		14,000					14,000
Net Income		27,000					27,000
	111,000	111,000	33,000	33,000			111,000	111,000

[1] To eliminate reciprocal accounts.

The following statements have been prepared from the Drexel Corp. worksheet for the year ended December 31, Year 1.

Drexel Corp.
Income Statement
Year Ended December 31, Year 1

Sales		$138,000
Less Cost of Goods Sold:		
Inventory, January 1	$ 18,000	
Add: Purchases	93,000	
Cost of Goods Available for Sale	$111,000	
Less: Inventory, December 31	16,000	
Cost of Goods Sold		95,000
Gross Margin		$ 43,000
Less: Expenses		16,000
Net Income		$ 27,000

Drexel Corp.
Retained Earnings
Year Ended December 31, Year 1

Retained Earnings, January 1	$14,000
Add: Net Income for Year	27,000
Retained Earnings, December 31	$41,000

Drexel Corp.
Balance Sheet
December 31, Year 1

ASSETS

Cash	$66,000	
Accounts Receivable	29,000	
Inventory	16,000	
Total Assets		$111,000

LIABILITIES AND SHAREHOLDERS' EQUITY

Accounts Payable		$ 20,000
Capital Stock	$50,000	
Retained Earnings	41,000	
Total Shareholders' Equity		91,000
Total Liabilities and Shareholders' Equity		$111,000

3.6 SHIPMENTS TO BRANCH BILLED IN EXCESS OF COST: YEAR 1

EXAMPLE 2. Assume the same data as in Example 1, except that the merchandise shipped to the branch is billed at 20 percent above cost. Thus the shipments to the branch are billed at $36,000 (120% of $30,000), and the final inventory at the branch will be reported by it as $7,200 (120 percent of $6,000).

The journal entries which follow summarize the transactions relating to Branch A for Year 1:

Home Office Books			*Branch Books*		
(a) Branch	10,000		Cash	10,000	
Cash		10,000	Home Office		10,000
(b) Branch	36,000		Shipments from Home Office	36,000	
Branch	000		Home Office		36,000
Allowance for Valuation of Branch Inventory		6,000			
(c)			Accounts Receivable	38,000	
			Sales		38,000
(d)			Cash	28,000	
			Accounts Receivable		28,000
(e)			Expenses	3,000	
			Cash		3,000
(f) Cash	18,000		Home Office	18,000	
Branch		18,000	Cash		18,000
(g) Branch	2,000		Expenses	2,000	
Expenses		2,000	Home Office		2,000
(h)			Inventory	7,200	
			Income Summary		7,200
(i)			Sales	38,000	
			Income Summary	3,000	
			Shipments from Home Office		36,000
			Expenses		5,000
(j) Branch	4,200		Income Summary	4,200	
Income Branch		4,200	Home Office		4,200
(k) Allowance for Valuation of Branch Inventory	4,800				
Income Branch		4,800			

The second entry—the account entitled Valuation of Branch Inventory—is credited by the home office for the excess of the billed price over the cost of the merchandise shipped. The excess amounted to $6,000 during Year 1 ($36,000 − $30,000). According to the branch records, the cost of goods sold would be $28,800 ($36,000 − $7,200). However, the actual cost of the goods sold by the branch is $24,000 ($30,000 − $6,000). Thus, $4,800 of the mark-up in shipments will have been realized as a result of the branch having sold these goods to outsiders. Entry (k), appearing only in the home office books, recognizes this adjustment to the net income reported by the branch. The net income of Branch A is thus $9,000 ($4,200 + $4,800).

The account entitled Allowance for Valuation of Branch Inventory in the home office ledger will appear as follows:

Allowance for Valuation of Branch Inventory

	Dr.	Cr.	Balance
Year 1—Mark-up of Merchandise Shipped to Branch: ($30,000 × 0.20)		6,000	6,000
Dec. 31—Realization of Mark-up in Goods Sold by Branch: ($28,000 − $24,000)	4,800		1,200

The balance in this account should equal the mark-up contained in the ending inventory of goods at the branch. Thus, $1,200 equals $7,200 × (0.20/1.20). In other words, the inventory at the branch at billed prices, $7,200, less the credit balance in the allowance valuation of branch inventory, $1,200, equals the actual cost of the inventory located at the branch. The actual cost of the ending inventory at the branch, $6,000, may be verified by comparing it to the ending inventory at the branch in Example 1, where all branch data are at cost.

In the home office ledger the account entitled branch will have a debit balance of $34,200, and will appear as follows:

Branch

	Dr.	Cr.	Balance
Cash to Branch	10,000		10,000
Merchandise to Branch	36,000		46,000
Cash Received from Branch		18,000	28,000
Expenses Applicable to Branch	2,000		30,000
Operating Income Reported by Branch	4,200		34,200

In the branch ledger, the account entitled Home Office will have a credit balance of $34,200, and will appear as follows:

Home Office

	Dr.	Cr.	Balance
Cash from Home Office		10,000	10,000
Merchandise from Home Office		36,000	46,000
Cash Sent to Home Office	18,000		28,000
Expenses Advanced by Home Office		2,000	30,000
Net Income for Period		4,200	34,200

The foregoing two accounts have balances which are equal. However, the branch account on the home office books has a debit balance of $34,200, while the home office account on the branch books has a credit balance of the same amount. Thus, these two accounts are reciprocal to each other.

In this example, the account entitled Shipments to Branch on the home office books and the account entitled Shipments from Home Office on the branch books are not reciprocal to each other; the former is at cost, while the latter is at billed prices.

The accompanying worksheet to prepare a combined income statement for Year 1 contains income statement data for the branch that is based on the transactions in this section and on assumed data for the home office. The purpose of journal entry (a) is to eliminate intracompany shipments at cost. Journal entry (b) eliminates the mark-up in the shipments from the home office; it also reduces the branch inventory at December 31 to cost; and it increases the net income of the branch from its reported figure to an amount based on cost. Journal entry (c) eliminates the net income of the branch already recorded by the home office; that is, it avoids double counting of net income earned by the branch.

The accompanying worksheet to prepare a combined balance sheet as of December 31, Year 1, contains balance sheet data for the branch that is based on the transactions in this section and on assumed data for the home office. Journal entry (1) combines the allowance for valuation of branch inventory with the inventory at December 31, so that inventory at the branch will be included at cost. Journal entry (2) eliminates reciprocal accounts in the two trial balances, which have no place in a combined balance sheet.

Since the data have all been reduced or adjusted to cost, statements prepared from these worksheets should be exactly the same as those prepared from the worksheets in the previous example.

Drexel Corp.
Worksheet to Combine Income Statements
Year Ended December 31, Year 1

	Home Office Dr.	Home Office Cr.	Branch Dr.	Branch Cr.	Adjustments & Eliminations		Combined Statements	
Sales		100,000		38,000				138,000
Inventory—Jan. 1	18,000						18,000	
Purchases	93,000						93,000	
Shipments to Branch		30,000			[a]30,000			
Shipments from Home Office			36,000			{[b] 6,000 / [a]30,000		
Inventory—Dec. 31		10,000		7,200	[b] 1,200			16,000
Expenses	11,000		5,000				16,000	
Income: Branch		9,000			[c] 9,000			
Totals	122,000	149,000	41,000	45,200			127,000	154,000
Net Income	27,000		4,200		[b] 4,800	[c] 9,000	27,000	
	149,000	149,000	45,200	45,200			154,000	154,000

[a] To eliminate intracompany shipments at cost.

[b] To eliminate intracompany mark-up in shipments during Year 1, and in inventory at end of year. Also to increase income of branch for mark-up realized during Year 1.

[c] To eliminate net income of branch already recorded by home office.

Drexel Corp.
Worksheet to Combine Balance Sheets
December 31, Year 1

	Home Office		Branch		Adjustments & Eliminations		Combined Statements	
	Dr.	Cr.	Dr.	Cr.				
Cash	49,000		17,000				66,000	
Accounts Receivable	19,000		10,000				29,000	
Inventory	10,000		7,200			[1] 1,200	16,000	
Branch	34,200					[2] 34,200		
Allowance for Valuation of Branch Inventory		1,200			[1] 1,200			
Accounts Payable		20,000						20,000
Home Office				34,200	[2] 34,200			
Capital Stock		50,000						50,000
Retained Earnings		14,000						14,000
Net Income		27,000						27,000
	112,200	112,200	34,200	34,200			111,000	111,000

[1] To eliminate intracompany mark-up in branch inventory at end of year.
[2] To eliminate reciprocal accounts.

3.7 SHIPMENTS TO BRANCH BILLED IN EXCESS OF COST: YEAR 2

EXAMPLE 3. Example 3 is a continuation of the previous example into Year 2. The income statements of the home office and branch of the Drexel Corp. are condensed in the first four columns of the accompanying worksheet to prepare a combined income statement for Year 2.

The income reported by the branch for Year 2 was $9,800. However, this amount must be adjusted by the home office for the excess of billed prices over cost realized by sales to outsiders. The relationship of billed prices, actual cost, and mark-up is presented in the following schedule, which indicates that $9,200 of intracompany mark-up has been realized in goods sold by the Branch.

	Billed Price	Cost	Mark-up
Inventory, January 1	$ 7,200	$ 6,000	$ 1,200
Shipments from Home Office	60,000	50,000	10,000
Available for Sale	$67,200	$56,000	$11,200
Inventory, December 31	12,000	10,000	2,000
Merchandise Sold	$55,200	$46,000	
Mark-up Realized			$ 9,200

If it is assumed that the oldest merchandise was sold first, then the intracompany mark-up realized by branch sales during Year 2 may be analyzed as follows:

Mark-up in Inventory at January 1	$1,200
Mark-up in Shipments Received and Sold	8,000
Total Mark-up Realized	$9,200

These data are the basis for the following entry, in the home office journal:

Allowance for Valuation of Branch Inventory	9,200	
Branch Income		9,200

To recognize intracompany mark-up realized by branch as a result
of sales of merchandise in Year 2 (20/120 × $55,200).

The account entitled Allowance for Valuation of Branch Inventory in the home office ledger for Year 2 will appear as follows:

Allowance for Valuation of Branch Inventory

	Dr.	Cr.	Balance
Jan. 1 Balance			1,200
Year 2 Mark-up of Merchandise Shipped to Branch ($50,000 × 0.20)		10,000	11,200
Dec. 31 Realization of Mark-up in Goods Sold by Branch ($55,200 − $46,000)	9,200		2,000

In the worksheet to prepare a combined income statement for Year 2, journal entry (a) eliminates the cost of intracompany shipments during the year. Journal entry (b) reduces the branch inventory as of January 1, Year 2, by the mark-up of $1,200, and recognizes that this amount was realized during Year 2 as a result of the sales of merchandise on hand at the beginning of the year. Journal entry (c) eliminates the mark-up in intracompany shipments during Year 2; it reduces the ending inventory at the branch to its cost; and it increases the real earnings of the branch by the mark-up in sales of current shipments, $8,000 [($60,000 − $12,000) × (0.20/1.20)].

Some accountants would prefer to combine the last two journal entries, as follows:

Inventory, Dec. 31 ($12,000 × 0.20/1.20)	2,000	
Net Income: Branch	9,200	
Inventory, Jan. 1 ($7,000 × 0.20/1.20)		1,200
Shipments from Home Office ($60,000 − $50,000)		10,000

Journal entry (d) eliminates the income from the branch, which has already been recorded by the home office in order to avoid double counting.

In the worksheet to prepare a combined balance sheet as of December 31, Year 2, journal entry (1) combines the allowance for valuation of branch inventory with the inventory in order to reduce the branch inventory to cost. Journal entry (2) eliminates the home office and branch reciprocal accounts.

Finally, the three statements have been prepared from the Drexel Corp. worksheets for the Year ended December 31, Year 2: the income statement, the statement of retained earnings, and the balance sheet.

Drexel Corp.
Worksheet to Combine Income Statements
Year Ended December 31, Year 2

	Home Office		Branch		Adjustments & Eliminations		Combined Statements	
	Dr.	Cr.	Dr.	Cr.				
Sales		135,000		75,000				210,000
Inventory—Jan. 1	10,000		7,200			b 1,200	16,000	
Purchases	140,000						140,000	
Shipments to Branch		50,000			a50,000			
Shipments from Home Office			60,000			{ c10,000		
						{ a50,000		
Inventory—Dec. 31		14,000		12,000	c 2,000			24,000
Expenses	13,000		10,000				23,000	
Income: Branch		19,000			d19,000			
Totals	163,000	218,000	77,200	87,000			179,000	234,000
Net Income	55,000		9,800		{ c 8,000	d19,000	55,000	
					{ b 1,200			
	218,000	218,000	87,000	87,000			234,000	234,000

a To eliminate intracompany shipments at cost.

b To eliminate intracompany mark-up in branch inventory at beginning of Year 2, and to recognize its realization in Year 2.

c To eliminate intracompany mark-up in shipments during Year 2, and in inventory at end of Year 2. Also, to increase income of branch for mark-up realized during Year 2.

d To eliminate net income of branch already recorded by home office.

Drexel Corp.
Worksheet to Combine Balance Sheets
December 31, Year 2

	Home Office		Branch		Adjustments & Eliminations		Combined Statements	
	Dr.	Cr.	Dr.	Cr.				
Cash	39,000		12,000				51,000	
Accounts Receivable	42,800		15,000				57,800	
Inventory	24,000		12,000			1 2,000	34,000	
Branch	39,000					239,000		
Allowance for Valuation of Branch Inventory		2,000			1 2,000			
Accounts Payable		11,800						11,800
Home Office				39,000	239,000			
Capital Stock		50,000						50,000
Retained Earnings—Jan. 1		41,000						41,000
Net Income		55,000						55,000
Dividends	15,000						15,000	
	159,800	159,800	39,000	39,000			157,800	157,800

1 To eliminate intracompany mark-up in branch inventory at end of year.

2 To eliminate reciprocal accounts.

Drexel Corp.
Income Statement
Year Ended December 31, Year 2

Sales		$210,000
Less Cost of Goods Sold:		
Inventory, January 1	$ 16,000	
Add: Purchases	140,000	
Cost of Goods Available for Sale	$156,000	
Less: Inventory, December 31	24,000	
Cost of Goods Sold		132,000
Gross Margin		$ 78,000
Less: Expenses		23,000
Net Income		$ 55,000

Drexel Corp.
Retained Earnings
Year Ended December 31, Year 2

Retained Earnings, January 1	$ 41,000
Add: Net Income for Year	55,000
	$ 96,000
Less: Dividends	15,000
Retained Earnings, December 31	$ 81,000

Drexel Corp.
Balance Sheet
December 31, Year 2

ASSETS

Cash	$51,000	
Accounts Receivable	67,800	
Inventory	24,000	
Total Assets		$142,800

LIABILITIES AND SHAREHOLDERS' EQUITY

Accounts Payable		$ 11,800
Capital Stock	$50,000	
Retained Earnings	81,000	
Total Shareholders' Equity		131,000
Total Liabilities and Shareholders' Equity		$142,800

3.8   COMPANY USES PERPETUAL INVENTORY

In the previous examples in this chapter, it was assumed that the firm uses the periodic inventory method; i.e., physical inventories are recorded at the end of each accounting period.

In this section the journal entries will illustrate the appropriate treatment when the perpetual inventory method is used.

EXAMPLE 4. Assume the same transactions as in Example 1 except for the fact that the company uses the perpetual inventory method. The following journal entries summarize the transactions relating to Branch A for Year 1:

	Home Office Books			*Branch Books*		
(a)	Branch	10,000		Cash	10,000	
	Cash		10,000	Home Office		10,000
(b)	Branch	30,000		Merchandise	30,000	
	Merchandise		30,000	Home Office		30,000
(c)				Accounts Receivable	38,000	
				Sales		38,000
				Cost of Goods Sold	24,000	
				Merchandise		24,000
(d)				Cash	28,000	
				Accounts Receivable		28,000
(e)				Expenses	3,000	
				Cash		3,000
(f)	Cash	18,000		Home Office	18,000	
	Branch		18,000	Cash		18,000
(g)	Branch	2,000		Expenses	2,000	
	Expenses		2,000	Home Office		2,000
(h)				(no entry)		
(i)				Sales	38,000	
				Cost of Goods Sold		24,000
				Expenses		5,000
				Income Summary		9,000
(j)	Branch	9,000		Income Summary	9,000	
	Branch Net			Home Office		9,000
	Income		9,000			

EXAMPLE 5. Assume the same data as in Example 2, except that the company uses the perpetual inventory method. The journal entries for Year 1 may be summarized as follows:

	Home Office Books			*Branch Books*		
(a)	Branch	10,000		Cash	10,000	
	Cash		10,000	Home Office		10,000
(b)	Branch	36,000		Merchandise	36,000	
	Merchandise		30,000	Home Office		36,000
	Allowance for Valuation					
	of Branch Inventory		6,000			
(c)				Accounts Receivable	38,000	
				Sales		38,000
				Cost of Goods Sold	28,800	
				Merchandise		28,800

(Entries continued on next page.)

Home Office Books			*Branch Books*		
(d)			Cash	28,000	
			Accounts Receivable		28,000
(e)			Expenses	3,000	
			Cash		3,000
(f) Cash	18,000		Home Office	18,000	
Branch		18,000	Cash		18,000
(g) Branch	2,000		Expenses	2,000	
Expenses		2,000	Home Office		2,000
(h)			(no entry)		
(i)			Sales	38,000	
			Cost of Goods Sold		28,800
			Expenses		5,000
			Income Summary		4,200
(j) Branch	4,200		Income Summary	4,200	
Income: Branch		4,200	Home Office		4,200
(k) Allowance for Valuation					
of Branch Inventory	4,800				
Income: Branch		4,800			

3.9 FREIGHT TO BRANCHES

Freight inward on merchandise or on other goods received by a branch is properly includable in the branch cost. If goods are shipped from one branch to another, however, the second branch should include only such an amount of freight as would have been paid if the goods had been shipped directly from the home office. Any excess freight is normally treated as a period expense of the home office.

It is generally not desirable for one branch to keep accounts with another branch. Thus, any transshipment of goods will generally involve the accounts of the home office and of the particular branches involved.

EXAMPLE 6. Freight of $500 was paid by Branch A on $5,000 of merchandise received from the home office. In the ensuing months it was found that the merchandise was selling poorly at Branch A, so management decided to transship 40 percent of the merchandise to Branch B. The additional freight paid by Branch B amounted to $250. If the goods, which originally cost $2,000, had been shipped directly from the home office, the freight would have amounted to $350.

Journal entries to summarize these transactions follow:

Home Office Books

Branch A	5,000	
Shipments to Branch A		5,000
Shipments to Branch A	2,000	
Shipments to Branch B		2,000
Branch B	2,100	
Transhipment Freight Expense ($450 − $350)	100	
Branch A		2,200

Branch A

Shipments from Home Office	5,000	
Freight In	500	
Home Office		5,000
Cash		500
Home Office (40% of $5,500)	2,200	
Shipments from Home Office		2,000
Freight In		200

Branch B

Shipments from Home Office	2,000	
Freight In	350	
Home Office		2,100
Cash		250

3.10 RECONCILIATION OF RECIPROCAL ACCOUNTS

The accounts on the home office books which represent the investment in a branch should, in theory, always agree with the branch accounts which indicate the branch's accountability with the home office. In actual practice, these records may not always agree because of items in transit. For example, a remittance to the home office will immediately reduce the balances on the branch books, but the receipt may not be recorded by the home office for several days.

Lack of agreement between reciprocal accounts may be tolerable during the accounting period, but adjusting entries should be made to bring them into agreement before work papers are prepared. By way of illustration, assume that merchandise which cost $20,000 was shipped to Branch D on June 29. If the branch does not receive and enter this until July 3, there will be a difference between the two reciprocal accounts as of June 30. If the goods are billed at cost the following adjusting entry should be made on the branch books:

Merchandise in Transit	20,000	
Home Office		20,000

When the branch enters the receipt of the merchandise in July, it will probably be entered in the customary manner. In such a case, the above journal entry would then be reversed.

Summary

(1) When a separate branch ledger is maintained there is no formal proprietorship account. In lieu of a proprietorship account there is an account labeled _____.

(2) When combining home office and branch ledger accounts _____ accounts are always eliminated.

(3) When branch books are closed the balance of its income summary account is transferred to the _____ account.

(4) Freight inward on goods received by a branch is properly _____ in the branch inventory.

(5) When goods are transferred from one branch to another, the branch receiving the goods should include in its inventory valuation an amount of freight which would have been incurred if the goods had been shipped directly from the _____.

(6) The home office bills Branch C for cost plus 25 percent. A physical inventory of goods at the branch amounts to $25,000 (excluding freight). The cost of these goods to the firm was $_____.

(7) A home office bills its one branch at 130 percent of cost. The allowance for valuation of branch inventory, after adjustments, is $6,000. The branch inventory, at billed prices, should be _____.

(8) The home office and branch reciprocal accounts of the Epsilon Corp. do not agree at the end of the fiscal period. Such lack of agreement is most likely to be the result of errors and/or _____.

Answers: (1) home office; (2) reciprocal; (3) home office; (4) included; (5) home office; (6) $20,000; (7) $26,000; (8) items in transit.

Solved Problems

3.1 The Hampshire Corp. maintains a branch office in Richmond. Merchandise is ordered by the main office for direct shipment to either office. However, all vendors' invoices are paid from the main office. All fixed asset records are centralized in the main office.

During the month of June, 19X1, the following selected transactions occurred:

June 1 Hampshire office issued its check to Richmond Realty Corp., $250 for rent of branch office.

3 The branch received $5,432 of merchandise from vendors. After checking the shipment, the branch sent a duplicate of the receiving memorandum and the vendors' invoices to the main office.

7 The Hampshire office sent out advertising for a direct mail campaign. Readings of the postage meter indicated total postage of $400, of which $80 was applicable to the branch.

10 The branch received $7,154, resulting from collections of its accounts receivable in amount of $7,300 less sales discounts.

12 The branch returned $216 of defective merchandise to the vendors and sent a memorandum to the main office.

15 The Hampshire office drew a transfer check for $10,000 on the branch bank account and deposited the check in the main office bank account. The branch was notified.

17 The branch made sales on credit of $8,735.

28 The home office bookkeeper recorded depreciation expense for the first half of 19X1 in the amount of $1,000, of which $300 was applicable to the Richmond branch.

Required:

Prepare entries for the foregoing transactions on both main office and branch books in general journal form.

SOLUTION

Main Office				Branch		

June 1

Main Office			Branch		
Branch	250		Rent Expense	250	
Cash		250	Main Office		250

June 3

Branch	5,432		Purchases	5,432	
Accounts Payable		5,432	Main Office		5,432

June 7

Advertising Expense	320		Advertising Expense	80	
Branch	80		Main Office		80
Postage		400			

June 10

			Cash	7,154	
			Sales Discount	146	
			Accounts Receivable		7,300

June 12

Accounts Payable	216		Main Office	216	
Branch		216	Purchases (Returns)		216

June 15

Cash	10,000		Main Office	10,000	
Branch		10,000	Cash		10,000

June 17

			Accounts Receivable	8,735	
			Sales		8,735

June 28

Depreciation Expense	700		Depreciation Expense	300	
Branch	300		Main Office		300
Allowance for Depreciation		1,000			

3.2 The Turner Corporation established its Milford branch in March, 19X1. During the first year of operations the home office shipped to the branch merchandise which had cost $40,000. Three-quarters of this merchandise was sold by the branch for $47,000. Operating expenses of the branch amounted to $9,000 during 19X1.

Required:

Determine the net income the branch will report if merchandise is billed to the branch:

(*a*) at cost;

(*b*) at 25 percent above cost.

SOLUTION

(a)

Sales	$47,000
Cost of Goods Sold ($\frac{3}{4} \times$ $40,000)	30,000
Gross Margin	$17,000
Less: Operating Expenses	9,000
Net Income	$ 8,000

(b)

Sales	$47,000
Cost of Goods Sold ($\frac{3}{4} \times$ $50,000)	37,500
Gross Margin	$ 9,500
Less: Operating Expenses	9,000
Net Income	$ 500

3.3 The Moran Corporation established the Bucksrock branch on February 15, 19X2. During the balance of the year, Moran shipped to the branch goods which cost $100,000. The branch was billed at 125 percent of cost. Freight charges totalling $20,000 were paid by the home office.

During 19X2 the branch sold goods for $180,000, all of which was collected. The branch incurred expenses of $30,000, of which $6,000 was still owed at December 31. At the end of the year, the branch physical inventory, at billed prices, amounted to $25,000.

The company uses the periodic inventory method.

Required:

Write journal entries on both home office and branch books to record the shipment of merchandise, payment of freight, year-end inventory, net income of branch, and any other related entries.

SOLUTION

Home Office		
Branch	125,000	
Shipments to Branch		100,000
Allowance for Valuation		
of Branch Inventory		25,000
Branch	20,000	
Cash		20,000

Branch		
Shipments from		
Home Office	125,000	
Home Office		125,000
Freight In	20,000	
Home Office		20,000
Accounts Receivable	180,000	
Sales		180,000
Cash	180,000	
Accounts Receivable		180,000

(Entries continued on next page.)

	Home Office			Branch		

			Expenses	30,000	
			Expenses Payable		6,000
			Cash		24,000
			Merchandise Inventory ($25,000 + $4,000)	29,000	
			Income Summary		29,000
			Sales	180,000	
			Expenses		30,000
			Shipments from H.O.		125,000
			Freight In		20,000
			Income Summary		5,000
Branch	34,000		Income Summary	34,000	
Income: Branch		34,000	Home Office		34,000
Allowance for Valuation of Branch Inventory	20,000				
Income: Branch (80/100 × $25,000)		20,000			

3.4   The Exter Company operates one branch in Baltimore.   The trial balances of the home office and the branch, prior to closing the books, are included in the accompanying worksheets to combine the statements for the year ended December 31, 19X6.   All goods shipped to the branch are marked up according to a uniform percentage.

Required:

(a)   Determine the percentage mark-up.

(b)   Write the elimination entries needed to properly combine the respective statements.

(c)   Complete the worksheets to prepare combined statements for year ended December 31, 19X6.

Exter Company
Worksheet to Combine Income Statements
Year Ended December 31, 19X6

	Home Office		Branch		Eliminations		Combined Statements
	Dr.	Cr.	Dr.	Cr.	Dr.	Cr.	
Sales		75,000		25,000			
Inventory—Jan. 1	11,000		6,000				
Purchases	60,000						
Shipments to Branch		15,000					
Shipments from H.O.			18,000				
Inventory—Dec. 31		9,000		7,200			
Expenses	12,000		4,600				
Totals	83,000	99,000	28,600	32,200			
Net Income	16,000		3,600				
	99,000	99,000	32,200	32,200			

Exter Company
Worksheet to Combine Balance Sheets
December 31, 19X6

	Home Office		Branch		Eliminations		Combined Statements
	Dr.	Cr.	Dr.	Cr.	Dr.	Cr.	
Cash	18,400		8,800				
Accounts Receivable	24,200		9,000				
Inventory	9,000		7,200				
Branch	21,400						
Allowance for Valuation of Branch Inventory		4,000					
Accounts Payable		21,000					
Home Office				21,400			
Capital Stock		5,000					
Retained Earnings—Jan. 1		27,000					
Net Income		16,000		3,600			
	73,000	73,000	25,000	25,000			

SOLUTION

(a) $\dfrac{\text{Shipments from home office}}{\text{Shipments to branch}} = \dfrac{\$18,000}{\$15,000} = 120\% = 20\%$ mark-up

(b) *Entries to combine income statements:*

Entry (a)

| Net Income | 1,000 | |
| Inventory—Jan. 1 | | 1,000 |

To recognize realization of mark-up in opening inventory as a result of sales in Year 19X6.

Entry (b)

Shipments to Branch	15,000	
Net Income	3,000	
Shipments from Home Office		18,000

To eliminate intracompany shipments and mark-up thereon.

Entry (c)

| Inventory—Dec. 31 | 1,200 | |
| Net Income | | 1,200 |

To eliminate unrealized mark-up in ending inventory (20/120 × $7,200).

Entries to combine balance sheets: see entry (c) above, and:

Entry (1)

| Allowance for Valuation of Branch Inventory | 2,800 | |
| Net Income | | 2,800 |

To recognize realization of mark-up in Year 2 ($4,000 − $1,200).

Entry (2)

Home Office		21,400
Branch		21,400

To eliminate reciprocal accounts.

(c)

Exter Company
Worksheet to Combine Income Statements
Year Ended December 31, 19X6

	Home Office		Branch		Eliminations		Combined Statements
	Dr.	Cr.	Dr.	Cr.	Dr.	Cr.	
Sales		75,000		25,000			100,000
Inventory—Jan. 1	11,000		6,000			[a] 1,000	16,000
Purchases	60,000						60,000
Shipments to Branch		15,000			[b]15,000		
Shipments from H.O.			18,000			[b]18,000	
Inventory—Dec. 31		9,000		7,200	[c] 1,200		15,000
Expenses	12,000		4,600				16,600
Totals	83,000	99,000	28,600	32,200			92,600	115,000
Net Income	16,000		3,600		{ [b] 3,000 [a] 1,000	[c] 1,200	22,400
	99,000	99,000	32,200	32,200			115,000	115,000

[a] To recognize realization of mark-up in opening inventory as a result of sales in Year 19X6.
[b] To eliminate intracompany shipments during Year 19X6 and mark-up thereon.
[c] To eliminate unrealized mark-up in ending inventory: $1,200 (20/120 × $7,200).

Exter Company
Worksheet to Combine Balance Sheets
December 31, 19X6

	Home Office		Branch		Eliminations		Combined Statements
	Dr.	Cr.	Dr.	Cr.	Dr.	Cr.	
Cash	18,400		8,800				27,200
Accounts Receivable	24,200		9,000				33,200
Inventory	9,000		7,200			[c] 1,200	15,000
Branch	21,400					[1]21,400	
Allowance for Valuation of Branch Inventory		4,000			{ [1] 2,800 [c] 1,200		
Accounts Payable		21,000					21,000
Home Office				21,400	[2]21,400		
Capital Stock		5,000					5,000
Retained Earnings— Jan. 1		27,000					27,000
Net Income		16,000		3,600		[1] 2,800	22,400
	73,000	73,000	25,000	25,000			75,400	75,400

[1] To recognize mark-up realized as a result of sales in Year 19X6: $2,800; (20/120) × ($6,000 + $18,000 − $7,200).
[2] To eliminate reciprocal accounts.

3.5 The Brite Sales Corp. maintains several branches throughout the United States. As of December 31, 19X9 a discrepancy was noted between the Rider branch account balance of $93,172 (on the main office books) and the main office account balance of $60,487 (on the Rider branch books). A summary of the two accounts follows.

Rider Branch Current

Dec. 1	Balance	43,617	Dec. 12	Remittance	6,300
7	Shipment to Branch	16,720	26	Remittance	11,100
10	Freight on Shipment	235			
14	Shipment to Branch	27,150			
28	Shipment to Branch	18,800			
31	Advertising	2,100			
31	Rent	1,950			

Main Office Current

Dec. 11	Remittance	6,300	Dec. 1	Balance	43,617
23	Remittance	11,100	10	Merchandise	16,720
31	Remittance	9,600	18	Merchandise	27,150

An examination of the records disclosed the following additional information:

1. Merchandise has been billed to all branches at cost.
2. The freight charged to the Rider branch on December 10 was recorded in error; it should have been charged to the Earleton branch.
3. Advertising and rent charged to the Rider branch on December 31 represent allocated portions of main office expenses chargeable to branch operations.
4. The Rider branch records for the year ended December 31, 19X9, showed Sales—$389,100; Merchandise from Main Office—$311,600; Inventory at January 1, 19X9—$23,900; Operating Expenses—$27,395; and Inventory at December 31, 19X9—$32,290.

Required:

(a) Prepare a reconciliation of the current account balances.

(b) In general journal form, write the entries necessary to correct the accounts.

(c) Write the journal entries to close the books of the Rider branch for the year.

SOLUTION

(a) *Reconciliation:*

	Rider Branch Current		Main Office Current	
	Dr.	Cr.	Dr.	Cr.
Balance Main Office Ledger	$93,172			
Balance Branch Ledger				$60,487
Transfer Freight to Earleton		$ 235		
Record Branch Share of:				
Advertising Expense				2,100
Rent Expense				1,950
Record Shipment in Transit				18,800
Record Remittance in Transit		9,600		
Totals	$93,172	$ 9,835		$83,337
Corrected Balances		83,337	83,337	
	$93,172	$93,172	$83,337	$83,337

(b)	1.	*Journal entry to correct main office books:*

Earleton Branch Current	235	
Cash in Transit	9,600	
Rider Branch Current		9,835

    2.	*Journal entry to correct Rider branch books:*

Operating Expenses (Advertising)	2,100	
Operating Expenses (Rent)	1,950	
Shipment in Transit	18,800	
Main Office Current		22,850

(c)	*Journal entries to close Rider branch for year:*

Cost of Goods Sold	303,210	
Merchandise Inventory (Dec. 31)	32,290	
Merchandise Inventory (Jan. 1)		23,900
Shipments from Main Office		311,600
Sales	389,100	
Cost of Goods Sold		303,210
Operating Expenses		27,395
Income Summary		58,495
Income Summary	58,495	
Main Office Current		58,495

3.6	The Sales Corp. of New York maintains a branch at Tacoma, Washington. The trial balances of their separate ledgers at December 31, 19X6, were as follows:

	Main Office		Branch	
Cash in Bank	$ 14,000		$ 6,000	
Accounts Receivable	31,000		15,000	
Merchandise Inventory	22,000		12,000	
Furniture and Equipment	12,000			
Branch Current	57,000			
Purchases	255,000			
Selling Expense Control	18,000		10,000	
Administrative Expense Control	16,000		5,000	
Allowance for Depreciation		$ 5,000		
Sales		210,000		$133,000
Accounts Payable		22,000		
Capital Stock		20,000		
Retained Earnings		26,000		
Allowance for Valuation of Branch Inventory		2,000		
Shipments to Branch		96,000		
Remittances from Branch	44,000			
Remittances to Main Office			46,000	
Shipments from Main Office			96,000	
Main Office Current				57,000
	$425,000	$425,000	$190,000	$190,000

Additional data:

1. Inventory, December 31, 19X6—main office, $20,000; branch, $9,000.
2. Merchandise shipped to branch at 20 percent above cost.
3. Check for $2,000 mailed by branch on December 30 was not received in the main office until January 3, 19X7.
4. Administrative expense on the main office books includes $1,500 of insurance premiums applicable to branch. Of this amount, $740 is applicable to periods after December 31, 19X6.
5. Furniture and equipment include $3,000 located at the branch.
6. Depreciation is computed at 8 percent per year.

Required:

Present the adjusting and closing entries for the main office and the branch in parallel columns.

SOLUTION

Main Office			*Branch Office*		
Merchandise Inventory	20,000		Merchandise Inventory	9,000	
Income Summary		20,000	Income Summary		9,000
Shipments to Branch	96,000				
Purchases		80,000			
Allowance for Valuation of					
Branch Inventory		16,000			
Cash in Transit	2,000				
Remittances from Branch		2,000			
Branch Current	760		Administrative Expense Control	760	
Prepaid Insurance	740		Main Office Current		760
Administrative Expense					
Control		1,500			
Administrative Expense			Administrative Expense Control	240	
Control	720		Main Office Current		240
Branch Control	240				
Allowance for Depreciation		960			
Remittances from Branch			Main Office Current	46,000	
($44,000 + $2,000)	46,000		Remittances to Main Office		46,000
Branch Current		46,000			
Sales	210,000		Sales	133,000	
Income Summary	20,220		Income Summary		9,000
Merchandise Inventory		22,000	Merchandise Inventory		12,000
Purchases		175,000	Selling Expense Control		10,000
Selling Expense Control		18,000	Administrative Expense Control		6,000
Administrative Expense			Shipments from Main Office		96,000
Control		15,220			
Branch Current	18,000		Income Summary	18,000	
Income: Branches		18,000	Main Office Current		18,000

(Entries continued on next page.)

	Main Office			Branch Office
Allowance for Valuation of				
Branch Inventory*	16,500			
Income: Branches		16,500		
Income: Branches	34,500			
Income Summary		220		
Retained Earnings		34,280		

*($12,000 + $96,000 − $9,000) × (0.20/1.20)

3.7 The River Corporation bills all goods shipped to its branch at 125 percent of cost, and is the only source of supply for the branch. These shipments are recorded as follows:

Dr. Branch Current	XXXX	
Cr. Shipments to Branch		XXXX

All ledger accounts have been adjusted to the end of 19X6 except the allowance for valuation of branch inventory, which has not been adjusted since December 31, 19X5. The following data are from the ledgers of the River Corporation as of December 31, 19X6.

	Home Office		Branch	
Cash in Transit from Branch	10,000			
Branch Current	104,000			
Allowance for Valuation of				
Branch Inventory		3,640		
Merchandise Inventory	38,000		21,000	
Dividends Declared	10,000			
Sales		600,000		400,000
Cost of Goods Sold	360,000		300,000	
Shipments to Branch		306,800		
Shipments in Transit			4,000	
Home Office Current				104,000
Expense Control	91,000		68,000	

Required:

(a) Prepare journal entries to close the branch ledger for 19X6.

(b) Prepare journal entries to record the branch profit on home office books. Prepare adjusting entry(ies) if necessary.

SOLUTION

(a)	Sales		400,000	
	Cost of Goods Sold			300,000
	Expense Control			68,000
	Home Office Current			32,000
(b)	Shipments to Branch ($306,800 × 0.20)		61,360	
	Income Summary ($300,000 × 0.20)			60,000
	Allowance for Valuation of Branch Inventory			1,360
	Branch Current		32,000	
	Income: Branch			32,000

3.8 The Hill Corp. opened its first branch on August 1, 19X8. The branch obtained merchandise solely from the home office, and billings were made at 125 percent of cost. The shipment of merchandise to the branch was recorded by credits to the sales account at the invoice price.

The branch manager calculated the profit at $15,000 and sent a check in this amount to the home office, the first transfer of funds from the branch to the home office. The home office bookkeeper did not know how to enter this transfer properly; he credited a new suspense account.

The following trial balances are available.

	Home Office		Branch	
	Dr.	Cr.	Dr.	Cr.
Sales		$400,000		$160,000
Cost of Sales	$220,000		$120,000	
Expenses	100,000		25,000	
Retained Earnings, Jan. 1		55,000		
Cash	24,000		16,000	
Accounts Receivable	105,000		110,000	
Merchandise Inventory	30,000		8,000	
Equipment	138,000			
Allowance for Depreciation		100,000		
Branch Office	128,000			
Suspense		15,000		
Vouchers Payable		75,000		6,000
Home Office				113,000
Capital Stock $10 par		100,000		
	$745,000	$745,000	$279,000	$279,000

Required:

Write the journal entries that are necessary to correct the books.

SOLUTION

Suspense	15,000	
Branch Office		15,000
Sales ($120,000 + $8,000)	128,000	
Cost of Sales		102,400
Allowance for Valuation of Branch Inventory		25,600
Allowance for Valuation of Branch Inventory	24,000	
Income: Branch (25/125 × $120,000)		24,000
Branch Office	15,000	
Income: Branch		15,000

Examination I

Chapters 1–3

1   A statement of partners' capital accounts for the year ended December 31, 19X8 appears below. Complete the answers to the questions based on this statement:

	Rady	Steem	Total
Balance, January 1	$100,000	$ 80,000	$180,000
Add:			
Additional Investments	20,000	10,000	30,000
Net Income for Year:			
Salaries to Partners	20,000	10,000	30,000
Interest on Capitals	10,000	8,000	18,000
Remainder	16,000	16,000	32,000
Totals	$166,000	$124,000	$290,000
Deduct:			
Withdrawals	30,000	18,000	48,000
Balance, December 31	$136,000	$106,000	$242,000

Required:

(a)   What was the net profit of the partnership for the year?

(b)   At what percentage rate was interest allowed on beginning capitals?

(c)   Were the partners penalized for drawing out more than their "salaries"?

(d)   How much was Rady's total share of the profits for the year?

2   A partnership sells its entire business, exclusive of cash in bank, to the Ultima Corporation and receives stock of the corporation in return.

Required:

Detail the steps the partnership should take in order to divide the stock among the partners.

3   The partnership of Morse and Spring allows salaries of $10,400 and $9,600, respectively. Any amount withdrawn by a partner is debited to his salary account until the drawings equal the salary allowance. Withdrawals by a partner in excess of his salary are charged to a drawings account. The remainder of the profits or losses is divided 60 percent to Morse and 40 percent to Spring. A partial trial balance follows:

	Dr.	Cr.
Cash in Bank	$42,000	
Sales		$40,000
Cost of Sales	35,000	
Operating Expenses	17,000	
Morse, Salary	6,000	
Spring, Salary	6,000	

Required:

Write the journal entries to complete the closing of the books.

4 Roberts and Morris entered into an agreement to speculate in silver commodity contracts, each using approximately $10,000 of his own capital. The profits and losses are to be divided equally, and settlement is to be made at the end of the year after all positions have been liquidated. A summary of the various brokerage statements for the year follows:

	Roberts	Morris
Total of All Purchases	$90,000	$40,000
Total of All Sales	95,000	$37,000
Interest Charged on Margin Accounts	380	460

Required:

Prepare a schedule which will show how settlement should be made between Roberts and Morris at the end of the year.

5 The Berlain Company established a branch in Freedom, N.H., on July 3, 19X4. During 19X4 the home office shipped goods to the branch at billed prices totalling $125,000, which was 25 percent above cost.

On December 31, 19X4 the branch showed an inventory of $25,000 at billed prices.

The branch reported a net profit of $33,000 for 19X4 operations.

Required:

Determine the true net profit of the branch.

6 Acme and Burns are partners sharing profits and losses equally. On June 1, 19X1, their capital interests in the firm are as shown below:

Acme	$40,000
Burns	$50,000

On this date, Storey is admitted as a partner upon the investment of $30,000 in cash.

Required:

Write the journal entries necessary to record the investment by Storey under each of the following conditions:

(a) Storey is given a one-third interest and a bonus is recorded.
(b) Storey is given a one-fifth interest with goodwill being recorded.
(c) Storey is given a one-third interest with the total investment in the firm to be $120,000.

7 The home office bills its Bingham branch at 125 percent of cost. During the year 19X5, goods costing $150,000 were shipped to the branch. At the end of the year the balance in the account entitled Allowance for Valuation of Branch Inventory, after adjustment, was $7,000.

Required:

Determine the amount of the ending inventory:

(a) at billed price;
(b) at cost.

8   David Adams has been operating a roofing business for some years. He decided to go into partnership with his uncle, William Barton, who owns a large business building which he will bring into the business. Each partner is to be credited for the applicable amounts at January 1, 19X1, as shown below:

	Ledger Balances	Fair Value
Partners' Contributions		
Adams:		
Cash	$15,000	$ 15,000
Accounts Receivable (net)	35,000	30,000
Inventory	25,000	20,000
Equipment (net)	30,000	40,000
Payables	10,000	10,000
Barton:		
Building and Land	75,000	100,000

Barton is to invest sufficient cash to make both capital accounts equal.

Required:

Determine:

(a)   Adams's capital account at January 1, 19X1;

(b)   Barton's cash investment.

9   The capital accounts of M. A. Branning and J. S. Harris are $30,000 and $50,000, respectively, at December 31, 19X2. The partnership agreement calls for the sharing of earnings as follows:

(1)   Branning and Harris are to receive annual salaries of $23,000 and $14,000, respectively.

(2)   Each partner is to receive interest of 10 percent on his December 31, 19X2 capital.

(3)   The remainder of earnings are to be shared in a 2:3 ratio.

Required:

Compute the division of profits if the earnings are:

(a) $55,000;

(b) $30,000.

10   William Ripple and James Ripple Jr. have partnership capitals of $40,000 each. James Connell has agreed to become a partner and supply the needed capital by either (a) investing $25,000 and increasing the capital of the firm or (b) purchasing half of William Ripple's capital for $25,000.

Required:

Write the journal entry (entries) for each situation.

11   B. J. Herlo, D.V.M., owns the Lemon Bay Animal Shelter in Englewood. There is also a branch in Ft. Myers. During 19X5 the home office shipped supplies costing $40,000 to the branch at a billed price of 20 percent above cost. The inventories of supplies at the branch were as follows:

January 1, 19X5	$30,000
December 31, 19X5	$36,000

The home office holds inventories of $53,500 which include $3,500 held on consignment. Both locations use the periodic inventory method.

Required:

Prepare:

(a) journal entries for shipments to the branch and the adjustment to the valuation account;

(b) balance sheet presentation of inventories in a combined balance sheet at December 31, 19X5.

12   Girard and Horton are partners in a retail business, sharing profits and losses in a 1:2 ratio. On December 31, 19X3, when they decided to liquidate the business, the condensed trial balance was as follows:

	Debit	Credit
Sundry Assets	$108,000	
Accounts Payable		$ 26,000
Girard, Loan		2,000
Horton, Loan		4,000
Girard, Capital		22,000
Horton, Capital		54,000
	$108,000	$108,000

The sale of the sundry assets yielded cash of $60,000.

Required:

Prepare a worksheet to show how the cash should be distributed.

13   King and Kuehnle are partners in the Dearborn Marina. For 19X6 the earnings were $77,000 before deducting salaries, interest, and bonus. King is to receive a bonus equal to 10 percent of the profit after salaries, interest, and bonus. The remainder of the profit or loss is to be divided in the ratio of 3:2. Salaries and interest are as shown below:

	King	Kuehnle
Salaries	$25,000	$20,000
Interest	6,000	4,000

Required:

Prepare a schedule of distribution of earnings.

14   Albright, Bettinger, and Cummings are partners in the Englewood Casino, which is in the process of liquidation. The financial information is as follows:

Partner	Capital Balances	Profit & Loss Ratio
Albright	$80,000	40%
Bettinger	54,000	30%
Cummings	48,000	30%

The assets of the firm amount to $197,000.

Required:

Determine the following:

(a) the potential loss that would eliminate each partner—that is, the degree of vulnerability of each;

(b) how cash realized from liquidation of the firm's assets may be safely distributed.

15   The Don Hanson Company established a branch in Angleton on June 15, 19X3. During that year the home office shipped goods to the branch costing $180,000, at the billed price of 120 percent of cost. The home office paid freight of $15,000 on the shipments.

The branch sales were $265,000, of which $210,000 was collected by the branch during the fiscal year. Expenses of $52,000 were paid by the branch and $8,000 was owed at the end of the year. The ending inventory was $18,000 at billed prices. The periodic inventory method is used.

Required:

Write summary journal entries on both the branch and home office books.

16   The Dexter Company ships goods to its branch at 110 percent of cost. The income statements for Year 19X8 and the balance sheets as of December 31, 19X8 are condensed in the Worksheets which accompany this problem.

Required:

(a) Complete the following worksheet to prepare a combined income statement for the year.

(b) Complete the following worksheet to prepare a combined balance sheet as of December 31.

Dexter Company
Worksheet to Combine Income Statements
Year Ended December 31, 19X8

	Home Office		Branch		Adjustments & Eliminations		Combined Statements
	Dr.	Cr.	Dr.	Cr.			
Sales		150,000		50,000			
Inventory—Jan. 1	22,000		11,000				
Purchases	120,000						
Shipments to Branch		30,000					
Shipments from Home Office			33,000				
Inventory—Dec. 31		18,000		13,200			
Expenses	24,000		9,200				
Income: Branch		12,800					
Totals	166,000	210,800	53,200	63,200			
Net Income	44,800		10,000				
	210,800	210,800	63,200	63,200			

Dexter Company
Worksheet to Combine Balance Sheets
December 31, 19X8

	Home Office		Branch		Adjustments & Eliminations		Combined Statements	
	Dr.	Cr.	Dr.	Cr.				
Cash	36,700		17,600					
Accounts Receivable	41,500		18,000					
Inventory	18,000		13,200					
Branch	48,800							
Allowance for Valuation of Branch Inventory		1,200						
Accounts Payable		42,000						
Home Office				48,800				
Capital Stock—$10 par		10,000						
Retained Earnings—Jan. 1		54,000						
Net Income		44,800						
Dividends	7,000							
	152,000	152,000	48,800	48,800				

Answers to Examination I

1 (a) $80,000
   (b) 10 percent
   (c) No.
   (d) $46,000

2 (a) The stock received should be recorded at its fair value.
   (b) The gain or loss on the sale of the business should be divided among the partners in their profit- and loss-sharing ratio.
   (c) If one or more partners has a deficit, either the partner should invest cash to eliminate the deficit or the deficit(s) should be divided among the other partners using their ratio for dividing losses.
   (d) The stock (and cash, if any) should be distributed in a resultant capital ratio. (If fractional shares are not available, it will be necessary to distribute whole shares and make up the differences with cash equivalent to fractions of a share.)

3

Sales	40,000	
Income Summary	12,000	
Cost of Sales		35,000
Operating Expenses		17,000

	Morse, Capital	8,800	
	Spring, Capital	3,200	
	Income Summary		12,000

To divide net loss as follows:

	Morse	Spring	Total
Salary Allowance	10,400	9,600	20,000
Deficit 60:40	(19,200)	(12,800)	(32,000)
Totals	(8,800)	(3,200)	(12,000)

	Morse, Capital	6,000	
	Spring, Capital	6,000	
	Morse, Salary		6,000
	Spring, Salary		6,000

To transfer partners' drawings.

4

	Roberts	Morris	Total
Sales	95,000	37,000	132,000
Cost of Goods Sold	90,000	40,000	130,000
Interest Expense	380	460	840
Total Cost & Expense	90,380	40,460	130,840
Net Income (Loss)	4,620	(3,460)	1,160
Net Income Divided Equally	580	580	(1,160)
Roberts Should Pay to Morris	4,040	(4,040)	

5

Sales of Goods by Branch at Billed Price	
($125,000 − $25,000)	$100,000
Cost to Home Office ($100,000 ÷ 1.25)	80,000
Intracompany Mark-up Realized	20,000
Reported Net Profit	33,000
Total Net Profit	$ 53,000

6   (a)

	Cash	30,000	
	Acme, Capital	5,000	
	Burns, Capital	5,000	
	Storey, Capital		40,000

To record investment by Storey for a one-third interest in a total capital of $120,000.

(b)

	Goodwill	30,000	
	Acme, Capital		15,000
	Burns, Capital		15,000

To record goodwill developed by Acme and Burns.

Cash	30,000	
Storey, Capital		30,000

To record admission of Storey to a one-fifth interest in a total capital of $150,000.

(c)

Cash	30,000	
Acme, Capital	5,000	
Burns, Capital	5,000	
Storey, Capital		40,000

To record admission of Storey to a one-third interest in a total capital of $120,000.

7 (a) Merchandise at 25 percent of cost is equal to 20 percent of billed price (0.25 ÷ 1.25). Thus, $7,000 balance in valuation account is 20 percent of billed price.

$$\$7,000 \div 20\% = \$35,000$$

(b)
$$\$35,000 - \$7,000 = \$28,000$$

8 (a) Adam's capital should be equal to the sum of the fair values, or $115,000.

(b)

Adam's Capital	$115,000
Fair Value of Barton Building	100,000
Cash Investment	$ 15,000

9 (a)

	Branning	Harris	Total
Salaries	23,000	14,000	37,000
Interest	3,000	5,000	8,000
	26,000	19,000	45,000
Balance in 2:3 ratio	4,000	6,000	10,000
Division of earnings	30,000	25,000	55,000

(b)

	Branning	Harris	Total
Salaries	23,000	14,000	37,000
Interest	3,000	5,000	8,000
	26,000	19,000	45,000
Deficit in 2:3 ratio	(6,000)	(9,000)	(15,000)
Division of earnings	20,000	10,000	30,000

10 (a)

Cash	25,000	
J. Connell, Capital		25,000

(b)

W. Ripple, Capital	20,000	
J. Connell, Capital		20,000

The consideration passes outside of the business.

11 (a)

Ft. Myers Branch	48,000	
Shipments to Branch		40,000
Allowance for Valuation of Branch Inventory		8,000

Allowance for Valuation of Branch Inventory Account:

Jan. 1 Balance $30,000 (0.20 ÷ 1.20)	$ 5,000
Increase during Year	8,000
	$13,000
Dec. 31 Balance $36,000 (0.20 ÷ 1.20)	6,000
Adjustment Required	$ 7,000

Journal Entry:

Allowance for Valuation of Branch Inventory	7,000	
Income Summary—Branches		7,000

(b)	Combined Balance Sheet—Inventories	$80,000
	Home Office ($53,500 − $3,500)	$50,000
	Branch ($36,000 − $6,000)	30,000
	Total Inventory	$80,000

12

	Liabilities	Girard	Horton	Totals
		Equities		
Accounts Payable	26,000			26,000
Loans by Partners		2,000	4,000	6,000
Capital Balances		22,000	54,000	76,000
Totals	26,000	24,000	58,000	108,000
Realization Loss (1:2)		16,000	32,000	48,000
Distribution of Cash	26,000	8,000	26,000	60,000

13

	King	Kuehnle	Total
Salaries	$25,000	$20,000	$45,000
Interest	6,000	4,000	10,000
Subtotal	$31,000	$24,000	$55,000
Balance before Bonus, $22,000*			
Bonus	2,000	–	2,000**
Remainder (3:2)	12,000	8,000	20,000
Totals	$45,000	$32,000	$77,000

* $77,000 − $55,000 = $22,000
** Bonus calculation: Let X = base after bonus
$$X + 0.10 X = \$22,000$$
$$1.1 X = \$22,000$$
$$X = \$20,000$$
$$0.1 X = \$2,000$$

14

Partner	Partner's Capital	P & L Ratio	Maximum Loss	Degree of Vulnerability
Albright	$80,000	40%	$200,000	3
Bettinger	54,000	30%	180,000	2
Cummings	48,000	30%	160,000	1

Potential Distribution of Cash

Balances	Assets (Noncash)	Liabil- ities	Albright	Bettinger	Cummings
			Partner's Capital		
Before Realization	$197,000	$15,000†	$80,000	$54,000	$48,000
Most Vulnerable	160,000*		64,000	48,000	48,000
Subtotal	$ 37,000	$15,000	$16,000	$ 6,000	
Next Vulnerable	14,000**		8,000	6,000	
Distribution	$ 23,000	$15,000	$ 8,000		

  * Most vulnerable (Cummings)
 ** Next vulnerable (Bettinger)
  † Assets $197,000 − Capital ($80,000 + $54,000 + $48,000) = Liabilities $15,000

Summary of Plan for Division of Cash

		Albright	Bettinger	Cummings
First	$15,000	$15,000		
Next	8,000		$8,000	
Next	14,000		8,000	$6,000

Thereafter divide cash in ratio 40:30:20.

15   *Branch*

Shipments from Home Office	180,000	
Home Office		180,000
Freight In	15,000	
Home Office		15,000
Accounts Receivable	265,000	
Sales		265,000
Cash	210,000	
Accounts Receivable		210,000
Expenses	60,000	
Cash		52,000
Accounts Payable		8,000
Inventory ($18,000 + $1,500*)	19,500	
Sales	265,000	
Shipment from Home Office		180,000
Freight In		15,000
Expenses		60,000
Income Summary		29,500
Income Summary	29,500	
Home Office		29,500

* Freight in = 10% of $15,000

Home Office

Branch	180,000	
Shipments to Branch		150,000
Allowance for Valuation		
of Branch Inventory		30,000
Branch	15,000	
Cash		15,000
Branch	29,500	
Income—Branch		29,500
Allowance for Valuation of		
Branch Inventory	27,000	
Income—Branch		
[$30,000 − ($18,000 − $15,000)]		27,000

16

Dexter Company
Worksheet to Combine Income Statements
Year Ended December 31, 19X8

	Home Office Dr.	Home Office Cr.	Branch Dr.	Branch Cr.	Adjustments & Eliminations	Adjustments & Eliminations	Combined Statements	Combined Statements
Sales		150,000		50,000				200,000
Inventory—Jan. 1	22,000		11,000			b 1,000	32,000	
Purchases	120,000						120,000	
Shipments to Branch		30,000			a30,000			
Shipments from Home Office			33,000			c 3,000 / a30,000		
Inventory—Dec. 31		18,000		13,200	c 1,200			30,000
Expenses	24,000		9,200				33,200	
Income: Branch		12,800			d12,800			
Totals	166,000	210,800	53,200	63,200				
Net Income	44,800		10,000		c 1,800 / b 1,000	d12,800	44,800	
	210,800	210,800	63,200	63,200			230,000	230,000

a To eliminate intracompany shipments at cost.

b To eliminate intracompany mark-up in branch inventory at beginning of Year 8, and to recognize its realization in Year 8.

c To eliminate intracompany mark-up in shipments during Year 8, and in inventory at end of Year 2. Also, to increase income of branch for mark-up realized during Year 8.

d To eliminate net income of branch already recorded by home office.

Dexter Company
Worksheet to Combine Balance Sheets
December 31, 19X8

	Home Office Dr.	Home Office Cr.	Branch Dr.	Branch Cr.	Adjustments & Eliminations	Adjustments & Eliminations	Combined Statements	Combined Statements
Cash	36,700		17,600				54,300	
Accounts Receivable	41,500		18,000				59,500	
Inventory	18,000		13,200			1 1,200	30,000	
Branch	48,800					248,800		
Allowance for Valuation of Branch Inventory		1,200			1 1,200			
Accounts Payable		42,000						42,000
Home Office				48,800	248,800			
Capital Stock—$10 par		10,000						10,000
Retained Earnings—Jan. 1		54,000						54,000
Net Income		44,800						44,800
Dividends	7,000						7,000	
	152,000	152,000	48,800	48,800			150,800	150,800

1 To eliminate intracompany mark-up in branch inventory at end of year.

2 To eliminate reciprocal accounts.

Part II

Consolidated Statements

Chapters 4 through 12 comprise an integrated coverage of consolidation accounting. In general, the beginner should study the chapters in the sequence in which they are presented, although the cost method, Chapter 5, may be deferred. Students who have already had experience with consolidation and wish to pursue a particular topic will find that each chapter is a fairly complete unit.

Numerous annotated worksheets should enable the reader to follow the eliminations and adjustments necessary for consolidation of parent and subsidiary corporations. In recent years it has become the fashion for many textbook writers to utilize a "three-tier" format for worksheets. Accordingly, a dozen worksheets of this type are presented as alternate solutions to some of the problems.

Chapter 4

Consolidated Statements—
Balance Sheet
at Date of Acquisition

4.1 INTRODUCTION

Businesses expand in many different ways. One firm may purchase assets; another may construct a new store or plant. Two or more companies may combine into one new and larger company. Frequently, one corporation acquires control of a group of assets by acquiring the outstanding stock of another corporation which owns that group of assets.

Regardless of the legal procedure by which one business unit obtains control of the assets and liabilities of another business unit, accountants generally treat the resultant affiliation as a business combination. For accounting purposes, control is usually considered to be evidenced by acquisition of more than 50 percent of the outstanding voting stock of another corporation.

4.2 INVESTMENT IN STOCK OF ANOTHER CORPORATION

Small blocks of stock in a corporation are frequently paid for by check, but large investments are often paid for by the investor issuing its own securities. In the former instance the cost is readily established; in the latter instance it may be necessary to infer the cost of the acquisition from the value of the securities issued.

Acquisitions of investments of almost every type are generally recorded at cost, at least initially. When the investment account is maintained at cost, there is no adjustment except for a few unusual situations which will be discussed in a later chapter. Even when the investment account is maintained on the equity method (see Chapter 6), the starting point at date of acquisition is invariably cost.

The holding of more than 50 percent of the voting stock of one corporation by another corporation generally creates a parent-subsidiary relationship. Control of a corporation may often be achieved with less than 50 percent of the voting stock, but this would not be regarded as a basis for preparing consolidated statements. In the latter situation, the investment would generally be included with the noncurrent assets in the balance sheet of the investor.

When the parent corporation has no activity other than to hold the controlling interest in the outstanding stock of one or more subsidiaries, it is frequently referred to as a holding company.

4.3 CORPORATE AFFILIATIONS MAY CREATE ECONOMIC ENTITY

From a legal point of view, each corporation is a separate entity that keeps its own set of books and prepares its own financial statements. However, when one corporation owns more than 50 percent of the outstanding voting stock of one or more other corporations and these corporations are operated as one business, the consolidated statements of the economic group are usually more informative than the individual statements of each corporation.

The purpose of consolidated statements is to present the financial position and results of operations of the parent company and its subsidiaries as if the group were a single company with one or more branches. The standard technique for preparing consolidated statements is to take the individual statements to be consolidated and to combine them on a worksheet after eliminating all intercompany transactions and intercompany relationships. Since these worksheets are equivalent to a set of books, they should be preserved just as surely as the journals and ledgers of individual companies are preserved.

4.4 ADVANTAGES OF CONSOLIDATED STATEMENTS

Consolidated statements enable one to see the financial position and results of operations of an affiliated group of companies as though they constituted a single economic unit. The effect of intercompany relationships and the results of intercompany transactions will have been eliminated in the consolidation process.

Statements of subsidiaries should be consolidated with the parent company's statement whenever the parent has the ability to control the subsidiary's managerial decisions. Thus, the economic results of the subsidiary will be available to the parent company. In order to be consolidated, the subsidiary should also possess the following attributes:

(a) the operations should be similar, closely related, or complementary

(b) the assets and liabilities should be similar

(c) the fiscal year of each member should be the same, or else end within two, or at most, three months of each other.

All of the assets and liabilities of each company appear in the consolidated balance sheet—except for intercompany items, which are properly eliminated. When a portion of the subsidiary stock is owned by nonaffiliated parties, a special minority position in the shareholders' equity is established.

4.5 WHEN CONSOLIDATED STATEMENTS SHOULD BE AVOIDED

In some situations, a subsidiary may be in an entirely different line of business from the other affiliated companies. In such a situation, combining its results with those of the other affiliates may not increase the utility of the statements. For example, a manufacturing and mercantile group may also include a financing subsidiary. In such a case it is generally considered preferable to consolidate the manufacturing and mercantile affiliates and to *omit* the financing subsidiary. In practice the investment in the financing subsidiary appears as an asset in the consolidated balance sheet, and separate statements for the unconsolidated subsidiary are usually appended to the consolidated report if they are material.

When the control of a subsidiary is expected to be of short duration, consolidated statements are generally avoided. Also, consolidated statements involving foreign subsidiaries should be avoided when there are restrictions that limit the ability of the parent to control the subsidiary or that limit its ability to take assets out of the foreign country.

When a subsidiary is not consolidated, for whatever appropriate reason, the investment should be shown under noncurrent assets. Usually the investment account should be maintained on the equity method, which is discussed in Chapter 6.

The need for separate statements of a company in an affiliated group may be vital for those who have a primary interest in one of the affiliated companies. (For example, minority shareholders will undoubtedly continue to be interested in the individual company in which they hold stock.)

4.6 CONSOLIDATED BALANCE SHEET AT DATE OF ACQUISITION OF CONTROL (100%)

In the examples in this section, it will be assumed that one corporation purchases *all* of the outstanding stock of another corporation, thus creating a wholly owned subsidiary. It is also assumed that consolidated statements are prepared immediately following acquisition of the investment. At this date, a consolidated balance sheet is the only statement which can be prepared.

EXAMPLE 1. The condensed balance sheets of P Corp. and of S Corp. on January 1, Year 1, before the investment by P in stock of S, are as follows:

	P Corp.	S Corp.
Current Assets	$200,000	$ 55,000
Depreciable Assets—net	200,000	100,000
Land		25,000
Total Assets	$400,000	$180,000
Liabilities	$140,000	$ 30,000
Capital Stock	200,000	100,000
Retained Earnings	60,000	50,000
Total Liabilities and Shareholders' Equity	$400,000	$180,000

Let us now assume that P purchases all of the outstanding capital stock of S from its stockholders on January 1 of Year 1 for $150,000 cash. The assets and liabilities of S Corp. are valued at the amounts shown in its statement.

The balance sheets of the two corporations immediately following the investment by P are as follows:

	P Corp.	S Corp.
Current Assets	$ 50,000	$ 55,000
Investment in S Corp. Stock	150,000	
Depreciable Assets—net	200,000	100,000
Land		25,000
Total Assets	$400,000	$180,000
Liabilities	$140,000	$ 30,000
Capital Stock	200,000	100,000
Retained Earnings	60,000	50,000
Total Liabilities and Shareholders' Equity	$400,000	$180,000

Observe that the investment in the stock of S is recorded on P's books at its cost of $150,000, which equals the *net assets* (assets $180,000, less liabilities $30,000) of S Corp. In a consolidated balance sheet of P and S, the assets and liabilities of S will be combined with the assets and liabilities of P. The investment in S Corp. stock will be offset or eliminated against the capital stock and retained earnings of S Corp. The elimination entry and the entire worksheet procedure is illustrated in the following worksheet to consolidate P Corp. and subsidiary on January 1, Year 1.

P Corp. and Subsidiary
Worksheet—Consolidated Balance Sheet
January 1, Year 1

	P Corp.		S Corp.		Eliminations		Consolidated	
	Dr.	Cr.	Dr.	Cr.	Dr.	Cr.	Dr.	Cr.
Current Assets	50,000		55,000				105,000	
Investment in S Corp. Stock	150,000					[1]150,000		
Depreciable Assets—net	200,000		100,000				300,000	
Land			25,000				25,000	
Liabilities		140,000		30,000				170,000
Capital Stock—P		200,000						200,000
Retained Earnings—P		60,000						60,000
Capital Stock—S				100,000	[1]100,000			
Retained Earnings—S				50,000	[1]50,000			
	400,000	400,000	180,000	180,000			430,000	430,000

[1] To eliminate 100% of subsidiary's capital stock and retained earnings.

The foregoing worksheet is equivalent to a set of books for the consolidated group; some accountants refer to it as a synthetic set of books. The consolidated balance sheet immediately following the acquisition of control has been prepared from the last two columns of the worksheet, and is presented here:

P Corp. and Subsidiary
Consolidated Balance Sheet
January 1, Year 1

ASSETS

Current	$105,000	
Depreciable Assets—net	300,000	
Land	25,000	
Total Assets		$430,000

LIABILITIES AND SHAREHOLDERS' EQUITY

Liabilities		$170,000
Capital Stock	$200,000	
Retained Earnings	60,000	
Total Shareholders' Equity		260,000
Total Liabilities and Shareholders' Equity		$430,000

Observe that the capital stock and the retained earnings of the parent company only appear in the consolidated balance sheet. The capital stock and retained earnings of the subsidiary company have been eliminated against the investment account of the parent.

EXAMPLE 2. The T Corp. has recorded assets similar to those of the S Corp. However, the land which T had once recorded at a cost of $25,000 now has a fair market value of $50,000. As a result, the R Corp. is willing to pay $175,000 for 100 percent of the outstanding stock of T Corp. In other words, R pays $25,000 more than the recorded net assets, or book value, of T Corp.

In preparing a worksheet to consolidate the balance sheets of R and T immediately after acquisition of control, we cannot make a simple elimination of R's investment against the shareholders' equity of T because the $175,000 investment is greater than the sum of T's capital stock and retained earnings. The difference, of course, is due to the fact that R paid $25,000 more than the recorded net assets of T. In the worksheet, entry (1) reflects the increase in value of the asset land which T owns. After this adjustment has been made, entry (2) can be made to eliminate the balance of the investment account against the shareholders' equity of T.

The consolidated balance sheet of R Corp. and its subsidiary T immediately after acquisition of control by R has been prepared from the accompanying worksheet.

R Corp. and Subsidiary
Consolidated Balance Sheet
January 1, Year 1

ASSETS

Current	$105,000	
Depreciable—net	300,000	
Land	50,000	
Total Assets		$455,000

LIABILITIES AND SHAREHOLDERS' EQUITY

Liabilities		$195,000
Capital Stock	$200,000	
Retained Earnings	60,000	
Total Shareholders' Equity		260,000
Total Liabilities and Shareholders' Equity		$455,000

R Corp. and Subsidiary
Worksheet—Consolidated Balance Sheet
January 1, Year 1

	R Corp.		T Corp.		Adjustments & Eliminations		Consolidated	
	Dr.	Cr.	Dr.	Cr.			Dr.	Cr.
Current Assets	50,000		55,000				105,000	
Investment in T Corp. Stock	175,000					[2]175,000		
Depreciable Assets—net	200,000		100,000				300,000	
Land			25,000		[1]25,000		50,000	
Liabilities		165,000		30,000				195,000
Capital Stock—R		200,000						200,000
Retained Earnings—R		60,000						60,000
Capital Stock—T				100,000	[2]100,000			
Retained Earnings—T				50,000	[2]50,000			
	425,000	425,000	180,000	180,000				
Appraisal Capital—T					[2]25,000	[1]25,000		
							455,000	455,000

[1] To record increase in value of land owned by T Corp., based on price paid by R Corp. for stock of subsidiary.
[2] To eliminate 100% of subsidiary's capital stock, retained earnings, and appraisal capital.

Observe that land is presented in the consolidated balance sheet at its current value of $50,000 even though the books of T Corp. may still carry the land at its historical cost of $25,000. It is deemed appropriate to present land at the fair market value, which was presumably arrived at objectively, and in arm's-length bargaining between the shareholders of T Corp. and the representatives of R Corp.

An alternative procedure would be for the parent company to cause the subsidiary to recognize the increase in the value of the land on its books with an entry such as the following:

Land	25,000	
Appraisal Capital		25,000

If the above entry had been made on T's books, only one elimination entry would be necessary, as follows:

Capital Stock—T	100,000	
Retained Earnings—T	50,000	
Appraisal Capital—T	25,000	
Investment in T Corp.—Stock		175,000

The remainder of the worksheet and the consolidated balance sheet would be the same as previously presented. If the subsidiary does not recognize the increase in value of the land on its books, it will be necessary to enter the increase in the value of the subsidiary's land each time a consolidation worksheet is prepared.

4.7 EXCESS OF COST OVER BOOK VALUE

When the acquisition cost of an investment in a subsidiary is greater than the book value of the underlying net assets of the subsidiary, the reasons for the excess of cost over book value should be ascertained. Occasionally, the excess may be due to a single cause, such as in Example 2 (Section 4.6), where the land had doubled in value since acquisition by the subsidiary. The longer the subsidiary has been in business, the more likely it is that the amounts recorded on the subsidiary's books will vary from the amount which an investor would be willing to recognize.

Until recently the excess of cost over book value was frequently not identified; it was often labeled *goodwill*, or simply *excess of cost over book value*. However, current practice requires that the *reasons* for the difference between cost and book value be ascertained and identified, if possible. Some reasons an investor may pay more than book value for the stock of another corporation are:

1. The subsidiary may have properly recorded its assets at cost, or other basis, but as time goes by the market value of such assets may have increased so that the investor will consider the market value at the time of making the investment rather than the historical cost to the subsidiary.

2. The subsidiary may have followed depreciation or amortization practices which may have been reasonable at the time of adoption but in retrospect appear to have been too conservative. As a result, these assets are undervalued when the book values are compared with present market values.

3. Estimated liabilities may turn out to have been too high, thus understating the net assets of the firm.

4. Superior earning power of a subsidiary may also account for an investor's willingness to pay more than the net asset value. As *goodwill* is not normally recorded unless purchased or determined in some objective fashion, such an asset may not appear in the subsidiary's books or in its statements.

5. Even when the assets and liabilities of the subsidiary are properly stated, and the net assets equal the values the parent placed on the net assets of the subsidiary, an investor may still expect that the advantages of the combination will enable it to earn more than the two companies could earn separately. Therefore, the investor may be willing to pay an additional amount which is, in effect, a bonus for control of the subsidiary. Thus the parent investor may cause an intangible asset of a subsidiary to be recognized as a result of acquisition of control of the subsidiary. In the past this was often referred to as *consolidation goodwill*; a better term would be *excess of cost over book value of investment in subsidiary*. This should be distinguished from goodwill due to superior earnings of the subsidiary. By way of illustration, goodwill of the subsidiary might be recorded on the subsidiary's books, whereas the *excess of cost over book value of investment in subsidiary* should never be recorded on the subsidiary's books. This excess might be recorded on the parent's books by separating the investment cost into two parts, but usually it appears only on the worksheet to consolidate the statements of parent and subsidiary and in the consolidated statements.

The unallocated excess of cost over book value of investment is treated as an *intangible asset*, which should be amortized over its estimated life. The amortization will affect the income statement of the parent in this and in succeeding years. Further discussion of this matter will be deferred to Chapter 5.

4.8   EXCESS OF BOOK VALUE OVER COST

When a majority of the stock of a subsidiary is acquired for an amount which is less than the book value of the underlying net assets of the subsidiary, the treatment of the excess of book value over cost will depend on the reason which should be assigned for the difference. Several of the more common reasons an investor may pay less than the book value of the net assets of a subsidiary are listed here.

1. The subsidiary may have recorded its assets at cost, or some other basis, but with the passage of time the fair value of such assets may have declined to a level which requires the investor to recognize that the net assets are worth less than book value.

2. The subsidiary may have followed depreciation or amortization policies which may have been deemed appropriate at the time, but now the carrying value of these assets is greater than the fair value of such assets.

3. Estimated liabilities may have seemed reasonable as they had been based on previous experience, but the liabilities may now appear to be inadequate to the investor.

4. Goodwill acquired at some time in the past is not considered by the parent to be of value, or the parent may value it at a lesser amount than appears on the subsidiary's books.

When the price paid by the parent is less than the net assets of the subsidiary, it is generally accepted as evidence that the net assets of the subsidiary are overvalued. The amount of each overvaluation should be identified and subtracted from the appropriate asset or added to the appropriate liability. If the overvaluation is assigned to an asset which is normally depreciated or amortized then the overvaluation will also be depreciated or amortized over the appropriate useful life.

EXAMPLE 3.   On January 1, Year 1, the P Corp. paid $130,000 for all of the outstanding stock of the U Corp. The net assets of the U Corp., according to its books, amount to $150,000, computed as follows:

Assets − liabilities = $165,000 − $15,000 = $150,000, or
Capital stock + retained earnings = $100,000 + $50,000 = $150,000.

Thus, P Corp. has paid $20,000 less than the book value of subsidiary U. It is ascertained that land which had been acquired by U Corp. some ten years earlier had declined in value because a nearby railroad has since discontinued operations, and the exit of the new expressway is a long distance from the site.

The condensed balance sheets of P and U immediately after the acquisition by P of its investment in subsidiary U are shown in the first four columns of the accompanying worksheet to prepare a consolidated balance sheet on January 1, Year 1. Entry (1) reduces the land owned by U by the excess of historical cost over present value. The land is reduced by $20,000, and the shareholders' equity of U Corp. is similarly reduced. The offsetting debit is to the retained earnings of U. If there had been appraisal capital on the books of U, the debit could have been to that account. If there is no appraisal capital or some similar account to which the decrease in U's equity could be debited, however, the charge must fall to retained earnings. Entry (2) eliminates the capital stock of U Corp. and its retained earnings, as adjusted, against the investment of the parent company.

The consolidated balance sheet, which has been prepared from the worksheet, is presented here:

P Corp. and Subsidiary
Consolidated Balance Sheet
January 1, Year 1

ASSETS

Current	$ 95,000
Depreciable Assets—net	300,000
Land	20,000
Total Assets	$415,000

LIABILITIES AND SHAREHOLDERS' EQUITY

Liabilities		$155,000
Capital Stock	$200,000	
Retained Earnings	60,000	
Total Shareholders' Equity		260,000
Total Liabilities & Shareholders' Equity		$415,000

P Corp. and Subsidiary
Worksheet—Consolidated Balance Sheet
January 1, Year 1

	P Corp.		U Corp.		Adjustments & Eliminations	Consolidated	
	Dr.	Cr.	Dr.	Cr.		Dr.	Cr.
Current Assets	70,000		25,000			95,000	
Investment in U Corp. Stock	130,000				[2]130,000		
Depreciable Assets—net	200,000		100,000			300,000	
Land			40,000		[1]20,000	20,000	
Liabilities		140,000		15,000			155,000
Capital Stock—P		200,000					200,000
Retained Earnings—P		60,000					60,000
Capital Stock—U				100,000	[2]100,000		
Retained Earnings—U				50,000	{ [2]30,000 { [1]20,000		
	400,000	400,000	165,000	165,000		415,000	415,000

[1] To adjust for overvalued asset of U Corp.
[2] To eliminate 100% of subsidiary's capital stock and retained earnings as adjusted.

4.9 PARTIALLY OWNED SUBSIDIARIES

When a parent company owns more than 50 percent but less than 100 percent of the voting stock of another corporation, control over the latter corporation's affairs may be just as effective as when all of the voting stock is owned by the parent company. If the two corporations constitute an economic unit, *all* of the subsidiary's assets and liabilities will be included in the consolidated balance sheet. As all of the shareholders' equity of the subsidiary is not represented by the investment of the parent, that component of the shareholders' equity which is not controlled by the parent is set off as a *minority interest*.

EXAMPLE 4. This illustration is based on the same pre-acquisition balance sheets as in Example 1 (Section 4.6), except that instead of purchasing all of the subsidiary's stock for $150,000 only 90 percent of the stock is acquired—for $135,000. Thus, the current assets of the parent are $15,000 more after the investment than in Example 1 (Section 4.6).

The balance sheets of the two corporations after affiliation are included in the first four columns of the accompanying worksheet. Entry (1) eliminates the investment in S Corp. stock against 90 percent of the capital stock and retained earnings of S Corp. Entry (2) classifies the remaining 10 percent of the capital stock and retained earnings of S Corp. as the equity of the minority shareholders.

A tabulation of the parent and minority interests in the shareholders' equity of S Corp. is as follows:

	Total	*90%*	*10%*
Capital Stock—S	$100,000	$ 90,000	$10,000
Retained Earnings—S	50,000	45,000	5,000
	$150,000	$135,000	$15,000

The consolidated balance sheet of P Corp. and S Corp. immediately after affiliation is prepared from the last two columns of the accompanying worksheet and is presented here in condensed form:

P Corp. and Subsidiary
Consolidated Balance Sheet
January 1, Year 1

ASSETS

Current	$120,000	
Depreciable Assets—net	300,000	
Land	25,000	
Total Assets		$445,000

LIABILITIES AND SHAREHOLDERS' EQUITY

Liabilities		$170,000
Minority Interest in Subsidiary		15,000
Capital Stock	$200,000	
Retained Earnings	60,000	
Total Shareholders' Equity		260,000
Total Liabilities and Shareholders' Equity		$445,000

In theory, the minority interest should be part of the owners' equity in the consolidated balance sheet. However, in practice the minority interest in consolidated subsidiaries is usually placed between the liability and the shareholders' equity sections of the balance sheet. The minority interest, however, is not an obligation of any sort. The practice of placing the minority interest in limbo, between the liabilities and the shareholders' equity, can perhaps be best defended on the ground of conservatism.

P Corp. and Subsidiary
Worksheet—Consolidated Balance Sheet
January 1, Year 1

	P Corp.		S Corp.		Eliminations		Consolidated	
	Dr.	Cr.	Dr.	Cr.	Dr.	Cr.	Dr.	Cr.
Current Assets	65,000		55,000				120,000	
Investment in S Corp. Stock	135,000					[1]135,000		
Depreciable Assets—net	200,000		100,000				300,000	
Land			25,000				25,000	
Liabilities		140,000		30,000				170,000
Capital Stock—P		200,000						200,000
Retained Earnings—P		60,000						60,000
Capital Stock—S				100,000	{ [2]10,000 { [1]90,000			
Retained Earnings—S				50,000	{ [2]5,000 { [1]45,000			
	400,000	400,000	180,000	180,000				
Minority Interest—S						[2]15,000		15,000
							445,000	445,000

[1] To eliminate 90% of subsidiary's capital stock and retained earnings.
[2] To classify the 10% interest of the minority stockholders.

4.10 PURCHASE OF 90% OF SUBSIDIARY'S STOCK
INVESTMENT COST GREATER THAN BOOK VALUE

EXAMPLE 5. This illustration is based on the same pre-acquisition balance sheets as in Example 2 (Section 4.6). However, instead of purchasing all of the outstanding stock of T Corp., R Corp. here purchases 90 percent of T's stock for $157,500. Thus, R's current assets, after acquisition of control of the subsidiary, amount to $67,500, or $17,500 more than in Example 2.

The balance sheets of the two corporations after affiliation have been placed in the first four columns of the accompanying worksheet. Entry (1) in this worksheet sets up the increase in the value of the land owned by T. This adjusting entry is equivalent to the following journal entry, which might have been made on the books of T:

Land (Appraisal Increment)	25,000	
Appraisal Capital		25,000

The price of $157,500, paid by R for 90 percent of the net assets of T, may be accepted as evidence that 100 percent of the net assets would be worth $175,000. Assume that all of the assets except land are worth book value, and that the liabilities properly reflect the obligations of T Corp. If the land is worth $25,000 more than the amount recorded on the books of T, the above entry gives appropriate recognition to this fact. Entry (2) eliminates the investment against 90 percent of the capital stock, retained earnings, and appraisal capital of T Corp. Entry (3) groups 10 percent of the foregoing elements of the shareholders' equity of T Corp. and classifies the total as the *minority interest*.

R Corp. and Subsidiary
Worksheet—Consolidated Balance Sheet
January 1, Year 1

	R Corp.		T Corp.		Adjustments & Eliminations		Consolidated	
	Dr.	Cr.	Dr.	Cr.			Dr.	Cr.
Current Assets	67,500		55,000				122,500	
Investment in T Corp. Stock	157,500					¹157,500		
Depreciable Assets—net	200,000		100,000				300,000	
Land			25,000		¹25,000		50,000	
Liabilities		165,000		30,000				195,000
Capital Stock—R		200,000						200,000
Retained Earnings—R		60,000						60,000
Capital Stock—T				100,000	{³10,000 ²90,000}			
Retained Earnings—T				50,000	{³5,000 ²45,000}			
	425,000	425,000	180,000	180,000				
Appraisal Capital—T					{³2,500 ²22,500}	¹25,000		
Minority Interest—T						³17,500		17,500
							472,500	472,500

¹ To record increase in value of land owned by T Corp. based on price paid by P Corp. for 90% of stock of T Corp.
² To eliminate 90% of subsidiary's capital stock, retained earnings, and appraisal capital.
³ To classify the 10% interest of minority stockholders.

If the management of T Corp. was required to revalue its land on its books, as in the foregoing journal entry, then the worksheet needs only elimination entries (2) and (3). If the land revaluation is not recorded on T's books, however, then entry (1) will have to be made on the worksheet each time a consolidation is to be performed.

EXAMPLE 6. Assume the same balance sheets of R Corp. and of T Corp. immediately following the purchase by R of a 90 percent interest in T, as in Example 5, but in this case it is ascertained that the assets and liabilities of T are properly represented by the book amounts. Why might R pay more than $135,000 for 90 percent of the stock of T? One possible explanation is that the advantages of affiliation are such that R is willing to pay $22,500 more than 90 percent of the net assets are worth. There may be expected advantages from centralized control over both companies; perhaps their activities can be coordinated for the maximum advantage to the economic group. An affiliate may achieve a steady source of material or an outlet for production.

Until recently the difference between cost of the investment and the book value of the net assets of the subsidiary was often labelled as *goodwill from consolidation* or simply *consolidation goodwill*. At present, the preferred terminology is *excess of cost over book value*, which is to be amortized over the number of years which are expected to benefit from this excess amount. This categorization should be used only when it is not possible to identify the reason for the excess with any of the assets or liabilities of the subsidiary.

A worksheet to consolidate the balance sheets of R Corp. and of T Corp. immediately after affiliation accompanies this section. Observe that there is no revaluation of the assets or liabilities of either company. There is, of course, a new intangible asset, *excess of cost over fair value of interest in subsidiary*, in the amount of $22,500. It does not appear on the statement of either company; if it is to be associated with either company, it must be with the parent, as it was the parent company which paid out the *excess* of its own volition.

There is no revaluation of the minority shareholders' interest; it remains at 10 percent of $150,000, or $15,000. This is the same amount as the minority interest in Example 4.

R Corp. and Subsidiary
Worksheet—Consolidated Balance Sheet
January 1, Year 1

	R Corp.		T Corp.		Eliminations		Consolidated	
	Dr.	Cr.	Dr.	Cr.	Dr.	Cr.	Dr.	Cr.
Current Assets	67,500		55,000				122,500	
Investment in T Corp. Stock	157,500					[2]135,000 [1]22,500		
Depreciable Assets—net	200,000		100,000				300,000	
Land			25,000				25,000	
Liabilities		165,000		30,000				195,000
Capital Stock—R		200,000						200,000
Retained Earnings—R		60,000						60,000
Capital Stock—T				100,000	[3]10,000 [2]90,000			
Retained Earnings—T				50,000	[3]5,000 [2]45,000			
	425,000	425,000	180,000	180,000				
Excess of Cost over Fair Value of Interest in Subsidiary					[1]22,500		22,500	
Minority Interest in T						[3]15,000		15,000
							470,000	470,000

[1] To record excess of cost of investment in 90% of stock of T Corp. over its value.
[2] To eliminate 90% of subsidiary's capital stock and retained earnings.
[3] To classify 10% interest of minority stockholders.

The consolidated balance sheet of R Corp. and its subsidiary T Corp. immediately following affiliation is prepared from the last two columns of the accompanying worksheet and is presented here:

R Corp. and Subsidiary
Consolidated Balance Sheet
January 1, Year 1

ASSETS

Current		$122,500
Depreciable Assets—net		300,000
Land		25,000
Excess of Cost over Value of Interest in Subsidiary		22,500
Total Assets		$470,000

LIABILITIES AND SHAREHOLDERS' EQUITY

Liabilities		$195,000
Minority Interest in Subsidiary		15,000
Capital Stock	$200,000	
Retained Earnings	60,000	
Total Shareholders' Equity		260,000
Total Liabilities and Shareholders' Equity		$470,000

4.11   PURCHASE OF 90% OF SUBSIDIARY'S STOCK, BOOK VALUE GREATER THAN COST

EXAMPLE 7. Assume that P Corp. and U Corp. have the same pre-affiliation balance sheets as in Example 3 (Section 4.8). The land which U owns is carried on its books at the historical cost of $40,000. However, the management of P deems it to be worth only $20,000. Accordingly, when P acquires a 90 percent interest in the stock of U, the cost to P is $117,000, or 90 percent of $130,000 ($150,000 − $20,000).

The balance sheets of the two corporations immediately after affiliation have been entered in the first four columns of the accompanying worksheet. Entry (1) reduces the land from cost to the fair value on which the price of the investment was based; the offsetting debit is to retained earnings of U. If there had been appraisal capital on the books of U, the debit could have been made to that account. Lacking any other suitable account to which the decrease in capital could be charged, the debit must fall to retained earnings. The adjusted shareholders' equity of U is now $130,000. Entry (2) eliminates 90 percent, or $117,000, against the investment; the remaining 10 percent, or $13,000, is classified as the minority interest.

P Corp. and Subsidiary
Worksheet—Consolidated Balance Sheet
January 1, Year 1

	P Corp. Dr.	P Corp. Cr.	U Corp. Dr.	U Corp. Cr.	Adjustments & Eliminations	Consolidated Dr.	Consolidated Cr.
Current Assets	83,000		25,000			108,000	
Investment in U Corp. Stock	117,000				[2]117,000		
Depreciable Assets—net	200,000		100,000			300,000	
Land			40,000		[1]20,000	20,000	
Liabilities		140,000		15,000			155,000
Capital Stock—P		200,000					200,000
Retained Earnings—P		60,000					60,000
Capital Stock—U				100,000	{ [3]10,000 { [2]90,000		
Retained Earnings—U				50,000	{ [2]27,000 { [1]20,000 { [3]3,000		
	400,000	400,000	165,000	165,000			
Minority Interest in U					[3]13,000		13,000
						428,000	428,000

[1] To adjust for overvalued asset of U Corp.
[2] To eliminate 90% of subsidiary's capital stock and retained earnings as adjusted.
[3] To classify the 10% interest of the minority stockholders.

4.12   CONSOLIDATED BALANCE SHEET AT DATE OF AFFILIATION— EXPANDED ILLUSTRATION

EXAMPLE 8. The previous examples in this chapter have been condensed in order to draw attention to the principles and techniques of consolidation. In this section an expanded worksheet and an expanded balance sheet are presented. The illustration is based on the data from Example 7. However, sufficient additional details have been added so that a realistic example results. The adjustments and eliminations in this worksheet are identical with those in Example 7, so no further explanation is needed. After the adjusting and eliminating entries have been entered in the worksheet, each line is combined according to the basic rules of debit and credit, and the result is placed in the appropriate column for the consolidated balance sheet.

The consolidated balance sheet is similar to the balance sheet of any corporation except for the title and the minority interest in the equity of the subsidiary corporation. In practice, the minority interest is often included with the liabilities, or is placed in between the liability and shareholders' equity sections. However, it is not in any sense a liability of the subsidiary or of the consolidated group. The minority interest represents an ownership outside of the parent or controlling group. Minority shareholders should look to the individual statements of the subsidiary corporation for data concerning their holdings. In an individual statement of U Corp. their equity would be represented by 10 percent of $150,000, or $15,000. The fact that the consolidated balance sheet shows the minority interest as $13,000 does not in any way affect the minority shareholders.

P Corp. and Subsidiary
Worksheet—Consolidated Balance Sheet
January 1, Year 1

	P Corp.		U Corp.		Adjustments & Eliminations		Consolidated	
	Dr.	Cr.	Dr.	Cr.			Dr.	Cr.
Cash in Bank	28,000		5,000				33,000	
Accounts Receivable	32,000		10,500				42,500	
Allowance for Bad Debts		1,000		500				1,500
Merchandise (at FIFO Cost)	20,500		9,000				29,500	
Prepaid Expenses	3,500		1,000				4,500	
Investment in U Corp. Stock	117,000					[2]117,000		
Machinery and Equipment	260,000		135,000				395,000	
Accumulated Depreciation		60,000		35,000				95,000
Land			40,000			[1]20,000	20,000	
Accounts Payable		27,000		11,000				38,000
Taxes Payable		8,000		2,500				10,500
Expenses Payable		4,000		1,500				5,500
Mortgage Payable (due Year 9)		101,000						101,000
Capital Stock—P		200,000						200,000
Retained Earnings—P		60,000						60,000
Capital Stock—U				100,000	[3]10,000 [2]90,000			
Retained Earnings—U				50,000	[2]27,000 [1]20,000 [3]3,000			
	461,000	461,000	200,500	200,500				
Minority Interest in U						[3]13,000		13,000
							524,500	524,500

[1] To adjust for overvalued asset of U Corp.
[2] To eliminate 90% of subsidiary's capital stock and retained earnings as adjusted.
[3] To classify the 10% interest of the minority stockholders.

P Corp. and Subsidiary
Consolidated Balance Sheet
January 1, Year 1

ASSETS

CURRENT

Cash in Banks		$ 33,000	
Accounts Receivable	$42,500		
Less: Allowance for Doubtful Accounts	1,500	41,000	
Merchandise (at FIFO Cost)		29,500	
Prepaid Expenses		4,500	
Total Current Assets			$108,000

LONG-TERM

Machinery and Equipment		$395,000	
Less: Accumulated Depreciation		95,000	
		$300,000	
Land		20,000	
Total Long-Term Assets			320,000
Total Assets			$428,000

LIABILITIES AND SHAREHOLDERS' EQUITY

CURRENT LIABILITIES

Accounts Payable	$ 38,000	
Taxes Payable	10,500	
Expenses Payable	5,500	
Total Current Liabilities		$ 54,000
Mortgage Payable (Due in Year 9)		101,000
Total Liabilities		$155,000
Minority Interest in U Corp.		13,000

SHAREHOLDERS' EQUITY

Common Stock—$10 par (Authorized 50,000 Shares)	$200,000	
Retained Earnings	60,000	260,000
Total Liabilities and Shareholders' Equity		$428,000

Summary

(1) In order to prepare consolidated statements, the parent should own more than _____ percent of another corporation's voting stock.

(2) One objective of a consolidated balance sheet is to prepare the financial position of a group of affiliated corporations as if they constituted an _____ entity; legal distinctions are ignored.

(3) The phrase *net assets* means _____ minus _____.

(4) *Net assets* can also be measured by adding the elements of _____.

(5) The capital stock which appears in a consolidated balance sheet is that of the _____ corporation.

(6) In a consolidated balance sheet the retained earnings which appears is that of the _____ corporation.

(7) When a parent corporation owns 80 percent of a subsidiary's voting stock, _____ percent of the subsidiary's assets will be included in the asset section of the consolidated balance sheet.

(8) A parent corporation which owns a controlling interest in one or more subsidiaries, but which is not an operating company, is also known as a _____ company.

(9) Goodwill is normally not recorded in the accounts of a firm unless it had been purchased or it had been determined in some other _____ manner.

(10) A minority interest in a consolidated balance sheet may be presented in three possible ways:
    (*a*) _____
    (*b*) _____
    (*c*) _____

Answers: (1) 50;   (2) economic;   (3) assets, liabilities;   (4) shareholders' equity;   (5) parent;
(6) parent;   (7) 100;   (8) holding;   (9) objective;   (10) (*a*) liability, (*b*) shareholders' equity,
(*c*) between liabilities and shareholders' equity

Solved Problems

4.1 The condensed balance sheets of Polk Corp. and Sack Corp. immediately after Polk acquired 90 percent of the voting stock of Sack on December 31 of Year 1 were as follows:

	Polk Corp.	Sack Corp.
ASSETS		
Cash in Banks	$ 34,000	$ 27,000
Accounts Receivable—net	47,000	24,000
Merchandise	62,000	29,000
Investment in Sack Corp.—Stock	225,000	
Machinery & Equipment—net	335,000	220,000
	$703,000	$300,000
LIABILITIES AND SHAREHOLDERS' EQUITY		
Current Liabilities	$101,000	$ 80,000
Capital Stock—$10 par	400,000	120,000
Premium on Common Stock		33,000
Retained Earnings	202,000	67,000
	$703,000	$300,000

Required:

Prepare a worksheet to consolidate Polk and its subsidiary Sack. Assume that any excess of cost of investment over book value of subsidiary is to be considered as:

(*a*)   an amount paid to achieve control;

(*b*)   fully amortized patent rights of Sack Corp.

(*a*)

Polk Corp. and Subsidiary
Worksheet—Consolidated Balance Sheet
End of Year 1

	Polk Corp.		Sack Corp.		Eliminations		Consolidated	
	Dr.	Cr.	Dr.	Cr.	Dr.	Cr.	Dr.	Cr.
Cash in Banks	34,000		27,000					
Accounts Receivable—net	47,000		24,000					
Merchandise	62,000		29,000					
Invest. in Sack Corp.—Stock	225,000							
Machinery and Equipment—net	335,000		220,000					
Current Liabilities		101,000		80,000				
Capital Stock; $10 par—Polk		400,000						
Retained Earnings—Polk		202,000						
Capital Stock; $10 par—Sack				120,000				
Prem. on Capital Stock—Sack				33,000				
Retained Earnings—Sack				67,000				
	703,000	703,000	300,000	300,000				
Minority Interest								

(*b*)

Polk Corp. and Subsidiary
Worksheet—Consolidated Balance Sheet
End of Year 1

	Polk Corp.		Sack Corp.		Eliminations		Consolidated	
	Dr.	Cr.	Dr.	Cr.	Dr.	Cr.	Dr.	Cr.
Cash in Banks	34,000		27,000					
Accounts Receivable—net	47,000		24,000					
Merchandise	62,000		29,000					
Invest. in Sack Corp.—Stock	225,000							
Machinery and Equipment—net	335,000		220,000					
Current Liabilities		101,000		80,000				
Capital Stock; $10 par—Polk		400,000						
Retained Earnings—Polk		202,000						
Capital Stock; $10 par—Sack				120,000				
Prem. on Capital Stock—Sack				33,000				
Retained Earnings—Sack				67,000				
	703,000	703,000	300,000	300,000				
Minority Interest								

SOLUTION

(a)

Polk Corp. and Subsidiary
Worksheet—Consolidated Balance Sheet
End of Year 1

	Polk Corp.		Sack Corp.		Eliminations		Consolidated	
	Dr.	Cr.	Dr.	Cr.	Dr.	Cr.	Dr.	Cr.
Cash in Banks	34,000		27,000				61,000	
Accounts Receivable—net	47,000		24,000				71,000	
Merchandise	62,000		29,000				91,000	
Invest. in Sack Corp.—Stock	225,000					[2]198,000 [1]27,000		
Machinery and Equipment—net	335,000		220,000				555,000	
Current Liabilities		101,000		80,000				181,000
Capital Stock; $10 par—Polk		400,000						400,000
Retained Earnings—Polk		202,000						202,000
Capital Stock; $10 par—Sack				120,000	[3]12,000 [2]108,000			
Prem. on Capital Stock—Sack				33,000	[3]3,300 [2]29,700			
Retained Earnings—Sack				67,000	[3]6,700 [2]60,300			
	703,000	703,000	300,000	300,000				
Excess of Cost Over Fair Value of Interest in Subsidiary					[1]27,000		27,000	
Minority Interest						[3]22,000		22,000
					247,000	247,000	805,000	805,000

[1] To record excess of cost of investment over 90% of book value of Sack Corp.: $225,000 − $198,000.
[2] To eliminate 90% of subsidiary's capital stock, premium on capital stock, and retained earnings.
[3] To classify 10% interest of minority stockholders.

(b)

Polk Corp. and Subsidiary
Worksheet—Consolidated Balance Sheet
End of Year 1

	Polk Corp.		Sack Corp.		Eliminations		Consolidated	
	Dr.	Cr.	Dr.	Cr.	Dr.	Cr.	Dr.	Cr.
Cash in Banks	34,000		27,000				61,000	
Accounts Receivable—net	47,000		24,000				71,000	
Merchandise	62,000		29,000				91,000	
Invest. in Sack Corp.—Stock	225,000					[2]225,000		
Machinery and Equipment—net	335,000		220,000				555,000	
Current Liabilities		101,000		80,000				181,000
Capital Stock; $10 par—Polk		400,000						400,000
Retained Earnings—Polk		202,000						202,000
Capital Stock; $10 par—Sack				120,000	[3]12,000 [2]108,000			
Prem. on Capital Stock—Sack				33,000	[3]3,300 [2]29,700			
Retained Earnings—Sack				67,000	[3]6,700 [2]60,300			
Appraisal Capital—Sack					[3]3,000 [2]27,000	[1]30,000		
	703,000	703,000	300,000	300,000				
Patent					[1]30,000		30,000	
Minority Interest						[2]25,000		25,000
					280,000	280,000	808,000	808,000

[1] Total value of Sack Corp.: $225,000 = $250,000. Value of patent: $250,000 − $220,000 = $30,000.
[2] To eliminate 90% of subsidiary's capital stock, premium on capital stock, retained earnings, and appraisal capital.
[3] To classify 10% interest of minority stockholders.

4.2   The Salvador Corp. balance sheet at June 30, 19XX includes the following items of liabilities and shareholders' equity:

Estimated Federal Income Tax Liability	$180,000
Capital Stock, $5 par—	
Authorized, 1,000,000 Shares	
Issued, 100,000 Shares	500,000
Premium on Capital Stock	110,000
Reserve for Contingencies	100,000
Retained Earnings	290,000

Any differential between the book value of the subsidiary and the cost of the investment is due to the difference between the market value and the recorded value of the land.

Required:

Prepare elimination entries to consolidate Pratt and Salvador immediately after the purchase of Salvador's stock by Pratt, under each of the following conditions.

(a)   Purchased 100,000 shares from stockholders for $1,000,000.

(b)   Purchased 100,000 shares from stockholders for $950,000.

(c)   Purchased 95,000 shares from stockholders for $925,000.

(d)   Purchased 80,000 shares from stockholders for $836,000.

(e)   Purchased 40,000 shares from stockholders for $209,000.

(f)   Purchased 150,000 shares of stock from the Salvador Corp. at $12 per share.

SOLUTION

(a)	Capital Stock	500,000	
	Premium on Capital Stock	110,000	
	Reserve for Contingencies	100,000	
	Retained Earnings	290,000	
	Investment in Salvador Corp.—Stock		1,000,000
(b)	Capital Stock	500,000	
	Premium on Capital Stock	110,000	
	Reserve for Contingencies	100,000	
	Retained Earnings	290,000	
	Investment in Salvador Corp.—Stock		950,000
	Land		50,000
(c)	Capital Stock	500,000	
	Premium on Capital Stock	110,000	
	Reserve for Contingencies	100,000	
	Retained Earnings	290,000	
	Investment in Salvador Corp.—Stock		925,000
	Land*		26,316
	Minority Interests ($973,684 × 5%)		48,684

---

* $925,000 ÷ 95% = $973,684

$1,000,000 − $973,684 = $26,316

(d)   Capital Stock   500,000
       Premium on Capital Stock   110,000
       Reserve for Contingencies   100,000
       Retained Earnings   290,000
       Land   45,000
             Investment in Salvador Corp.—Stock   836,000
             Minority Interests   209,000

(e) 40 percent—not sufficient for consolidation

(f)

       Capital Stock*   1,250,000
       Premium on Capital Stock**   1,160,000
       Reserve for Contingencies   100,000
       Retained Earnings   290,000
       Land   200,000
             Investment in Salvador Corp.—Stock
                 (150,000 shares × $12)   1,800,000
             Minority Interests
                 (100,000 shares × $12)   1,200,000

-----

* Capital Stock:
    $500,000 + $750,000 = $1,250,000
** Premium on Capital Stock:
    $110,000 + $1,050,000 = $1,160,000

4.3   The condensed balance sheets of P Corp. and S Corp. on January 1, Year 1, before P Corp.'s investment in stock of S Corp. are as follows:

	P Corp.	S Corp.
Current Assets	$200,000	$ 55,000
Depreciable Assets—net	200,000	100,000
Land		25,000
Total Assets	$400,000	$180,000
Liabilities	$140,000	$ 30,000
Capital Stock	200,000	100,000
Retained Earnings	60,000	50,000
Total Liabilities and Shareholders' Equity	$400,000	$180,000

Assume that P purchases 90 percent of the outstanding capital stock of S from its stockholders on January 1, Year 1, for $162,000 cash. The recorded assets and liabilities of S Corp. are valued at the amounts shown in its statement; however, it is deemed that S Corp. has unrecorded goodwill.

Required:

Prepare a worksheet to consolidate the balance sheets of P Corp. and S Corp. immediately after the investment by P Corp. in the stock of S Corp.

P Corp. and Subsidiary
Worksheet—Consolidated Balance Sheet
January 1, Year 1

	P Corp.		S Corp.		Eliminations		Consolidated	
	Dr.	Cr.	Dr.	Cr.	Dr.	Cr.	Dr.	Cr.
Current Assets	38,000		55,000					
Investment in S Corp.	162,000							
Depreciable Assets—net	200,000		100,000					
Land			25,000					
Liabilities		140,000		30,000				
Capital Stock—P		200,000						
Retained Earnings—P		60,000						
Capital Stock—S				100,000				
Retained Earnings—S				50,000				
	400,000	400,000	180,000	180,000				
Goodwill								
Minority Interest in S								

SOLUTION

P Corp. and Subsidiary
Worksheet—Consolidated Balance Sheet
January 1, Year 1

	P Corp.		S Corp.		Eliminations		Consolidated	
	Dr.	Cr.	Dr.	Cr.	Dr.	Cr.	Dr.	Cr.
Current Assets	38,000		55,000				93,000	
Investment in S Corp.	162,000					{ [2]135,000 [1]27,000		
Depreciable Assets—net	200,000		100,000				300,000	
Land			25,000				25,000	
Liabilities		140,000		30,000				170,000
Capital Stock—P		200,000						200,000
Retained Earnings—P		60,000						60,000
Capital Stock—S				100,000	{ [3]10,000 [2]90,000			
Retained Earnings—S				50,000	{ [3]5,000 [2]45,000			
	400,000	400,000	180,000	180,000				
Goodwill					[1]30,000		30,000	
Minority Interest in S						[3]15,000 } [1]3,000 }		18,000
							448,000	448,000

[1] To record goodwill of S based on price paid by P Corp. for 90% of stock of subsidiary.
[2] To eliminate 90% of subsidiary's capital stock and retained earnings as of Jan. 1, Yr. 1.
[3] To classify 10% interest of minority stockholders.

4.4	The condensed balance sheets of Pale, Sale, and Tale corporations, at the date of acquisition by Pale of controlling interests in Sale and Tale, are shown below:

	Pale Corp.	Sale Corp.	Tale Corp.
ASSETS			
Current Assets	$ 44,000	$ 70,000	$ 95,000
Investment in Sale Corp.— 9,000 shares	144,000		
Investment in Tale Corp.—16,000 shares	72,000		
Land	40,000	22,000	40,000
Other Assets	264,000	68,000	45,000
	$564,000	$160,000	$180,000
EQUITIES			
Liabilities	$ 64,000	$ 20,000	$ 60,000
Capital Stock—$100 par	400,000		
Capital Stock—$10 par		100,000	200,000
Retained Earnings	100,000	40,000	
Deficit			(80,000)
	$564,000	$160,000	$180,000

The cost of the investments in the respective subsidiaries reflects acceptance of the recorded asset and liabilities except for land. The implied current value of the subsidiaries' land is to be shown in the consolidated balance sheet.

Required:

Complete the consolidated worksheet of the three corporations immediately after acquisition of control.

Pale Corp. and Subsidiaries
Worksheet—Consolidated Balance Sheet
Date of Acquisition

	Pale Corp.		Sale Corp.		Tale Corp.		Eliminations		Consolidated	
	Dr.	Cr.	Dr.	Cr.	Dr.	Cr.	Dr.	Cr.	Dr.	Cr.
Current Assets	44,000		70,000		95,000					
Investment in Sale Corp.— 9,000 sh.	144,000									
Investment in Tale Corp.— 18,000 sh.	72,000									
Land	40,000		22,000		40,000					
Other Assets	264,000		68,000		45,000					
Liabilities		64,000		20,000		60,000				
Capital Stock; $100 par—P		400,000								
Retained Earnings—P		100,000								
Capital Stock; $10 par—S				100,000						
Retained Earnings—S				40,000						
Capital Stock: $10 par—T						200,000				
Deficit—T					80,000					
	564,000	564,000	160,000	160,000	260,000	260,000				

SOLUTION

Pale Corp. and Subsidiaries
Worksheet—Consolidated Balance Sheet
Date of Acquisition

	Pale Corp.		Sale Corp.		Tale Corp.		Eliminations		Consolidated	
	Dr.	Cr.	Dr.	Cr.	Dr.	Cr.	Dr.	Cr.	Dr.	Cr.
Current Assets	44,000		70,000		95,000				209,000	
Investment in Sale Corp.— 9,000 sh.	144,000							[2]144,000		
Investment in Tale Corp.— 18,000 sh.	72,000							[5]72,000		
Land	40,000		22,000		40,000		[1]20,000	[4]30,000	92,000	
Other Assets	264,000		68,000		45,000				377,000	
Liabilities		64,000		20,000		60,000				144,000
Capital Stock; $100 par—P		400,000								400,000
Retained Earnings—P		100,000								100,000
Capital Stock; $10 par—S				100,000			{[3]10,000 [2]90,000			
Retained Earnings—S				40,000			{ [3]4,000 [2]36,000			
Capital Stock; $10 par—T						200,000	{[6]40,000 [5]160,000			
Deficit—T					80,000		[4]30,000	{[6]22,000 [5]88,000		
	564,000	564,000	160,000	160,000	260,000	260,000				
Appraisal Capital—S							{[3]2,000 [2]18,000}	[1]20,000		
Minority Interests								{[6]18,000 [3]16,000}		34,000
									678,000	678,000

[1] Total value of sale: $144,000 ÷ 90% = $160,000. Increase in land: $160,000 − $140,000 = $20,000.
[2] To eliminate 90% of Sale's equity accounts.
[3] To classify 10% minority interest in Sale's equity accounts.
[4] Total value of Tale: $72,000 ÷ 80% = $90,000. Decrease in land: $120,000 − $90,000 = $30,000.
[5] To eliminate 80% of Tale's equity accounts.
[6] To classify 20% minority interest in Tale's equity accounts.

4.5 On March 31 of 19XX, the Petro Corp. purchased 9,000 shares of the Sutro Corp. common stock for $230,000 and $100,000 of Sutro Corp. bonds at par (plus accrued interest). The condensed trial balances which appear below were taken from the books of the two corporations.

The acquisition of Sutro was motivated by the fact that Sutro had recently completed the installation of a substantial amount of highly specialized machinery. To acquire this machinery from the manufacturers and install it would take about two years. Petro felt that immediate control of Sutro would give the group a substantial economic advantage.

An examination of the books revealed that Petro owed Sutro $95,000 for merchandise purchased during February and March.

Required:

Complete the worksheet to prepare a consolidated balance sheet at the close of business on March 31.

	Petro Corp.	Sutro Corp.	
Cash	27,000	13,000	
Accrued Interest Receivable	1,500		
Other Current Assets	98,000	159,000	
Investment in Sutro Corp.—Stock	230,000		
Investment in Sutro Corp.—Bonds	100,000		
Machinery and Equipment	210,000	700,000	
Accumulated Depreciation		185,000		66,000
Other Assets	101,000	14,000	
Vouchers Payable		205,000		145,000
Accrued Interest Payable				6,000
Other Current Liabilities		17,000		69,000
Bonds Payable: 9% Interest Payable Feb. 1 and Aug. 1				400,000
Capital Stock—$100 par		200,000	
Retained Earnings		160,500	
Capital Stock—$10 par				100,000
Retained Earnings				100,000
	767,500	767,500	886,000	886,000

Petro Corp. and Subsidiary
Worksheet—Consolidated Balance Sheet
March 31, 19XX

	Petro Corp.		Sutro Corp.		Eliminations		Consolidated	
	Dr.	Cr.	Dr.	Cr.	Dr.	Cr.	Dr.	Cr.
Cash	27,000		13,000					
Accrued Interest Receivable	1,500							
Other Current Assets	98,000		159,000					
Investment in Sutro Corp.—Stock	230,000							
Investment in Sutro Corp.—Bonds	100,000							
Machinery and Equipment	210,000		700,000					
Accumulated Depreciation		185,000		66,000				
Other Assets	101,000		14,000					
Vouchers Payable		205,000		145,000				
Accrued Interest Payable				6,000				
Other Current Liabilities		17,000		69,000				
Bonds Payable: 9% 2/1 and 8/1				400,000				
Capital Stock—$100 par		200,000						
Retained Earnings—Petro		160,500						
Capital Stock—$10 par				100,000				
Retained Earnings—Sutro				100,000				
	767,500	767,500	886,000	886,000				

SOLUTION

Petro Corp. and Subsidiary
Worksheet—Consolidated Balance Sheet
March 31, 19XX

	Petro Corp.		Sutro Corp.		Eliminations		Consolidated	
	Dr.	Cr.	Dr.	Cr.	Dr.	Cr.	Dr.	Cr.
Cash	27,000		13,000				40,000	
Accrued Interest Receivable	1,500					[5]1,500		
Other Current Assets	98,000		159,000			[6]95,000	162,000	
Investment in Sutro Corp.—Stock	230,000					{ [2]180,000 [1]50,000		
Investment in Sutro Corp.—Bonds	100,000					[4]100,000		
Machinery and Equipment	210,000		700,000				910,000	
Accumulated Depreciation		185,000		66,000				251,000
Other Assets	101,000		14,000				115,000	
Vouchers Payable		205,000		145,000	[6]95,000			255,000
Accrued Interest Payable				6,000	[5]1,500			4,500
Other Current Liabilities		17,000		69,000				86,000
Bonds Payable: 9% 2/1 and 8/1				400,000	[4]100,000			300,000
Capital Stock—$100 par		200,000						200,000
Retained Earnings—Petro		160,500						160,500
Capital Stock—$10 par				100,000	{ [3]10,000 [2]90,000			
Retained Earnings—Sutro				100,000	{ [3]10,000 [2]90,000			
	767,500	767,500	886,000	886,000				
Excess of Cost Over Fair Value of Interest in Subsidiary					[1]50,000		50,000	
Minority Interest						[3]20,000		20,000
					446,500	446,500	1,277,000	1,277,000

[1] To record excess of cost of investment over 90% of book value of Sutro Corp.: $230,000 − (0.90)($200,000).
[2] To eliminate 90% of subsidiary's capital stock and retained earnings.
[3] To classify 10% interest of minority stockholders.
[4] To eliminate reciprocal bondholdings.
[5] To eliminate reciprocal interest on bonds.
[6] To eliminate reciprocal receivable and payables.

Chapter 5

Consolidated Statements—
After Date of Acquisition:
Cost Method

5.1 EARNINGS OF SUBSIDIARY

The net income or loss of a subsidiary is generally included in a consolidated income statement which is prepared for periods after the affiliation has been established. If a subsidiary is less than 100 percent owned, an appropriate portion of the net income or loss must be allocated to the minority interests.

When the investment account is maintained at *cost*, the balance of the account is rarely changed except for a return of investment or for an additional investment. The cost method is the one which will be followed in this chapter.

Some investors attempt to increase the investment balance in order to recognize the parent's share of the subsidiary's earnings and to decrease the investment balance for the parent's share of the subsidiary's losses and dividends. This method, generally referred to as the *equity* or accrual method, will be the subject of the following chapter.

5.2 DIVIDENDS OF SUBSIDIARY

There are various ways by which assets may be moved from a subsidiary to a parent company. One of the most common methods is a distribution of profits—that is, a dividend—usually in the form of cash.

Dividends paid or declared by a corporation are generally based on current or accumulated profits, and thus reduce the retained earnings of the declaring corporation. In those infrequent situations where there is no accumulation of income retained in the business or some other surplus on which to base a dividend, the distribution may be considered a return of capital in whole or in part.

Dividends are normally treated as income by the receiver, whereas dividends are *not* an expense to the distributing corporation. Thus, in consolidating income statements of a parent and of a subsidiary, attention must be directed to eliminating dividend income received from an affiliated corporation in order to avoid double counting of income actually earned by the companies.

Assume that the results of operations of a parent and a subsidiary company during the first year of operations, after the parent had purchased 100 percent of the subsidiary's stock are condensed as follows:

	Parent	*Subsidiary*
Income from Operations	$19,000	$20,000
Dividend Income—from Subsidiary	10,000	
Net Income	$29,000	$20,000

Assume further that there were no intercompany transactions except for the $10,000 received by the parent company from its subsidiary. In order to consolidate the two income statements, the following elimination entry (or its equivalent) must be made to avoid double counting of the income from subsidiary:

Dividend Income	10,000	
Net Income		10,000

After the effect of this elimination entry has been recognized in the consolidation worksheet, all the other items in the respective income statements can be combined to arrive at a consolidated income statement, which should result in the consolidated net income of $39,000. The same result would have been obtained if the income from operations of the two companies had been combined directly. This is not to say that finding the consolidated net income is always so simple, however. Frequently it is necessary to adjust one or more of the data utilized to arrive at an individual company's income.

5.3 CONSOLIDATED STATEMENTS AT END OF FIRST YEAR OF CONTROL

In the next three examples it will be assumed that one corporation purchased all of the outstanding stock of another corporation and one full year of operations has occurred.

EXAMPLE 1. The balance sheets of the two corporations immediately following the investment by P Corp. in 100 percent of the stock of S Corp. are as follows:

	P Corp.	S Corp.
Current Assets	$ 50,000	$ 55,000
Investment in S Corp. Stock	150,000	
Depreciable Assets—net	200,000	100,000
Land		25,000
Total Assets	$400,000	$180,000
Liabilities	$140,000	$ 30,000
Capital Stock	200,000	100,000
Retained Earnings	60,000	50,000
Total Liabilities and Shareholders' Equity	$400,000	$180,000

The respective balance sheets at the end of Year 1 are included in the first four columns of the accompanying worksheet to consolidate the balance sheets at the end of Year 1.

The results of operations of the two corporations for the first twelve months after P Corp. had acquired 100 percent of the stock of S Corp. are condensed as follows:

	P Corp.	S Corp.
Sales	$120,000	$116,000
Cost of Goods Sold	70,000	75,000
Gross Profit	$ 50,000	$ 41,000
Selling Expenses	$ 16,000	$ 12,000
General Expenses	15,000	9,000
Total Expenses	$ 31,000	$ 21,000
Income from Operations	$ 19,000	$ 20,000
Dividend Income from S Corp.	10,000	
Net Income	$ 29,000	$ 20,000

The schedule of retained earnings for the above twelve-month period follows:

	P Corp.	S Corp.
Balance, January 1	$60,000	$50,000
Add: Net Income—Year 1	29,000	20,000
Total	$89,000	$70,000
Less: Dividends—Year 1	15,000	10,000
Balance, December 31	$74,000	$60,000

The worksheet to consolidate the income statements of the two corporations for Year 1 (p. 120) contains the appropriate data condensed from the respective books after actual or constructive closings. In order to include the net income, which results from an excess of credits over debits, the amount of net income is inserted as a balancing figure on the debit, or smaller, side. To complete the picture, the offsetting credit goes to the respective retained earnings account. It is thus equivalent to the debit side of the following journal entry, which an individual corporation would make to transfer net income to the retained earnings account at the end of a year:

Income Summary	XXXX	
Retained Earnings		XXXX

In order to avoid double counting of the dividends received by P Corp. from S Corp., in addition to the net income of S Corp., it is necessary to eliminate this intercompany transaction by elimination entry (a) in the accompanying worksheet to prepare a consolidated income statement. In general journal form, the entry is as follows:

Dividend Income	10,000	
Net Income		10,000

Entry (b) transfers the net income of S Corp. so as to combine the net income of both corporations on the same line. After these elimination entries have been entered in the eliminations columns of the worksheet, the remaining items can be combined and extended.

The worksheet to prepare a consolidated balance sheet at the end of the first year of operations is presented in condensed form in order to highlight those items which have special significance in the consolidation process. It is assumed that all accounts of each corporation have been closed, except net income and dividends (or dividends declared), which have not been transferred to determine the final retained earnings. Elimination entries (a) and (b) are similar to those same-lettered entries in the worksheet to consolidate the income statements, and perform the same functions.

Entry (1), which eliminates 100 percent of the subsidiary's capital stock and retained earnings as of January 1 of Year 1, is exactly the same as entry (1) in Example 1 of the previous chapter (Section 4.6).

Condensed consolidated statements prepared from the accompanying worksheets appear here:

P Corp. and Subsidiary
Consolidated Income Statement
Year 1

Sales	$236,000	
Cost of Goods Sold	145,000	
Gross Profit		$91,000
Selling Expenses	$ 28,000	
General Expenses	24,000	52,000
Net Income		$39,000

(*Note:* As an alternate approach, a three-tier worksheet is included in this problem.)

P Corp. and Subsidiary
Worksheet—Consolidated Income Statement
Year 1

	P Corp.		S Corp.		Eliminations		Consolidated	
	Dr.	Cr.	Dr.	Cr.	Dr.	Cr.	Dr.	Cr.
Sales		120,000		116,000				236,000
Cost of Goods Sold	70,000		75,000				145,000	
Selling Expenses	16,000		12,000				28,000	
General Expenses	15,000		9,000				24,000	
Dividend Income		10,000			[a]10,000			
	101,000	130,000	96,000	116,000			197,000	236,000
Net Income—P	29,000				[b]20,000	[a]10,000	39,000	
Net Income—S			20,000			[b]20,000		
	130,000	130,000	116,000	116,000			236,000	236,000

[a] To eliminate dividend received by parent from subsidiary.
[b] To combine net income of two corporations.

P Corp. and Subsidiary
Worksheet—Consolidated Balance Sheet
December 31, Year 1

	P Corp.		S Corp.		Eliminations		Consolidated	
	Dr.	Cr.	Dr.	Cr.	Dr.	Cr.	Dr.	Cr.
Current Assets	103,000		56,000				159,000	
Investment in S Corp.	150,000					[1]150,000		
Depreciable Assets—net	190,000		110,000				300,000	
Land			25,000				25,000	
Liabilities		169,000		31,000				200,000
Capital Stock—P		200,000						200,000
Retained Earnings (Jan. 1)—P		60,000						60,000
Net Income—P		29,000			[a]10,000	[b]20,000		39,000
Dividends—P	15,000						15,000	
Capital Stock—S				100,000	[1]100,000			
Retained Earnings (Jan. 1)—S				50,000	[1]50,000			
Net Income—S				20,000	[b]20,000			
Dividends—S			10,000			[a]10,000		
	458,000	458,000	201,000	201,000			499,000	499,000

[1] To eliminate 100% of subsidiary's capital stock and retained earnings as of Jan. 1, Yr. 1.

P Corp. and Subsidiary
Consolidated Workpapers
Year 1

	Company		Adjustments & Eliminations		Consoli-dated
	P	S			
INCOME STATEMENT					
Revenue					
Sales	120,000	116,000			236,000
Dividend Income	10,000		[a]10,000		
Total Revenue	130,000	116,000			236,000
Costs and Expenses					
Cost of Goods Sold	70,000	75,000			145,000
Selling Expenses	16,000	12,000			28,000
General Expenses	15,000	9,000			24,000
Total Costs and Expenses	101,000	96,000			197,000
Net Income	29,000	20,000			39,000
RETAINED EARNINGS					
Balance (1/1)—P	60,000				60,000
Balance (1/1)—S		50,000	[1]50,000		
Net Income	29,000	20,000			39,000
Total	89,000	70,000			99,000
Less: Dividends—P	15,000				15,000
Dividends—S		10,000		[a]10,000	
Balance (12/31)	74,000	60,000			84,000
BALANCE SHEET					
Assets					
Current Assets	103,000	56,000			159,000
Investment in S Corp. Stock	150,000			[1]150,000	
Depreciable Assets—net	190,000	110,000			300,000
Land		25,000			25,000
Total Assets	443,000	191,000			484,000
Equities					
Liabilities	169,000	31,000			200,000
Capital Stock—P	200,000				200,000
Retained Earnings—P	74,000				84,000
Capital Stock—S		100,000	[1]100,000		
Retained Earnings—S		60,000			
Total Equities	443,000	191,000			484,000

P Corp. and Subsidiary
Consolidated Balance Sheet
December 31, Year 1

ASSETS

Current Assets	$159,000	
Depreciable Assets—net	300,000	
Land	25,000	
Total Assets		$484,000

LIABILITIES AND SHAREHOLDERS' EQUITY

Liabilities			$200,000
Capital Stock		$200,000	
Retained Earnings:			
January 1	$60,000		
Add: Net Income	39,000		
	$99,000		
Less: Dividends	15,000		
December 31		84,000	
Total Shareholders' Equity			284,000
Total Liabilities and Shareholders' Equity			$484,000

Observe that only the parent company's capital stock and dividends appear in the consolidated balance sheet. The starting point for the consolidated retained earnings is the retained earnings of the parent company as of the date of affiliation. However, the net income added to it is the consolidated net income for the year. But the dividends which are deducted are those of the parent company only. In Year 2, the opening consolidated retained earnings will be $84,000—the same amount as of the end of Year 1.

5.4 COST OF INVESTMENT GREATER THAN BOOK VALUE OF SUBSIDIARY

Each identifiable asset acquired and each liability assumed should be assigned a portion of the net cost of the investment as of the date of acquisition. Any excess of cost of the investment over the aggregate of the identifiable net assets will generally be regarded as goodwill if associated with excess earning power. Otherwise, a more suitable title will generally be the excess of cost of investment over the fair value of interest in net assets of subsidiary.

The cost of each asset, tangible or intangible, should be depreciated or amortized by systematic charges over the years expected to be benefited. However, in no case should the period of amortization of an intangible asset exceed 40 years.

EXAMPLE 2. The R Corp. purchased 100 percent of the outstanding stock of T Corp. on January 1, Year 1 for $175,000. As of that date the book value of the recorded assets of T Corp. was fairly shown on its books, except for a fully amortized patent which R Corp. was interested in. R Corp. paid more than the recorded value of T Corp. because this patent right was estimated to be worth $25,000 and to have four years of additional economic life to the consolidated group. For consolidation purposes it is necessary to recognize the value of this asset and also the annual amortization expense of $6,250 per year, assuming straight-line amortization.

The condensed trial balances of the two corporations immediately after affiliation are as follows:

	R Corp.		T Corp.	
Current Assets	$ 50,000		$ 55,000	
Investment in T Corp.—Stock	175,000			
Depreciable Assets—net	200,000		100,000	
Land			25,000	
Liabilities		$165,000		$ 30,000
Capital Stock		200,000		100,000
Retained Earnings		60,000		50,000
	$425,000	$425,000	$180,000	$180,000

The results of operations of the two corporations for the first year after affiliation appear in the first four columns of the worksheet to prepare a consolidated income statement (p. 124). Entry (a) eliminates the intercompany dividend and, in effect, indicates that only $19,000 of the income of R Corp. has been generated from its own operations. Entry (b) records the annual amortization of patent expense and thus reduces T's income, for consolidation purposes, by $6,250 per year ($25,000 ÷ 4 years). This consolidation adjustment will have to be repeated for the next three years, until the entire patent amount of $25,000 is fully amortized. Entry (c) combines the adjusted net income of the two corporations to indicate that the consolidated net income is $32,750.

The consolidated net income may be computed as follows:

Reported Net Income of R	$29,000	
Less: Dividend from Subsidiary	10,000	
Net Income from Own Operations		$19,000
Net Income of T	$20,000	
Less: Amortization of Patent	6,250	
Net Income of T for Consolidation		13,750
Consolidated Net Income		$32,750

The balance sheets of R Corp. and T Corp. at the end of Year 1 are condensed in the first four columns of the accompanying worksheet to prepare a consolidated balance sheet at the end of Year 1. Elimination entries (a) and (b) are similar to these lettered entries in the worksheet to consolidate the income statements, and perform the same functions. Entry (1) records the patent at the value of $25,000 as determined at the date of acquisition of the investment in T Corp. The combined effect of entries (1) and (b) is that the amortized value of the patent as of the end of Year 1 will be $18,750. Entry (c) combines the adjusted net income of subsidiary T with the adjusted net income of the parent. It should be noted that the consolidated net income per the worksheet to consolidate the balance sheet is the same as the consolidated net income per the worksheet to consolidate the income statements. This is a logical result, since the eliminations and consolidations have been based on the same data.

Entry (2) eliminates the cost of the investment against the shareholders' equity of the subsidiary corporation as of the beginning of Year 1.

A condensed consolidated income statement may be prepared from the worksheet as follows:

R Corp. and Subsidiary
Consolidated Income Statement
Year 1

Sales	$236,000	
Cost of Goods Sold	145,000	
Gross Profit		$91,000
Selling Expenses	$ 28,000	
General Expenses	24,000	
Amortization of Patent	6,250	
Total Expenses		58,250
Net Income		$32,750

R Corp. and Subsidiary
Worksheet—Consolidated Income Statement
Year 1

	R Corp.		T Corp.		Eliminations		Consolidated	
	Dr.	Cr.	Dr.	Cr.	Dr.	Cr.	Dr.	Cr.
Sales		120,000		116,000				236,000
Cost of Goods Sold	70,000		75,000				145,000	
Selling Expenses	16,000		12,000				28,000	
General Expenses	15,000		9,000				24,000	
Amortization of Patent					[b]6,250		6,250	
Dividend Income		10,000			[a]10,000			
	101,000	130,000	96,000	116,000				
Net Income—R	29,000				[c]13,750	[a]10,000	32,750	
Net Income—T			20,000			{[c]13,750 [b]6,250		
	130,000	130,000	116,000	116,000			236,000	236,000

[a] To eliminate intercompany dividend.
[b] To amortize patent for one year; rate 25%.
[c] To combine the adjusted net income of the two corporations.

R Corp. and Subsidiary
Worksheet—Consolidated Balance Sheet
December 31, Year 1

	R Corp.		T Corp.		Eliminations		Consolidated	
	Dr.	Cr.	Dr.	Cr.	Dr.	Cr.	Dr.	Cr.
Current Assets	78,000		85,000				163,000	
Investment in T	175,000					[2]175,000		
Depreciable Assets—net	190,000		90,000				280,000	
Land			25,000				25,000	
Patent					[1]25,000	[b]6,250	18,750	
Liabilities		169,000		40,000				209,000
Capital Stock—R		200,000						200,000
Retained Earnings (Jan. 1)—R		60,000						60,000
Net Income—R		29,000			[a]10,000	[c]13,750		32,750
Dividends—R	15,000						15,000	
Capital Stock—T				100,000	[2]100,000			
Retained Earnings (Jan. 1)—T				50,000	[2]50,000			
Net Income—T				20,000	{[c]13,750 [b]6,250			
Dividends—T			10,000			[a]10,000		
Appraisal Capital—T					[2]25,000	[1]25,000		
	458,000	458,000	210,000	210,000			501,750	501,750

[1] To record value of patent, $25,000, based on price paid by R Corp. for stock of subsidiary.
[2] To eliminate 100% of subsidiary's capital stock and retained earnings, and appraisal capital.

5.5 COST OF INVESTMENT LESS THAN BOOK VALUE OF SUBSIDIARY'S NET ASSETS

EXAMPLE 3. The condensed trial balances of P Corp. and U Corp. as of January 1, the date of affiliation, are given in the tabulation at the top of p. 125. Two worksheets—one to prepare consolidated income statements for Year 1, the other to prepare a consolidated balance sheet at the end of Year 1—are also presented.

	P Corp.		U Corp.	
Current Assets	$ 70,000		$ 25,000	
Investment in U Corp. Stock	130,000			
Depreciable Assets—net	200,000		100,000	
Patents			40,000	
Liabilities		$140,000		$ 15,000
Capital Stock		200,000		100,000
Retained Earnings		60,000		50,000
	$400,000	$400,000	$165,000	$165,000

P Corp. and Subsidiary
Worksheet—Consolidated Income Statement
Year 1

	P Corp.		T Corp.		Eliminations		Consolidated	
	Dr.	Cr.	Dr.	Cr.	Dr.	Cr.	Dr.	Cr.
Sales		120,000		116,000				236,000
Cost of Goods Sold	70,000		75,000				145,000	
Selling Expense	16,000		10,000				26,000	
General Expense	15,000		7,000				22,000	
Amortization of Patent			4,000			b2,000	2,000	
Dividend Income		10,000			a10,000			
	101,000	130,000	96,000	116,000				
Net Income—P	29,000				c22,000	a10,000	41,000	
Net Income—U			20,000		b2,000	c22,000		
	130,000	130,000	116,000	116,000			236,000	236,000

[a] To eliminate intercompany dividend.
[b] To adjust the amortization of patent from 10% of $40,000 to 10% of $20,000.
[c] To transfer the adjusted net income of U Corp.

P Corp. and Subsidiary
Worksheet—Consolidated Balance Sheet
December 31, Year 1

	P Corp.		U Corp.		Eliminations		Consolidated	
	Dr.	Cr.	Dr.	Cr.	Dr.	Cr.	Dr.	Cr.
Current Assets	105,000		51,000				156,000	
Investment in U Corp. Stock	130,000					2130,000		
Depreciable Assets—net	190,000		90,000				280,000	
Patent			36,000		b2,000	120,000	18,000	
Liabilities		151,000		17,000				168,000
Capital Stock—P		200,000						200,000
Retained Earnings (Jan. 1)—P		60,000						60,000
Net Income—P		29,000			a10,000	c22,000		41,000
Dividends—P	15,000						15,000	
Capital Stock—U				100,000	2100,000			
Retained Earnings (Jan. 1)—U				50,000	{230,000 ⎰120,000			
Net Income—U				20,000	c22,000	b2,000		
Dividends—U			10,000			a10,000		
	440,000	440,000	187,000	187,000			469,000	469,000

[1] To reduce patents as of Jan. 1, Yr. 1, to $20,000.
[2] To eliminate 100% of subsidiary's capital stock and adjusted retained earnings as of Jan. 1, Yr. 1.

P Corp. considers that the book value of the patents to be $20,000 in excess of their fair value; i.e., that the patents are worth only $20,000. The recorded amortization expense of the patent on the books of U Corp. is $4,000, based on the cost to U Corp. and on a remaining estimated life of ten years from January 1 of Year 1.

Data from the condensed income statements of the two companies have been entered in the first four columns of the accompanying worksheet to prepare consolidated income statements for Year 1 after affiliation. Entry (a) eliminates the intercompany dividend. Entry (b) reduces the annual amortization of the patent by $2,000; that is, from $4,000 to $2,000, based on the fair value of the patent as determined at the date of acquisition of the investment in U Corp. The result of this elimination adjustment is to increase the income of the subsidiary by $2,000. Entry (c) transfers the adjusted net income of U Corp. to the same line as the net income of P Corp., so that they may be conveniently combined and extended as one amount.

The condensed balance sheets as of the end of Year 1 appear in the first four columns of the worksheet to prepare a consolidated balance sheet as of that date. The lettered entries in this worksheet correspond to the respective entries in the worksheet to consolidate the income statements. Note that U Corp. has continued to amortize its patents at the rate of $4,000 per year. As a result, the book value of patents on the books of U Corp. at the end of Year 1 is $36,000 ($40,000 − $4,000). The purpose of entry (1) is to reduce the value of the patents by $20,000 as of the date of acquisition. Thus the amortization, for consolidation purposes, should be only $2,000 per year, which has been accomplished by entry (b). When the balance of the patents is extended to the consolidated balance sheet column the amount is $18,000, which is equal to an adjusted cost of $20,000 less one year's amortization of $2,000. Entry (2) eliminates the cost of the investment against the shareholders' equity accounts as of January 1 of Year 1.

5.6 CONSOLIDATED STATEMENTS AFTER DATE OF CONTROL: INVESTMENT IN 90% OF SUBSIDIARY'S STOCK

At the date of acquisition of control of a subsidiary, the accumulated income, less losses and dividends to date (retained earnings), is allocated to the parent and to the minority interest in the same ratio as their capital stock holdings. The amount allocated to the parent is considered to have been *purchased* by it, and thereafter this amount is continuously eliminated against all or a portion of the amount of the parent's investment. Of course, the amount considered to have been purchased by the parent may be subject to special adjustments for consolidation purposes.

The parent's share of the subsidiary's income accumulated after the date of acquisition of control is generally included in the consolidated retained earnings. Decreases in subsidiary retained earnings due to net losses after the affiliation date naturally reduce the consolidated retained earnings. Dividends of the subsidiary are automatically distributed to the parent and to the minority in proportion to their stockholdings.

EXAMPLE 4. P Corp. purchased 90 percent of the outstanding stock of S Corp. on January 1 of Year 1 for $135,000. The results of operations and dividends distributed in Year 1 are similar to those in Example 1 of this chapter (Section 5.3). However, since P Corp. now owns only 90 percent of the stock of S Corp., the share of dividends which will go to P Corp. will amount to $9,000 (90 percent of $10,000).

The result of operations for the first twelve months after affiliation are condensed as follows:

	P Corp.	S Corp.
Sales	$120,000	$116,000
Cost of Goods Sold	70,000	75,000
Gross Profit	$ 50,000	$ 41,000
Selling Expenses	$ 16,000	$ 12,000
General Expenses	15,000	9,000
Total Expenses	$ 31,000	$ 21,000
Income from Operations	$ 19,000	$ 20,000
Dividend Income from S Corp.	9,000	
Net Income	$ 28,000	$ 20,000

The schedule of retained earnings for the above twelve-month period is as follows:

	P Corp.	S Corp.
Balance, January 1	$60,000	$50,000
Add: Net Income	28,000	20,000
Total	$88,000	$70,000
Less: Dividends	15,000	10,000
Balance, December 31	$73,000	$60,000

In consolidating the income statements of the two corporations, the earnings of S Corp. must be allocated to the shareholders of P Corp. and to the minority in the ratio of 90:10. Thus, 90 percent of $20,000 ($18,000) will be included in the consolidated net income. Since P Corp. has already included $9,000 of intercompany dividend income in determining its net income, this dividend income must be eliminated in preparing the consolidated net income in order to avoid double counting.

In order to focus attention on the allocations of the minority and controlling interests in the first year of affiliated operations, the following schedule has been prepared:

	Elimination Ref., Amount		Minority Interest	Consolidated Income	Consolidated Shareholders' Equity
January 1, Year 1:					
Retained Earnings—					
Parent $60,000					$ 60,000
Subsidiary $50,000	(1)	$45,000			
	(2)		$ 5,000		
Net Income, Year 1—					
Parent $28,000					
Eliminate Dividend					
from Subsidiary	(a)	9,000			
Balance				$19,000	
Subsidiary $20,000	(b)		2,000	18,000	
Dividends, Year 1—					
Parent ($15,000)					(15,000)
Subsidiary ($10,000)	(a)	(9,000)	(1,000)		
Consolidated Net Income				$37,000	37,000
December 31, Year 1:					
Consolidated Retained Earnings					$ 82,000
Capital Stock—					
Parent $200,000					200,000
Subsidiary $100,000	(1)	90,000			
	(2)		10,000		
Consolidated Shareholders' Equity,					
End of Year 1					$282,000
Total Minority Interest			$16,000		

Observe that the outstanding capital stock has not changed during the year, therefore elimination entry (1) is the same as it was at January 1, Year 1. (See Example 4, Section 4.9.)

The worksheet to prepare a consolidated income statement and the worksheet to prepare a consolidated balance sheet follow (p. 128); as an alternate approach, a three-tier worksheet is also included (p. 129).

P Corp. and Subsidiary
Worksheet—Consolidated Income Statement
Year 1

	P Corp.		S Corp.		Eliminations		Consolidated	
	Dr.	Cr.	Dr.	Cr.	Dr.	Cr.	Dr.	Cr.
Sales		120,000		116,000				236,000
Cost of Goods Sold	70,000		75,000				145,000	
Selling Expenses	16,000		12,000				28,000	
General Expenses	15,000		9,000				24,000	
Dividend Income		9,000			[a]9,000			
	101,000	129,000	96,000	116,000				
Net Income—P	28,000				[b]18,000	[a]9,000	37,000	
Net Income—S			20,000			[b]20,000		
	129,000	129,000	116,000	116,000				
Minority Interest					[b]2,000		2,000	
							236,000	236,000

[a] To eliminate intercompany dividend.
[b] To allocate the net income of S Corp.

P Corp. and Subsidiary
Worksheet—Consolidated Balance Sheet
December 31, Year 1

	P Corp.		S Corp.		Eliminations		Consolidated	
	Dr.	Cr.	Dr.	Cr.	Dr.	Cr.	Dr.	Cr.
Current Assets	103,000		56,000				159,000	
Investment in S Corp. Stock	135,000					[1]135,000		
Depreciable Assets—net	190,000		110,000				300,000	
Land			25,000				25,000	
Liabilities		155,000		31,000				186,000
Capital Stock—P		200,000						200,000
Retained Earnings (1/1)—P		60,000						60,000
Net Income—P		28,000			[a]9,000	[b]18,000		37,000
Dividends—P	15,000						15,000	
Capital Stock—S				100,000	{[2]10,000 {[1]90,000			
Retained Earnings (1/1)—S				50,000	{[2]5,000 {[1]45,000			
Net Income—S				20,000	[b]20,000			
Dividends—S			10,000			[a]10,000		
	443,000	443,000	201,000	201,000				
Minority Interest—S					[a]1,000	{[b]2,000 {[2]15,000		16,000
							499,000	499,000

[1] To eliminate 90% of subsidiary's capital stock and retained earnings.
[2] To classify the 10% interest of the minority stockholders.

P Corp. and Subsidiary
Consolidated Workpapers (3-tier)
Year 1

	Company		Adjustments & Eliminations		Consoli-dated
	P	S			
INCOME STATEMENT					
Revenue					
Sales	120,000	116,000			236,000
Dividend Income	9,000		[a]9,000		
Total Revenue	129,000	116,000			236,000
Costs and Expenses					
Cost of Goods Sold	70,000	75,000			145,000
Selling Expenses	16,000	12,000			28,000
General Expenses	15,000	9,000			24,000
Total Costs and Expenses	101,000	96,000			197,000
					39,000
Minority Interest in Income (10% of $20,000)			[b]2,000		2,000
Net Income	28,000	20,000			37,000
RETAINED EARNINGS					
Balance (1/1)—P	60,000				60,000
Balance (1/1)—S		50,000	{ [2]5,000 [1]45,000		
Net Income	28,000	20,000			37,000
Total	88,000	70,000			97,000
Less: Dividends—P	15,000				15,000
Dividends—S		10,000		[a]10,000	
Balance (12/31)	73,000	60,000			82,000
BALANCE SHEET					
Assets					
Current Assets	103,000	56,000			159,000
Investment in S Corp. Stock	135,000			[1]135,000	
Depreciable Assets—net	190,000	110,000			300,000
Land		25,000			25,000
Total Assets	428,000	291,000			484,000
Equities					
Liabilities	155,000	31,000			186,000
Capital Stock—P	200,000				200,000
Retained Earnings—P	73,000				82,000
Capital Stock—S		100,000	{ [2]10,000 [1]90,000		
Retained Earnings—S		60,000			
Minority Interest			[a]1,000	{ [b]2,000 [2]15,000 }	16,000
Total Equities	428,000	291,000			484,000

Condensed statements prepared from the accompanying worksheets are presented below:

P Corp. and Subsidiary
Consolidated Income Statement
Year 1

Sales	$236,000	
Cost of Goods Sold	145,000	
Gross Profit		$91,000
Selling Expenses	$ 28,000	
General Expenses	24,000	
Total Expenses		52,000
Net Income, before Minority Interest		$39,000
Minority Interest in Subsidiary		2,000
Net Income		$37,000

P Corp. and Subsidiary
Consolidated Balance Sheet
December 31, Year 1

ASSETS

Current	$159,000	
Depreciable Assets—net	300,000	
Land	25,000	
Total Assets		$484,000

LIABILITIES AND SHAREHOLDERS' EQUITY

Liabilities		$186,000
Minority Interest in Subsidiary		16,000
Capital Stock	$200,000	
Retained Earnings	82,000	
Total Shareholders' Equity		282,000
Total Liabilities and Shareholders' Equity		$484,000

5.7 PURCHASE OF 90% OF SUBSIDIARY'S STOCK— INVESTMENT GREATER THAN BOOK VALUE

EXAMPLE 5. This illustration is based on the same pre-affiliation balance sheets as in Example 2 of this chapter (Section 5.4). However, in this example the R Corp. purchased only 90 percent of the outstanding stock of T Corp., for which investment the R Corp. paid $157,500 on January 1, Year 1. All the assets were considered to be worth the recorded book values, and the recorded liabilities properly reflected the obligation of T Corp. as of that date, except that in addition to the recorded assets T Corp. owned the rights to a fully amortized patent, which R Corp. established to have an additional four years of economic life from the beginning of Year 1.

The investment cost of $157,500 for 90 percent of the net assets of T Corp. may be accepted as evidence that 100 percent of its net assets were considered to have a fair value of $175,000. This latter amount was $25,000 higher than the recorded net assets of T Corp. as of the date of acquisition (January 1, Year 1). As in Example 2, the patent must be recognized in the consolidated balance sheet, and amortization expense must be recognized in the consolidated income statement.

In the accompanying worksheet to prepare a consolidated income statement for the first year of operations of R Corp. and T Corp. (p. 131), adjustment entry (a) eliminates the intercompany dividend of $9,000. Entry (b)

R Corp. and Subsidiary
Worksheet—Consolidated Income Statement
Year 1

	R Corp.		T Corp.		Eliminations		Consolidated	
	Dr.	Cr.	Dr.	Cr.	Dr.	Cr.	Dr.	Cr.
Sales		120,000		116,000				236,000
Cost of Goods Sold	70,000		75,000				145,000	
Selling Expenses	16,000		12,000				28,000	
General Expenses	15,000		9,000				24,000	
Amortization of Patent					[b]6,250		6,250	
Dividend Income		9,000			[a]9,000			
	101,000	129,000	96,000	116,000				
Net Income—R	28,000				[c]12,375	[a]9,000	31,375	
Net Income—T			20,000			{ [c]13,750 [b]6,250		
	129,000	129,000	116,000	116,000				
Minority Interest					[c]1,375		1,375	
							236,000	236,000

[a] To eliminate intercompany dividend.
[b] To amortize patent for one year: 25% of $25,000.
[c] To allocate net income of T Corp. as adjusted.

R Corp. and Subsidiary
Worksheet—Consolidated Balance Sheet
December 31, Year 1

	R Corp.		T Corp.		Eliminations		Consolidated	
	Dr.	Cr.	Dr.	Cr.	Dr.	Cr.	Dr.	Cr.
Current Assets	84,500		85,000				169,500	
Investment in T Corp.	157,500					[2]157,500		
Depreciable Assets—net	190,000		90,000				280,000	
Land			25,000				25,000	
Patent					[1]25,000	[b]6,250	18,750	
Liabilities		159,000		40,000				199,000
Capital Stock—R		200,000						200,000
Retained Earnings (1/1)—R		60,000						60,000
Net Income—R		28,000			[a]9,000	[c]12,375		31,375
Dividends—R	15,000						15,000	
Capital Stock—T				100,000	{ [3]10,000 [2]90,000			
Retained Earnings (1/1)—T				50,000	{ [3]5,000 [2]45,000			
Net Income—T				20,000	{ [c]13,750 [b]6,250			
Dividends—T			10,000			[a]10,000		
	447,000	447,000	210,000	210,000				
Appraisal Capital—T					{ [3]2,500 [2]22,500	[1]25,000		
Minority Interest					[a]1,000	{ [3]17,500 [c]1,375		17,875
							508,250	508,250

[1] To record value of patent based on cost of 90% of stock of subsidiary.
[2] To eliminate 90% of subsidiary's capital stock, retained earnings, and appraisal capital as of Jan. 1, Yr. 1.
[3] To classify the 10% interest of the minority stockholders as of Jan. 1, Yr. 1.

records the annual amortization of patent expense, based on a four-year useful life remaining from the date of affiliation. Thus, T's net income for consolidation purposes is reduced by $6,250 for the year. Entry (c) allocates the adjusted net income of T Corp. of $13,750 ($20,000 − $6,250) as indicated in the following elimination entry:

Net Income—R	12,375	
Minority Interest in T (income)	1,375	
Net Income—T		13,750

The balance sheets of R Corp. and of T Corp. at the end of Year 1 are condensed in the first four columns of the accompanying worksheet to prepare a consolidated balance sheet as of that date. Elimination entries bearing the letters (a), (b), and (c) are *similar* to the entries in the worksheet to consolidate the income statements for Year 1, and perform the same functions. However, entry (a) now allocates the entire dividends of $10,000: 90 percent ($9,000) to parent R and 10 percent ($1,000) to the minority interests in T. Entry (1) recognizes the patent at the value of $25,000, which was determined as of the date of acquisition of the stock of T Corp. As in Example 2, the combined effect of entries (1) and (b) is that the amortized value of the patent for consolidation purposes at the end of the first year is $18,750. Entry (2) eliminates the cost of the investment in T Corp. against 90 percent of the shareholders' equity of T Corp. as of January 1, Year 1. Entry (3) classifies the remaining 10 percent of the shareholders' equity as the minority interest at the beginning of the year.

The minority interest in T Corp. as of December 31, Year 1, totals $17,875, which may be verified from the following table.

	Total	Minority
Capital Stock	$100,000	$10,000
Retained Earnings, January 1	50,000	5,000
Appraisal Capital	25,000	2,500
Net Income—Year 1 (as adjusted)	13,750	1,375
Dividends	(10,000)	(1,000)
Totals	$178,750	$17,875

A consolidated income statement for Year 1, prepared from the accompanying worksheet on p. 131, would appear as follows:

R Corp. and Subsidiary
Consolidated Income Statement
Year 1

Sales	$236,000	
Cost of Goods Sold	145,000	
Gross Profit		$91,000
Less Expenses:		
Selling	$ 28,000	
General	24,000	
Amortization of Patent	6,250	
Total Expenses		58,250
Net Income, before Minority Interest		$32,750
Minority Interest in Income		1,375
Net Income		$31,375

The amount of consolidated net income for Year 1 may be calculated from an analysis of each corporation's contribution to the consolidation as follows:

R Corp., Reported Net Income	$28,000	
Less: Dividend from Subsidiary	9,000	
Income from Own Operations		$19,000
T Corp., Reported Net Income	$20,000	
Less: Amortization of Patent	6,250	
Adjusted Net Income	$13,750	
Less: Minority Interest in Income	1,375	
Income Available for Controlling Interest		12,375
Consolidated Net Income		$31,375

The consolidated balance sheet of R Corp. and its subsidiary T has been prepared from the last two columns of the accompanying worksheet (p. 131):

R Corp. and Subsidiary
Consolidated Balance Sheet
December 31, Year 1

ASSETS

Current Assets	$169,500	
Depreciable Assets—net	280,000	
Patent—net	18,750	
Land	25,000	
Total Assets		$493,250

LIABILITIES AND SHAREHOLDERS' EQUITY

Liabilities		$199,000
Minority Interest		17,875
Capital Stock	$200,000	
Retained Earnings (See schedule below.)	76,375	
Total Shareholders' Equity		276,375
Total Liabilities and Shareholders' Equity		$493,250

A supporting schedule of consolidated retained earnings for Year 1 follows:

Retained Earnings, Jan. 1	$60,000
Add: Consolidated Net Income, Year 1	31,375
Total	$91,375
Less: Dividends	15,000
Retained Earnings, Dec. 31	$76,375

The consolidated retained earnings as of the end of Year 1 may be verified by analyzing the "contribution" of each corporation, as in the following schedule:

R Corp.:

Retained Earnings,
December 31, Year 1 $73,000

T Corp.:

Retained Earnings,
December 31, Year 1 $60,000

Less: Amortization of Patent
for Year 1   6,250

Balance, after Amortization
of Patent $53,750

Less: Minority Interests
(10% of $53,750)   5,375

Balance $48,375

Purchased by acquisition of
90% of stock (90% of
$50,000) as of January 1,
Year 1   45,000

Parent's share of increase
in T's Retained Earnings,
January 1, Year 1   3,375

Consolidated Retained Earnings,
December 31, Year 1 $76,375

In order to focus attention on the allocations of the retained earnings and the net income for the first year of affiliation, the following schedule has been prepared:

	Elimination Ref., Amount		Minority Interest	Consolidated Income	Consolidated Retained Earnings
January 1, Year 1:					
Retained Earnings:					
Parent $60,000					$60,000
Subsidiary $50,000	(2)	$45,000			
	(3)		$5,000		
Net Income, Year 1:					
Parent $28,000					
Eliminate dividend from subsidiary	(a)	9,000			
Balance				$19,000	
Subsidiary $20,000					
Deduct amortization of patent	(b)	6,250			
Balance $13,750	(c)		1,375	12,375	
Dividends, Year 1:					
Parent ($15,000)					(15,000)
Subsidiary ($10,000)	(a)	(9,000)	(1,000)		
Consolidated Net Income, Year 1				$31,375	31,375

(Schedule continued on following page.)

	Elimination Ref., Amount	Minority Interest	Consolidated Income	Consolidated Retained Earnings
December 31, Year 1:				
Minority Interest in Retained Earnings		$5,375		
Consolidated Retained Earnings				$76,375

5.8 PURCHASE OF 90% OF SUBSIDIARY'S STOCK— INVESTMENT COST GREATER THAN FAIR VALUE

There are situations where the assets of a subsidiary are fairly valued, but the parent will pay more than the amount of the subsidiary's book value for expected future benefits of the affiliation. Such excess must be amortized over a reasonable period of time (not to exceed 40 years). Amortization of this type of excess of cost over book value affects the net income of the controlling interest only, whereas amortization of goodwill or other increments associated with the subsidiary assets will also affect the minority interest.

EXAMPLE 6. Assume the same condition as in the previous example except that it has been ascertained that the assets and liabilities of T Corp. were fairly reflected by the book amounts as of the date of acquisition. The R Corp. willingly paid $22,500 in excess of 90 percent of the net assets of the T Corp. because it expected the combination to achieve financial benefits that result from centralized control and direction. The amount paid for the potential benefits of affiliation as of January 1, Year 1 may be computed as follows:

Net Assets of T Corp.	$150,000	
90% of Net Asset Value of T Corp.		$135,000
Cost of Investment by R Corp.		157,500
Excess of Cost of Investment Over Fair Value of Interest in Subsidiary		$ 22,500

The Board of Directors of R Corp. has decided that it would be appropriate to amortize this intangible asset over ten years. Thus, entry (b) records the amortization of $2,250 in the consolidation working papers. Amortization of goodwill applicable to the subsidiary would affect a minority interest. However, amortization of an excess paid by the parent for expected benefits affects only the net income of the controlling interests. Entry (a) eliminates the intercompany dividends, and entry (c) allocates the net income of the subsidiary in the ratio of 90:10.

Entry (1) in the worksheet to prepare a consolidated balance sheet identifies the excess of cost of investment over fair value of interest in subsidiary. This is the same entry that was recognized as of the date of acquisition, one year earlier. (See Example 6 of Chapter 4, Section 4.10.) A similar adjustment would have to be made each time a consolidated balance sheet is to be prepared until this excess of cost over value of interest in subsidiary is fully amortized.

Other consolidation adjustments and elimination entries correspond to previous examples in this chapter; listing them again is not necessary. Furthermore, each worksheet entry is identified in the lower section of the respective worksheet.

R Corp. and Subsidiary
Worksheet—Consolidated Income Statement
Year 1

	R Corp. Dr.	R Corp. Cr.	T Corp. Dr.	T Corp. Cr.	Adjustments & Eliminations		Consolidated Dr.	Consolidated Cr.
Sales		120,000		116,000				236,000
Cost of Goods Sold	70,000		75,000				145,000	
Selling Expenses	16,000		12,000				28,000	
General Expenses	15,000		9,000				24,000	
Dividend Income		9,000			[a]9,000			
	101,000	129,000	96,000	116,000				
Net Income—R	28,000				[c]18,000	[b]2,250 [a]9,000	34,750	
Net Income—T			20,000			[c]20,000		
	129,000	129,000	116,000	116,000				
Amortization of Excess of Cost Over Fair Value of Subsidiary					[b]2,250		2,250	
Minority Interest in T					[c]2,000		2,000	
							236,000	236,000

[a] To eliminate intercompany dividend.
[b] To amortize intangible asset: 10% of $2,250.
[c] To allocate net income of T Corp.

R Corp. and Subsidiary
Worksheet—Consolidated Balance Sheet
December 31, Year 1

	R Corp. Dr.	R Corp. Cr.	T Corp. Dr.	T Corp. Cr.	Adjustments & Eliminations		Consolidated Dr.	Consolidated Cr.
Current Assets	84,500		75,000				159,500	
Investment in T Corp.	157,500					[2]135,000 [1]22,500		
Depreciable Assets—net	190,000		100,000				290,000	
Land			25,000				25,000	
Liabilities		159,000		40,000				199,000
Capital Stock—R		200,000						200,000
Retained Earnings (1/1)—R		60,000						60,000
Net Income—R		28,000			[b]2,250 [a]9,000	[c]18,000		34,750
Dividends—R	15,000						15,000	
Capital Stock—T				100,000	[3]10,000 [2]90,000			
Retained Earnings (1/1)—T				50,000	[3]5,000 [2]45,000			
Net Income—T				20,000	[c]20,000			
Dividends—T			10,000			[a]10,000		
	447,000	447,000	210,000	210,000				
Excess of Cost Over Fair Value of Interest in Subsidiary					[1]22,500	[b]2,250	20,250	
Minority Interest in T					[a]1,000	[3]15,000 [c]2,000		16,000
							509,750	509,750

[1] To record excess of cost of investment in stock of T over 90% of the book value of T Corp.
[2] To eliminate 90% of subsidiary's capital stock and retained earnings.
[3] To classify 10% interest of minority stockholders.

5.9 PURCHASE OF 90% OF SUBSIDIARY'S STOCK—
INVESTMENT GREATER THAN FAIR VALUE, YEAR 2

EXAMPLE 7.   Previous examples in this chapter have illustrated worksheets for the preparation of consolidated income statements for the first year of affiliation and balance sheets at the end of the first year of affiliation.   The purpose of this example is to illustrate what happens in the subsequent year, Year 2.   Example 7 is a continuation of Example 5 (Section 5.7) through the end of Year 2.   The results of operations of R Corp. and T Corp. are condensed in the first four columns of the accompanying worksheet to consolidate income statements for Year 2.   The lettered entries (a), (b), and (c) perform the same function as in Year 1.   For convenience they are briefly explained in the lower section of the worksheet.

A consolidated income statement of R Corp. and its subsidiary for Year 2 has been arranged from the accompanying worksheet to prepare a consolidated income statement for the second year of affiliation.

R Corp. and Subsidiary
Consolidated Income Statement
Year 2

Sales	$400,000	
Cost of Goods Sold	275,000	
Gross Profit		$125,000
Less Expenses:		
Selling	$ 37,000	
General	31,000	
Amortization of Patent	6,250	
Total Expenses		74,250
Net Income, before Minority Interest		$ 50,750
Minority Interest in Income		2,075
Net Income		$ 48,675

The amount of the consolidated net income for Year 2 may be substantiated by an analysis of the contribution of each of the two companies to the consolidated picture, as follows:

R Corp., Reported Net Income	$48,000	
Less: Dividend from Subsidiary	18,000	
Income from Own Operations		$30,000
T Corp., Reported Net Income	$27,000	
Less: Amortization of Patent	6,250	
Adjusted Net Income	$20,750	
Less: Minority Interest in Income	2,075	
Income Available for Controlling Interest		18,675
Consolidated Net Income		$48,675

The condensed balance sheets of R Corp. and of T Corp. at the end of the second year of affiliation are presented in the first four columns of the accompanying worksheet to consolidate these balance sheets.

In preparing consolidating worksheets for years after the first, it is necessary to recognize the changes in the parent's share of the changes in the subsidiary's retained earnings from the date of acquisition of control to the date of the consolidation.   Since the current year's changes are usually detailed in a worksheet to consolidate the current year's income statement, a common practice is to summarize the changes in the subsidiary's retained earnings up to the beginning of the current year. Entry (3) in the accompanying worksheet to prepare a consolidated balance sheet as of December 31, Year 2, accomplished this as follows:

Investment in T Corp.	3,375	
Retained Earnings (Jan. 1, Yr. 2)—R		3,375

Retained Earnings—T		
Dec. 31, Yr. 1	$60,000	
Less: Amortization of		
Patent, Yr. 1	6,250	
	$53,750	
Less: Minority Interests	5,375	
Balance	$48,375	
Purchased at Date of Acquisition		
(90% of $50,000)	45,000	
Parent's Equity in Increase of		
T's Retained Earnings in Yr. 1	$ 3,375	

Other entries in the worksheet to consolidate the balance sheets as of the end of Year 2 are similar to those entries of one year earlier. Brief explanations are found in the lower portion of the worksheet.

R Corp. and Subsidiary
Worksheet—Consolidated Income Statement
Year 2

	R Corp.		T Corp.		Eliminations		Consolidated	
	Dr.	Cr.	Dr.	Cr.	Dr.	Cr.	Dr.	Cr.
Sales		200,000		200,000				400,000
Cost of Goods Sold	130,000		145,000				275,000	
Selling Expenses	22,000		15,000				37,000	
General Expenses	18,000		13,000				31,000	
Amortization of Patent					[b]6,250		6,250	
Dividend Income		18,000			[a]18,000			
Net Income—R	48,000				[c]18,675	[a]18,000	48,675	
Net Income—T			27,000			{ [c]20,750		
						{ [b]6,250		
	218,000	218,000	200,000	200,000				
Minority Interest					[c]2,075		2,075	
							400,000	400,000

[a] To eliminate intercompany dividend.
[b] To amortize patent for one year: 25% of $25,000.
[c] To allocate net income of T Corp. as adjusted.

R Corp. and Subsidiary
Worksheet—Consolidated Balance Sheet
December 31, Year 2

	R Corp.		T Corp.		Eliminations		Consolidated	
	Dr.	Cr.	Dr.	Cr.	Dr.	Cr.	Dr.	Cr.
Current Assets	79,500		95,000				174,500	
Investment in T Corp.	157,500				[3]3,375	[4]160,875		
Depreciable Assets—net	180,000		80,000				260,000	
Land			25,000				25,000	
Patent					[1]25,000	$\left\{\begin{array}{l}{}^{b}6,250\\{}^{2}6,250\end{array}\right\}$	12,500	
Liabilities		121,000		33,000				154,000
Capital Stock—R		200,000						200,000
Retained Earnings (1/1)—R		73,000				[3]3,375		76,375
Net Income—R		48,000			[a]18,000	[c]18,675		48,675
Dividends—R	25,000						25,000	
Capital Stock—T				100,000		$\left\{\begin{array}{l}{}^{5}10,000\\{}^{4}90,000\end{array}\right.$		
Retained Earnings (1/1)—T				60,000		$\left\{\begin{array}{l}{}^{5}5,375\\{}^{4}48,375\\{}^{2}6,250\end{array}\right.$		
Net Income—T				27,000		$\left\{\begin{array}{l}{}^{c}20,750\\{}^{b}6,250\end{array}\right.$		
Dividends—T			20,000			[a]20,000		
	442,000	442,000	220,000	220,000				
Appraisal Capital					$\left.\begin{array}{l}{}^{2}2,500\\{}^{4}22,500\end{array}\right\}$	[1]25,000		
Minority Interest					[a]2,000	$\left\{\begin{array}{l}{}^{5}17,875\\{}^{c}2,075\end{array}\right\}$		17,950
							497,000	497,000

[1] To record value of patent based on cost of 90% of stock of subsidiary.
[2] To record prior year's amortization of patent.
[3] To add to investment account R's share of growth in T Company during Year 1, as adjusted: 90% of $3,750.
[4] To eliminate 90% of subsidiary's capital stock, retained earnings, and appraisal capital as of Jan. 1, Yr. 2.
[5] To classify the 10% interest of the minority stockholders as of Jan. 1, Yr. 2.

The consolidated balance sheet of R Corp. and its subsidiary T Corp. has been prepared from the last two columns of the accompanying worksheet.

R Corp. and Subsidiary
Consolidated Balance Sheet
December 31, Year 2

ASSETS

Current Assets	$174,500
Depreciable Assets—net	260,000
Patent—net	12,500
Land	25,000
Total Assets	$472,000

LIABILITIES AND SHAREHOLDERS' EQUITY

Liabilities		$154,000
Minority Interest		17,950
Capital Stock	$200,000	
Retained Earnings (See schedule below.)	100,050	
Total Shareholders' Equity		300,050
Total Liabilities and Shareholders' Equity		$472,000

A supporting schedule of consolidated retained earnings for Year 2 follows:

Retained Earnings, January 1	$ 76,375
Add: Consolidated Net Income, Year 2	48,675
Total	$125,050
Less: Dividends, Year 2	25,000
Retained Earnings, December 31	$100,050

The consolidated retained earnings as of the end of Year 2 may be verified by analyzing the "contribution" of each corporation, as in the following schedule:

R Corp.:		
Retained Earnings, December 31, Year 2		$ 96,000
T Corp.:		
Retained Earnings, December 31, Year 2	$67,000	
Less: Amortization of Patent for Years 1 and 2	12,500	
Balance, after Amortization of Patent	$54,500	
Less: Minority Interests (10% of $54,500)	5,450	
Balance	$49,050	
Purchased by Acquisition of 90% of Stock (90% of $50,000) as of January 1, Year 1	45,000	
Parent's Share of Increase in T's Retained Earnings since January 1, Year 1		4,050
Consolidated Retained Earnings, December 31, Year 2		$100,050

Summary

(1) When the investment account is maintained on the cost method, dividends received by the parent are credited to the _____ account.

(2) When a subsidiary corporation declares a dividend, the _____ account should be debited.

(3) Any excess of cost of investment in a subsidiary corporation over the aggregate of the identifiable net assets will generally be regarded as _____ if associated with excess earning power.

(4) Excess of cost of investment over the fair value of interest in net assets of a subsidiary should be _____ over a reasonable period of time. This period of time should not, however, exceed _____ years.

(5) In consolidating the income statements of a parent and subsidiary, intercompany dividend revenue should always be _____.

(6) The net income of a subsidiary, after suitable adjustments, should be allocated between the parent company and _____ interests in proportion to their respective stockholdings.

(7) Consolidated statements are generally prepared from the point of view of the _____ interests.

(8) In a consolidated statement of retained earnings, the dividends of the _____ corporation only are deducted.

(9) Subsequent to investment in the stock of a subsidiary, it is necessary to recognize changes in the parent's share of the increase (or decrease) in the subsidiary's _____ from the date of acquisition of control to the date of the consolidated balance sheet.

Answers: (1) dividend income (or revenue);   (2) retained earnings;   (3) goodwill;   (4) amortized, 40;   (5) eliminated;   (6) minority;   (7) controlling (or parent);   (8) parent;   (9) retained earnings

Solved Problems

5.1   The consolidated income statement of Pride Corp. and its 80 percent owned subsidiary follows:

Pride Corp. and Subsidiary
Consolidated Income Statement
Year Ended December 31, 19X4

Sales Revenue	$134,000
Cost of Goods Sold	82,000
Gross Profit	$ 52,000
Operating Expenses	27,000
Combined Net Income	$ 25,000
Minority Interest in Income	2,000
Consolidated Net Income	$ 23,000

Required:

(a) Determine how much of the consolidated net income was the result of operations of the subsidiary.

(b) Determine how much of the consolidated net income was earned by the parent company from its own operations.

SOLUTION

(a)   Minority interest in income of $2,000 = 20% of net income of subsidiary

$$\$2,000 \div 20\% = \$10,000$$

Therefore,   Subsidiary net income = $10,000

Subsidiary Net Income	$10,000
Less: Minority Interest in Net Income	2,000
Portion of Consolidated Net Income Attributable to Operations of Subsidiary	$ 8,000

(b)

Consolidated Net Income	$23,000
Less: Subsidiary Net Income Included ($10,000 − $2,000)	8,000
Net Income of Parent from Own Operations	$15,000

5.2   The Ross Corp. purchased 80 percent of the outstanding stock of Tone Corp. on January 2, Year 1, at a cost of $440,000. The book value of Tone's net assets was approximately equal to its fair value at the date of acquisition. However, in order to gain prompt control of Tone's assets, the board of directors of Ross Corp. decided to pay an amount in excess of the book value of Tone and to amortize this additional cost in the consolidated statements over a ten-year period.

The income statements of the individual companies for Year 1 and the balance sheets at the end of Year 1 are condensed in the following worksheets.

Required:

(a) Complete the worksheet to prepare a consolidated income statement for Year 1.

(b) Complete the worksheet to prepare a consolidated balance sheet at the end of Year 1.

(c) Prepare a statement of consolidated retained earnings for the year ended December 31, Year 1.

(a)
Ross Corp. and Subsidiary
Worksheet—Consolidated Income Statement
Year 1

	Ross Corp.		Tone Corp.		Eliminations		Consolidated	
	Dr.	Cr.	Dr.	Cr.	Dr.	Cr.	Dr.	Cr.
Sales		500,000		230,000				
Cost of Goods Sold	300,000		120,000					
Selling Expenses	94,000		42,000					
General Expenses	30,000		24,000					
Dividend Income		24,000						
Net Income—Ross	100,000							
Net Income—Tone				44,000				
	524,000	524,000	230,000	230,000				
Amortization—Excess of Cost Over Value of Interest in Subsidiary								
Minority Interest								

(b)
Ross Corp. and Subsidiary
Worksheet—Consolidated Balance Sheet
December 31, Year 1

	Ross Corp.		Tone Corp.		Eliminations		Consolidated	
	Dr.	Cr.	Dr.	Cr.	Dr.	Cr.	Dr.	Cr.
Current Assets	31,000		109,000					
Investment in Tone Stock	440,000							
Depreciable Assets—net	190,000		260,000					
Land	100,000		140,000					
Liabilities		11,000		45,000				
Capital Stock—Ross		300,000						
Retained Earnings (1/1)—Ross		390,000						
Net Income—Ross		100,000						
Dividends—Ross	40,000							
Capital Stock—Tone				400,000				
Retained Earnings (1/1)—Tone				50,000				
Net Income—Tone				44,000				
Dividends—Tone			30,000					
	801,000	801,000	539,000	539,000				
Excess of Cost Over Fair Value of Interest in Subsidiary								
Minority Interest in Tone								

SOLUTION
(a)

Ross Corp. and Subsidiary
Worksheet—Consolidated Income Statement
Year 1

	Ross Corp.		Tone Corp.		Eliminations		Consolidated	
	Dr.	Cr.	Dr.	Cr.	Dr.	Cr.	Dr.	Cr.
Sales		500,000		230,000				730,000
Cost of Goods Sold	300,000		120,000				420,000	
Selling Expenses	94,000		42,000				136,000	
General Expenses	30,000		24,000				54,000	
Dividend Income		24,000			[a]24,000			
Net Income—Ross	100,000				[c]35,200	{[b]8,000 / [a]24,000}	103,200	
Net Income—Tone			44,000			[c]44,000		
	524,000	524,000	230,000	230,000				
Amortization—Excess of Cost Over Value of Interest in Subsidiary					[b]8,000		8,000	
Minority Interest						[c]8,800	8,800	
							730,000	730,000

[a] To eliminate intercompany dividend.
[b] To amortize intangible asset: 10% of $80,000.
[c] To allocate net income of subsidiary.

(b)

Ross Corp. and Subsidiary
Worksheet—Consolidated Balance Sheet
December 31, Year 1

	Ross Corp.		Tone Stock		Eliminations		Consolidated	
	Dr.	Cr.	Dr.	Cr.	Dr.	Cr.	Dr.	Cr.
Current Assets	31,000		109,000				140,000	
Investment in Tone Stock	440,000					{[2]360,000 / [1]80,000}		
Depreciable Assets—net	190,000		260,000				450,000	
Land	100,000		140,000				240,000	
Liabilities		11,000		45,000				56,000
Capital Stock—Ross		300,000						300,000
Retained Earnings (1/1)—Ross		390,000						390,000
Net Income—Ross		100,000			{[b]8,000 / [a]24,000}	[c]35,200		103,200
Dividends—Ross	40,000						40,000	
Capital Stock—Tone				400,000	{[3]80,000 / [2]320,000}			
Retained Earnings (1/1)—Tone				50,000	{[3]10,000 / [2]40,000}			
Net Income—Tone				44,000	[c]44,000			
Dividends—Tone			30,000			[a]30,000		
	801,000	801,000	539,000	539,000				
Excess of Cost Over Fair Value of Interest in Subsidiary					[1]80,000	[b]8,000	72,000	
Minority Interest in Tone					[a]6,000	{[3]90,000 / [c]8,800}		92,800
							942,000	942,000

[1] To reclassify excess of cost ($440,000) over book value of investment, $360,000 (or 80% of $450,000) as of date of purchase.
[2] To eliminate 80% of Tone's capital stock and retained earnings, as of Jan. 1, Yr. 1.
[3] To classify 20% interest of minority stockholders, as of Jan. 1, Yr. 1.

(c)
Ross Corp. and Subsidiary
Consolidated Retained Earnings
Year 1

Retained Earnings, Jan. 1, Year 1	$390,000*
Add: Consolidated Net Income, Year 1	103,200
	$493,200
Less: Dividends	40,000*
Retained Earnings, Dec. 31, Year 1	$453,200

* Parent company only

5.3 The Ross Corp. purchased 80 percent of the outstanding stock of the Tone Corp. on January 2, Year 1 at a cost of $440,000. The book value of Tone's net assets was roughly equal to its fair value at the date of acquisition. However, in order to achieve prompt control of Tone Corp. the board of directors of Ross Corp. decided to invest an amount in excess of the value of Tone's net assets and to amortize the additional cost in the consolidated statements over a ten-year period.

The income statements of the individual companies for Year 2 and the balance sheets at the end of Year 2 are condensed in the following worksheets.

Required:

(a) Complete the worksheet to prepare a consolidated income statement for Year 2.

(b) Complete the worksheet to prepare a consolidated balance sheet at the end of Year 2.

(c) Prepare a statement of consolidated retained earnings for the year ended December 31, Year 2.

SOLUTION

(a) An incomplete worksheet to prepare a consolidated income statement for Year 2 appears on p. 146; the completed worksheet appears on p. 147.

(b) An incomplete worksheet to prepare a consolidated balance sheet at the end of Year 2 appears on p. 146; the completed worksheet appears on p. 147.

(c)
Ross Corp. and Subsidiary
Consolidated Retained Earnings
Year 2

Retained Earnings, Jan. 1, Year 2	$453,200
Add: Consolidated Net Income, Year 2	108,800
	$562,000
Less: Dividends	50,000
Retained Earnings, Dec. 31, Year 2	$512,000

(a)

Ross Corp. and Subsidiary
Worksheet—Consolidated Income Statement
Year 2

	Ross Corp.		Tone Corp.		Eliminations		Consolidated	
	Dr.	Cr.	Dr.	Cr.	Dr.	Cr.	Dr.	Cr.
Sales		701,200		290,000				
Cost of Goods Sold	420,000		158,000					
Selling Expenses	115,000		50,000					
General Expenses	91,000		30,000					
Dividend Income		28,800						
Net Income—Ross	104,000							
Net Income—Tone			52,000					
	730,000	730,000	290,000	290,000				
Amortization—Excess Cost Over Value of Interest in Subsidiary								
Minority Interest								

(b)

Ross Corp. and Subsidiary
Worksheet—Consolidated Balance Sheet
December 31, Year 2

	Ross Corp.		Tone Corp.		Eliminations		Consolidated	
	Dr.	Cr.	Dr.	Cr.	Dr.	Cr.	Dr.	Cr.
Current Assets	210,000		160,000					
Investment in Tone Stock	440,000							
Depreciable Assets—net	180,000		251,000					
Land	100,000		140,000					
Liabilities		126,000		71,000				
Capital Stock—Ross		300,000						
Retained Earnings (1/1)—Ross		450,000						
Net Income—Ross		104,000						
Dividends—Ross	50,000							
Capital Stock—Tone				400,000				
Retained Earnings (1/1)—T				64,000				
Net Income—Tone				52,000				
Dividends—Tone			36,000					
	980,000	980,000	587,000	587,000				
Excess Cost Over Fair Value of Interest in Subsidiary								
Minority Interest in Tone								

(a)

Ross Corp. and Subsidiary
Worksheet—Consolidated Income Statement
Year 2

	Ross Corp.		Tone Corp.		Eliminations		Consolidated	
	Dr.	Cr.	Dr.	Cr.	Dr.	Cr.	Dr.	Cr.
Sales		701,200		290,000				991,200
Cost of Goods Sold	420,000		158,000				578,000	
Selling Expenses	115,000		50,000				165,000	
General Expenses	91,000		30,000				121,000	
Dividend Income		28,800			[a]28,800			
Net Income—Ross	104,000				[c]41,600	{ [b]8,000 [a]28,800 }	108,800	
Net Income—Tone			52,000			[c]52,000		
	730,000	730,000	290,000	290,000				
Amortization—Excess Cost Over Value of Interest in Subsidiary					[b]8,000		8,000	
Minority Interest					[c]10,400		10,400	
							991,200	991,200

[a] To eliminate intercompany dividend.
[b] To amortize intangible asset: 10% of $80,000.
[c] To allocate net income of subsidiary.

(b)

Ross Corp. and Subsidiary
Worksheet—Consolidated Balance Sheet
December 31, Year 2

	Ross Corp.		Tone Corp.		Eliminations		Consolidated	
	Dr.	Cr.	Dr.	Cr.	Dr.	Cr.	Dr.	Cr.
Current Assets	210,000		160,000				370,000	
Investment in Tone Stock	440,000				[2]11,200	{ [3]371,200 [1]80,000 }		
Depreciable Assets—net	180,000		251,000				431,000	
Land	100,000		140,000				240,000	
Liabilities		126,000		71,000				197,000
Capital Stock—Ross		300,000						300,000
Retained Earnings (1/1)—Ross		450,000			[b]8,000	[2]11,200		453,200
Net Income—Ross		104,000			{ [b]8,000 [a]28,800 }	[c]41,600		108,800
Dividends—Ross	50,000						50,000	
Capital Stock—Tone				400,000	{ [c]80,000 [3]320,000 }			
Retained Earnings (1/1)—T				64,000	{ [4]12,800 [3]51,200 }			
Net Income—Tone				52,000	[c]52,000			
Dividends—Tone			36,000			[a]36,000		
	980,000	980,000	587,000	587,000				
Excess Cost Over Fair Value of Interest in Subsidiary					[1]80,000	[b]16,000	64,000	
Minority Interest in Tone					[a]7,200	{ [4]92,800 [c]10,400 }		96,000
							1,155,000	1,155,000

[1] To reclassify excess of cost ($440,000) over book value of investment, $360,000 (or 80% of $450,000) as of date of purchase.
[2] To add to investment account R's share of growth in T during Year 1: 80% of $14,000 = $11,200.
[3] To eliminate 80% of subsidiary's capital stock and retained earnings as of Jan. 1, Yr. 1.
[4] To classify 20% interest of minority stockholders as of Jan. 1, Yr. 2.

5.4 On July 1, 19X2 the Root Corp. purchased 90 percent of the voting common stock of Trim, Inc., for $238,500. When consolidated statements were prepared at the end of the year, the consolidated net income for the six-month period July 1 to December 31, 19X2 was $34,500. The net income for Root Corp. was $30,000.

From July 1, 19X2 to December 31, 19X2, the following payments were made to stockholders as a result of dividends declared by the boards of directors:

Root Corp., paid	$10,000
Trim Corp., paid	5,000

For the year 19X3, the following data were extracted from the books of account:

	Root	Trim
Capital Stock—$10 par	$400,000	$150,000
Premium on Capital Stock	275,000	50,000
Retained Earnings, Jan. 1	115,000	55,000
Net Income—19X3	45,000	15,000
Dividends Declared	20,000	10,000

Required:

(a) Determine retained earnings of each corporation as of July 1, 19X2.

(b) Prepare an elimination journal entry to consolidate the balance sheets as of July 1, 19X2.

(c) Determine the consolidated net income for year 19X3.

(d) Compute the consolidated retained earnings as of December 31, 19X3.

(e) Determine the minority interest as of December 31, 19X3.

SOLUTION

(a)   1. Calculation of net income, July–Dec. 19X2.

Net Income Reported by Root	$ 30,000	
Less: Dividend from Trim (90% of $5,000)	4,500	
Net Income from Own Operations	$ 25,500	
Consolidated Net Income	34,500	
Contribution of Trim	$ 9,000	
Net Income Reported by Trim ($9,000 = 90%)		$10,000

2. Retained earnings.

	Root	Trim
Retained Earnings:		
Jan. 1, 19X3 (Dec. 31, 19X2)	$115,000	$55,000
Less: Net Income, July–Dec. 19X2	30,000	10,000
	$ 85,000	$45,000
Add: Dividends, July–Dec. 19X2	10,000	5,000
Retained Earnings, July 1, 19X2	$ 95,000	$50,000

(b)   *July 1, 19X2*

Capital Stock—$10 par		
(90% of $150,000)	135,000	
Premium on Capital Stock		
(90% of $50,000)	45,000	
Retained Earnings		
(90% of $50,000)	45,000	
Excess of Cost over Fair Value of		
Interest in Subsidiary	13,500	
Investment in Trim Corp.—Stock		238,500

To eliminate 90% of equity of subsidiary and to set up intangible asset on acquisition.

(c)

Root Corp., Reported Income 19X3	$45,000	
Less: Income from Trim		
(90% of $10,000)	9,000	
Root's Income from Own Operations	$36,000	
Less: Amortization of Excess of Cost over		
Fair Value ($13,500 ÷ 40 years)	338	
Parent's Contribution to		
Consolidated Net Income		$35,662
Trim Corp., Reported Income 19X3	$15,000	
Less: Minority Interest		
(10% of $15,000)	1,500	
Parent's Share of Subsidiary Income		13,500
Consolidated Net Income, 19X3		$49,162

(d)

Consolidated Retained Earnings, July 1, 19X2	
(Retained earnings of parent at date of acquisition)	$ 95,000
Add: Consolidated Net Income, July–Dec., 19X2	34,500
	$129,500
Less: Dividends of Root, July–Dec., 19X2	10,000
Consolidated Retained Earnings, Dec. 31, 19X2	$119,500
Add: Consolidated Net Income, 19X2 [see (c)]	49,162
	$168,662
Less: Dividends of Root, 19X3	20,000
Consolidated Retained Earnings, Dec. 31, 19X3	$148,662

(e) 1.

Trim Corp. Retained Earnings, Jan. 1, 19X3	$ 55,000
Add: Net Income, 19X3	15,000
	$ 70,000
Less: Dividends, 19X3	10,000
Retained Earnings, Dec. 31, 19X3	$ 60,000

2. Allocation of shareholders' equity, Dec. 31, 19X3

Trim Corp.	Total	90%	10%
Capital Stock	$150,000	$135,000	$15,000
Premium on Capital Stock	50,000	45,000	5,000
Retained Earnings	60,000	54,000	6,000
Total Shareholders' Equity	$260,000		
Parent's Share		$234,000	
Minority Interest			$26,000

5.5 The Frost Corp. purchased 80 percent of the capital stock of Stream Corp. on January 1, 19X1 and also 90 percent of the capital stock of Delta Corp. on January 1, 19X2. The following data have been summarized from the books of the three corporations:

	Frost	Stream	Delta
Retained Earnings, Jan. 1, 19X1	$140,000	$80,000	$70,000
Net Income—19X1	24,000	10,000	15,000
Dividends Paid in 19X1	–0–	9,000	2,500
Net Income—19X2	11,900	7,500	10,000
Dividends Paid in 19X2	25,000	3,000	5,000

Required:

(a) Determine the consolidated net income for years 19X1 and 19X2.

(b) Determine the consolidated retained earnings as of December 31, 19X2.

SOLUTION

(a) Determination of consolidated net income.

19X1

	Frost	Stream	Delta	Consolidated
Reported Net Income	$24,000	$10,000		
Less: Intercompany Dividend Revenue (80% of $9,000)	7,200*			
Income Own Operations				$ 16,800
Less: Minority Interest (20% of $10,000)		2,000*		
Parent's Share of Subsidiary Income				8,000
Consolidated Net Income, 19X1				$ 24,800

_____
* Deduction

19X2

	Frost	Stream	Delta	Consolidated
Reported Net Income	$11,900	$ 7,500	$10,000	
Less: Intercompany Dividend Revenue				
(80% of $3,000)	2,400*			
(90% of $5,000)	4,500*			
Income Own Operations				$ 5,000
Minority Interest in Subsidiaries:				
Stream (20% of $7,500)		1,500*		
Delta (10% of $10,000)			1,000*	
Parent's Share of Subsidiary Income:				
Stream				6,000
Delta				9,000
Consolidated Net Income, 19X2				$ 20,000

* Deduction

(b) Consolidated retained earnings.

Balance—Jan. 1, 19X1 (Frost only)	$140,000
Add: Consolidated Net Income, 19X1	24,800
	$164,800
Less: Dividends, 19X1 (Frost only)	–0–
Consolidated Retained Earnings, Dec. 31, 19X1	$164,800
Add: Consolidated Net Income, 19X2	20,000
	$184,800
Less: Dividends, 19X2 (Frost only)	25,000
Consolidated Retained Earnings, Dec. 31, 19X2	$159,800

Chapter 6

Consolidated Statements—
After Date of Acquisition:
Equity Method

6.1 EARNINGS OF A SUBSIDIARY

The net income or loss of a subsidiary company ordinarily is included in consolidated statements prepared after the date of acquisition of control by the parent company. In order to harmonize the data to be consolidated, adjustments and eliminations may have to be made in various revenue and expense items. When a subsidiary's stock is less than 100 percent owned by the parent, a portion of the subsidiary income, as adjusted, should be allocated to the minority interests.

When the investment account is maintained on the *equity* (accrual) method, the parent's share of the subsidiary earnings, losses, and dividends are recognized in the parent's accounts. Thus, the carrying value of the investment in a subsidiary is increased or decreased in accordance with increases and decreases in the subsidiary's net assets, which underlie the investment and presumably give value to it.

Assume that a corporation had purchased 100 percent of the stock of a subsidiary for $100,000 and that the subsidiary earned $20,000 in Year 1 after affiliation; also that it paid dividends amounting to $10,000. The entries, on the parent's books, in summary form are as follows:

Investment in Subsidiary	20,000	
Income from Subsidiary		20,000

To record net income reported by subsidiary.

Cash	10,000	
Investment in Subsidiary		10,000

To record receipt of dividends from subsidiary.

As a result of the foregoing transactions, the parent company's investment account would reflect an increase in the subsidiary's equity of $10,000. The parent company's revenue, however, would show an increase of $20,000 as a result of the subsidiary's earnings, regardless of whether any dividends had been declared or paid by the subsidiary. The investment and income accounts are summarized as follows:

Investment in Subsidiary Corp.—Stock

	Dr.	Cr.	Balance
Cost of Investment	100,000		100,000
Earnings of Subsidiary	20,000		120,000
Dividends		10,000	110,000

Income from Subsidiary

	Dr.	Cr.	Balance
Dec. 31, Yr. 1 Net Income		20,000	20,000

Assume further that the results of operations of the parent and the subsidiary during Year 1 of operations after the parent had purchased 100 percent of the subsidiary's voting stock are condensed as follows:

	Parent	Subsidiary
Income from Operations	$19,000	$20,000
Equity in Net Income of Subsidiary	20,000	
Net Income	$39,000	$20,000

There were no intercompany transactions other than the dividends received by the parent from the subsidiary. In consolidating the two income statements, the following *elimination* entry or its equivalent must be made in order to avoid double counting of the earnings of the subsidiary.

Income from Subsidiary	20,000	
Net Income (parent)		20,000

To eliminate income from subsidiary already included in parent's income.

6.2 COMPARISON OF COST AND EQUITY METHODS

The initial entry to record an investment in a subsidiary is the same under both the cost and equity methods. By way of illustration, assume that P Corp. purchased all of the outstanding stock of Sub Corp. for $150,000. The entry under either method would be:

Investment in Sub Corp.	150,000	
Cash, Notes Payable, etc.		150,000

During the first year of operations following acquisition of control, the subsidiary showed a net income of $20,000. Under the cost method no entry would be made on the parent's books. Under the equity method, however, the following entry should be made:

Investment in Subsidiary	20,000	
Income from Subsidiary		20,000

An alternative title for the latter account is Equity in Net Income of Subsidiary, or some variation thereof.

Assume further that the subsidiary corporation paid a dividend of $10,000. Following the cost method, the entry on the parent's books would be as follows:

Cash	10,000	
Dividend Revenue		10,000

However, under the equity method the entry would be as follows:

Cash	10,000	
Investment in Sub Corp.		10,000

At the end of the year, after all nominal accounts have been transferred to the account entitled income summary (or profit and loss), the parent company's own income will be augmented by the income from the subsidiary. Under the cost method the increase would be $10,000, representing only the dividends from subsidiary. Under the equity method, the increase would be $20,000, which represents the parent's share in the income earned by the subsidiary.

Under the cost method the investment account is unaffected by these transactions; it remains at $150,000. Under the equity method, however, there are changes in the investment account, which may be summarized as follows:

Investment in Sub Corp.—Stock

	Dr.	Cr.	Balance
Cash	150,000		150,000
Dividends Received		10,000	140,000
Net Income of Sub Corp.	20,000		160,000

One advantage of the equity method is that it tends to show the entire income of a parent company and of another company in which the parent has a controlling interest through ownership of voting stock. The usual precaution against recognizing income prior to realization is not warranted in this situation because the parent company decides when and how dividends are to be declared and distributed. Many accountants recommend that the equity method be used even when the investment in another company is in the 20 to 50 percent range if the investor's block of stock represents control of the investee. Below the 50 percent range, consolidated statements are normally not acceptable.

The reader will observe that consolidated statements are not affected by the method utilized for the investment account. Consolidated statements should be identical regardless of which method is used internally by the parent company or even what technique may be utilized in the consolidating workpapers.

Choice of the equity method will probably be dictated chiefly when the investment account is not to be consolidated, either because the investment is 50 percent or less or because although the investment is more than 50 percent, there are economic or financial reasons for not consolidating. For example, although a manufacturing company is consolidated with its industrial subsidiaries, its finance subsidiary is ordinarily not consolidated; it is shown as an unconsolidated investment.

There are occasions when a subsidiary distributes a dividend that is based on retained earnings or some other surplus that was accumulated prior to acquisition of control by the investor. In such a case, the distribution, now in the hands of the investor, should be considered a return of the investment, and that account should be credited. This happens automatically when the equity method is followed; the same treatment should prevail when the cost method is utilized. This is one situation where the proper entry is the same under both methods.

All of the examples in this chapter are based on the assumption that the parent company utilizes the equity method for its investment account. Each of the first seven examples parallels its like-numbered example in Chapter 5, and while the worksheets may appear different in some details, the last pair of columns of each worksheet in this chapter contain the same data as the final pair of columns of the like-numbered example in the previous chapter. Thus, the statements prepared from these worksheets should be identical, regardless of which method is used in the accounts of the parent company.

6.3   CONSOLIDATED STATEMENTS AT END OF FIRST YEAR OF CONTROL

In the next three illustrations it will be assumed that one corporation purchased all of the outstanding stock of another corporation and one full year of operations has occurred.

EXAMPLE 1.   The balance sheets of the two corporations immediately following the investment by P Corp. in 100 percent of the stock of S Corp. are the same as those found in Example 1 of Chapter 5 (Section 5.3).

The respective balance sheets at the end of Year 1 are included in the first four columns of the accompanying worksheet to consolidate the balance sheets at the end of Year 1.

The results of operations of the two corporations for the first year after P Corp. acquires 100 percent of the stock of S Corp. are condensed as follows:

	P Corp.	S Corp.
Sales	$120,000	$116,000
Cost of Goods Sold	70,000	75,000
Gross Profit	$ 50,000	$ 41,000
Selling Expenses	$ 16,000	$ 12,000
General Expenses	15,000	9,000
Total Expenses	$ 31,000	$ 21,000
Income from Operations	$ 19,000	$ 20,000
Income from Subsidiary	20,000	
Net Income	$ 39,000	$ 20,000

The schedule of retained earnings for this first year follows:

	P Corp.	S Corp.
Balance, January 1	$60,000	$50,000
Add: Net Income—Year 1	39,000	20,000
Total	$99,000	$70,000
Less: Dividends—Year 1	15,000	10,000
Balance, December 31	$84,000	$60,000

The worksheet to consolidate the income statements of the two corporations for Year 1 contains the appropriate condensed data from the respective books after actual, or constructive, closings. In order to include the net income that results from an excess of credits over debits, the amount of net income is inserted as a balancing figure on the debit, or smaller side. To complete the picture, the offsetting credit goes to the respective retained earnings account. It is thus equivalent to the debit side of the following journal entry, which an individual corporation would make to transfer net income to the retained earnings account at the end of a year:

Income Summary	XXXX	
Retained Earnings		XXXX

In order to avoid double counting of the subsidiary income recognized by P Corp. in addition to the net income of S Corp. from its own operations, it is necessary to construct elimination entry (a) in the accompanying worksheet to prepare a consolidated income statement. In general journal form, the entry is as follows:

| Income from Subsidiary | 20,000 | |
| Net Income | | 20,000 |

After this elimination entry has been entered in the elimination columns of the worksheet, the remaining items can be combined and extended.

The worksheet to prepare a consolidated balance sheet at the end of the first year of operations is presented in condensed form in order to highlight those items which have special significance in the consolidation process. It is assumed that all accounts of each corporation have been closed except that net income and dividends (or dividends declared) have not been transferred to determine the final retained earnings.

It is now practical to eliminate the investment account, on the equity basis, directly against the shareholders' equity of the subsidiary corporation at the end of the year, since the investment account has been increased by the parent's share of the subsidiary's net increase in its equity. Thus, entry (1) eliminates 100 percent of the shareholders' equity of the subsidiary corporation as of December 31 of Year 1 against the carrying value of the investment.

If the income summary and dividend accounts of S Corp. had been transferred to retained earnings at the end of the year, its retained earnings account would show a closing balance of $60,000. In such a case, elimination entry (1) would be as follows:

Capital Stock—S	100,000	
Retained Earnings (12/31)—S	60,000	
Investment in S Corp.		160,000

Condensed consolidated statements prepared from the accompanying worksheets will be the same as those in Example 1 of Chapter 5 (Section 5.3).

P Corp. and Subsidiary
Worksheet—Consolidated Income Statement
Year 1

	P Corp.		S Corp.		Eliminations		Consolidated	
	Dr.	Cr.	Dr.	Cr.	Dr.	Cr.	Dr.	Cr.
Sales		120,000		116,000				236,000
Cost of Goods Sold	70,000		75,000				145,000	
Selling Expenses	16,000		12,000				28,000	
General Expenses	15,000		9,000				24,000	
Income from Subsidiary		20,000			a20,000			
	101,000	140,000	96,000	116,000				
Net Income—P	39,000						39,000	
Net Income—S			20,000			a20,000		
	140,000	140,000	116,000	116,000			236,000	236,000

a To eliminate income from subsidiary previously recorded by P Corp. This eliminates double counting of income of S Corp.

P Corp. and Subsidiary
Worksheet—Consolidated Balance Sheet
December 31, Year 1

	P Corp.		S Corp.		Eliminations		Consolidated	
	Dr.	Cr.	Dr.	Cr.	Dr.	Cr.	Dr.	Cr.
Current Assets	103,000		56,000				159,000	
Investment in S Corp.	160,000					[1]160,000		
Depreciable Assets—net	190,000		110,000				300,000	
Land			25,000				25,000	
Liabilities		169,000		31,000				200,000
Capital Stock—P		200,000						200,000
Retained Earnings (1/1)—P		60,000						60,000
Net Income—P		39,000						39,000
Dividends—P	15,000						15,000	
Capital Stock—S				100,000	[1]100,000			
Retained Earnings (1/1)—S				50,000	[1]50,000			
Net Income—S				20,000	[1]20,000			
Dividends—S			10,000			[1]10,000		
	468,000	468,000	201,000	201,000			499,000	499,000

[1] To eliminate 100% of subsidiary's shareholders' equity as of Dec. 31, Yr. 1.

The capital stock of only the parent company appears in the consolidated balance sheet. The starting point for the consolidated retained earnings is the retained earnings account of the parent company as of the date of affiliation. Net income that is added to it is the consolidated net income for the year; dividends that are deducted, however, are those of the parent company only. At the beginning of Year 2, consolidated retained earnings will be $84,000—the same amount as at the end of Year 1.

6.4 COST OF INVESTMENT GREATER THAN BOOK VALUE OF SUBSIDIARY

The situation described in this section is identical to the situation described in Section 5.4, with one important exception: it is now assumed that the equity method has been followed by the parent company.

EXAMPLE 2. Refer to the data for Example 2 of Chapter 5. For the sake of convenience, the condensed trial balances of the two corporations immediately after affiliation are repeated here:

	R Corp.		T Corp.	
Current Assets	$ 50,000		$ 55,000	
Investment in T Corp.—Stock	175,000			
Depreciable Assets—net	200,000		100,000	
Land			25,000	
Liabilities		$165,000		$ 30,000
Capital Stock		200,000		100,000
Retained Earnings		60,000		50,000
	$425,000	$425,000	$180,000	$180,000

(Text continued on p. 160.)

R Corp. and Subsidiary
Worksheet—Consolidated Income Statement
Year 1

	R Corp.		T Corp.		Eliminations		Consolidated	
	Dr.	Cr.	Dr.	Cr.	Dr.	Cr.	Dr.	Cr.
Sales		120,000		116,000				236,000
Cost of Goods Sold	70,000		75,000				145,000	
Selling Expenses	16,000		12,000				28,000	
General Expenses	15,000		9,000				24,000	
Income from Subsidiary		20,000			[a]20,000			
	101,000	140,000	96,000	116,000				
Net Income—R	39,000				[c]13,750	[a]20,000	32,750	
Net Income—T			20,000			{ [c]13,750 [b]6,250		
	140,000	140,000	116,000	116,000				
Amortization of Patent					[b]6,250		6,250	
							236,000	236,000

[a] To eliminate income of T Corp. previously recorded by R Corp.
[b] To amortize patent for one year: 25% of $25,000.
[c] To transfer net income of T Corp.

R Corp. and Subsidiary
Worksheet—Consolidated Balance Sheet
December 31, Year 1

	R Corp.		T Corp.		Eliminations		Consolidated	
	Dr.	Cr.	Dr.	Cr.	Dr.	Cr.	Dr.	Cr.
Current Assets	78,000		85,000				163,000	
Investment in T Corp.—Stock	185,000					[2]185,000		
Depreciable Assets—net	190,000		90,000				280,000	
Land			25,000				25,000	
Liabilities		169,000		40,000				209,000
Capital Stock—R		200,000						200,000
Retained Earnings (1/1)—R		60,000						60,000
Net Income—R		39,000			[b]6,250			32,750
Dividends—R	15,000						15,000	
Capital Stock—T				100,000	[2]100,000			
Retained Earnings (1/1)—T				50,000	[2]50,000			
Net Income—T				20,000	[2]20,000			
Dividends—T			10,000			[2]10,000		
	468,000	468,000	210,000	210,000				
Patent					[1]25,000	[b]6,250	18,750	
Appraisal Capital—T					[2]25,000	[1]25,000		
							501,750	501,750

[1] To record value of patent: $25,000, based on price paid by R Corp. for stock of subsidiary.
[2] To eliminate 100% of shareholders' equity in T Corp. as of Dec. 31, Yr. 1.

R Corp. and Subsidiary
Consolidated Workpapers (3-tier)
Year 1

	Company		Adjustments & Eliminations		Consolidated
	R	T			
INCOME STATEMENT					
Revenue					
Sales	120,000	116,000			236,000
Income from Subsidiary	20,000		[2]20,000		
Total Revenue	140,000	116,000			236,000
Costs and Expenses					
Cost of Goods Sold	70,000	75,000			145,000
Selling Expenses	16,000	12,000			28,000
General Expenses	15,000	9,000			24,000
Amortization of Patent			[b]6,250		6,250
Total Costs and Expenses	101,000	96,000			203,250
Net Income	39,000	20,000			32,750
RETAINED EARNINGS					
Balance (1/1)—R	60,000				60,000
Balance (1/1)—T		50,000	[2]50,000		
Net Income	39,000	20,000			32,750
Total	99,000	70,000			92,750
Less: Dividends—R	15,000				15,000
Dividends—T		10,000		[2]10,000	
Balance (12/31)	84,000	60,000			77,750
BALANCE SHEET					
Assets					
Current Assets	78,000	85,000			163,000
Investment in T Corp.	185,000			[2]185,000	
Depreciable Assets—net	190,000	90,000			280,000
Land		25,000			25,000
Patent			[1]25,000	[b]6,250	18,750
Total Assets	453,000	200,000			486,750
Equities					
Liabilities	169,000	40,000			209,000
Capital Stock—R	200,000				200,000
Retained Earnings—R	84,000				77,750
Capital Stock—T		100,000	[2]100,000		
Retained Earnings—T		60,000			
Appraisal Capital—T			[2]25,000	[1]25,000	
Total Equities	453,000	200,000			486,750

The results of operations of the two corporations for the first year after affiliation appear in the first four columns of the worksheet to prepare a consolidated income statement (p. 158). Entry (a) eliminates the income from subsidiary in order to avoid double counting of subsidiary income. Entry (b) records the first-year amortization of patent expense, $6,250, and thus reduces T's income, for consolidation purposes, to $13,750 in Year 1. This consolidation adjustment must be repeated for the next three years until the entire amount of $25,000 originally assigned to the patent is fully amortized. Entry (c) combines the adjusted net income of the two corporations to indicate that the consolidated net income is $32,750.

The balance sheets of R Corp. and T Corp. at the end of Year 1 are condensed in the first four columns of the accompanying worksheet to prepare a consolidated balance sheet at end of Year 1. The investment account has increased by $10,000 as a result of transactions summarized in the following ledger account on the parent's books:

Investment in T Corp.—Stock

	Dr.	Cr.	Balance
Cost of Stock	175,000		175,000
Year 1 Dividends		10,000	165,000
12/31, Yr. 1 Net Income of T	20,000		185,000

Elimination entry (b) is similar to entry (b) in the worksheet to consolidate the income statements and performs the same function. Entry (1) records the patent at the value of $25,000, determined as of the date of acquisition of the investment in T Corp. The combined effect of entries (1) and (b) is that the carrying value of the patent at the end of Year 1 will be $18,750.

Entry (2) eliminates the carrying value of the investment against the shareholders' equity of the subsidiary corporation as of the end of Year 1.

Condensed consolidated statements from these worksheets would be the same as those obtained from the worksheets in Section 5.4.

(*Note:* As an alternate solution, a three-tier worksheet is presented on p. 159.)

6.5 COST OF INVESTMENT LESS THAN BOOK VALUE OF SUBSIDIARY'S NET ASSETS

EXAMPLE 3. This example is based on data identical to that found in Example 3 of Chapter 5 (Section 5.5).

Data from the condensed income statements of the two companies have been entered in the first four columns of the accompanying worksheet to prepare the consolidated income statement for Year 1 after affiliation. Entry (a) eliminates the income from subsidiary, which P Corp. had already recognized in its accounts. Entry (b) reduces the annual amortization of the patents by $2,000; that is, from $4,000 to $2,000, based on the fair value of the patents as determined as of the date of acquisition of the investment in U Corp. The result of this elimination adjustment is to increase the income of the subsidiary for consolidation purposes by $2,000. Entry (c) transfers the adjusted net income of U Corp., $22,000, to the same line as the net income of P Corp. so that they may be conveniently combined and extended as one amount.

The investment account on the books of the parent company as of the end of Year 1 is summarized as follows:

Investment in U Corp.—Stock

	Dr.	Cr.	Balance
1/1, Yr. 1 Cost	130,000		130,000
Year 1 Dividends		10,000	120,000
12/31, Yr. 1 Net Income of U	20,000		140,000

The condensed balance sheets as of the end of Year 1 appear in the first four columns of the worksheet to prepare a consolidated balance sheet as of that date. The lettered entry (b) in this worksheet corresponds to entry (b) in the worksheet to consolidate the income statements. Note that the U Corp. has continued to amortize its patents at the rate of 4,000 per year; as a result, the book value of patents on the books of U Corp. at the end of Year 1 is $36,000 ($40,000 − $4,000). The purpose of entry (1) is to reduce the value of the patents by $20,000 as of the date of acquisition. Thus the amortization, for consolidation purposes, should be only $2,000 per year, which is accomplished by entry (b). When the balance of the patents is extended to the Consolidated Balance Sheet columns, the consolidated carrying value of the patent becomes $18,000, which is equal to an adjusted cost of $20,000 less one year's amortization of $2,000. Entry (2) eliminates the carrying value of the investment against the shareholders' equity accounts as of December 31, Year 1.

P Corp. and Subsidiary
Worksheet—Consolidated Income Statement
Year 1

	P Corp.		U Corp.		Eliminations		Consolidated	
	Dr.	Cr.	Dr.	Cr.	Dr.	Cr.	Dr.	Cr.
Sales		120,000		116,000				236,000
Cost of Goods Sold	70,000		75,000				145,000	
Selling Expenses	16,000		10,000				26,000	
General Expenses	15,000		7,000				22,000	
Amortization of Patent			4,000			b2,000	2,000	
Income from Subsidiary		20,000			a20,000			
	101,000	140,000	96,000	116,000				
Net Income—P	39,000				c22,000	a20,000	41,000	
Net Income—U				20,000	b2,000	c22,000		
	140,000	140,000	116,000	116,000			236,000	236,000

a To eliminate income of U Corp. previously recorded by P Corp.
b To reduce amortization of patent from $4,000 (10% of $40,000) to $2,000 (10% of $20,000).
c To transfer the net income of U Corp. as adjusted.

P Corp. and Subsidiary
Worksheet—Consolidated Balance Sheet
December 31, Year 1

	P Corp.		U Corp.		Eliminations		Consolidated	
	Dr.	Cr.	Dr.	Cr.	Dr.	Cr.	Dr.	Cr.
Current Assets	105,000		51,000				156,000	
Investment in U Corp.	140,000					2140,000		
Depreciable Assets—net	190,000		90,000				280,000	
Patent			36,000		b2,000	120,000	18,000	
Liabilities		151,000		17,000				168,000
Capital Stock—P		200,000						200,000
Retained Earnings (1/1)—P		60,000						60,000
Net Income—P		39,000				b2,000		41,000
Dividends—P	15,000						15,000	
Capital Stock—U				100,000	2100,000			
Retained Earnings (1/1)—U				50,000	{230,000 120,000			
Net Income—U				20,000	222,000	b2,000		
Dividends—U			10,000			210,000		
	450,000	450,000	187,000	187,000			469,000	469,000

1 To reduce patents to $20,000 as of Jan. 1, Yr. 1.
2 To eliminate 100% of shareholders' equity in U Corp. as of Dec. 31, Yr. 1.

6.6 CONSOLIDATED STATEMENTS AFTER DATE OF CONTROL— INVESTMENT IN 90% OF SUBSIDIARY STOCK

At the date of acquisition of control of a subsidiary, the accumulated income, less losses and dividends to date (retained earnings), is allocated to the parent and to the minority interest in the same ratio as their capital stockholdings. The amount allocated to the parent is considered to have been *purchased* by it, and thereafter this amount is continuously eliminated against all or a portion of the amount of the parent's investment. The amount considered to have been purchased by the parent may, of course, be subject to special adjustments for consolidation purposes.

When the equity method is used, the parent's share of the subsidiary's net income each year after the date of acquisition of control is generally included in the parent's net income and thus is included almost automatically in the consolidated retained earnings. Decreases in subsidiary retained earnings due to net losses after the affiliation date similarly reduce the consolidated retained earnings. Dividends of the subsidiary would automatically be distributed to the parent and to the minority in proportion to their stockholdings. Under the equity method, dividends from a subsidiary would reduce the parent's investment account.

EXAMPLE 4. P Corp. purchased 90 percent of the outstanding stock of S Corp. on January 1 of Year 1 for $135,000. The results of operations and dividends distributed in Year 1 are similar to those in Example 1 of this chapter (Section 6.3). However, since P Corp. now owns only 90 percent of the stock of S Corp., the parent company's share of S's net income amounts to $18,000 (90 percent of $20,000).

The results of operations for the first year after affiliation are condensed as follows:

	P Corp.	S Corp.
Sales	$120,000	$116,000
Cost of Goods Sold	70,000	75,000
Gross Profit	$ 50,000	$ 41,000
Selling Expenses	$ 16,000	$ 12,000
General Expenses	15,000	9,000
Total Expenses	$ 31,000	$ 21,000
Income from Operations	$ 19,000	$ 20,000
Income from Subsidiary	18,000	
Net Income	$ 37,000	$ 20,000

The schedule of retained earnings for the first year after affiliation is as follows:

	P Corp.	S Corp.
Balance, January 1	$60,000	$50,000
Add: Net Income	37,000	20,000
Total	$97,000	$70,000
Less: Dividends	15,000	10,000
Balance, December 31	$82,000	$60,000

In the worksheet to consolidate the income statements of the two corporations, the earnings of S Corp. must be allocated to the shareholders of P Corp. and to the minority in the ratio of 90:10. Thus, $18,000 (90 percent of $20,000) will be included in the consolidated net income. Since P Corp. has already included this $18,000 as income from subsidiary in determining its net income, this amount must be eliminated in preparing the consolidated net income in order to avoid double counting. This step is accomplished in entry (a). Entry (b) allocates the net income of S Corp. in proportion to the stockholdings: 90 percent to the parent company and 10 percent to the minority interests.

The investment account for Year 1 on the parent's books follows:

Investment in S Corp.—Stock

	Dr.	Cr.	Balance
1/1, Yr. 1 Cost	135,000		135,000
Year 1 Dividends		9,000	126,000
12/31, Yr. 1 90% of Net Income	18,000		144,000

The balance sheets of the two corporations as of the end of Year 1 are contained in the first four columns of the worksheet to prepare a consolidated balance sheet. Entry (1) eliminates the balance of the investment as of December 31, Year 1 against 90 percent of the shareholders' equity of the subsidiary corporation as of that date. Entry (2) classifies the remaining 10 percent as the minority interest at the end of the year.

P Corp. and Subsidiary
Worksheet—Consolidated Income Statement
Year 1

	P Corp.		S Corp.		Eliminations		Consolidated	
	Dr.	Cr.	Dr.	Cr.	Dr.	Cr.	Dr.	Cr.
Sales		120,000		116,000				236,000
Cost of Goods Sold	70,000		75,000				145,000	
Selling Expenses	16,000		12,000				28,000	
General Expenses	15,000		9,000				24,000	
Income from Subsidiary		18,000			[a]18,000			
	101,000	138,000	96,000	116,000				
Net Income—P	37,000				[b]18,000	[a]18,000	37,000	
Net Income—S			20,000			[b]20,000		
	138,000	138,000	116,000	116,000				
Minority Interest						[b]2,000		2,000
							236,000	236,000

[a] To eliminate income from subsidiary previously recorded by P Corp.
[b] To allocate the net income of S Corp.: 90% to parent and 10% to minority.

P Corp. and Subsidiary
Worksheet—Consolidated Balance Sheet
December 31, Year 1

	P Corp.		S Corp.		Eliminations		Consolidated	
	Dr.	Cr.	Dr.	Cr.	Dr.	Cr.	Dr.	Cr.
Current Assets	103,000		56,000				159,000	
Investment in S Corp.—Stock	144,000					[1]144,000		
Depreciable Assets—net	190,000		110,000				300,000	
Land			25,000				25,000	
Liabilities		155,000		31,000				186,000
Capital Stock—P		200,000						200,000
Retained Earnings (1/1)—P		60,000						60,000
Net Income—P		37,000						37,000
Dividends—P	15,000						15,000	
Capital Stock—S				100,000	[2]10,000 [1]90,000			
Retained Earnings (1/1)—S				50,000	[2]5,000 [1]45,000			
Net Income—S				20,000	[2]2,000 [1]18,000			
Dividends—S			10,000			[2]1,000 [1]9,000		
	452,000	452,000	201,000	201,000				
Minority Interest						[2]16,000		16,000
							499,000	499,000

[1] To eliminate 90% of shareholders' equity of S Corp. as of Dec. 31, Yr. 1.
[2] To classify 10% interest of minority shareholders.

The condensed statements prepared from the accompanying worksheets would be the same as those found in Section 5.6.

6.7 PURCHASE OF 90% OF SUBSIDIARY STOCK— INVESTMENT COST GREATER THAN BOOK VALUE

EXAMPLE 5. The preaffiliation balance sheets in this example are the same as those in Example 2 of this chapter (Section 6.4) and Example 2 of Chapter 5 (Section 5.4). Refer to the accompanying worksheet to prepare a consolidated income statement for the first year of operations of the two corporations. Adjustment entry (a) eliminates the income from subsidiary, which the parent has already recorded on its own books and thus included in its income. Entry (b) records the annual amortization of patent expense, based on a four-year useful life remaining from the date of affiliation. Thus, T's net income for consolidation purposes is reduced by $6,250 for Year 1. Entry (c) allocates the adjusted net income of T Corp., $13,750 ($20,000 − $6,250), as indicated in the following entry:

Net Income—R	12,375	
Minority Interest in T	1,375	
Net Income—T		13,750

The investment account on the parent company's books appears as follows:

Investment in T Corp.—Stock

	Dr.	Cr.	Balance
1/1, Yr. 1 Cost	157,500		157,500
Year 1 Dividend		9,000	148,500
12/31, Yr. 1 Net Income	18,000		166,500

The balance sheets of R Corp. and of T Corp. at the end of Year 1 are condensed in the first four columns of the accompanying worksheet to prepare a consolidated balance sheet as of that date. Entry (b) is similar to the same-lettered entry in the worksheet to consolidate the income statements for Year 1 and it performs the same function. Entry (1) recognizes the patent at the value of $25,000, which was determined as of the date of acquisition of 90 percent of the stock of T Corp. As in Example 2 (Section 6.4), the combined effect of entries (1) and (b) is that the amortized value of the patent, for consolidation purposes, at the end of the first year is $18,750.

The purpose of entry (2) is to reduce the parent company's investment account by $5,625, 90 percent of the $6,250 reduction made to the net income of T Corp. as a result of the annual amortization of the patent. The patent and the amortization thereof will normally appear only in the consolidated workpapers and in the consolidated statements.

If the subsidiary had recorded the patent on its books, it would have recorded the annual amortization; the net income of T Corp. for Year 1 would have been reported at $13,750. The parent would have picked up only $12,375 (90 percent of $13,750). In such case worksheet entries (b), (1), and (2) would not be necessary. There may be sound reasons for not entering the appraisal value of the patent on the books of T Corp. For example, management may prefer that the ledger account balances harmonize with the tax basis when feasible. In any case, there are accountants who feel that the parent company should record $12,375 rather than $18,000 as its proper share of the subsidiary net income. Such accountants would argue that in this example the smaller figure is more in harmony with the equity method. If that had been done in this example, the necessity for entry (2) would be obviated.

Entry (3) eliminates the adjusted cost of the investment in T Corp. against 90 percent of the shareholders' equity of T Corp. as of the end of Year 1, and entry (4) classifies the remaining 10 percent as the minority interest.

The minority interest in T Corp. as of December 31, Year 1, totals $17,875. For the details, refer to the table in Example 5 of the previous chapter (Section 5.7). Likewise, refer to Section 5.7 for the consolidated income statement for Year 1 and the consolidated balance sheet as of December 31, Year 1.

R Corp. and Subsidiary
Worksheet—Consolidated Income Statement
Year 1

	R Corp.		T Corp.		Eliminations		Consolidated	
	Dr.	Cr.	Dr.	Cr.	Dr.	Cr.	Dr.	Cr.
Sales		120,000		116,000				236,000
Cost of Goods Sold	70,000		75,000				145,000	
Selling Expenses	16,000		12,000				28,000	
General Expenses	15,000		9,000				24,000	
Income from Subsidiary		18,000			[a]18,000			
	101,000	138,000	96,000	116,000				
Net Income—R	37,000				[c]12,375	[a]18,000	31,375	
Net Income—T				20,000		[c]13,750 [b]6,250		
	138,000	138,000	116,000	116,000				
Amortization of Patent					[b]6,250		6,250	
Minority Interest					[c]1,375		1,375	
							236,000	236,000

[a] To eliminate income of T Corp. previously recorded by R Corp.

[b] To amortize patent for one year: 25% of $25,000.

[c] To allocate net income of T Corp. as adjusted.

R Corp. and Subsidiary
Worksheet—Consolidated Balance Sheet
December 31, Year 1

	R Corp.		T Corp.		Eliminations		Consolidated	
	Dr.	Cr.	Dr.	Cr.	Dr.	Cr.	Dr.	Cr.
Current Assets	84,500		85,000				169,500	
Investment in T Corp.	166,500					[3]160,875 [2]5,625		
Depreciable Assets—net	190,000		90,000				280,000	
Land			25,000				25,000	
Liabilities		159,000		40,000				199,000
Capital Stock—R		200,000						200,000
Retained Earnings (1/1)—R		60,000						60,000
Net Income—R		37,000			[2]5,625			31,375
Dividends—R	15,000						15,000	
Capital Stock—T				100,000	[4]10,000 [3]90,000			
Retained Earnings (1/1)—T				50,000	[4]5,000 [3]45,000			
Net Income—T				20,000	[3]12,375 [b]6,250 [4]1,375			
Dividends—T			10,000			[4]1,000 [3]9,000		
	456,000	456,000	210,000	210,000				
Patent					[1]25,000	[b]6,250	18,750	
Appraisal Capital—T					[4]2,500 [3]22,500	[1]25,000		
Minority Interest						[4]17,875		17,875
							508,250	508,250

[1] To record value of patent: $25,000 based on price paid by R Corp. for 90% of stock of subsidiary.

[2] To correct R's investment and net income for 90% of reduction in T's net income for Year 1: $5,625 (90% of $6,250).

[3] To eliminate 90% of shareholders' equity in T Corp. as of Dec. 31, Yr. 1.

[4] To classify 10% interest of minority shareholders.

6.8 PURCHASE OF 90% OF SUBSIDIARY STOCK—INVESTMENT COST GREATER THAN FAIR VALUE

EXAMPLE 6. Assume the same conditions as in the previous example, except that it has been ascertained that the assets and liabilities of T Corp. were fairly reflected by the book amounts as of the date of acquisition. The R Corp. willingly paid $22,500 in excess of 90 percent of the net assets of the T Corp. because it was expected that the combination would achieve financial benefits from centralized control and direction. The amount paid for the potential benefits of affiliation as of January 1, Year 1, may be computed as follows:

Net Assets of T Corp.		$150,000
90% of Net Asset Value		$135,000
Cost of Investment		157,500
Excess of Cost of Investment over Fair Value of Interest in Subsidiary		$ 22,500

The board of directors of R Corp. has decided that it would be appropriate to amortize this intangible asset over ten years. Thus, entry (b) records this amortization in the consolidation workpapers. Note that the minority interest is not affected by this amortization expense; it concerns the accounts of the parent company only.

In the worksheet to prepare a consolidated income statement entry (a) eliminates the income from subsidiary to avoid double counting of the subsidiary's earnings. Entry (b) records the amortization of 10 percent of the excess of cost over fair value of interest in subsidiary. If the parent company had recorded this amortization in its books the net income of R Corp. would have been reported at $34,750 ($37,000 − $2,250) and entry (b) would not be required. Entry (c) allocates the net income of the subsidiary in the ratio of parent and minority shareholdings.

R Corp. and Subsidiary
Worksheet—Consolidated Income Statement
Year 1

	R Corp.		T Corp.		Eliminations		Consolidated	
	Dr.	Cr.	Dr.	Cr.	Dr.	Cr.	Dr.	Cr.
Sales		120,000		116,000				236,000
Cost of Goods Sold	70,000		75,000				145,000	
Selling Expenses	16,000		12,000				28,000	
General Expenses	15,000		9,000				24,000	
Income from Subsidiary		18,000			[a]18,000			
	101,000	138,000	96,000	116,000				
Net Income—R	37,000				[c]18,000	{ [b]2,250 [a]18,000 }	34,750	
Net Income—T			20,000			[c]20,000		
	138,000	138,000	116,000	116,000				
Amortization of Excess of Cost Over Value of Interest in Subsidiary					[b]2,250		2,250	
Minority Interest					[c]2,000		2,000	
							236,000	236,000

[a] To eliminate income from subsidiary previously recorded by R Corp.
[b] To amortize intangible asset: 10% of $22,500.
[c] To allocate net income of T Corp.

The income statement of R Corp. and its consolidated subsidiary has been prepared from the last two columns of the worksheet.

R Corp. and Subsidiary
Worksheet—Consolidated Balance Sheet
December 31, Year 1

	R Corp.		T Corp.		Eliminations		Consolidated	
	Dr.	Cr.	Dr.	Cr.	Dr.	Cr.	Dr.	Cr.
Current Assets	84,500		75,000				159,500	
Investment in T Corp.—Stock	166,500					{²144,000 ¹22,500		
Depreciable Assets—net	190,000		100,000				290,000	
Land			25,000				25,000	
Liabilities		159,000		40,000				199,000
Capital Stock—R		200,000						200,000
Retained Earnings (1/1)—R		60,000						60,000
Net Income—R		37,000			ᵇ2,250			34,750
Dividends—R	15,000						15,000	
Capital Stock—T				100,000	{³10,000 ²90,000			
Retained Earnings (1/1)—T				50,000	{³5,000 ²45,000			
Net Income—T				20,000	{³2,000 ²18,000			
Dividends—T			10,000			{³1,000 ²9,000		
	456,000	456,000	210,000	210,000				
Excess of Cost Over Value of Interest in Subsidiary					¹22,500	ᵇ2,250	20,250	
Minority Interest						³16,000		16,000
							509,750	509,750

¹ To record excess of cost of investment, $157,500, over book value of investment, $135,000 (90% of $150,000).

² To eliminate 90% of shareholders' equity in T Corp. as of Dec. 31, Yr. 1.

³ To classify 10% interest of minority shareholders.

The investment account on the parent's books would be the same as in Example 5.

Entry (1) in the worksheet to prepare a consolidated balance sheet segregates the excess of cost of investment over fair value of interest in subsidiary. This is the same entry that was recognized as of the date of acquisition one year earlier. (See Example 6 of Chapter 4, Section 4.10.) A similar adjustment would have to be made each time a consolidated balance sheet is to be prepared until this excess of cost over fair value of interest in subsidiary is fully amortized.

The combination of entries (1) and (b) results in a balance of this intangible asset of $20,250, which should appear in the consolidated balance sheet at the end of Year 1. As an alternative procedure, the excess cost over value of interest in subsidiary might have been immediately identified in a separate account in the parent's ledger and the amortization recorded directly in the accounts. In such a case, entries (b) and (1) would not be required in the worksheet.

Entry (2) eliminates the balance of the investment account against 90 percent of the shareholders' equity in T Corp. as of the end of Year 1, and entry (3) classifies the remaining 10 percent as the minority interest.

R Corp. and Subsidiary
Consolidated Income Statement
Year Ended December 31, Year 1

Sales	$236,000	
Cost of Goods Sold	145,000	
Gross Profit		$91,000
Less Expenses:		
Selling	$ 28,000	
General	24,000	
Amortization of Excess of Cost over Value of Interest in Subsidiary	2,250	
Total Expenses		54,250
Net Income before Minority Interest		$36,750
Minority Interest in Income		2,000
Net Income		$34,750

6.9   PURCHASE OF 90% OF SUBSIDIARY STOCK— INVESTMENT COST GREATER THAN FAIR VALUE, YEAR 2

EXAMPLE 7.   Previous examples in this chapter have illustrated worksheets for the preparation of consolidated income statements for the first year of affiliation and balance sheets at the end of the first year of affiliation.   The purpose of this example is to illustrate what happens in a subsequent year.   This example is a continuation of Example 5 (Section 6.7) through the end of Year 2.

The results of operations of R Corp. and T Corp. for Year 2 are condensed in the first four columns of the accompanying worksheet to prepare a consolidated income statement (p. 170).   The entries (a), (b), and (c) perform the same functions as in Year 1.   For convenience, however, they are briefly explained in the lower section of the worksheet.

A consolidated income statement for the second year of affiliation may be found in Section 5.9 (Chapter 5); the statement should be the same for the same set of facts, regardless of the methodology used to assemble the data.

The investment account on the parent's books at the end of two years affiliation is summarized below.   It is based on reported net income by T Corp. in Year 2 of $27,000 and dividends paid of $20,000.

Investment in T Corp.—Stock

	Dr.	Cr.	Balance
1/1, Yr. 1 Cost	157,000		157,000
Year 1 Dividends		9,000	148,500
12/31, Yr. 1 Net Income	18,000		166,500
Year 2 Dividends		18,000	148,500
12/31, Yr. 2 Net Income	24,300		172,800

The parent's retained earnings account for the first two years of affiliation is summarized as follows:

Retained Earnings

	Dr.	Cr.	Balance
1/1, Yr. 1 Balance		60,000	60,000
Year 1 Dividends	15,000		45,000
12/31, Yr. 1 Net Income:			
Own Operations	19,000		
Subsidiary	18,000	37,000	82,000
Year 2 Dividends	25,000		57,000
12/31, Yr. 2 Net Income:			
Own Operations	30,000		
Subsidiary	24,300	54,300	111,300

The condensed balance sheets of R Corp. and of T Corp. at the end of the second year of affiliation are presented in the first four columns of the accompanying worksheet to prepare a consolidated balance sheet as of December 31, Year 2.

Entry (1) records the value of the patent as determined at January 1, Year 1, the date of purchase of 90 percent of T stock. Entry (b) reduces the net income of T by $6,250, the amortization of the patent for Year 2. [This is the same as entry (b) in Year 1.] However, since the adjustment for amortization in the first year had been entered only in the worksheet, it is necessary to repeat that entry again. Since last year's reduction in net income would reduce the retained earnings at the end of Year 1, entry (2) now reduces the retained earnings at the beginning of Year 2. In general journal form, the entry is as follows:

Retained Earnings (1/1, Yr. 2)—T	6,250	
Patent		6,250

The purpose of entry (3) is to correct the investment account by 90 percent of the reduction in T's net income for both Years 1 and 2. The journal entry follows;

Retained Earnings (1/1, Yr. 2)—R	5,625	
Net Income—R	5,625	
Investment in T Corp.—R		11,250

Entry (4) eliminates the adjusted balance of the investment account against 90 percent of the adjusted shareholders' equity of the subsidiary corporation as of December 31, Year 2. Entry (5) allocates the remaining 10 percent to the minority interests. The determination of these amounts is best shown by the tabulation of the shareholders' equity accounts of the T Corp. as of December 31, Year 2, which follows:

T Corporation
Shareholders' Equity Accounts
December 31, Year 2

	Trial Balance	Adjusted Balances		
		Total	90%	10%
Capital Stock	$100,000	$100,000	$ 90,000	$10,000
Retained Earnings (1/1)	60,000(2)	53,750	48,375	5,375
Net Income—Year 2	27,000(b)	20,750	18,675	2,075
Appraisal Capital	25,000	25,000	22,500	2,500
Dividends—Year 2	(20,000)	(20,000)	(18,000)	(2,000)
Totals	$192,000	$179,500	$161,550	$17,950

(*Note*: As an alternate approach, a three-tier worksheet is included in this example.)

R Corp. and Subsidiary
Worksheet—Consolidated Income Statement
Year 2

	R Corp.		T Corp.		Eliminations		Consolidated	
	Dr.	Cr.	Dr.	Cr.	Dr.	Cr.	Dr.	Cr.
Sales		200,000		200,000				400,000
Cost of Goods Sold	130,000		145,000				275,000	
Selling Expenses	22,000		15,000				37,000	
General Expenses	18,000		13,000				31,000	
Income from Subsidiary		24,300			[a]24,300			
	170,000	224,300	173,000	200,000				
Net Income—R	54,300				[c]18,675	[a]24,300	48,675	
Net Income—T			27,000			{[c]20,750 [b]6,250		
	224,300	224,300	200,000	200,000				
Amortization of Patent						[b]6,250	6,250	
Minority Interest						[c]2,075	2,075	
							400,000	400,000

[a] To eliminate income from subsidiary previously recorded by R Corp.
[b] To amortize patent for one year: 25% of $25,000.
[c] To allocate net income of T Corp. as adjusted.

R Corp. and Subsidiary
Worksheet—Consolidated Balance Sheet
December 31, Year 2

	R Corp.		T Corp.		Eliminations		Consolidated	
	Dr.	Cr.	Dr.	Cr.	Dr.	Cr.	Dr.	Cr.
Current Assets	79,500		95,000				174,500	
Investment in T Corp.—Stock	172,800					{[4]161,550 [3]11,250		
Depreciable Assets—net	180,000		80,000				260,000	
Land			25,000				25,000	
Liabilities		121,000		33,000				154,000
Capital Stock—R		200,000						200,000
Retained Earnings (1/1)—R		82,000			[3]5,625			76,375
Net Income—R		54,300			[3]5,625			48,675
Dividends—R	25,000						25,000	
Capital Stock—T				100,000	{[5]10,000 [4]90,000			
Retained Earnings (1/1)—T				60,000	{[5]5,375 [4]48,375 [2]6,250			
Net Income—T				27,000	{[5]2,075 [4]18,675 [b]6,250			
Dividends—T			20,000			{[5]2,000 [4]18,000		
	457,300	457,300	220,000	220,000				
Patent					[1]25,000	{[2]6,250 [b]6,250}	12,500	
Appraisal Capital					{[5]2,500 [4]22,500}	[1]25,000		
Minority Interest						[5]17,950		17,950
							497,000	497,000

[1] To record value of patent: $25,000 as of Jan. 1, Yr. 1, based on price paid by R Corp. for 90% of stock of subsidiary.
[2] To re-enter amortization of patent for prior year.
[3] To reduce R's investment for 90% of reduction in T's net income for years 1 and 2: $5,625 each year.
[4] To eliminate 90% of shareholders' equity in T Corp. as of Dec. 31, Yr. 2.
[5] To classify 10% interest of minority shareholders.

R Corp. and Subsidiary
Consolidated Workpapers (3-tier)
Year 2

	Company R	Company T	Adjustments & Eliminations		Consolidated
INCOME STATEMENT					
Revenue					
Sales	200,000	200,000			400,000
Income from Subsidiary	24,300		[4]24,300		
Total Revenue	224,300	200,000			400,000
Costs and Expenses					
Cost of Goods Sold	130,000	145,000			275,000
Selling Expenses	22,000	15,000			37,000
General Expenses	18,000	13,000			31,000
Amortization of Patent			[b]6,250		6,250
Total Costs and Expenses	170,000	173,000			349,250
					50,750
Minority Interest in Income [10% of ($27,000 − $6,250)]			[5]2,075		2,075
Net Income	54,300	27,000			48,675
RETAINED EARNINGS					
Balance (1/1)—R	82,000		[2]5,625		76,375
Balance (1/1)—T		60,000	[4]54,000 [2]625 [5]5,375		
Net Income	54,300	27,000			48,675
Total	136,300	87,000			125,050
Less: Dividends—R	25,000				25,000
Dividends—T		20,000		[5]2,000 [4]18,000	
Balance (12/31)	111,300	67,000			100,050
BALANCE SHEET					
Assets					
Current Assets	79,500	95,000			174,500
Investment in T Corp.	172,800			[4]172,800	
Depreciable Assets—net	180,000	80,000			260,000
Land		25,000			25,000
Patent			[1]25,000	[2]6,250 [b]6,250	12,500
Total Assets	432,300	200,000			472,000
Equities					
Liabilities	121,000	33,000			154,000
Capital Stock—R	200,000				200,000
Retained Earnings—R	111,300				100,050
Capital Stock—T		100,000	[5]10,000 [4]90,000		
Retained Earnings—T		67,000			
Appraisal Capital—T			[5]2,500 [4]22,500	[1]25,000	
Minority Interest				[5]17,950	17,950
Total Equities	432,300	200,000			472,000

6.10 PURCHASE OF 90% OF SUBSIDIARY'S STOCK— INVESTMENT GREATER THAN BOOK VALUE, YEAR 2, ALTERNATIVE

When the investment account is maintained on the equity basis, some firms recognize only that portion of the subsidiary's gains and losses which would accrue to the parent company after intercompany relationships and adjustments have been recognized. It is thought that this makes the change in the investment account more realistic.

EXAMPLE 8. This example is based on the same transactions and events as those in Example 7. However, it is now assumed that the R Corp. recognized all pertinent parent-subsidiary relationships when recording the parent's share of subsidiary income. Specifically, the R Corp. reduced T's reported earnings in Years 1 and 2 by $6,250 each year (the annual amortization of patent) before recording 90 percent of the balance as the parent's share of the subsidiary's increase in equity.

The worksheets that follow are similar to those in the previous example but fewer adjustments are now required because the parent had, in effect, made some adjustments in recording income from subsidiary. Explanations will be found at the foot of the respective worksheet.

The investment and the retained earnings accounts as they would appear in the parent's ledger are summarized as follows:

Investment in T Corp.—Stock

	Dr.	Cr.	Balance
1/1, Yr. 1 Cost of Stock	157,500		157,500
Year 1 Dividends from T		9,000	148,500
12/31, Yr. 1 Share of T's Net Income:			
90% ($20,000 − $6,250)	12,375		160,875
Year 2 Dividends from T		18,000	142,875
12/31, Yr. 2 Share of T's Net Income:			
90% ($27,000 − $6,250)	18,675		161,550

Retained Earnings

	Dr.	Cr.	Balance
1/1, Yr. 1 Balance		60,000	60,000
Year 1 Dividends Declared	15,000		45,000
12/31, Yr. 1 Net Income:			
Own Operations	19,000		
Subsidiary	12,375	31,375	76,375
Year 2 Dividends Declared	25,000		51,375
12/31, Yr. 2 Net Income:			
Own Operations	30,000		
Subsidiary	18,675	48,675	100,050

R Corp. and Subsidiary
Worksheet—Consolidated Income Statement
Year 2

	R Corp.		T Corp.		Eliminations		Consolidated	
	Dr.	Cr.	Dr.	Cr.	Dr.	Cr.	Dr.	Cr.
Sales		200,000		200,000				400,000
Cost of Goods Sold	130,000		145,000				275,000	
Selling Expenses	22,000		15,000				37,000	
General Expenses	18,000		13,000				31,000	
Income from Subsidiary		18,675			[b]18,675			
	170,000	218,675	173,000	200,000				
Net Income—R	48,675						48,675	
Net Income—T			27,000			{ [b]20,750 [a]6,250		
	218,675	218,675	200,000	200,000				
Amortization of Patent					[a]6,250		6,250	
Minority Interest					[b]2,075		2,075	
							400,000	400,000

[a] To amortize patent for one year: 25% of $25,000.

[b] To allocate net income of T Corp. as adjusted.

R Corp. and Subsidiary
Worksheet—Consolidated Balance Sheet
December 31, Year 2

	R Corp.		T Corp.		Eliminations		Consolidated	
	Dr.	Cr.	Dr.	Cr.	Dr.	Cr.	Dr.	Cr.
Current Assets	79,500		95,000				174,500	
Investment in T Corp.—Stock	161,550					[3]161,550		
Depreciable Assets—net	180,000		80,000				260,000	
Land			25,000				25,000	
Patent					25,000	{ [2]6,250 [a]6,250	12,500	
Liabilities		121,000		33,000				154,000
Capital Stock—R		200,000						200,000
Retained Earnings (1/1)—R		76,375						76,375
Net Income—R		48,675						48,675
Dividends—R	25,000						25,000	
Capital Stock—T				100,000	{ [4]10,000 [3]90,000			
Retained Earnings (1/1)—T				60,000	{ [4]5,375 [3]48,375 [2]6,250			
Net Income—T				27,000	{ [4]2,075 [3]18,675 [b]6,250			
Dividends—T			20,000			{ [4]2,000 [3]18,000		
	446,050	446,050	220,000	220,000				
Appraisal Capital					{ [4]2,500 [3]22,500	[1]25,000		
Minority Interest						[4]17,950		17,950
							497,000	497,000

[1] To record value of patent: $25,000 as of Jan. 1, Yr. 1.

[2] To record effect of amortization of patent in prior year.

[3] To eliminate 90% of shareholders' equity in T Corp. as of Dec. 31, Yr. 2.

[4] To classify 10% interest of minority shareholders.

Summary

(1) When an investment account is maintained on the equity basis, dividends received by the parent should be credited to the _____ account.

(2) In consolidating income statements of a parent and a subsidiary, _____ revenue should be eliminated.

(3) In a consolidated statement of retained earnings, the dividends of only the _____ corporation should be deducted.

(4) The realization criterion is not considered applicable when the investment account is maintained on the _____ method.

(5) When following the equity method, all cash dividends received by the parent are treated as if they were _____ dividends.

(6) The equity method refers to a situation where the parent company adjusts the _____ account for its share of changes in the subsidiary's equity.

(7) The equity method is based on the concept that accounting for an investment in a _____ should be similar to accounting for an investment in a branch.

(8) A parent company recognizes its share of the net income of a subsidiary by debiting its _____ account and crediting an appropriate revenue account.

(9) The initial debit entry to the parent's investment is based on the _____ of the subsidiary stock acquired.

(10) In general the _____ method is preferred for those subsidiaries which are not consolidated.

(11) An 80 percent owned subsidiary earned $40,000 in the first year after affiliation and paid dividends of $10,000. The investment should be increased by $_____ under the equity method.

Answers: (1) investment; (2) intercompany; (3) parent; (4) equity; (5) liquidating; (6) investment; (7) subsidiary; (8) investment; (9) cost; (10) equity; (11) $24,000

Solved Problems

6.1 The shareholders' equity of the Pack Corp. and its 90 percent owned subsidiary are as follows at the beginning of 19X1:

	Pack Corp.	Bark Corp.
Capital Stock, $10 par	$700,000	$500,000
Amounts Paid-in in Excess of Par	100,000	200,000
Retained Earnings	90,000	100,000
	$890,000	$800,000

AFTER DATE OF ACQUISITION: EQUITY METHOD

The Pack Corp. purchased 90 percent of the stock of Bark Corp. on January 2, 19X1, for $820,000. During the next two years Bark's net income and dividends paid were as follows:

	19X1	19X2
Net Income	$60,000	$ 5,000
Dividends Declared (and paid)	50,000	30,000

The parent company had recorded the investment on January 1, 19X1 by means of the following entry:

Investment in Bark Corp.—Stock	720,000	
Excess of Cost Over Fair Value		
of Interest in Subsidiary	100,000	
Cash		820,000

The investment account is maintained on the equity method. The excess of cost of investment in subsidiary over 90 percent of its fair value is being amortized over 20 years.

Required:

(a) Show how the investment account would appear on the parent's books for the two years ended December 31, 19X2.

(b) In connection with the investment in the Bark Corp., what balances, if any, should appear in a consolidated balance sheet as of this date?

SOLUTION

(a) *Investment in Bark Corp.—Stock*

	Dr.	Cr.	Balance
1/2/X1 Cost—90% of Bark Stock	720,000		720,000
19X1 90% of Dividends		45,000	675,000
12/31/X1 90% of Net Income	54,000		729,000
19X2 90% of Dividends		27,000	702,000
12/31/X2 90% of Net Income	4,500		706,500

(b) Consolidated balance sheet will include:

Assets: Noncurrent

Excess of Cost over Fair Value		
of Interest in Subsidiary	$100,000	
Less: Amortization (2 years at		
$5,000 per year)	10,000	
		$90,000

6.2 The Fab Corp. purchased 80 percent of the outstanding stock of the Cate Corp. on January 2, 19X3, for $180,000 cash. On that date the net assets recorded on the books of Cate amounted to $200,000, the par value of its stock was $150,000, and the retained earnings amounted to $50,000. The excess above book value paid by Fab was considered an indication of goodwill belonging to Cate. The goodwill of Cate was immediately recorded in its books and has been amortized at the rate of 10 percent per year.

In 19X3, Cate earned $57,500 and paid dividends of $6,000. In 19X4, Cate reported a net loss of $12,500 and paid dividends amounting to $3,000.

Required:

(a) Prepare the investment account as it should appear on the books of Fab Corp.

(b) Prepare adjusting and elimination entries for the worksheet to prepare a consolidated balance sheet, as of: (1) December 31, 19X3; and (2) December 31, 19X4.

SOLUTION

(a)   *Investment in Cate Corp.—Stock*

			Dr.	*Cr.*	*Balance*
1/2/X3	Cost—80% of Stock		180,000		180,000
19X3	Dividends (80% of $6,000)			4,800	175,200
12/31/X3	Net Income (80% of $57,500)		46,000		221,200
19X4	Dividends (80% of $3,000)			2,400	218,800
12/31/X4	Net Loss (80% of $12,500)			10,000	208,800

(b) 1.   *Worksheet Entries, Dec. 31, 19X3*

Capital Stock—Cate	150,000	
Retained Earnings (1/1/X3) Cate	50,000	
Appraisal Capital—Cate	25,000*	
Net Income—Cate	57,500	
Dividends Declared—Cate		6,000
Investment in Cate		221,200
Minority Interest [20% of $276,500]		55,300

2.   *Worksheet Entries, Dec. 31, 19X4*

Capital Stock—Cate	150,000	
Retained Earnings (1/1/X4)—Cate		
[$50,000 + $57,500 − $6,000]	101,500	
Appraisal Capital	25,000	
Net Income (Loss)—Cate		12,500
Dividends Declared—Cate		3,000
Investment in Cate		208,800
Minority Interest [20% of $261,000]		52,200

---

*Calculation of Appraisal Capital (Goodwill):

Total value of Cate, 1/1/X3, $180,000 ÷ 80% =	$225,000
Recorded net assets of Cate	200,000
Goodwill as of 1/1/X3	$ 25,000

6.3 The Fab Corp. purchased 80 percent of the outstanding stock of the Cate Corp. on January 2, 19X3, for $180,000. On that date the net assets of Cate were $200,000, and its statement disclosed that the par value of the outstanding stock was $150,000 and the retained earnings were $50,000. Any excess above book value paid by Fab was an indication of goodwill belonging to Cate.

In 19X3, Cate reported net income of $60,000 and paid dividends of $6,000. In 19X4, Cate reported a net loss of $10,000 and paid dividends of $3,000.

The Fab Corp. maintains its investment account on the equity method. Goodwill of the subsidiary has been amortized in the consolidated workpapers at the rate of 10 percent per annum; that is, goodwill had not been recorded on the books of the subsidiary.

Required:

(a) Prepare the investment account as it might appear on the books of Fab Corp. on December 31, 19X4.

(b) Prepare adjusting and elimination entries for a worksheet to consolidate the balance sheets as of December 31, 19X3.

(c) Prepare adjusting and elimination entries for a worksheet to consolidate the balance sheets as of December 31, 19X4.

SOLUTION

(a)   *Investment in Cate Corp.—Stock*

		Dr.	Cr.	Balance
1/2/X3	Cost—80% of Stock	180,000		180,000
19X3	Dividends (80% of $6,000)		4,800	175,200
12/31/X3	Net Income (80% of $60,000)	48,000		223,200
19X4	Dividends (80% of $3,000)		2,400	220,800
12/31/X4	Net Loss (80% of $10,000)		8,000	212,800

(b)   *Worksheet Entries, Dec. 31, 19X3*

Goodwill*	25,000	
Appraisal Capital—Cate		25,000
Net Income—Cate	2,500	
Goodwill		2,500
Net Income—Fab [80% of $2,500]	2,000	
Investment in Cate		2,000
Capital Stock—Cate	150,000	
Retained Earnings (1/1/X3)—Cate	50,000	
Appraisal Capital—Cate	25,000	
Net Income—Cate [$60,000 − $2,500]	57,500	
Dividends Declared—Cate		6,000
Investment in Cate [$223,200 − $2,000]		221,200
Minority Interest [20% of $276,500]		55,300

---

*Calculation of Goodwill:

Total value of Cate, 1/1/X3, $180,000 ÷ 80% =	$225,000
Recorded net assets of Cate	200,000
Goodwill as of 1/1/X3	$ 25,000

(c)   *Worksheet Entries, Dec. 31, 19X4*

Goodwill	25,000	
Appraisal Capital—Cate		25,000
Retained Earnings (1/1/X4)—Cate	2,500	
Net Income (Loss)—Cate	2,500	
Goodwill		5,000
Retained Earnings (1/1/X4)—Fab [80% of $2,500]	2,000	
Net Income—Fab [80% of $2,500]	2,000	
Investment in Cate		4,000
Capital Stock—Cate	150,000	
Retained Earnings (1/1/X4)—Cate		
($50,000 + $60,000 − $6,000 − $2,500)	101,500	
Appraisal Capital—Cate	25,000	
Dividends Declared—Cate		3,000
Net Income (Loss)—Cate [$10,000 + $2,500]		12,500
Investment in Cate [$212,800 − $4,000]		208,800
Minority Interest [20% of $261,000]		52,200

6.4 The Farrell Corp. purchased 7,500 shares of the voting common stock of the Toy Co., Inc., as of January 2, 19X3, for $210,000 in cash and notes. The following condensed trial balances are available as of December 31, 19X3.

	Farrell Corp.		Toy Co., Inc.	
Current Assets	$104,000		$ 16,000	
Investment in Toy Co.—Stock	240,000			
Depreciable Assets—net	87,000		91,000	
Land	33,000		100,000	
Building Site			90,000	
Liabilities		$ 97,000		$ 17,000
Capital Stock—$20 par		200,000		200,000
Retained Earnings, Jan. 1		128,000		40,000
Dividends Declared	40,000		20,000	
Sales		236,000		222,000
Income from Subsidiary		45,000		
Cost of Goods Sold	174,000		130,000	
Operating Expenses	26,000		32,000	
Interest Expense	2,000			
	$706,000	$706,000	$479,000	$479,000

The chief purpose of the acquisition was to gain control of a building site which Toy owned that was contiguous to Farrell's plant.

Required:

Complete the worksheet(s) to consolidate:

(*a*) income statements for 19X3;

(*b*) balance sheets as of December 31, 19X3.

(a)

Farrell Corp. and Subsidiary
Worksheet—Consolidated Income Statement
Year 19X3

	Farrell Corp.		Toy Co., Inc.		Eliminations		Consolidated	
	Dr.	Cr.	Dr.	Cr.	Dr.	Cr.	Dr.	Cr.
Sales		236,000		222,000				
Cost of Goods Sold	174,000		130,000					
Interest Expense	2,000							
Operating Expenses	26,000		32,000					
Income from Subsidiary		45,000						
	202,000	281,000	162,000	222,000				
Net Income—Farrell	79,000							
Net Income—Toy			60,000					
	281,000	281,000	222,000	222,000				

(b)

Farrell Corp. and Subsidiary
Worksheet—Consolidated Balance Sheet
December 31, 19X3

	Farrell Corp.		Toy Co., Inc.		Eliminations		Consolidated	
	Dr.	Cr.	Dr.	Cr.	Dr.	Cr.	Dr.	Cr.
Current Assets	104,000		16,000					
Investment in Toy	240,000							
Depreciable Assets—net	87,000		91,000					
Land	33,000		100,000					
Building Site			90,000					
Liabilities		97,000		17,000				
Capital Stock—F		200,000						
Retained Earnings (1/1)—F		128,000						
Net Income—F		79,000						
Dividends Declared—F	40,000							
Capital Stock—T				200,000				
Retained Earnings (1/1)—T				40,000				
Net Income—T				60,000				
Dividends Declared—T			20,000					
	504,000	504,000	317,000	317,000				

SOLUTION
(a)

Farrell Corp. and Subsidiary
Worksheet—Consolidated Income Statement
Year 19X3

	Farrell Corp.		Toy Co., Inc.		Eliminations		Consolidated	
	Dr.	Cr.	Dr.	Cr.	Dr.	Cr.	Dr.	Cr.
Sales		236,000		222,000				458,000
Cost of Goods Sold	174,000		130,000				304,000	
Interest Expense	2,000						2,000	
Operating Expenses	26,000		32,000				58,000	
Income from Subsidiary		45,000			[a]45,000			
	202,000	281,000	162,000	222,000				
Net Income—Farrell	79,000				[b]45,000	[a]45,000	79,000	
Net Income—Toy			60,000			[b]60,000		
	281,000	281,000	222,000	222,000				
Minority Interest						[b]15,000	15,000	
							458,000	458,000

[a] To eliminate income from subsidiary previously recorded by parent.
[b] To allocate net income of subsidiary; 75% to parent and 25% to minority.

(b)

Farrell Corp. and Subsidiary
Worksheet—Consolidated Balance Sheet
December 31, 19X3

	Farrell Corp.		Toy Co., Inc.		Eliminations		Consolidated	
	Dr.	Cr.	Dr.	Cr.	Dr.	Cr.	Dr.	Cr.
Current Assets	104,000		16,000				120,000	
Investment in Toy Co.	240,000					[2]240,000		
Depreciable Assets—net	87,000		91,000				178,000	
Land	33,000		100,000				133,000	
Building Site			90,000		[1]40,000		130,000	
Liabilities		97,000		17,000				114,000
Capital Stock—F		200,000						200,000
Retained Earnings (1/1)—F		128,000						128,000
Net Income—F		79,000						79,000
Dividends Declared—F	40,000						40,000	
Capital Stock—T				200,000	[3]50,000 [2]150,000			
Retained Earnings (1/1)—T				40,000	[3]10,000 [2]30,000			
Net Income—T				60,000	[3]15,000 [2]45,000			
Dividends Declared—T			20,000			[3]5,000 [2]15,000		
	504,000	504,000	317,000	317,000				
Appraisal Capital—T					[3]10,000 [2]30,000	[1]40,000		
Minority Interest						[3]80,000		80,000
							601,000	601,000

[1] To assign excess of cost of investment over book value to building site based on price paid for 75% of stock of subsidiary: $210,000 − (75% of $240,000) = $30,000. Increment to building site = $40,000 ($30,000 ÷ 75%).
[2] To eliminate 75% of shareholders' equity as of Dec. 31, 19X3.
[3] To classify 25% interest of minority shareholders as of Dec. 31, 19X3.

ALTERNATE SOLUTION
(b)

Farrell Corp. and Subsidiary
Worksheet—Consolidated Balance Sheet
December 31, 19X3

	Farrell Corp.		Toy Co., Inc.		Eliminations		Balance Sheet	
	Dr.	Cr.	Dr.	Cr.	Dr.	Cr.	Dr.	Cr.
Current Assets	104,000		16,000				120,000	
Investment in Toy Co.	240,000					{²210,000 ¹30,000		
Depreciable Assets—net	87,000		91,000				178,000	
Land	33,000		100,000				133,000	
Building Site			90,000		¹30,000		120,000	
Liabilities		97,000		17,000				114,000
Capital Stock—F		200,000						200,000
Retained Earnings (1/1)—F		128,000						128,000
Net Income—F		79,000						79,000
Dividends—F	40,000						40,000	
Capital Stock—T				200,000	{³50,000 ²150,000			
Retained Earnings (1/1)—T				40,000	{³10,000 ²30,000			
Net Income—T				60,000	{³15,000 ²45,000			
Dividends Declared—T			20,000			{³5,000 ²15,000		
	504,000	504,000	317,000	317,000				
Minority Interest						³70,000		70,000
							591,000	591,000

¹ To assign excess of cost of investment over book value to building site: $30,000 ($210,000 − $180,000)
² To eliminate 75% of shareholders' equity as of Dec. 31, 19X3.
³ To classify 25% interest of minority shareholders as of Dec. 31, 19X3.

6.5   The Bart Corp. purchased four investments on January 2, 19X3, with costs as follows:

> 90% of the voting stock of W Corp. $280,000
> 80% of the voting stock of X Corp.   120,000
> 70% of the voting stock of Y Corp.   64,000
> 30% of the voting stock of Z Corp.   50,000

The investment accounts are carried on the equity basis.
Additional data concerning these corporations are contained in the following schedule.

	Bart	W	X	Y	Z
Capital Stock—$10 par	$400,000	$200,000	$50,000	$40,000	$50,000
Retained Earnings— Jan. 1, 19X3	200,000	100,000	40,000	20,000	40,000
Net Income—19X3	170,000	80,000	40,000		40,000
Net Loss—19X3				10,000	
Dividends—19X3	20,000	10,000	8,000		

Required:

(a) Write summary journal entries on the books of Bart Corp. to reflect its transactions with or interest in W, X, Y, and Z corporations.

(b) Determine the consolidated net income for year 19X3 and the net income (or loss) of Bart Corp. from its own operations.

(c) Determine the minority interests in net income for year in the subsidiary corporations.

(d) Prepare a schedule of minority interests in the retained earnings of the subsidiary corporations as of December 31, 19X3.

SOLUTION

(a) *Journal entries:*

Investment in W Corp.	280,000	
Investment in X Corp.	120,000	
Investment in Y Corp.	64,000	
Investment in Z Corp.	50,000	
Cash		514,000
Cash	15,400	
Investment in W Corp.		9,000
Investment in X Corp.		6,400
Investment in W Corp.	72,000	
Subsidiary Income		72,000
Investment in X Corp.	32,000	
Subsidiary Income		32,000
Subsidiary Loss	7,000	
Investment in Y Corp.		7,000
Investment in Z Corp.	12,000	
Income from Investments—		
(unconsolidated)		12,000

(b)   Consolidated Net Income

Reported by Bart, 19X3		$170,000
Less: Equity in 19X3 Net Income (Loss) of		
W—90% of $80,000	$72,000	
X—80% of 40,000	32,000	
Y—70% of 10,000 Loss	(7,000)	
Z—30% of 40,000	12,000	109,000
Net Income from Bart's Own Operations		$ 61,000

(c)   Minority Interests in Subsidiary Income, 19X3

W—10% of $80,000	$8,000
X—20% of 40,000	8,000
Y—30% of 10,000 Loss	(3,000)
Z—(not a subsidiary)	—
Total Minority Interest in Income	$13,000

(d)

Co.	Retained Earnings 1/1/X3	Net Income (Loss) 19X3	Dividends 19X3	Retained Earnings 12/31/X3	Minority Interests %	Minority Interests Amount
W	$100,000	$80,000	$10,000	$170,000	10	$17,000
X	40,000	40,000	8,000	72,000	20	14,400
Y	20,000	(10,000)	—	10,000	30	3,000
Z	(Not a subsidiary)					
Total Minority Interests in Retained Earnings						$34,400

Chapter 7

Consolidated Statements—
Intercompany Sales and Services

7.1 INTRODUCTION

Affiliated corporations frequently engage in transactions with one another. When completed, these transactions are properly reported in each company's books and statements. However, when consolidated statements are prepared, the effects of most intercompany transactions must be eliminated or, perhaps, modified in order to present the consolidated statements from the point of view of a single economic entity.

Sales, services, and other transactions between a home office and a branch of one company are generally eliminated in order to present a combined statement for the company. Likewise, sales, services, and other transactions between two or more affiliates are eliminated in preparing consolidated statements. Frequently, transactions that may be considered as completed by one company or that result in realized income by one company may be considered incomplete or not realized when a consolidated viewpoint is adopted.

7.2 INTERCOMPANY REVENUE AND EXPENSE

One of the common goals of affiliation is the corporation's ability to specialize beyond those limits which might otherwise not be considered prudent. For example, an affiliate might specialize in marketing, manufacturing, holding of real estate, research, or some other service activity. Sometimes the sole activity of an affiliate is to provide goods or services to another affiliate.

EXAMPLE 1. P Corp. purchased 90 percent of the outstanding stock of S Corp. on January 1, Year 1, for $135,000. The balance sheets of the two corporations immediately following the investment by P Corp. are as follows:

	P Corp.	S Corp.
Current Assets	$ 65,000	$ 55,000
Investment in S Corp. Stock	135,000	
Depreciable Assets—net	200,000	100,000
Land		25,000
Total Assets	$400,000	$180,000
Liabilities	$140,000	$ 30,000
Capital Stock	200,000	100,000
Retained Earnings	60,000	50,000
Total Liabilities and Shareholders' Equity	$400,000	$180,000

The respective balance sheets at the end of Year 1 are included in the first four columns of the accompanying worksheet to consolidate the balance sheets at the end of Year 1.

The investment account on the parent's books, which is kept on the equity basis, is summarized as follows:

Investment in S Corp.—Stock

Date	Dr.	Cr.	Balance
1/1, Yr. 1 Cost	135,000		135,000
Year 1 Dividends		9,000	126,000
12/31, Yr. 1 Net Income of S (90%)	18,000		144,000

The results of operations for the first twelve months after affiliation are condensed as follows:

	P Corp.	S Corp.
Sales	$120,000	$109,000
Rent Income		7,000
Income from Subsidiary	18,000	
Total Revenue	$138,000	$116,000
Cost of Goods Sold	$ 70,000	$ 75,000
Selling Expenses	16,000	12,000
General Expenses	15,000	9,000
Total Costs and Expenses	$101,000	$ 96,000
Net Income	$ 37,000	$ 20,000

The schedule of retained earnings for the above twelve-month period is as follows:

	P Corp.	S Corp.
Balance, January 1	$60,000	$50,000
Add: Net Income	37,000	20,000
Total	$97,000	$70,000
Less: Dividends	15,000	10,000
Balance, December 31	$82,000	$60,000

The general expenses of P Corp. include $7,000 rent for premises leased from S Corp. During Year 1, P paid $5,000 to S, and $2,000 is included in P's liabilities at the end of the year. In the worksheet to prepare a consolidated income statement for Year 1 (p. 186), the intercompany expense and revenue are eliminated by entry (a). In general journal form, the entry is as follows:

Rent Income—S	7,000	
General Expenses—P		7,000

It should be observed that the effect of this entry is to restate the income and expenses of the two corporations as if they constituted one economic entity. However, this elimination does not in itself affect the consolidated net income. Entry (b) eliminates the income from subsidiary which had been previously recorded by the parent. Entry (c) allocates the net income of the subsidiary between the parent and the minority interests in the ratio of their stockholdings (90:10).

In the worksheet to prepare a consolidated balance sheet, entry (1) eliminates the intercompany receivables and payables. In general journal form, the entry is as follows:

Liabilities	2,000	
Current Assets		2,000

Entry (2) eliminates 90 percent of the subsidiary's capital stock and retained earnings against the balance of the investment account. Entry (3) classifies the 10 percent interest of the minority stockholders.

Cost Method

P Corp. and Subsidiary
Worksheet—Consolidated Income Statement
Year 1

	P Corp.		S Corp.		Eliminations		Consolidated	
	Dr.	Cr.	Dr.	Cr.	Dr.	Cr.	Dr.	Cr.
Sales		120,000		109,000				229,000
Cost of Goods Sold	70,000		75,000				145,000	
Selling Expenses	16,000		12,000				28,000	
General Expenses	15,000		9,000			[a]7,000	17,000	
Rent Income				7,000	[a]7,000			
Income from Subsidiary		18,000			[b]18,000			
	101,000	138,000	96,000	116,000				
Net Income—P	37,000				[c]18,000	[b]18,000	37,000	
Net Income—S			20,000			[c]20,000		
	138,000	138,000	116,000	116,000				
Minority Interest					[c]2,000		2,000	
							229,000	229,000

[a] To eliminate intercompany rent.
[b] To eliminate intercompany income.
[c] To allocate net income of S Corp.

Cost Method

P Corp. and Subsidiary
Worksheet—Consolidated Balance Sheet
December 31, Year 1

	P Corp.		S Corp.		Eliminations		Consolidated	
	Dr.	Cr.	Dr.	Cr.	Dr.	Cr.	Dr.	Cr.
Current Assets	103,000		56,000			[1]2,000	157,000	
Investment in S Corp.	144,000					[2]144,000		
Depreciable Assets—net	190,000		110,000				300,000	
Land			25,000				25,000	
Liabilities		155,000		31,000	[1]2,000			184,000
Capital Stock—P		200,000						200,000
Retained Earnings (1/1)—P		60,000						60,000
Net Income—P		37,000						37,000
Dividends—P	15,000						15,000	
Capital Stock—S				100,000	[3]10,000 [2]90,000			
Retained Earnings (1/1)—S				50,000	[3]5,000 [2]45,000			
Net Income—S				20,000	[3]2,000 [2]18,000			
Dividends—S			10,000			[3]1,000 [2]9,000		
	452,000	452,000	201,000	201,000				
Minority Interest						[3]16,000		16,000
							497,000	497,000

[1] To eliminate intercompany receivable and payable.
[2] To eliminate 90% of subsidiary's capital stock and retained earnings as of Dec. 31, Yr. 1.
[3] To classify the 10% interest of the minority stockholders as of Dec. 31, Yr. 1.

7.3 INTERCOMPANY SALES AND PURCHASES

Merchandise is often transferred between affiliates for resale, for further processing, or for use in the purchaser's business. Each company would normally record the purchase or sale in the same manner as transfers to or from outsiders. The price to affiliates may be the same as those to third parties or it may be the result of special negotiations. Regardless of the pricing mechanism, all intercompany movements of goods and the effects thereof must be eliminated when preparing consolidated statements. If any goods acquired from an affiliate remain unsold at a statement date, the mark-up above cost should be considered as unrealized profit to the seller. The excess above cost should be considered realized, or confirmed, only when the goods have been resold to outsiders, directly or indirectly. Thus, for consolidation purposes, such goods on hand should be reduced to the cost to the vendor. However, items like intercompany freight, which bring the goods closer to the point of sale, may be included in the consolidated cost.

Sales by one affiliate may include items which are used by the purchasing affiliate for selling, manufacturing, or other purposes. Thus, the transfer price may appear in an expense or asset account of the transferee. If the items are still on hand at statement date, the elimination entry will have to take them into account. The remainder of this chapter will be devoted to transfers of merchandise for resale; transfers of machinery, land, etc., will be considered in the next chapter.

7.4 INTERCOMPANY PROFIT—MERCHANDISE (YEAR 1): COST METHOD

The general rule for merchandise owned by an affiliate is that all intercompany profit is eliminated from inventory on hand, and a like amount is eliminated from the profit of the affiliate which sold the goods.

Assume that F sold merchandise which cost it $60,000 to a wholly owned subsidiary H for $100,000. The records of Company F indicate a gross profit of $40,000. Company H sold 80 percent of these goods for $105,000; thus goods which cost H $20,000 remain in its inventory at the end of the fiscal period. These data are abbreviated in the schedule that follows:

	Company F		Company H	
Sales		$100,000		$105,000
Purchases	XXXX		$100,000	
Less: Inventory at End	XXXX		20,000	
Cost of Goods Sold		60,000		80,000
Gross Profit		$ 40,000		$ 25,000

From a consolidated point of view, the sales to be reported are the sales to outsiders, or $105,000, and the consolidated cost of goods sold amounts to $48,000 (80 percent of $60,000). Thus the consolidated gross profit is $57,000 ($105,000 − $48,000).

The ending inventory of H consists entirely of goods which were purchased from F at a price of $20,000. Company F data indicates a gross profit ratio of 40 percent on its sales ($40,000 ÷ $100,000). Thus there is $8,000 (40 percent of $20,000) of gross profit in the inventory which H owns at the end of the fiscal year. This amount must be eliminated from the individual statements in order to prepare consolidated statements.

An alternate calculation of the unrealized gross profit to be eliminated may be based on the cost percentage of the seller. Company F's cost is 60 percent of its selling price ($60,000 ÷ $100,000). Applying this percentage to H's ending inventory, the unrecovered cost is $12,000 (60 percent of $20,000). The recorded cost of $20,000 less the cost to the vendee of $12,000 yields $8,000 as the gross profit to be eliminated.

EXAMPLE 2.   B Corp. purchased 9,000 shares of stock of Q Corp. on January 1, Year 1, for $162,000. At that date, Q Corp. had 10,000 shares of stock outstanding, each with a par of $10, and accumulated profits retained in the business of $80,000.

The results of operations of the two corporations for the first year of affiliation are summarized in the accompanying worksheet to prepare a consolidated income statement for Year 1. During the year, B Corp. sold merchandise to Q Corp. amounting to $100,000. At the end of Year 1, $20,000 of these goods remain in the inventory of Q Corp. The dividend income received by B Corp. was the result of distributions by Q Corp. During Year 1, Q Corp. had paid B for all intercompany purchases.

In the worksheet to prepare a consolidated income statement, entry (a) eliminates the intercompany movement of goods: sales by B and purchases by Q. Assume that B sold all goods at a gross profit of 25 percent ($75,000* ÷ $300,000); the merchandise that Q owns, which had been purchased from its parent company, includes $5,000 (25 percent of $20,000) of unrealized gross profit from a consolidated viewpoint. This is eliminated in entry (b), which reduces the merchandise inventory of Q and the net income of B. Until these goods are resold, no gross profit is deemed to be realized by the affiliated group. No adjustment is needed for other merchandise which B had sold to Q, as these goods had been resold to outsiders and the profits are considered to have been realized, or confirmed, to the consolidated group. Entry (c) eliminates the intercompany dividend, and entry (d) allocates the net income of Q between the parent company and the minority interests in proportion to their holdings of Q stock.

The balance sheets of B Corp. and of Q Corp. at the end of Year 1 are condensed in the first four columns of the worksheet to prepare a consolidated balance sheet. Entry (b) reduces the ending inventory of Q by the unrealized gross profit of $5,000. Entry (b) also reduces the net income of B by the same amount. Again, for consolidation purposes this amount is not considered earned until the goods are resold to third parties. Entry (c) now allocates the dividends paid by the subsidiary, between the parent company and the minority interests in proportion to their stockholdings (90:10). Entry (d) allocates the net income of Q in the same ratio.

Entry (1) in the worksheet to consolidate the balance sheets at the end of Year 1 eliminates the cost of the investment in Q Corp. against 90 percent of the shareholders' equity of Q Corp. as of January 1, Year 1. Entry (2) classifies the remaining 10 percent of the shareholders' equity as the minority interest as of the beginning of the year.

* Sales	$300,000	100%
Cost of Goods Sold	225,000	75%
Gross Profit	$ 75,000	25%

Cost Method

B Corp. and Subsidiary
Worksheet—Consolidated Income Statement
Year 1

	B Corp.		Q Corp.		Eliminations		Consolidated	
	Dr.	Cr.	Dr.	Cr.	Dr.	Cr.	Dr.	Cr.
Sales		300,000		200,000	ª100,000			400,000
Merchandise Inventory (1/1)	70,000		10,000				80,000	
Purchases	240,000		195,000			ª100,000	335,000	
Merchandise Inventory (12/31)		85,000		50,000	ᵇ5,000			130,000
Selling Expenses	27,000		12,000				39,000	
General Expenses	30,000		19,000				49,000	
Income from Dividends		9,000			ᶜ9,000			
	367,000	394,000	236,000	250,000				
Net Income—B	27,000				ᵈ12,600	{ᶜ9,000 ᵇ5,000}	25,600	
Net Income—Q			14,000			ᵈ14,000		
	394,000	394,000	250,000	250,000				
Minority Interest					ᵈ1,400		1,400	
							530,000	530,000

ª To eliminate intercompany purchases and sales.
ᵇ To eliminate unrealized profit in final inventory of Q (25% of $20,000).
ᶜ To eliminate intercompany dividend.
ᵈ To allocate net income of Q Corp.

Cost Method

B Corp. and Subsidiary
Worksheet—Consolidated Balance Sheet
December 31, Year 1

	B Corp.		Q Corp.		Eliminations		Consolidated	
	Dr.	Cr.	Dr.	Cr.	Dr.	Cr.	Dr.	Cr.
Accounts Receivable	103,000		98,000				201,000	
Merchandise Inventory	85,000		50,000			[b]5,000	130,000	
Other Current Assets	17,000		28,000				45,000	
Investment in Q Corp. [cost]	162,000					[1]162,000		
Depreciable Assets—net	88,000		70,000				158,000	
Accounts Payable		57,000		44,000				101,000
Other Liabilities		22,000		18,000				40,000
Capital Stock, $10 par—B		250,000						250,000
Retained Earnings (1/1)—B		111,000						111,000
Net Income—B		27,000			[c]9,000 [b]5,000	[d]12,600		25,600
Dividends—B	12,000						12,000	
Capital Stock, $10 par—Q				100,000	[2]10,000 [1]90,000			
Retained Earnings (1/1)—Q				80,000	[2]8,000 [1]72,000			
Net Income—Q				14,000	[d]14,000			
Dividends—Q			10,000			[c]10,000		
	467,000	467,000	256,000	256,000				
Minority Interest					[c]1,000	[2]18,000 [d]1,400		18,400
							546,000	546,000

[1] To eliminate 90% of subsidiary's capital stock and retained earnings as of Jan. 1, Yr. 1.
[2] To classify the 10% interest of the minority stockholders as of Jan. 1, Yr. 1.

7.5 INTERCOMPANY PROFIT—MERCHANDISE (YEAR 2): COST METHOD

EXAMPLE 3. Example 3 is a continuation of the previous example into Year 2. The results of operation of B Corp. and Q Corp. are condensed in the first four columns of the accompanying worksheet to prepare a consolidated income statement for Year 2 (p. 190). Entry (a) eliminates sales of $120,000 by B to Q. In general journal form, the entry is as follows:

Sales—B	120,000	
Purchases—Q		120,000

During the second year B achieved a gross profit of 30 percent ($93,000 ÷ $310,000) based on sales. The inventory of Q at December 31, Year 2 included $40,000 of merchandise acquired from B. Applying the gross profit percentage of B to the goods on hand at the end of Year 2 in the inventory of Q, the unrealized gross profit in Q's inventory is $12,000 (30 percent of $40,000). Entry (b) reduces the merchandise inventory at the end of Year 2 and also reduces the net income of B. In general journal form, the entry is as follows:

Merchandise Inventory (12/31)—Q	12,000	
Net Income—B		12,000

The merchandise inventory at the beginning of Year 2, is the same as the ending inventory of Year 1. Thus, worksheet adjustments and eliminations which had been required at the end of Year 1 in connection with this inventory are also required at the beginning of Year 2. In the previous example it was determined that Q's inventory at the end of Year 1 contained $5,000 of gross profit unrealized by B, and a suitable elimination was made in the worksheet. A similar reduction must now be applied to the goods on hand at January 1, Year 2. The opening inventory is a debit balance in the income accounts, thus a reduction of this opening inventory requires a credit to the account balance. The offsetting debit is to the net income of B, the seller. In general journal form, entry (c) is as follows:

Net Income—B	5,000	
Merchandise Inventory (1/1)—Q		5,000

The foregoing credit reduces the cost of goods sold in Year 2, and thus results in an increase in the net income of Year 2. The increase in income is assigned to B because recognition of profit of $5,000 was deferred from Year 1, when the goods had been transferred to an affiliate, to Year 2, when the goods were sold to outsiders. It is reasonable to assume that all of the goods on hand at January 1, Year 2, were sold before the end of Year 2. However, if that were not the case, the unrealized gross profit would have been eliminated again in entry (b).

Entry (d) eliminates the intercompany dividends from Q to B, and entry (e) allocates the net income of Q in proportion to the stockholdings of the parent and minority interests.

The balance sheets at the end of Year 2 are condensed in the first four columns of the accompanying worksheet to prepare a consolidated balance sheet as of that date. Elimination entries bearing letters (b), (c), (d), and (e) are similar to the entries in the worksheet to consolidate the income statements for Year 2, and perform the same functions. However, entry (d) now allocates the entire dividend of Q Corp.

Entry (1) eliminates the intercompany receivable and payable as of the end of Year 2. Entry (2) recognizes the parent's share of the increase in Q's retained earnings from January 1, Year 1 (the date of acquisition of control), to January 1, Year 2. The changes in Q's retained earnings for the current Year 2 are detailed in the worksheet, and no special treatment is required under the cost method. The retained earnings of Q increased during Year 1 from $80,000 to $84,000. Thus, entry (3) increases the investment account by $3,600 (90% of the $4,000 increment). Entry (3) also eliminates 90 percent of the shareholders' equity of Q as of January 1, Year 1. Entry (4) classifies the remaining 10 percent as the minority interest.

Cost Method

B Corp. and Subsidiary
Worksheet—Consolidated Income Statement
Year 2

	B Corp.		Q Corp.		Eliminations		Consolidated	
	Dr.	Cr.	Dr.	Cr.	Dr.	Cr.	Dr.	Cr.
Sales		310,000		240,000	[a]120,000			430,000
Merchandise Inventory (1/1)	85,000		50,000			[c]5,000	130,000	
Purchases	220,000		190,000			[a]120,000	290,000	
Merchandise Inventory (12/31)		88,000		57,000	[b]12,000			133,000
Selling Expenses	28,000		14,000				42,000	
General Expenses	31,000		20,000				51,000	
Income from Dividends		18,000			[d]18,000			
	364,000	416,000	274,000	297,000				
Net Income—B	52,000				[e]20,700 [c]5,000	[d]18,000 [b]12,000	47,700	
Net Income—Q			23,000			[e]23,000		
	416,000	416,000	297,000	297,000				
Minority Interest					[e]2,300		2,300	
							563,000	563,000

[a] To eliminate intercompany purchases and sales.
[b] To eliminate intercompany profit in final inventory of Q; $12,000 (30% of $40,000).
[c] To eliminate intercompany profit in inventory of Q as of Jan. 1, Yr. 2.
[d] To eliminate intercompany dividend.
[e] To allocate net income of Q Corp.

Cost Method

B Corp. and Subsidiary
Worksheet—Consolidated Balance Sheet
December 31, Year 2

	B Corp.		Q Corp.		Eliminations		Consolidated	
	Dr.	Cr.	Dr.	Cr.	Dr.	Cr.	Dr.	Cr.
Accounts Receivable	110,000		101,000			[1]20,000	191,000	
Merchandise Inventory	88,000		57,000			[b]12,000	133,000	
Other Current Assets	36,000		30,000				66,000	
Investment in Q Corp. [cost]	162,000				[2]3,600	[3]165,600		
Depreciable Assets—net	82,000		65,000				147,000	
Accounts Payable		59,000		47,000	[1]20,000			86,000
Other Liabilities		21,000		19,000				40,000
Capital Stock—B		250,000						250,000
Retained Earnings—B		126,000			[c]5,000	[2]3,600		124,600
Net Income—B		52,000			{[d]18,000 [b]12,000	[e]20,700} [c]5,000}		47,700
Dividends—B	30,000						30,000	
Capital Stock—Q				100,000	{[4]10,000 [3]90,000			
Retained Earnings—Q				84,000	{[4]8,400 [3]75,600			
Net Income—Q				23,000	[e]23,000			
Dividends—Q			20,000			[d]20,000		
	508,000	508,000	273,000	273,000				
Minority Interest					[d]2,000	{[4]18,400 [e]2,300}		18,700
							567,000	567,000

[1] To eliminate intercompany receivable and payable.
[2] To add to investment account B's share of growth in Q Corp. during Year 1: 90% of $4,000.
[3] To eliminate 90% of subsidiary's capital stock and retained earnings as of Jan. 1, Yr. 2.
[4] To classify 10% of interest of minority stockholders as of Jan. 1, Yr. 2.

7.6 INTERCOMPANY PROFIT—MERCHANDISE (YEAR 1): EQUITY METHOD

EXAMPLE 4. P Corp. purchased 90 percent of the stock of S Corp. on January 1 of Year 1 for $180,000. On that date the outstanding capital stock of S Corp. was $100,000, and the earnings accumulated in the business were $50,000. The excess amount above the fair value of P's share in the equity of S Corp. was attributed to above-average earnings of the subsidiary.

The S Corp. immediately recorded goodwill in its books by means of the following entry:

Goodwill	50,000	
Appraisal Capital		50,000

The amount of goodwill was ascertained by the following calculation:

Amount Paid by Parent for 90% of S Stock	$180,000	
Fair Value of 100% of S Stock ($180,000 ÷ 90%)		$200,000
Book Value of S Corp.		150,000
Goodwill		$ 50,000

The board of directors decided that the goodwill should be amortized over 20 years and that the straight-line method should be used.

During Year 1, S sold $40,000 of merchandise to P. At the end of the year, P had $15,000 of this merchandise in inventory on which S had recorded a gross profit of $6,000. The accounts payable of P included $10,000 due to S on these goods.

The result of operations for the first year after affiliation are condensed as follows:

	P Corp.	S Corp.
Sales	$120,000	$116,000
Cost of Goods Sold	70,000	75,000
Gross Profit	$ 50,000	$ 41,000
Selling Expenses	$ 16,000	$ 12,000
General Expenses	15,000	9,000
Total Expenses	$ 31,000	$ 21,000
Income from Operations	$ 19,000	$ 20,000
Less: Amortization of Goodwill		2,500
Income from Subsidiary	10,350	
Net Income	$ 29,350	$ 17,500

The income from subsidiary recognized by the parent in its books was determined as follows:

Net Income Reported by S Corp.	$17,500
Less: Unrealized Gross Profit in Unsold Merchandise on Hand at End of Year	6,000
Net Income of S Corp., for Consolidation Purposes	$11,500
Parent's Share—90%	$10,350
Minority Share—10%	$ 1,150

The schedule of retained earnings for Year 1 is summarized as follows:

	P Corp.	S Corp.
Balance, January 1	$ 80,000	$50,000
Add: Net Income	29,350	17,500
Total	$109,350	$67,500
Less: Dividends	15,000	10,000
Balance, December 31	$ 94,350	$57,500

In the worksheet to consolidate the income statements for Year 1 (p. 194), (a) eliminates the intercompany sales and purchases. Entry (b) reduces the net income of S by the amount of the unrealized gross profit in the merchandise which it sold to P and which still remains in the latter's inventory at the end of Year 1. In general journal form, the entries would be as follows:

Sales—S	40,000	
Cost of Goods Sold—P		40,000

To eliminate intercompany sales and purchases.

Cost of Goods Sold—P	6,000	
Net Income—S		6,000

To eliminate unrealized gross profit in inventory.

Many accountants would prefer to combine the foregoing entries, particularly when a company uses perpetual inventory procedures. The compound entry would be as follows:

Sales—S	40,000	
Cost of Goods Sold—P		34,000
Net Income—S		6,000

In consolidating the income statements of the two corporations, the earnings of S Corp. must be allocated to the shareholders of P Corp. and to the minority in the ratio of 90:10. P Corp. has already included $10,350 as its share under the heading of Income from Subsidiary. Therefore, in determining its net income this amount is eliminated in entry (c) to determine the consolidated net income; this avoids double counting. Entry (d) allocates the adjusted net income of S between the parent and minority interest in proportion to their stockholdings.

The investment account for Year 1 on the parent's books is summarized as follows:

Investment in S Corp.—Stock

	Dr.	Cr.	Balance
1/1, Yr. 1 Cost	180,000		180,000
Year 1 Dividends		9,000	171,000
12/31, Yr. 1 90% of Net Income as adjusted	10,350		181,350

The balance sheets of the two corporations as of the end of Year 1 are contained in the first four columns of the worksheet to prepare a consolidated balance sheet. Entry (1) eliminates $10,000 of intercompany accounts receivable by S against the accounts payable of P. Entry (2) eliminates the balance of the investment as of December 31, Year 1, against 90 percent of the shareholders' equity of the subsidiary corporation as of that date. Entry (3) classifies the remaining 10 percent as the minority interest at the end of the year. (*Note*: As an alternate approach, a three-tier worksheet is included in this example.)

Equity Method

P Corp. and Subsidiary
Worksheet—Consolidated Income Statement
Year 1

	P Corp.		S Corp.		Eliminations		Consolidated	
	Dr.	Cr.	Dr.	Cr.	Dr.	Cr.	Dr.	Cr.
Sales		120,000		116,000	[a]40,000			196,000
Cost of Goods Sold	70,000		75,000		[b]6,000	[a]40,000	111,000	
Selling Expenses	16,000		12,000				28,000	
General Expenses	15,000		9,000				24,000	
Amortization of Goodwill			2,500				2,500	
Income from Subsidiary		10,350			[c]10,350			
	101,000	130,350	98,500	116,000				
Net Income—P	29,350				[d]10,350	[c]10,350	29,350	
Net Income—S			17,500			{[d]11,500 [b]6,000		
	130,350	130,350	116,000	116,000				
Minority Interest					[d]1,150		1,150	
							196,000	196,000

[a] To eliminate intercompany purchases and sales.
[b] To eliminate unrealized gross profit in final inventory of P.
[c] To eliminate income from subsidiary previously recorded by P.
[d] To allocate net income of S Corp.: 90% to parent and 10% to minority.

Equity Method

P Corp. and Subsidiary
Worksheet—Consolidated Balance Sheet
December 31, Year 1

	P Corp.		S Corp.		Eliminations		Consolidated	
	Dr.	Cr.	Dr.	Cr.	Dr.	Cr.	Dr.	Cr.
Accounts Receivable	26,000		23,000			[1]10,000	39,000	
Merchandise Inventory	35,000		30,000			[b]6,000	59,000	
Other Current Assets	28,000		16,000				44,000	
Investment in S Corp. [equity]	181,350					[2]181,350		
Depreciable Assets—net	130,000		140,000				270,000	
Goodwill			47,500				47,500	
Accounts Payable		85,000		30,000	[1]10,000			105,000
Other Liabilities		21,000		19,000				40,000
Capital Stock—P		200,000						200,000
Retained Earnings (1/1)—P		80,000						80,000
Net Income—P		29,350						29,350
Dividends—P	15,000						15,000	
Capital Stock—S				100,000	{[3]10,000 [2]90,000			
Retained Earnings (1/1)—S				50,000	{[3]5,000 [2]45,000			
Net Income—S				17,500	{[3]1,150 [2]10,350 [b]6,000			
Dividends—S			10,000			{[3]1,000 [2]9,000		
Appraisal Capital				50,000	{[3]5,000 [2]45,000			
	415,350	415,350	266,500	266,500				
Minority Interests						[3]20,150		20,150
							474,500	474,500

[1] To eliminate intercompany receivable and payable.
[2] To eliminate 90% of shareholders' equity as of Dec. 31, Yr. 1.
[3] To classify 10% interest of minority shareholders as of Dec. 31, Yr. 1.

Equity Method

P Corp. and Subsidiary
Consolidated Workpapers (3-tier)
Year 1

	Company		Adjustments & Eliminations		Consolidated
	P	S			
INCOME STATEMENT					
Revenue					
Sales	120,000	116,000	ª40,000		196,000
Income from Subsidiary	10,350		²10,350		
Total Revenue	130,350	116,000			196,000
Costs and Expenses					
Cost of Goods Sold	70,000	75,000	ᵇ6,000	ª40,000	111,000
Selling Expenses	16,000	12,000			28,000
General Expenses	15,000	9,000			24,000
Amortization of Goodwill		2,500			2,500
Total Costs and Expenses	101,000	98,500			165,500
					30,500
Minority Interest in Income [10% of ($17,500 − $6,000)]			³1,150		1,150
Net Income	29,350	17,500			29,350
RETAINED EARNINGS					
Balance (1/1)—P	80,000				80,000
Balance (1/1)—S		50,000	{ ³5,000 ²45,000		
Net Income	29,350	17,500			29,350
Total	109,350	67,500			109,350
Less: Dividends—P	15,000				15,000
Dividends—S		10,000	{ ³1,000 ²9,000		
Balance (12/31)	94,350	57,500			94,350
BALANCE SHEET					
Assets					
Accounts Receivable	26,000	23,000		¹10,000	39,000
Merchandise Inventory	35,000	30,000		ᵇ6,000	59,000
Other Current Assets	28,000	16,000			44,000
Investment in S Corp.	181,350			²181,350	
Depreciable Assets—net	130,000	140,000			270,000
Goodwill		47,500			47,500
Total Assets	400,350	256,500			459,500
Equities					
Accounts Payable	85,000	30,000	ª10,000		105,000
Other Liabilities	21,000	19,000			40,000
Capital Stock—P	200,000				200,000
Retained Earnings—P	94,350				94,350
Capital Stock—S		100,000	{ ³10,000 ²90,000		
Retained Earnings—S		57,500			
Appraisal Capital—S		50,000	{ ³5,000 ²45,000		
Minority Interest				³20,150	20,150
Total Equities	400,350	256,500			459,500

7.7 INTERCOMPANY PROFIT—MERCHANDISE (YEAR 2): EQUITY METHOD

EXAMPLE 5. Example 5 is a continuation of the previous example into Year 2, utilizing the equity method. The results of operations of P Corp. and of S Corp. for Year 2 are condensed in the first four columns of the accompanying worksheet to prepare a consolidated income statement.

During the second year of affiliation, S made sales of $50,000 to P. At the end of Year 2, P had $20,000 of these goods in its inventory, on which S had recorded a gross profit of $8,000. At the end of Year 2, P still owed $12,000 to S.

During Year 2, the parent company recognized income from subsidiary in the amount of $18,900, which was determined as follows:

Net Income Reported by S Corp.	$23,000
Add: Unrealized Profit at End of Year 1 in Goods Sold in Year 2	6,000
Total	$29,000
Less: Unrealized Gross Profit in Unsold Merchandise at December 31, Year 2	8,000
Net Income of S Corp., for Consolidation Purposes	$21,000
Parent's Share (90% of $21,000)	$18,900
Minority Share (10% of $21,000)	$ 2,100

In the worksheet to consolidate the income statements for Year 2 (p. 198), (a) eliminates the intercompany sales and purchases. Entry (b) reduces the net income of S by the amount of the unrealized gross profit in the merchandise which it had sold to P, but which still remains in the parent's inventory at the end of Year 2.

Entry (c) restores to income in Year 2 the $6,000 which had been considered unrealized at the end of Year 1. In general journal form, the entry is as follows:

Net Income—S	6,000	
Cost of Goods Sold—P		6,000

The effects of the foregoing entries on the cost of goods sold are summarized in the following schedule.

1/1/2 Inventories (S & P)	$ 65,000	
Less: Unrealized Profit (b)	6,000	
		$ 59,000
Year 2 Gross Purchases (S & P)	$287,000*	
Less: Intercompany Items (a)	50,000	
		237,000
Goods Available for Sale (Consolidated)		$296,000
12/31/2 Deduct Inventories (S & P)	$ 90,000	
Less: Unrealized Profit (c)	8,000	
		82,000
Cost of Goods Sold (Consolidated)		$214,000

---

*Inventories at Dec. 31, Yr. 2, $90,000, plus cost of goods sold, $262,000 ($138,000 + $124,000), indicates that cost of goods available for sale was $352.000. The inventories at Jan. 1, Yr. 2 amounted to $65,000 ($35,000 + $30,000). Therefore the gross purchases of both companies were $287,000.

Entry (d) eliminates the income from subsidiary previously recorded by the parent company. Entry (e) allocates the net income of the subsidiary, as adjusted, between the parent and the minority interests.

The investment account for the first two years of affiliation is summarized as follows:

Investment in S Corp.—Stock

		Dr.	Cr.	Balance
1/1, Yr. 1	Cost	180,000		180,000
Year 1	Dividends		9,000	171,000
12/31, Yr. 1	90% of Net Income —as adjusted	10,350		181,350
Year 2	Dividends		18,000	163,350
12/31, Yr. 2	90% of Net Income —as adjusted	18,900		182,250

The balance sheets of the two corporations as of the end of Year 2 are condensed in the first four columns of the worksheet to prepare a consolidated balance sheet. Entry (1) eliminates the intercompany receivable and payable in the amount of $12,000. Entry (2) eliminates 90 percent of the shareholders' equity of the subsidiary against the balance in the investment account as of the end of Year 2. Entry (3) segregates the remaining 10% of the equity of S Corp. as the minority interest at the balance sheet date. (*Note*: As an alternate approach, a three-tier worksheet is included in this example.)

Equity Method

P Corp. and Subsidiary
Worksheet—Consolidated Income Statement
Year 2

	P Corp.		S Corp.		Eliminations		Consolidated	
	Dr.	Cr.	Dr.	Cr.	Dr.	Cr.	Dr.	Cr.
Sales		200,000		180,000	[a]50,000			330,000
Cost of Goods Sold	138,000		124,000		[b]8,000	{[c]6,000 [a]50,000}	214,000	
Selling Expenses	22,000		16,500				38,500	
General Expenses	17,900		14,000				31,900	
Amortization of Goodwill			2,500				2,500	
Income from Subsidiary		18,900			[d]18,900			
	177,900	218,900	157,000	180,000				
Net Income—P	41,000				[e]18,900	[d]18,900	41,000	
Net Income—S			23,000		[c]6,000	{[e]21,000 [b]8,000}		
	218,900	218,900	180,000	180,000				
Minority Interest						[e]2,100	2,100	
							330,000	330,000

[a] To eliminate intercompany purchases and sales.
[b] To eliminate unrealized gross profit in final inventory of P.
[c] To eliminate intercompany profit in inventory of P as of Jan. 1, Yr. 2.
[d] To eliminate income from subsidiary previously recorded by P.
[e] To allocate net income of S Corp.: 90% to parent and 10% to minority.

Equity Method

P Corp. and Subsidiary
Worksheet—Consolidated Balance Sheet
December 31, Year 2

	P Corp.		S Corp.		Eliminations		Consolidated	
	Dr.	Cr.	Dr.	Cr.	Dr.	Cr.	Dr.	Cr.
Accounts Receivable	34,000		24,000			[1]12,000	46,000	
Merchandise Inventory	48,000		42,000			[c]8,000	82,000	
Other Current Assets	27,000		20,000				47,000	
Investment in S Corp.	182,250					[2]182,250		
Depreciable Assets—net	120,000		130,500				250,500	
Goodwill			45,000				45,000	
Accounts Payable		77,000		31,000	[1]12,000			96,000
Other Liabilities		23,000		20,000				43,000
Capital Stock—P		200,000						200,000
Retained Earnings (1/1)—P		95,250						95,250
Net Income—P		41,000						41,000
Dividends—P	25,000						25,000	
Capital Stock—S				100,000	{[3]10,000 [2]90,000}			
Retained Earnings (1/1)—S				57,500	{[3]5,150 [2]46,350 [b]6,000}			
Net Income—S				23,000	{[3]2,100 [2]18,900 [c]8,000}	[b]6,000		
Dividends—S			20,000			{[3]2,000 [2]18,000}		
Appraisal Capital				50,000	{[3]5,000 [2]45,000}			
	436,250	436,250	281,500	281,500				
Minority Interest						[3]20,250		20,250
							495,500	495,500

[1] To eliminate intercompany receivable and payable.
[2] To eliminate 90% of shareholders' equity as of Dec. 31, Yr. 2.
[3] To classify 10% interest of minority shareholders as of Dec. 31, Yr. 2.

Equity Method

P Corp. and Subsidiary
Consolidated Workpapers (3-tier)
Year 2

	Company		Adjustments & Eliminations		Consolidated
	P	S			
INCOME STATEMENT					
Revenue					
Sales	200,000	180,000	[a]50,000		330,000
Income from Subsidiary	18,900		[2]18,900		
Total Revenue	218,900	180,000			330,000
Costs and Expenses					
Cost of Goods Sold	138,000	124,000	[b]8,000	{ [c]6,000 [a]50,000 }	214,000
Selling Expenses	22,000	16,500			38,500
General Expenses	17,900	14,000			31,900
Amortization of Goodwill		2,500			2,500
Total Costs and Expenses	177,900	157,000			286,900
					43,100
Minority Interest in Income [10% of ($23,000 + $6,000 − $8,000)]			[3]2,100		2,100
Net Income	41,000	23,000			41,000
RETAINED EARNINGS					
Balance (1/1)—P	95,250				95,250
Balance (1/1)—S		57,500	{ [2]46,350 [c]6,000 [3]5,150		
Net Income	41,000	23,000			41,000
Total	136,250	80,500			136,250
Less: Dividends—P	25,000			{ [3]2,000 [2]18,000 }	25,000
Dividends—S		20,000			
Balance (12/31)	111,250	60,500			111,250
BALANCE SHEET					
Assets					
Accounts Receivable	34,000	24,000		[1]12,000	46,000
Merchandise Inventory	48,000	42,000		[b]8,000	82,000
Other Current Assets	27,000	20,000			47,000
Investment in S Corp.	182,250			[2]182,250	
Depreciable Assets—net	120,000	130,500			250,500
Goodwill		45,000			45,000
Total Assets	411,250	261,500			470,500
Equities					
Accounts Payable	77,000	31,000	[1]12,000		96,000
Other Liabilities	23,000	20,000			43,000
Capital Stock—P	200,000				200,000
Retained Earnings—P	111,250				111,250
Capital Stock—S		100,000	{ [3]10,000 [2]90,000 }		
Retained Earnings—S		60,500			
Appraisal Capital—S		50,000	{ [3]5,000 [2]45,000 }		
Minority Interest				[3]20,250	20,250
Total Equities	411,250	261,500			470,500

7.8   100% ELIMINATION CONCEPT

The chief object in preparing consolidated statements is to restate the results of operations and other statements as if the group were one company. For example, transfers between members of a group have no meaning vis-a-vis outsiders, thus all intercompany sales and purchases should be eliminated.

The general rule for the elimination of intercompany profits in inventories is to remove 100 percent of the gross profit* from the company which sold the goods and to reduce the inventory of the company which holds the goods. The rule is the same regardless of whether a parent had sold to a subsidiary, a subsidiary had sold to a parent, or one subsidiary had sold to another. It does not matter how many times the goods may have been transferred from one affiliate to another; the rule is to be universally applied.

If the merchandise on hand had been acquired prior to affiliation, there is ordinarily no elimination of gross profit, on the theory that sales and purchases during such a period had been made at arm's length.

Consolidated Financial Statements (Accounting Research Bulletin No. 51), August 1959. In "Original Pronouncements as of July 1, 1978." Stamford, Conn.: Financial Accounting Standards Board, 1978.

Summary

(1)   When merchandise is transferred between affiliates, each company should record the transaction in the same manner that it records similar transactions with _____.

(2)   Intercompany movements of goods should be _____ when consolidated statements are prepared.

(3)   Merchandise on hand that a parent had acquired from a subsidiary should be valued at the cost to the _____.

(4)   A parent company sold merchandise to a subsidiary for $1,000; the subsidiary resold these goods for $1,250. The consolidated sales amount to $_____.

(5)   A subsidiary company purchased goods for $1,000 which is later sold to the parent company for $1,400. These goods are in the parent company's inventory at the end of the fiscal year. For consolidation purposes, they should be valued at the cost to the _____ company.

(6)   The general rule for the elimination of intercompany profit in inventories is to remove 100 percent of the _____ profit.

(7)   The amount of intercompany profit to be eliminated is not affected by the existence of _____ interests.

(8)   Transportation costs incurred in transferring goods between affiliated companies should be _____ in the cost of unsold merchandise when the goods have been brought closer to the point of ultimate sale.

(9)   Intercompany profit is realized, or confirmed, when the merchandise has been transferred to _____ parties.

Answers: (1) outsiders;   (2) eliminated;   (3) subsidiary;   (4) $1,250;   (5) subsidiary;   (6) gross;
(7) minority;   (8) included;   (9) third

Solved Problems

7.1 The Plan Corporation owns 80 percent of the stock of the Save Corp. and 85 percent of the stock of Tar Corp. The investment accounts are carried at cost. Intercompany sales are made at a gross profit of 30 percent of selling price.

Required:

In each of the following cases, calculate the amount at which merchandise should be carried in a consolidated balance sheet at the end of the period.

Case 1. Merchandise held by Plan which had been acquired from Save for $20,000.

Case 2. Merchandise held by Save which had been acquired from Plan for $20,000.

Case 3. Merchandise held by Save which had been acquired from Tar for $30,000.

Case 4. Merchandise held by Tar which it had acquired from Save for $40,000. This merchandise had originally been acquired by Save from Plan.

Case 5. Merchandise held by Plan which it had acquired from Save for $40,000. This merchandise had originally been purchased by Save from Tar.

SOLUTION

 1. $14,000 (70% of $20,000)

 2. $14,000 (70% of $20,000)

 3. $21,000 (70% of $30,000)

 4. $19,600 [70% of (70% of $40,000)]
     Merchandise held by Tar:
       Cost to Save—70% of $40,000 = $28,000
       Original Cost to Plan—70% of $28,000 = $19,600

 5. $19,6000 [70% of (70% of $40,000)]
     Merchandise held by Plan:
       Cost to Save—70% of $40,000 = $28,000
       Original Cost to Tar—70% of $28,000 = $19,600

Note: In each case, the merchandise inventory should be stated at the cost to the first affiliate that acquired it from an outsider.

7.2 An 80 percent owned subsidiary sold goods to a 90 percent owned subsidiary at a mark-up of $4,000. The latter sold it to a 70 percent owned subsidiary at a mark-up of $6,000. The third subsidiary sold the goods to the parent company at a mark-up of $3,000. The goods are in the parent company's inventory at the end of the year.

Required:

Determine how much of the mark-up should be eliminated from the inventory when a consolidated statement is to be prepared.

SOLUTION

Mark-ups to be eliminated:

$4,000 + $6,000 + $3,000 = $13,000

7.3   The Jar Corp. owns 83 percent of the outstanding stock of Kar Co., Inc.   Kar sells merchandise to Jar at a gross profit of 25 percent (based on sales price).   On January 1, 19XX, Jar's inventory included $200,000 of goods purchased from Kar.   At the end of the year, Jar's inventory included $300,000 of goods purchased from Kar.

Required:

Write the elimination entries needed to consolidate in general journal form:

(a)   the income statements for the year 19XX, and

(b)   the balance sheets at December 31, 19XX.

SOLUTION

(a)   *To consolidate income statements for Year 19XX:*

Net Income—K	50,000	
Merchandise Inventory (1/1)—J*		50,000

To eliminate intercompany gross profit in opening inventory.

Merchandise Inventory (12/31)—J*	75,000	
Net Income—K		75,000

To eliminate intercompany gross profit in closing inventory.

(b)   *To consolidate balance sheets at December 31, 19XX:*

Retained Earnings (1/1)—K	50,000	
Net Income—K		50,000

To eliminate unrealized gross profit in opening inventory.

Net Income—K	75,000	
Merchandise Inventory—J		75,000

To eliminate unrealized gross profit in closing inventory.

---

*Alternative: Cost of Goods Sold.

7.4   The Onibar Corp. acquired an 80 percent interest in Exade Corp. at a date when Exade had
retained earnings of $250,000. The Onibar Corp. also purchased 70 percent of the outstanding
stock of Avis Company when it had retained earnings of $25,000. The investment accounts
have been kept on the cost basis. A schedule of retained earnings of the three corporations
for 19X4 follows:

	Onibar	Exade	Avis
Retained Earnings, Jan. 1	$488,000	$421,500	$341,000
Add: Net Income, 19X4	290,000	180,000	120,000
Total	$778,000	$601,500	$461,000
Less: Dividends Paid, 19X4	125,000	100,000	75,000
Retained Earnings, Dec. 31	$653,000	$501,500	$386,000

The Avis Company sells parts to Onibar where they become components of subassemblies. Onibar then sells the subassemblies to Exade.

Intercompany profits, in inventories, at the beginning and end of 19X4 are as follows:

	January 1	December 31
As a result of sales from Avis to Onibar	$45,000	$17,500
As a result of sales from Onibar to Exade	26,000	59,000

Required:

(a) Compute the consolidated net income for 19X4.

(b) Prepare a statement of consolidated retained earnings for the year 19X4.

SOLUTION

(a)

	Onibar Corp.	Exade Corp.	Avis Corp.
Net Income, as reported	$290,000	$180,000	$120,000
Less: Intercompany Dividends—			
by Exade (80% of $100,000)	(80,000)		
by Avis (70% of $75,000)	(52,500)		
Intercompany Profits in Inventories at December 31—			
Sales by Avis to Onibar			(17,500)
Sales by Onibar to Exade	(59,000)		
Add: Intercompany Profits in Inventories at January 1—			
Sales by Avis to Onibar			45,000
Sales by Onibar to Exade	26,000		
Net Income, Own Operations	$124,500	$180,000	$147,500
Add: 80% of Exade Income	144,000		
70% of Avis Income	103,250		
Consolidated Net Income, 19X4	$371,750		

(b)

	Onibar Corp.	Exade Corp.	Avis Corp.
Retained Earnings, January 1, as reported	$488,000	$421,500	$341,000
Less: Intercompany profits in Inventories at January 1—			
Sales by Avis to Onibar			(45,000)
Sales by Onibar to Exade	(26,000)		
Retained Earnings at Date of Acquisition of Control by Onibar		(250,000)	(25,000)
Increase in Subsidiary Earnings Since Date of Acquisition of Control by Onibar		$171,500	$271,000
Parent's Share of Growth in Exade (80% of $171,500)	137,200		
Parent's Share of Growth in Avis (70% of $271,000)	189,700		
Consolidated Retained Earnings, as of January 1	$788,900		

Onibar Corp. and Subsidiaries
Consolidated Statement of Retained Earnings
Year Ended December 31, 19X4

January 1, 19X4	$ 788,900
Add: Consolidated Net Income, 19X4	371,750
	$1,160,650
Less: Dividends, 19X4	125,000
December 31, 19X4	$1,035,650

7.5 The financial statements of Pad Corp. and of its 80 percent owned subsidiary, the Sac Corp., for the year ended December 31, 19X6 are summarized in the worksheets accompanying this problem. The Pad Corp. has maintained its investment account in the subsidiary under the equity method. The parent followed the practice of recording its share of the subsidiary income as reported by the treasurer of Sac Corp.

The inventory of Pad on January 1, 19X6, included merchandise of $20,000 purchased from Sac; these goods had cost the subsidiary $13,750. The inventory of Pad on December 31 included merchandise of $25,000 which had cost the subsidiary $15,625. During the year 19X6, the subsidiary sold goods to the parent amounting to $62,500, and on December 31, 19X6 the parent owed $11,250 for these goods.

The Pad Corp. acquired 80 percent of the stock of Sac on July 1, 19X1. At that date, the price paid by Pad was based on the book value of the recorded assets of Sac plus an additional $36,000 assigned to the value of its land.

Required:

(a) Complete the worksheet to consolidate the income statements.

(b) Complete the worksheet to consolidate the balance sheets at the end of 19X6.

Note: Be sure to clearly show the minority interest(s).

(a)

Pad Corp. and Subsidiary
Worksheet—Consolidated Income Statement
Year Ended December 31, 19X6

	Pad Corp.		Sac Corp.		Eliminations		Consolidated	
	Dr.	Cr.	Dr.	Cr.	Dr.	Cr.	Dr.	Cr.
Sales		1,000,000		325,000				
Merchandise Inventory (1/1)	85,000		30,000					
Purchases	650,000		190,000					
Merchandise Inventory (12/31)		60,000		20,000				
Selling Expenses	75,000		30,000					
General Expenses	205,000		70,000					
Income from Subsidiary		20,000						
	1,015,000	1,080,000	320,000	345,000				
Net Income—Pad	65,000							
Net Income—Sac			25,000					
	1,080,000	1,080,000	345,000	345,000				

(b)

Pad Corp. and Subsidiary
Worksheet—Consolidated Balance Sheet
December 31, 19X6

	Pad Corp.		Sac Corp.		Eliminations		Consolidated	
	Dr.	Cr.	Dr.	Cr.	Dr.	Cr.	Dr.	Cr.
Accounts Receivable	315,000		115,000					
Merchandise Inventory	60,000		20,000					
Other Current Assets	203,200		10,000					
Investment in Sac Corp. (Equity)	196,800							
Other Assets	500,000		130,000					
Accounts Payable		205,000		40,000				
Other Liabilities		100,000		25,000				
Capital Stock—Pad		750,000						
Retained Earnings (1/1)—Pad		192,500						
Net Income—Pad		65,000						
Dividends—Pad	37,500							
Capital Stock—Sac				200,000				
Retained Earnings (1/1)—Sac			5,000					
Net Income—Sac				25,000				
Dividends—Sac			10,000					
	1,312,500	1,312,500	290,000	290,000				

SOLUTION
(a)

Pad Corp. and Subsidiary
Worksheet—Consolidated Income Statement
Year Ended December 31, 19X6

	Pad Corp.		Sac Corp.		Eliminations		Consolidated	
	Dr.	Cr.	Dr.	Cr.	Dr.	Cr.	Dr.	Cr.
Sales		1,000,000		325,000	[a]62,500			1,262,500
Merchandise Inventory (1/1)	85,000		30,000			[b]6,250	108,750	
Purchases	650,000		190,000			[a]62,500	777,500	
Merchandise Inventory (12/31)		60,000		20,000	[c]9,375			70,625
Selling Expenses	75,000		30,000				105,000	
General Expenses	205,000		70,000				275,000	
Income from Subsidiary		20,000			[d]20,000			
	1,015,000	1,080,000	320,000	345,000				
Net Income—Pad	65,000				[e]17,500	[d]20,000		62,500
Net Income—Sac			25,000			[b]6,250		
						{[e]21,875 / [c]9,375}		
	1,080,000	1,080,000	345,000	345,000				
Minority Interest						[e]4,375	4,375	
							1,333,125	1,333,125

[a] To eliminate intercompany purchases and sales.
[b] To eliminate unrealized gross profit in inventory of Pad, as of 1/1/X6 ($20,000 − $13,750).
[c] To eliminate unrealized gross profit in inventory of Pad, as of 12/31/X6 ($25,000 − $15,625).
[d] To eliminate income from subsidiary previously recorded by parent.
[e] To allocate adjusted net income of Sac $21,875 ($25,000 + $6,250 − $9,375).

(b)

Pad Corp. and Subsidiary
Worksheet—Consolidated Balance Sheet
December 31, 19X6

	Pad Corp.		Sac Corp.		Eliminations		Consolidated	
	Dr.	Cr.	Dr.	Cr.	Dr.	Cr.	Dr.	Cr.
Accounts Receivable	315,000		115,000			[2]11,250	418,750	
Merchandise Inventory	60,000		20,000			[c]9,375	70,625	
Other Current Assets	203,200		10,000				213,200	
Investment in Sac Corp. (Equity)	196,800					{[5]189,300 / [4]7,500}		
Other Assets	500,000		130,000		[1]36,000		666,000	
Accounts Payable		205,000		40,000	[2]11,250			233,750
Other Liabilities		100,000		25,000				125,000
Capital Stock—Pad		750,000						750,000
Retained Earnings (1/1)—Pad		192,500			[3]5,000			187,500
Net Income—Pad		65,000			[4]7,500	[3]5,000		62,500
Dividends—Pad	37,500						37,500	
Capital Stock—Sac				200,000	{[6]40,000 / [5]160,000}			
Retained Earnings (1/1)—Sac			5,000		[b]6,250	{[6]2,250 / [5]9,000}		
Net Income—Sac				25,000	{[6]4,375 / [5]17,500 / [c]9,375}	[b]6,250		
Dividends—Sac			10,000			{[6]2,000 / [5]8,000}		
	1,312,500	1,312,500	290,000	290,000				
Appraisal Capital—Sac					{[6]7,200 / [5]28,800}	[1]36,000		
Minority Interest						[6]47,325		47,325
							1,406,075	1,406,075

[1] To record increment in value of land, $36,000.
[2] To eliminate intercompany receivable and payable, $11,250.
[3] To reduce Pad's retained earnings as of 1/1/X6 for 80% of Sac's unrealized profit in intercompany merchandise.
[4] To reduce investment by 80% of unrealized intercompany profit in merchandise at 12/31/X6 (80% of $9,375).
[5] To eliminate 80% of shareholders' equity of Sac, as of 12/31/X6.
[6] To classify 20% interest of minority shareholders as of 12/31/X6.

Chapter 8

Consolidated Statements—
Intercompany Transactions: Long-Term Assets

8.1 INTRODUCTION

Long-term assets owned by one affiliate may be sold to another affiliated company for legal, financial, or economic reasons. For example, real estate may be purchased by a wholly owned subsidiary from another subsidiary which has a minority large enough to hinder a prospective mortgaging of its real property. Or, by way of another example, an affiliate with excess funds may purchase some long-term asset as a means of transferring funds to the selling company.

When one company sells long-term assets to an affiliated company, the transfer price is usually based on fair market value. Thus, the selling company will record a gain or a loss on its books. When preparing consolidated statements, such gains or losses are generally considered to be unrealized and are therefore eliminated. Also, any asset should be adjusted so that it will be restated at the cost, or basis, to the selling company.

8.2 INTERCOMPANY SALE OF LAND

When land is sold to a nonaffiliated company, the gain or loss is generally fully recognized in the period of sale. The most notable exception would be a sale which is handled on the installment method. However, when land is sold to an affiliated company, no gain or loss is recognized in consolidated statements unless or until the land is resold to an entity outside of the affiliated group. Until such a time, any gain or loss which may have been properly recorded on the selling company's books should be eliminated. The land should be restated, for consolidating purposes, at the carrying value as of the date of sale. Such elimination of intercompany profit should be repeated each time consolidated statements are prepared.

At some later date, the affiliate which had purchased the land may resell it to a company outside of the affiliated group. At such a point, the gain or loss to be recognized by the consolidated group, is the difference between its original cost or other basis to the first affiliate and the selling price to the third party.

EXAMPLE 1. The B Corp. purchased 90 percent of the stock of T Corp. on January 2, Year 1, when T had retained earnings of $50,000. The investment account is kept on the cost method. During Year 4, T sold land to B for $125,000; this land had cost the subsidiary $100,000 in Year 2. Thus, the income statement of T for Year 4 should include $25,000 as gain on sale of land.

The condensed income statements of both companies for Year 4 appear in the accompanying worksheet to prepare a consolidated income statement (p. 208). Entry (a) eliminates the intercompany profit on the intercompany sale of land and restates the land at its original cost to T. In general journal form the entry is as follows:

Gain on Sale of Land—T	25,000	
Net Income—T		25,000

(Example continued on p. 210.)

Cost Method

B Corp. and Subsidiary
Worksheet—Consolidated Income Statement
Year 4

	B Corp.		T Corp.		Eliminations		Consolidated	
	Dr.	Cr.	Dr.	Cr.	Dr.	Cr.	Dr.	Cr.
Sales		130,000		116,000				246,000
Cost of Goods Sold	70,000		75,000				145,000	
Selling Expenses	16,000		12,000				28,000	
General Expenses	15,000		9,000				24,000	
Gain on Sale of Land				25,000	[a]25,000			
	101,000	130,000	96,000	141,000				
Net Income—B	29,000				[b]18,000		47,000	
Net Income—T			45,000			{[b]20,000 / [a]25,000		
	130,000	130,000	141,000	141,000				
Minority Interest					[b]2,000		2,000	
							246,000	246,000

[a] To eliminate intercompany profit on sale of land to affiliate.
[b] To allocate net income of T as adjusted.

Cost Method

B Corp. and Subsidiary
Worksheet—Consolidated Balance Sheet
December 31, Year 4

	B Corp.		T Corp.		Eliminations		Consolidated	
	Dr.	Cr.	Dr.	Cr.	Dr.	Cr.	Dr.	Cr.
Current Assets	205,000		202,000				407,000	
Investment in T Corp.	135,000					{[2]126,000 / [1]9,000		
Depreciable Assets—net	190,000		150,000				340,000	
Land	125,000					[a]25,000	100,000	
Liabilities		126,000		167,000				293,000
Capital Stock—B		300,000						300,000
Retained Earnings (1/1)—B		200,000			[1]9,000			191,000
Net Income—B		29,000				[b]18,000		47,000
Capital Stock—T				100,000	{[3]10,000 / [2]90,000			
Retained Earnings (1/1)—T				40,000	{[3]4,000 / [2]36,000			
Net Income—T				45,000	{[b]20,000 / [a]25,000			
	655,000	655,000	352,000	352,000				
Minority Interest						{[3]14,000 / [b]2,000}		16,000
							847,000	847,000

[1] To reduce investment for B's share of decrement in T Corp. as adjusted during Years 1, 2, and 3: 90% of $10,000.
[2] To eliminate 90% of shareholders' equity of T Corp. as of Jan. 1, Yr. 4.
[3] To classify 10% interest of minority stockholders as of Jan. 1, Yr. 4.

Cost Method

B Corp. and Subsidiary
Consolidated Workpapers (3-tier)
Year 4

	Company		Adjustments & Eliminations		Consolidated
	B	T			
INCOME STATEMENT					
Revenue					
Sales	130,000	116,000			246,000
Gain on Sale of Land		25,000	[a]25,000		
Total Revenue	130,000	141,000			246,000
Costs and Expenses					
Cost of Goods Sold	70,000	75,000			145,000
Selling Expenses	16,000	12,000			28,000
General Expenses	15,000	9,000			24,000
Total Costs and Expenses	101,000	96,000			197,000
					49,000
Minority Interest in Income [10% of ($45,000 − $25,000)]			[b]2,000		2,000
Net Income	29,000	45,000			47,000
RETAINED EARNINGS					
Balance (1/1)—B	200,000		[1]9,000		191,000
Balance (1/1)—T		40,000	$\begin{cases}{}^34,000 \\ {}^236,000\end{cases}$		
Net Income	29,000	45,000			47,000
Balance (12/31)	229,000	85,000			238,000
BALANCE SHEET					
Assets					
Current Assets	205,000	202,000			407,000
Investment in T Corp.	135,000			$\begin{cases}{}^2126,000 \\ {}^19,000\end{cases}$	
Depreciable Assets—net	190,000	150,000			340,000
Land	125,000			[a]25,000	100,000
Total Assets	655,000	352,000			847,000
Equities					
Liabilities	126,000	167,000			293,000
Capital Stock—B	300,000				300,000
Retained Earnings—B	229,000				238,000
Capital Stock—T		100,000	$\begin{cases}{}^310,000 \\ {}^290,000\end{cases}$		
Retained Earnings—T		85,000			
Minority Interest				$\left.\begin{array}{r}{}^314,000 \\ {}^b2,000\end{array}\right\}$	16,000
Total Equities	655,000	352,000			847,000

Entry (b) allocates the adjusted net income of T, $20,000 ($45,000 − $25,000), between the parent and the minority interests in proportion to their stockholdings.

The balance sheets of B Corp. and T Corp. are condensed in the worksheet to prepare a consolidated balance sheet as of the end of Year 4. Entry (a) reduces the land account by the unrecognized intercompany gain of $25,000; it also reduces the net income of T by the same amount. Thus, the land is restated at the basis to the economic entity. In general journal form, the entry is as follows:

Net Income—T	25,000	
Land—B		25,000

Entry (b) allocates the adjusted net income of T between the parent and the minority interests.

Since the investment account has been kept on the cost basis it is necessary to recognize the parent's share of the change in the subsidiary's earnings from the date of acquisition of control to the end of Year 3. This is accomplished in entry (1). The calculation is as follows:

Retained Earnings, 1/1, Year 4 (12/31, Year 3)	$40,000	
Retained Earnings, 1/2, Year 1	50,000	
Decrease	$10,000	
Parent's Share of Decrease (90% of $10,000)		$9,000

Entry (2) eliminates the balance of the investment account, as adjusted, against 90% of the shareholders' equity of T as of January 1, Year 4. Entry (3) classifies the minority interest as of the same date. (*Note*: As an alternate approach, a three-tier worksheet is included in this example.)

8.3 INTERCOMPANY SALE OF LAND—SUBSEQUENT YEAR

EXAMPLE 2. The income statements of B Corp. and T Corp. for years after Year 4 can be consolidated without any special treatment apropos the unrecognized gain on the intercompany sale of land in that year. However, in consolidating the balance sheets for any date after the ending date in the previous example, the land must be reduced by the unrecognized intercompany profit of $25,000; the accumulated profits of the selling company must also be reduced by a like amount.

In closing its accounts for Year 4, it may be assumed that the T Corp. transferred the gain on sale of land to its retained earnings account via an income summary or some similar account. Thus, after this point in time the following elimination entry will be required:

Retained Earnings—T	25,000	
Land—B		25,000

Assume that the balance sheets of the two corporations as of December 31, Year 8, are to be consolidated. The condensed balance sheets are contained in the accompanying worksheet to prepare a consolidated balance sheet as of that date. Entry (1), as above, reduces the land on the books of B to the affiliated basis; it also removes from the retained earnings of T an amount equal to the unrealized intercompany profit on the transfer of the land in Year 4.

It is necessary to recognize the parent's share of the change in the subsidiary's accumulated earnings from the date of acquisition of control to the beginning of Year 8 (the end of Year 7). The calculation of the increase is as follows:

Retained Earnings, 1/1, Year 8	$110,000
Less: Gain on Intercompany Sale of Land, Not Recognized	25,000
Retained Earnings, as adjusted, 1/1, Year 8	$ 85,000
Retained Earnings, 1/2, Year 1	50,000
Increase	$ 35,000
Parent's Share of Increase (90% of $35,000)	$31,500

Entry (2) recognizes this increment in the investment account and in B's retained earnings.

Entry (3) allocates the net income of the subsidiary for Year 8 between parent and minority interests according to their stockholdings. Entry (4) eliminates the revised balance of the investment account against 90 percent of the shareholders' equity of T as of January 1, Year 8 and entry (5) classifies the minority interest as of the same date.

Cost Method

B Corp. and Subsidiary
Worksheet—Consolidated Balance Sheet
December 31, Year 8

	B Corp.		T Corp.		Eliminations		Consolidated	
	Dr.	Cr.	Dr.	Cr.	Dr.	Cr.	Dr.	Cr.
Current Assets	267,000		178,000				445,000	
Investment in T Corp.	135,000				[2]31,500	[4]166,500		
Depreciable Assets—net	180,000		160,000				340,000	
Land	125,000					[1]25,000	100,000	
Liabilities		103,000		98,000				201,000
Capital Stock—B		300,000						300,000
Retained Earnings (1/1)—B		270,000				[2]31,500		301,500
Net Income—B		34,000				[3]27,000		61,000
Capital Stock—T				100,000	[5]10,000 [4]90,000			
Retained Earnings (1/1)—T				110,000	[4]76,500 [1]25,000 [5]8,500			
Net Income—T				30,000	[3]30,000			
	707,000	707,000	338,000	338,000				
Minority Interest						[4]18,500 [3]3,000		21,500
							885,000	885,000

[1] To eliminate intercompany gain on sale of land in Year 4.
[2] To add to investment account B's share of growth in T Co., as adjusted, during Years 1 through 7: 90% of $35,000.
[3] To allocate net income of subsidiary.
[4] To eliminate 90% of shareholders' equity of T Corp., as of Jan. 1, Yr. 8.
[5] To classify 10% interest of minority shareholders, as of Jan. 1, Yr. 8.

8.4 INTERCOMPANY SALE OF LAND—RESALE TO UNAFFILIATED COMPANY

EXAMPLE 3. This example is a continuation of the previous one into Year 11, in which year the B Corp. sold its land to an unaffiliated company. The income statements of the two corporations are condensed in the accompanying worksheet to prepare a consolidated income statement for Year 11. B Corp. sold its land for $160,000. B's basis has been $125,000, so it indicates a gain on sale of land in the amount of $35,000. However, the cost to the affiliated group was $100,000, as the land was originally acquired by T in Year 2 for this amount. Thus, the consolidated gain is $60,000 ($160,000 − $100,000).

In Year 4 the gain reported by T was eliminated, and each year thereafter the effect of this gain was eliminated by reducing the consolidated cost of the land and of T's retained earnings. Now that the land has been sold to an unaffiliated company it is appropriate to recognize (or confirm) that portion of the gain originally recorded by T. This is accomplished by entry (a) which, in general journal form, would appear as follows:

Net Income—T	25,000	
Gain on Sale of Land		25,000

The reader may observe that this entry is the reverse of entry (a) in Example 1 of this chapter.

Entry (b) allocates the net income, as adjusted, of T Corp. between the parent and the minority interests.

The condensed balance sheets of the two corporations as of December 31, Year 11 appear in the accompanying worksheet to prepare a consolidated balance sheet as of that date. Entries (a) and (b) perform the same functions as the similarly lettered entries in the worksheet to consolidate the income statements.

It is necessary to recognize the parent's share of the increase in the subsidiary's retained earnings from the date of acquisition of control to the beginning of Year 11; see entry (1) and the following schedule:

Retained Earnings, 1/1, Year 11 (12/31, Year 10)	$126,000	
Less: Gain on Intercompany Sale of Land, Not Recognized to Date	25,000	
Retained Earnings, as adjusted, 1/1, Year 11	$101,000	
Retained Earnings, 1/2, Year 1	50,000	
Increase	$ 51,000	
Parent's Share of Increase (90% of $51,000)		$45,900

Entry (2) eliminates the investment account, as adjusted, against 90 percent of the shareholders' equity as of January 1, Year 11. Entry (3) classifies the minority interest as of January 1, Year 11.

Cost Method

B Corp. and Subsidiary
Worksheet—Consolidated Income Statement
Year 11

	B Corp.		T Corp.		Eliminations		Consolidated	
	Dr.	Cr.	Dr.	Cr.	Dr.	Cr.	Dr.	Cr.
Sales		190,000		146,000				336,000
Cost of Goods Sold	120,000		85,000				205,000	
Selling Expenses	27,000		19,000				46,000	
General Expenses	24,000		12,000				36,000	
Gain on Sale of Land		35,000				[a]25,000		60,000
	171,000	225,000	116,000	146,000				
Net Income—B	54,000				[b]49,500		103,500	
Net Income—T			30,000		[a]25,000	[b]55,000		
	225,000	225,000	146,000	146,000				
Minority Interest						[b]5,500	5,500	
							396,000	396,000

[a] To measure gain on sale of land from original basis to affiliate of $100,000. Intercompany gain not recognized in Year 4.
[b] To allocate net income of T as adjusted.

Cost Method

B Corp. and Subsidiary
Worksheet—Consolidated Balance Sheet
December 31, Year 11

	B Corp.		T Corp.		Eliminations		Consolidated	
	Dr.	Cr.	Dr.	Cr.	Dr.	Cr.	Dr.	Cr.
Current Assets	435,000		184,000				619,000	
Investment in T Corp.	135,000				[1]45,900	[2]180,900		
Depreciable Assets—net	205,000		169,000				374,000	
Land								
Liabilities		111,000		97,000				208,000
Capital Stock—B		300,000						300,000
Retained Earnings (1/1)—B		310,000				[1]45,900		355,900
Net Income—B		54,000				[b]49,500		103,500
Capital Stock—T				100,000	[3]10,000 [2]90,000			
Retained Earnings (1/1)—T				126,000	[2]90,900 [a]25,000 [3]10,100			
Net Income—T				30,000	[b]55,000	[a]25,000		
	775,000	775,000	353,000	353,000				
Minority Interest						[3]20,100 [b]5,500		25,600
							993,000	993,000

[1] To add to investment account B's share of growth in T Corp., as adjusted, during Years 1 through 10: $45,900 (90% of $51,000).
[2] To eliminate 90% of shareholders' equity of T Corp. as of Jan. 1, Yr. 11.
[3] To classify 10% interest of minority stockholders as of Jan. 1, Yr. 11.

8.5 INTERCOMPANY SALES OF DEPRECIABLE ASSETS

Machinery, equipment, and other long-term assets subject to depreciation are often sold by one affiliate to another. The vendor generally records a gain or loss based on its cost or other basis. If the vendee utilizes the long-term asset in its operations, it normally records depreciation expense based on the transfer price. For consolidated income statements, however, the appropriate depreciation should be based on the *cost* or other basis to the original owner.

In consolidated statements, no gain or loss is recognized as a result of an intercompany transfer per se. However, as the asset is utilized by the vendee in the production of goods and services, a portion of the utility of the depreciating asset is transferred to the product or services which are sold or rendered to outsiders. In this manner, a portion of the intercompany profit equivalent to the amount of depreciation, is realized. The concept is that an amount of the intercompany gain equal to the depreciation on the increase in basis is considered to have been transferred to customers. For example, assume that a parent sold equipment to its subsidiary for $7,200. The equipment had a basis to the parent of $6,000. This equipment has an estimated service life of five years. In a consolidated statement as of the date of sale, the profit of $1,200 would be eliminated and the equipment would be shown at the consolidated basis of $6,000. Each month, depreciation expenses based on the transfer price would be recorded as $120 (1/60 of $7,200), whereas depreciation based on the consolidated basis would be $100 (1/60 of $6,000). The difference of $20 per month would be considered to have been, in effect, sold to the subsidiary's customers. In this fashion it is earned by, or confirmed to, the affiliated group.

8.6 INTERCOMPANY SALE OF DEPRECIABLE ASSET—DATE OF SALE

EXAMPLE 4. The D Corp. purchased 90 percent of the stock of U Corp. on January 1, Year 1, when U had retained earnings of $60,000. On the same date, D purchased equipment from U for $14,000. This equipment originally cost U $16,000, and accumulated depreciation amounted to $6,000.

The condensed trial balances of the D Corp. and of the U Corp. are included in the first four columns of the accompanying worksheet to prepare a consolidated balance sheet as of the close of business on January 1, Year 1. No other transactions took place on that date. Entry (1) eliminates the gross profit on the intercompany sale of equipment and restates the equipment at the basis of $10,000 ($16,000 − $6,000) to the economic entity. Entry (2) eliminates the cost of the investment against 90 percent of the shareholders' equity of U Corp., and entry (3) classifies the remaining 10 percent as the minority interest.

Cost Method

D Corp. and Subsidiary
Worksheet—Consolidated Balance Sheet
January 1, Year 1

	D Corp.		U Corp.		Eliminations		Consolidated	
	Dr.	Cr.	Dr.	Cr.	Dr.	Cr.	Dr.	Cr.
Current Assets	127,000		140,000				267,000	
Investment in U Corp.	144,000					^{2}144,000		
Depreciable Assets	204,000		130,000			^{1}4,000	330,000	
Accumulated Depreciation		25,000		11,000				36,000
Liabilities		100,000		95,000				195,000
Capital Stock—D		200,000						200,000
Retained Earnings (1/1)—D		150,000						150,000
Capital Stock—U				100,000	$\{^3$10,000 ^{2}90,000			
Retained Earnings (1/1)—U				60,000	$\{^3$6,000 ^{2}54,000			
Gain on Sale of Equipment				4,000	^{1}4,000			
	475,000	475,000	270,000	270,000				
Minority Interest						^{3}16,000		16,000
							597,000	597,000

^{1} To eliminate profit on intercompany sale of depreciable assets, $4,000 ($14,000 − $10,000).
^{2} To eliminate 90% of subsidiary's shareholders' equity.
^{3} To classify the 10% interest of minority shareholders.

8.7 INTERCOMPANY SALE OF DEPRECIABLE ASSET—COST METHOD: YEAR 1

EXAMPLE 5. This example is based on a continuation of the activity of D Corp. and its 90-percent-owned subsidiary, the U Corp., to the end of Year 1. Both corporations calculate depreciation utilizing a ten-year life and follow the straight-line method.

The condensed income statements of the two corporations for the first year of affiliation appear in the accompanying worksheet to prepare a consolidated income statement for Year 1 (p. 216). Depreciation expense has been separately stated in order to better focus on this item. Entry (a) eliminates the intercompany dividends received by D Corp. Entry (b) eliminates the gross profit on the intercompany sale of equipment by U Corp. to its parent company.

The equipment U had sold to D on January 1, Year 1, for $14,000 is included in D's depreciable assets. Thus, the depreciation recorded by D includes $1,400 (10 percent of $14,000) based on its acquisition price, whereas depreciation based on cost would be only $1,000 (10 percent of $10,000). The excess depreciation of $400 ($1,400 − $1,000) is considered to have been realized by or confirmed to U as a result of the sales and services by D to outsiders in Year 1. Entry (c) recognizes on one hand that $400 is excess depreciation expense to D, and on the other hand that U's income is to be augmented by this amount. In general journal form, the entry is as follows:

Net Income—U	400	
Depreciation Expense—D		400

One effect of the foregoing entry is to restate depreciation expense in the consolidated income statement as if the depreciable property had not been transferred.

From a consolidated point of view, the net income of U Corp. for Year 1 is determined in the following schedule:

Net Income of U Corp., per books	$30,000
Less: Profit on Intercompany Sale of Equipment	4,000
	$26,000
Add: Portion of Intercompany Profit Realized Through Sales and Services Rendered by D Corp. (1/10 of $4,000)	400
Net Income of U Corp. for Consolidation Purposes	$26,400

The net income of U, adjusted to a consolidated point of view, is allocated in entry (d) between the parent company and the minority interests in accordance with their stockholdings.

The balance sheets of D Corp. and of U Corp. at the end of Year 1 are condensed in the first four columns of the accompanying worksheet to prepare a consolidated balance sheet as of December 31, Year 1. Elimination entries (a), (b), (c), and (d) are similar to the like-lettered entries in the worksheet to consolidate the income statements for Year 1. Entry (a) now eliminates the entire amount of dividends of $10,000; 90 percent, or $9,000, to the parent company and 10 percent, or $1,000, to the minority stockholders in U. Entry (b) eliminates U's profit of $4,000 on the intercompany sale of equipment; it also reduces D's equipment by the same amount. Entry (c) reduces the accumulated depreciation of D by $400; it also recognizes $400 of income to U. Entry (d) allocates the net income of U, as adjusted, between the parent and the minority interests.

Entry (1) eliminates the cost of the investment in U Corp. against 90 percent of the shareholders' equity of U Corp. as of January 1, Year 1. Entry (2) classifies the remaining 10 percent of the shareholders' equity of U Corp. as the minority interest on January 1, Year 1.

The minority interest in U Corp. as of December 31, Year 1 amounts to $17,640, which may be verified from the following schedule.

	Total	Minority
Capital Stock—U	$100,000	$10,000
Retained Earnings, Jan. 1—U	60,000	6,000
Net Income, Year 1, as Adjusted—U	26,400	2,640
Dividends, Year 1—U	(10,000)	(1,000)
Totals	$176,400	$17,640

Cost Method

D Corp. and Subsidiary
Worksheet—Consolidated Income Statement
Year 1

	D Corp.		U Corp.		Eliminations		Consolidated	
	Dr.	Cr.	Dr.	Cr.	Dr.	Cr.	Dr.	Cr.
Sales		350,000		300,000				650,000
Cost of Goods Sold	215,000		189,000				404,000	
Selling Expenses	30,000		28,000				58,000	
General Expenses	42,000		44,000				86,000	
Depreciation Expense	20,400		13,000			c400	33,000	
Gain on Sale of Equipment				4,000	b4,000			
Dividend Income		9,000			a9,000			
	307,400	359,000	274,000	304,000				
Net Income—D	51,600				d23,760	a9,000	66,360	
Net Income—U			30,000		c400	{d26,400 b4,000}		
	359,000	359,000	304,000	304,000				
Minority Interest					d2,640		2,640	
							650,000	650,000

a To eliminate intercompany dividend.
b To eliminate gain on intercompany sale of equipment: $4,000.
c To eliminate excess depreciation by D: $400 (10% of $4,000).
d To allocate net income of U, as adjusted.

Cost Method

D Corp. and Subsidiary
Worksheet—Consolidated Balance Sheet
December 31, Year 1

	D Corp.		U Corp.		Eliminations		Consolidated	
	Dr.	Cr.	Dr.	Cr.	Dr.	Cr.	Dr.	Cr.
Current Assets	64,000		160,000				224,000	
Investment in T Corp.	144,000					1 144,000		
Depreciable Assets	204,000		130,000			b4,000	330,000	
Accumulated Depreciation		40,400		24,000	c400			64,000
Liabilities		90,000		86,000				176,000
Capital Stock—D		200,000						200,000
Retained Earnings (1/1)—D		60,000						60,000
Net Income—D		51,600			a9,000	d23,760		66,360
Dividends—D	30,000						30,000	
Capital Stock—U				100,000	{2 10,000 / 1 90,000}			
Retained Earnings (1/1)—U				60,000	{2 6,000 / 1 54,000}			
Net Income—U				30,000	{d26,400 / b4,000}	c400		
Dividends—U			10,000			a10,000		
	442,000	442,000	300,000	300,000				
Minority Interest					a1,000	{2 16,000 / d2,640}		17,640
							584,000	584,000

1 To eliminate 90% of subsidiary's shareholders' equity.
2 To classify the 10% interest of minority shareholders.

8.8   INTERCOMPANY SALE OF DEPRECIABLE ASSET—COST METHOD: YEAR 2

EXAMPLE 6.   This example is based on a continuation of the activity of D Corp. and its 90-percent-owned subsidiary, the U Corp., to the end of Year 2.   Both corporations continue to calculate depreciation utilizing a ten-year life and follow the straight-line method.   The condensed income statements of the two corporations for the second year of affiliation appear in the accompanying worksheet to prepare a consolidated income statement for Year 2 (p. 218).   Depreciation has again been separately stated in order to better focus on this item.

Entry (a) in the worksheet eliminates the intercompany dividend received by D Corp.   Entry (b) recognizes the $400 as excess depreciation expense to D and also that U's income is to be augmented by this amount.   In general journal form, the entry is as follows:

Net Income—U	400	
Depreciation Expense—D		400

From a consolidated point of view, the net income of U Corp. for Year 2 is determined in the following schedule:

Net Income of U Corp., per Books	$35,000
Add: Portion of Intercompany Profit Realized Through Sales and Services Rendered by D Corp. (1/10 of $4,000)	400
Net Income of U Corp., for Consolidation Purposes	$35,400

The net income of U, adjusted to a consolidated point of view, is allocated in entry (c) between the parent company and the minority interests in accordance with their stockholdings.

The condensed balance sheets of D Corp. and of U Corp. as of the end of Year 2 have been entered in the first four columns of the accompanying worksheet to prepare a consolidated balance sheet as of December 31, Year 2.   Elimination entries (a), (b), and (c) are similar to the like-lettered entries in the worksheet to consolidate the income statements for Year 1.   Entry (a) now eliminates the entire amount of dividends of $15,000: 90 percent, or $13,500, to the parent company, and 10 percent, or $1,500, to the minority stockholders in U.   Entry (b) reduces the accumulated depreciation of D by $400 and also recognizes $400 of income to U.   Entry (c) allocates the net income of U, as adjusted, between the parent and the minority interests.

In closing its general ledger for Year 1, it may be assumed that U Corp. transferred the gain on sale of equipment to its retained earnings account along with other revenue and expense balances.   For consolidation purposes it will be necessary to reduce the retained earnings of U as of January 1, Year 2, and also the basis of the equipment by $4,000.   This has been done in elimination entry (1).

The D Corp. had recorded depreciation based on its acquisition cost.   Thus its accumulated depreciation account at the end of Year 1 was $400 greater than the balance would have been if the depreciation expense had been calculated on the basis to the affiliated group.   The $400 was considered to have been earned by U as a result of the use of the transferred equipment in D's economic activities.   Thus entry (2) in effect repeats, for this worksheet, what had been recognized one year earlier in Example 5, entry (c) of the worksheet to prepare a consolidated income statement for Year 1.

The foregoing objectives may be accomplished in one compound entry, which in general journal form would be as follows:

Accumulated Depreciation—D	400	
Retained Earnings (1/1)—U	3,600	
Depreciable Assets—D		4,000

Since the investment account has been kept on the cost basis, it is necessary to recognize the parent's share of the change in U's retained earnings during Year 1.   The computation is as follows:

(Example continued on p. 219.)

Cost Method

D Corp. and Subsidiary
Worksheet—Consolidated Income Statement
Year 2

	D Corp.		U Corp.		Eliminations		Consolidated	
	Dr.	Cr.	Dr.	Cr.	Dr.	Cr.	Dr.	Cr.
Sales		380,000		330,000				710,000
Cost of Goods Sold	240,000		210,000				450,000	
Selling Expenses	31,000		30,000				61,000	
General Expenses	43,000		42,000				85,000	
Depreciation Expense	20,400		13,000			[b]400	33,000	
Dividend Income		13,500			[a]13,500			
	334,400	393,500	295,000	330,000				
Net Income—D	59,100				[c]31,860	[a]13,500	77,460	
Net Income—U			35,000		[b]400	[c]35,400		
	393,500	393,500	330,000	330,000				
Minority Interest					[c]3,540		3,540	
							710,000	710,000

[a] To eliminate intercompany dividend.
[b] To eliminate excess depreciation by D: $400 (10% of $4,000).
[c] To allocate net income of U, as adjusted.

Cost Method

D Corp. and Subsidiary
Worksheet—Consolidated Balance Sheet
December 31, Year 2

	D Corp.		U Corp.		Eliminations		Consolidated	
	Dr.	Cr.	Dr.	Cr.	Dr.	Cr.	Dr.	Cr.
Current Assets	104,900		199,000				303,900	
Investment in T Corp.	144,000				[3]14,760	[4]158,760		
Depreciable Assets	204,000		130,000			[1]4,000	330,000	
Accumulated Depreciation		60,800		36,000	[2]400 [b]400			96,000
Liabilities		87,000		93,000				180,000
Capital Stock—D		200,000						200,000
Retained Earnings (1/1)—D		81,000				[3]14,760		95,760
Net Income—D		59,100			[a]13,500	[c]31,860		77,460
Dividends—D	35,000						35,000	
Capital Stock—U				100,000	[5]10,000 [4]90,000			
Retained Earnings (1/1)—U				80,000	[4]68,760 [1]4,000 [5]7,640	[2]400		
Net Income—U				35,000	[c]35,400	[b]400		
Dividends—U			15,000			[a]15,000		
	487,900	487,900	344,000	344,000				
Minority Interest					[a]1,500	[5]17,640 [c]3,540		19,680
							668,900	668,900

[1] To eliminate intercompany gain on sale of equipment: $4,000.
[2] To reflect the realization, in Year 1, of 1/10 of above gain: $400.
[3] To add to investment account D's share of growth of U in Year 1: 90% of $16,400.
[4] To eliminate 90% of subsidiary's shareholders' equity as of Jan. 1, Yr. 2.
[5] To classify 10% interest of minority shareholders as of Jan. 1, Yr. 2.

Net Income, Year 1, as Adjusted for Consolidation Purposes [See Example 5, entry (d).]	$26,400	
Less: Dividends, Year 1	10,000	
Increase	$16,400	
Parent's Share of Increase (90% of $16,400)		$14,760

Entry (3) recognizes the parent's share of the increase in its subsidiary's retained earnings.

Entry (4) eliminates the cost of the investment in U Corp. against 90 percent of the shareholders' equity of U Corp. as of January 1, Year 2. Entry (5) classifies the remaining 10 percent of the shareholders' equity of U Corp. as the minority interest on January 1, Year 2.

The minority interest in U Corp. as of December 31, Year 2, amounts to $19,680, which may be verified from the following schedule:

	Total	Minority
Capital Stock—U	$100,000	$10,000
Retained Earnings, January 1, Year 2, as Adjusted—U	76,400	7,640
Net Income, Year 2, as Adjusted—U	35,400	3,540
Dividends, Year 2—U	(15,000)	(1,500)
Totals	$196,800	$19,680

8.9 INTERCOMPANY SALE OF DEPRECIABLE ASSET—EQUITY METHOD: YEAR 2

EXAMPLE 7. This example is based on the D Corp. and its 90-percent-owned subsidiary, the U Corp., for the second year of affiliation. However, it is now assumed that the parent company has been using the equity method for its investment account.

The investment account on D's books for the first two years of affiliation would appear as follows:

Investment in U Corp.—Stock

		Dr.	Cr.	Balance
1/1, Yr. 1	Cost	144,000		144,000
Year 1	Dividends		9,000	135,000
12/31, Yr. 1	Net Income of U (90% of $26,400)	23,760		158,760
Year 2	Dividends		13,500	145,260
12/31, Yr. 2	Net Income of U (90% of $35,400)	31,860		177,120

Utilizing the equity method, the retained earnings of D as of December 31, Year 1 would be $95,760, or $14,760 more than the balance obtained when utilizing the cost method. This is the result of recognizing $23,760 as income from subsidiary rather than only $9,000 of dividend income, which was the case when the cost method was utilized.

The income statements of the two corporations for the second year of affiliation are condensed in the accompanying worksheet to prepare a consolidated income statement for Year 2 (p. 220). Entry (a) eliminates the income from subsidiary that was previously recorded by the parent. Entry (b) recognizes that $400 (10% of $4,000) of excess depreciation recorded by D has been earned by U as a result of D's sales and services to third parties in Year 2. Entry (c) allocates the adjusted net income of U, $35,400, between the parent and the minority interests.

(Example continued on p. 222)

Equity Method

D Corp. and Subsidiary
Worksheet—Consolidated Income Statement
Year 2

	D Corp.		U Corp.		Eliminations		Consolidated	
	Dr.	Cr.	Dr.	Cr.	Dr.	Cr.	Dr.	Cr.
Sales		380,000		330,000				710,000
Cost of Goods Sold	240,000		210,000				450,000	
Selling Expenses	31,000		30,000				61,000	
General Expenses	43,000		42,000				85,000	
Depreciation Expense	20,400		13,000			[b]400	33,000	
Income from Subsidiary		31,860			[a]31,860			
	334,400	411,860	295,000	330,000				
Net Income—D	77,460				[c]31,860	[a]31,860	77,460	
Net Income—U				35,000	[b]400	[c]35,400		
	411,860	411,860	330,000	330,000				
Minority Interest					[c]3,540		3,540	
							710,000	710,000

[a] To eliminate income from subsidiary previously recorded by D Corp.
[b] To eliminate excess depreciation by parent: $400 (10% of $4,000).
[c] To allocate net income of U.

Equity Method

D Corp. and Subsidiary
Worksheet—Consolidated Balance Sheet
December 31, Year 2

	D Corp.		U Corp.		Eliminations		Consolidated	
	Dr.	Cr.	Dr.	Cr.	Dr.	Cr.	Dr.	Cr.
Current Assets	104,900		199,000				303,900	
Investment in U Corp.	177,120					[3]177,120		
Depreciable Assets	204,000		130,000			[1]4,000	330,000	
Accumulated Depreciation		60,800		36,000	[2]400 [b]400			96,000
Liabilities		87,000		93,000				180,000
Capital Stock—D		200,000						200,000
Retained Earnings (1/1)—D		95,760						95,760
Net Income—D		77,460						77,460
Dividends—D	35,000						35,000	
Capital Stock—U				100,000	[4]10,000 [3]90,000			
Retained Earnings (1/1)—U				80,000	[3]68,760 [1]4,000 [4]7,640	[2]400		
Net Income—U				35,000	[4]3,540 [3]31,860	[b]400		
Dividends—U			15,000			[4]1,500 [3]13,500		
	521,020	521,020	344,000	344,000				
Minority Interest						[4]19,680		19,680
							668,900	668,900

[1] To eliminate intercompany gain on sale of equipment: $4,000.
[2] To reflect realization in Year 1 of 1/10 of above gain: $400.
[3] To eliminate 90% of subsidiary's shareholders' equity as of Dec. 31, Yr. 2.
[4] To classify 10% interest of minority shareholders as of Dec. 31, Yr. 2.

Equity Method

D Corp. and Subsidiary
Consolidated Workpapers (3-tier)
Year 2

	Company		Adjustments & Eliminations		Consolidated
	D	U			
INCOME STATEMENT					
Revenue					
Sales	380,000	330,000			710,000
Income from Subsidiary	31,860		[3]31,860		
Total Revenue	411,860	330,000			710,000
Costs and Expenses					
Cost of Goods Sold	240,000	210,000			450,000
Selling Expenses	31,000	30,000			61,000
General Expenses	43,000	42,000			85,000
Depreciation Expense	20,400	13,000		[b]400	33,000
Total Costs and Expenses	334,400	295,000			629,000
					81,000
Minority Interest in Income [10% of ($35,000 + $400)]			[4]3,540		3,540
Net Income	77,460	35,000			77,460
RETAINED EARNINGS					
Balance (1/1)—P	95,760				95,760
Balance (1/1)—U		80,000	{ [3]68,760 [1]4,000 [4]7,640 }	[2]400	
Net Income	77,460	35,000			77,460
Total	173,220	115,000			173,220
Less: Dividends—D	35,000				35,000
Dividends—U		15,000		{ [4]1,500 [3]13,500 }	
Balance (12/31)	138,220	100,000			138,220
BALANCE SHEET					
Assets					
Current Assets	104,900	199,000			303,900
Investment in U Corp.	177,120			[3]177,120	
Depreciable Assets	204,000	130,000		[1]4,000	330,000
Accumulated Depreciation	(60,800)	(36,000)	{ [2]400 [b]400 }		(96,000)
Total Assets	425,220	293,000			537,900
Equities					
Liabilities	87,000	93,000			180,000
Capital Stock—D	200,000				200,000
Retained Earnings—D	138,220				138,220
Capital Stock—U		100,000	{ [4]10,000 [3]90,000 }		
Retained Earnings—U		100,000			
Appraisal Capital					
Minority Interest				[4]19,680	19,680
Total Equities	425,220	293,000			537,900

The balance sheets of D and U as of the end of Year 2 are condensed in the first four columns of the accompanying worksheet to prepare a consolidated balance sheet as of December 31, Year 2. Entry (1) eliminates the intercompany gain to U, which had resulted from the transfer of equipment in Year 1, and also reduces the equipment to a cost basis. In each of the two years, depreciation, based on the transfer price, causes the accumulated depreciation account to be overstated by $400 (10 percent of $4,000). On the other hand, the activities of D require the recognition of an equivalent amount of income to U. Entry (b) accomplishes the foregoing objectives based on the event in Year 2, and entry (2) accomplishes the same result for excess depreciation in Year 1. Entry (3) eliminates 90 percent of the shareholders' equity, as of December 31, Year 2, against the investment account. Entry (4) classifies the minority interests as of that date. (*Note*: As an alternate approach, a three-tier worksheet is included in this example.)

Summary

(1) A parent company owned land which had cost it $50,000. The land was sold to subsidiary A for $65,000. Subsidiary A then sold this land to subsidiary B for $85,000. In a consolidated balance sheet the land should be included at $_____. In an income statement covering the period of these sales, gain of $35,000 should be _____.

(2) When land is sold to an affiliated company, no gain or loss is recognized in consolidated statements unless and until the land is _____ to an entity _____ of the affiliated group.

(3) Subsidiary E manufactured machinery at a cost of $70,000 and sold it to subsidiary C for $100,000. Subsidiary C resold this machinery to subsidiary D for $120,000, where it remained and was used in its manufacturing process. In a consolidated balance sheet, this machinery should be included in the amount of $_____.

(4) The _____ profit of the selling affiliate should be eliminated in arriving at the amount at which long-term assets should be included in preparing consolidated statements.

(5) From a consolidated point of view, the intercompany profit on a sale of depreciable assets by one controlled company to another is realized over the useful life of the _____.

(6) In a worksheet to consolidate F and T, an elimination entry decreased the depreciation expense of F by $5,000 and increased the net income of T by the same amount. Company _____ was the seller of the depreciable asset to which the adjusting entry relates.

Answers: (1) $50,000, eliminated; (2) resold, outside; (3) $70,000; (4) gross; (5) depreciable asset; (6) T

Solved Problems

8.1 The following items have been selected from the trial balances of the Prexy Corp. and its subsidiary Sarbo Corp. as of December 31, 1976.

	Prexy Corp.	Sarbo Corp.
Sales	400,000	285,000
Cost of Goods Sold	280,000	185,000
Gain on Condemnation of Land	10,000	
Interest Expense	5,000	20,000
Machinery	120,000	80,000
Allowance for Depreciation	33,000	10,000
Investment in Sarbo Corp.	205,000	

Prexy has owned 80 percent of the outstanding stock of Sarbo since August 8, 1966. On January 1, 1975, Prexy sold machinery to Sarbo for $80,000, which included a profit to Prexy of $10,000. Sarbo uses the straight-line method of depreciation.

The land Prexy lost by condemnation in 1976 had been originally acquired by Sarbo in 1967 at a cost of $100,000. Sarbo sold it to Prexy, in 1971, for $150,000. In that year the board of directors of Sarbo decided that the profit was not normal to its operations and therefore the gain was credited directly to its retained earnings account. In 1976 the City of Erehwon condemned the land for municipal purposes and paid Prexy $160,000.

Required:

Write partial elimination entries to consolidate:

(a) The income statements for the year 1976.

(b) The balance sheets as of December 31, 1976.

SOLUTION

(a) *Journal entries to consolidate income statements.*

Net Income—Sarbo	50,000	
Gain on Condemnation of Land		50,000

To recognize the portion of gain which was not recognized in consolidated statements in 1969, but which is now realized as a result of disposition to third party.

Net Income—Prexy	625	
Depreciation—Sarbo		625

To eliminate excess depreciation by Sarbo, and to confirm earning by Prexy.

Supporting Calculations:

(1) Allowance for depreciation at end of two years $10,000, thus depreciation per year = $5,000. Therefore, the rate of depreciation equals 6.25% ($5,000 ÷ $80,000).

(2) Thus depreciation based on cost equals $4,375 (6.25% of $70,000).

(3) Therefore, excess depreciation equals $625 ($5,000 − $4,375).

(b) *Journal entries to consolidate balance sheets.*

Retained Earnings (Jan. 1)—Prexy	10,000	
Machinery—Sarbo		10,000

To eliminate intercompany gain on sale of machinery by Prexy to Sarbo on Jan. 1, 1975.

Allowance for Depreciation—Sarbo	1,250	
Retained Earnings, (Jan. 1)—Prexy		625
Net Income—Prexy		625

To reduce allowance for depreciation of machinery to the amount which it would be if the depreciation had been based on cost; and to confirm earning by Prexy of an amount equivalent to the excess depreciation in 1975 and in 1976.

Retained Earnings (Jan. 1)—Sarbo	50,000	
Net Income—Sarbo		50,000

To recognize that portion of the gain on sale of land which was not recognized in consolidated statements in 1971, but which is now realized as a result of disposition of land to an outsider.

8.2   The N Corp. purchased 80 percent of the capital stock of U Corp. at par on January 1, 19X1, the date of organization of U. On January 2, 19X2, U sold equipment to N for $120,000. This equipment had been manufactured by U at a cost of $80,000. N has been depreciating this equipment over a five-year life, using the straight-line method.

Condensed trial balances of the two corporations, as of December 31, 19X4, appear below:

	N Corp.		U Corp.	
Current Assets	$220,000		$170,000	
Investment in U Corp.	160,000			
Machinery and Equipment	600,000		560,000	
Allowance for Depreciation		$140,000		$ 90,000
Liabilities		60,000		180,000
Capital Stock—$10 par		600,000		200,000
Retained Earnings (1/1)		110,000		160,000
Net Income		70,000		100,000
	$980,000	$980,000	$730,000	$730,000

Required:

(a) Write, in general journal form, the necessary entries to consolidate the balance sheets of the two corporations as of December 31.

(b) Calculate the minority interests as of the balance sheet date.

(c) Determine the consolidated net income for the year 19X4.

SOLUTION

(a) *Journal entries to consolidate balance sheets.*

Allowance for Depreciation—N (3 × $8,000)	24,000	
Retained Earnings (1/1)—U ($40,000 + $16,000)	24,000	
Machinery and Equipment ($160,000 − $120,000)		40,000
Net Income—U		8,000

To remove unrealized portion of original $40,000 gain on sale of machinery, and to restate other accounts on cost basis.

Investment in U Corp.	108,800	
Retained Earnings (1/1)—N		108,800

To record parent's share of U's earnings since acquisition of control to January 1, 19X4 [80% of ($160,000 − $24,000)].

Net Income—U ($100,000 + $8,000)	108,000	
Net Income—N		86,400
Minority Interest in U		21,600

To allocate subsidiary's net income, as adjusted, according to stockholdings.

Capital Stock—U	160,000	
Retained Earnings (1/1)—U	108,800	
Investment in U Corp. ($160,000 + $108,800)		268,800

To eliminate 80% of subsidiary's shareholders' equity as of January 1, 19X4.

Capital Stock—U	40,000	
Retained Earnings (1/1)—U	27,200	
Minority Interest in U		67,200

To classify minority interests as of January 1, 19X4.

(b) *Minority interest as of December 31, 19X4.*

Balance as of January 1, 19X4	$67,200
Add: Minority Interest in 19X4 Income (20% of $108,000)	21,600
Total	$88,800

(c) *Consolidated net income—Year 19X4.*

Net Income of N	$ 70,000
Parent's Share of U's Net Income, as Adjusted (80% of $108,000)	86,400
Total	$156,400

8.3   Hat Corp. purchased 90 percent of the outstanding capital stock of the Rent Corp. on January 2, 1969. On January 1, 1974, a building which had cost the Rent Corp. $240,000 ten years earlier was sold to Hat Corp. for $280,000. Accumulated depreciation to the end of 1973, based on an estimated useful life of 60 years, amounted to $40,000. Net income reported by each of the companies in 1974 and 1975 was as follows:

	1974	1975
Hat Corp.	$160,000	$170,000
Rent Corp.	$152,000	$144,000

Required:

(a) Write elimination entries necessary to consolidate the income statements of the two corporations for 1974 and 1975.

(b) Write elimination entries necessary to consolidate the balance sheets of the two corporations as of December 31, 1974 and 1975.

(c) Calculate the consolidated net income for 1974 and 1975. Show the minority interest in income.

SOLUTION

(a) *Journal entries to consolidate income statements.*

	Year 1974		Year 1975	
Gain on Sale of Building—R	80,000			
Net Income—R		80,000		

Sale price	$280,000
Less: Book Value	200,000
Intercompany Gain	$ 80,000

	Year 1974		Year 1975	
Net Income—R	1,600		1,600	
Depreciation—H		1,600		1,600

Remaining Life: 50 Yrs. (2%)
2% of $80,000 = $1,600

(b) *Journal entries to consolidate balance sheets.*

	Dec. 31, 1974		Dec. 31, 1975	
Net Income—R	80,000			
Retained Earnings (1/1)—R			80,000	
Building—H		80,000		80,000

To eliminate intercompany gain.

	Dec. 31, 1974		Dec. 31, 1975	
Accumulated Depreciation—H	1,600		3,200	
Net Income—R		1,600		1,600
Retained Earnings				1,600

To reduce accumulated depreciation to consolidated basis, and to recognize portion of gain validated through usage of building by H.

(c) *Calculation of consolidated net income for 1974 and 1975.*

	Year 1974		Year 1975
Hat Corp., Inc:			
Net Income, as Reported		$160,000	$170,000
Rent Corp:			
Net Income, as Reported	$152,000		$144,000
Less: Gain on Intercompany			
Sale of Building	80,000		
	$ 72,000		
Add: Portion of Intercompany			
Gain Validated through			
Utilization of Building	1,600		1,600
Net Income, as adjusted		73,600	145,600
Consolidated Net Income			
before Minority Interests		$233,600	$315,600
Less: Minority Interests:			
(10% of $ 73,600)		7,360	
(10% of $145,600)			14,560
Consolidated Net Income		$226,240	$301,040

8.4   The Pab Corp. purchased 60 percent of the outstanding capital stock of Oz Corp. at the beginning of Year 11, for which Pab paid $528,000. The price was based on an appraisal which showed that Oz's land was worth $500,000 and that its building was worth $1,060,000 at that date.

Oz had paid $1,600,000 for the building on January 1, Year 1, and has been depreciating the building utilizing the straight-line method. It was originally estimated that the building had a useful life of twenty years from the date of purchase, and there has been no change in this estimate.

Simultaneous with the purchase of the stock of Oz, Pab entered into a lease with Oz for the remaining ten-year life of the building. As Pab did not need all of the space immediately, it sublet portions of the building to other industrial tenants.

The board of directors decided that in consolidated statements the property of Oz should be stated at the appraisal values and depreciation should be recognized on the same basis.

Pab maintains its investment account on the equity basis. It records its share of Oz's income based on reports issued by the subsidiary.

Required:

(a) Complete the worksheet to consolidate the income statements of the two corporations for Year 11.

(b) Complete the worksheet to consolidate the balance sheets of the two corporations as of December 31, Year 11.

(c) Prepare a schedule of consolidated retained earnings for Year 11.

(a)

Pab Corp. and Subsidiary
Worksheet—Consolidated Income Statement
Year 11

	Pab Corp.		Oz Corp.		Eliminations		Consolidated	
	Dr.	Cr.	Dr.	Cr.	Dr.	Cr.	Dr.	Cr.
Rental Income		408,000		212,000				
Income from Subsidiary		28,800						
Rent Expense	212,000							
Depreciation of Building			80,000					
Real Estate Taxes			20,000					
Other Taxes	14,800		4,000					
Gen. & Admin. Expenses	130,000		20,000					
Interest Expense			40,000					
	356,800	436,800	164,000	212,000				
Net Income—Pab	80,000							
Net Income—Oz			48,000					
	436,800	436,800	212,000	212,000				

(b)

Pab Corp. and Subsidiary
Worksheet—Consolidated Balance Sheet
December 31, Year 11

	Pab Corp.		Oz Corp.		Eliminations		Consolidated	
	Dr.	Cr.	Dr.	Cr.	Dr.	Cr.	Dr.	Cr.
Building			1,600,000					
Accumulated Depreciation				880,000				
Land			200,000					
Investment in Oz Corp.	552,000							
Current Assets	240,000		280,000					
Mortgage Note Payable				800,000				
Current Liabilities		180,000		40,000				
Capital Stock—Pab		500,000						
Retained Earnings (1/1)—Pab		72,000						
Net Income—Pab		80,000						
Dividends—Pab	40,000							
Capital Stock—Oz				200,000				
Retained Earnings (1/1)—Oz				120,000				
Net Income—Oz				48,000				
Dividends			8,000					
	832,000	832,000	2,088,000	2,088,000				

SOLUTION

(a)

Pab Corp. and Subsidiary
Worksheet—Consolidated Income Statement
Year 11

	Pab Corp.		Oz Corp.		Eliminations		Consolidated	
	Dr.	Cr.	Dr.	Cr.	Dr.	Cr.	Dr.	Cr.
Rental Income		408,000		212,000	c212,000			408,000
Income from Subsidiary		28,800			a28,800			
Rent Expense	212,000					c212,000		
Depreciation of Building			80,000		b26,000		106,000	
Real Estate Taxes			20,000				20,000	
Other Taxes	14,800		4,000				18,800	
Gen. & Admin. Expenses	130,000		20,000				150,000	
Interest Expense			40,000				40,000	
	356,800	436,800	164,000	212,000				
Net Income—Pab	80,000				d13,200	a28,800	64,400	
Net Income—Oz				48,000		{ d22,000 / b26,000		
	436,800	436,800	212,000	212,000				
Minority Interest					d8,800		8,800	
							408,000	408,000

a To eliminate income of Oz previously recorded by Pab.

b To record increase in depreciation of building based on appraisal increment: $26,000 (10% of $260,000); $1,060,000 − ½($1,600,000) = $260,000.

c To eliminate intercompany rent.

d To allocate net income of subsidiary as adjusted.

(b)

Pab Corp. and Subsidiary*
Worksheet—Consolidated Balance Sheet
December 31, Year 11

	Pab Corp.		Oz Corp.		Eliminations		Consolidated	
	Dr.	Cr.	Dr.	Cr.	Dr.	Cr.	Dr.	Cr.
Building			1,600,000		1260,000		1,860,000	
Accumulated Depreciation				880,000		b26,000		906,000
Land			200,000		1300,000		500,000	
Investment in Oz Corp.	552,000					{ 3536,400 / 215,600		
Current Assets	240,000		280,000				520,000	
Mortgage Note Payable				800,000				800,000
Current Liabilities		180,000		40,000				220,000
Capital Stock—Pab		500,000						500,000
Retained Earnings (1/1)—Pab		72,000						72,000
Net Income—Pab		80,000			215,600			64,400
Dividends—Pab	40,000						40,000	
Capital Stock—Oz				200,000	{ 480,000 / 3120,000			
Retained Earnings (1/1)—Oz				120,000	{ 448,000 / 372,000			
Net Income—Oz				48,000	{ 313,200 / b26,000 / 48,800			
Dividends—Oz			8,000			{ 43,200 / 34,800		
	832,000	832,000	2,088,000	2,088,000				
Appraisal Increment					{ 4224,000 / 3336,000	1560,000		
Minority Interest						4357,600		357,600
							2,920,000	2,920,000

* See p. 230 for additional explanatory notes.

1 To record appraisal increment $560,000 (building, $260,000 + land, $300,000).

2 To adjust investment account for parent's share of reduction in subsidiary income.

3 To eliminate 60% of subsidiary shareholders' equity as of Dec. 31, Yr. 11.

4 To classify minority interest as of Dec. 31, Yr. 11.

Explanatory Notes for Worksheet to Prepare Consolidated Balance Sheet (p. 229):

(1)   Revaluation of real estate as of January 1, Year 11.

	Book Value	Appraisal	Appraisal Increment
Building	$ 800,000	$1,060,000	$260,000
Land	200,000	500,000	300,000
Totals	$1,000,000	$1,560,000	$560,000

(2)   Increased valuation of building requires a proportionate increase in depreciation: 10% of $260,000 = $26,000. The parent's share of decrease in net income = $15,600 (60% of $26,000).

(3) and (4)   Equity of Oz, as   December 31, Year 11.

	Total	60%	40%
Capital Stock	$200,000	$120,000	$ 80,000
Retained Earnings (1/1)	120,000	72,000	48,000
Net Income—Year 11 as adjusted	22,000	13,200	8,800
Dividends	(8,000)	(4,800)	(3,200)
Appraisal Increment	560,000	336,000	224,000
Totals	$894,000	$536,400	$357,600

(c)

Pab Corp. and Subsidiary
Consolidated Retained Earnings
Year Ended December 31, Year 11

Balance, January 1	$ 72,000
Add: Consolidated Net Income	64,400
Total	$136,400
Less: Dividends	40,000
Balance, December 31	$ 96,400

8.5   The Banf Corp. purchased 90 percent of the outstanding capital stock of the Salvatore Corp. on January 1, 1971, for $324,000, when Salvatore had outstanding capital stock of $200,000 and retained earnings of $160,000.

On January 2, 1972, Salvatore sold its real estate to Banf for $250,000. The journal entry on Salvatore's books is condensed as follows:

Receivable from Banf Corp.	250,000	
Accumulated Depreciation	47,000	
Land		52,000
Building		198,000
Gain on Sale of Land		8,000
Gain on Sale of Building		39,000

The building had originally been purchased by Salvatore on January 2, 1962, and was estimated to have a total useful life of 40 years. Both corporations calculate depreciation on the straight-line method.

The parent company keeps the investment account on the cost basis.

Other data pertaining to the two corporations for 1972 and 1973 are condensed in the following schedules:

	Banf Corp.	Salvatore Corp.
Retained Earnings, Jan. 1, 1972	$330,000	$240,000
Add: Net Income, 1972	80,000	100,000
	$410,000	$340,000
Less: Dividends (cash), 1972	40,000	10,000
Retained Earnings, Dec. 31, 1972	$370,000	$330,000
Add: Net Income, 1973	60,000	40,000
	$430,000	$370,000
Less: Dividends, 1973:		
Cash	10,000	
Stock		20,000
Retained Earnings, Dec. 31, 1973	$420,000	$350,000
Capital Stock, $10 par, Jan. 1, 1972	$400,000	$200,000
Stock Dividend, issued July, 1973		20,000
Capital Stock, $10 par, Dec. 31, 1973	$400,000	$220,000

Required:

Calculate the consolidated net income for 1972 and 1973. Show the minority interest in income for each year.

SOLUTION

Consolidated Net Income

	1972		1973	
Banf's Reported Net Income	$ 80,000		$60,000	
Less: Cash Dividends from Salvatore	9,000		–0–	
Income from Own Operations		$ 81,000		$60,000
Salvatore's Reported Net Income	$100,000		$40,000	
Less: Gain on Intercompany Sale of Land and Building	47,000		–0–	
	$ 53,000		$40,000	
Add: Portion of Excess Depreciation Earned Through Use of Building (1/30 of $39,000)	1,300		1,300	
Adjusted Net Income, before Minority Interest	$ 54,300		$41,300	
Less: Minority Interest in Income (10% of $54,300)	5,430			
(10% of $41,300)			4,130	
		48,870		37,170
Consolidated Net Income		$129,870		$97,170

8.6   The Fab Corp. purchased 80 percent of the outstanding capital stock of the Ty Corp. The parent company has been maintaining its investment account by debiting it for 80 percent of the subsidiary's net income, and by crediting the investment account with the entire amount of dividends received from the subsidiary.

On January 1, Year 3, Fab purchased machinery from Ty for $110,000, which had a cost basis to Ty of $88,000. The parent company uses the straight-line method of depreciation and a twenty-year life for machinery.

The balance sheets as of the end of Year 5 are condensed in the first four columns of the following worksheet.

Required:

Complete the worksheet to consolidate the balance sheets as of December 31, Year 5.

Fab Corp. and Subsidiary
Worksheet—Consolidated Balance Sheet
December 31, Year 5

	Fab Corp.		Ty Corp.		Eliminations		Consolidated	
	Dr.	Cr.	Dr.	Cr.	Dr.	Cr.	Dr.	Cr.
Current Assets	366,000		556,000					
Investment in Ty Corp.	632,000							
Depreciable Assets	350,000		300,000					
Accumulated Depreciation		101,000		27,000				
Liabilities		51,000		39,000				
Capital Stock—Fab		600,000						
Retained Earnings—Fab		596,000						
Capital Stock—Ty				400,000				
Retained Earnings—Ty				390,000				
	1,348,000	1,348,000	856,000	856,000				

SOLUTION

Fab Corp. and Subsidiary
Worksheet—Consolidated Balance Sheet
December 31, Year 5

	Fab Corp. Dr.	Fab Corp. Cr.	Ty Corp. Dr.	Ty Corp. Cr.	Eliminations Dr.	Eliminations Cr.	Consolidated Dr.	Consolidated Cr.
Current Assets	366,000		556,000				922,000	
Investment in Ty Corp.	632,000					[4]617,040 [3]14,960		
Depreciable Assets	350,000		300,000			[1]22,000	628,000	
Accumulated Depreciation		101,000		27,000	[2]3,300			124,700
Liabilities		51,000		39,000				90,000
Capital Stock—Fab		600,000						600,000
Retained Earnings—Fab		596,000			[3]14,960			581,040
Capital Stock—Ty				400,000	[5]80,000 [4]320,000			
Retained Earnings—Ty				390,000	[4]297,040 [1]22,000 [5]74,260	[2]3,300		
	1,348,000	1,348,000	856,000	856,000				
Minority Interest						[5]154,260		154,260
							1,550,000	1,550,000

[1] To eliminate gain on intercompany sale of equipment: $22,000 ($110,000 − $88,000).
[2] To reflect realization in Years 3, 4, and 5 of 3/20 of intercompany gain: $3,300 (15% of $22,000).
[3] To eliminate parent's share of unrealized profit in subsidiary's equity: $14,960 [80% of ($22,000 − $3,300)].
[4] To eliminate 80% of subsidiary shareholders' equity as of Dec. 31, Year 5.
[5] To classify 20% interest of minority shareholders.

Chapter 9

Consolidated Statements—
Intercompany Transactions:
Long-term Debt

9.1 INTRODUCTION

Affiliated corporations frequently engage in transactions which result in intercompany receivables and payables. The results of these transactions may give rise to obligations on open account, notes, mortgages, or other instruments of long-term or short-term debt. Elimination of intercompany receivables and payables which arise from everyday sales of goods and services has been considered in Chapter 7. This chapter will concentrate on some of the problems which arise when an affiliated company holds long-term intercompany notes or bonds.

When a corporation holds short-term obligations of an affiliated corporation it is usually the result of an acquisition directly from the affiliate. The resulting accounts are usually reciprocal in amount and can be eliminated without much difficulty. When long-term debt of an affiliate is held, however, it is generally the result of an acquisition in the market place. Thus, the cost to the investor and the carrying value on the books of the issuer will almost always be different. Initially this difference is the measure of a constructive gain or loss. In subsequent periods, intercompany bond interest and related bond accounts are to be eliminated.

9.2 NOTE ACQUIRED FROM AN AFFILIATE

EXAMPLE 1. The P Corp. owned 80 percent of the outstanding stock of S Corp. Included in the balance sheets as of June 30, Year 5, were the following:

	P Corp.		S Corp.	
Notes Receivable	$70,000		$40,000	
Notes Receivable Discounted		$40,000		$40,000

Analysis of the above accounts indicates that P had received notes from its customers and that subsequently P discounted $40,000 of these notes with S. At a later date, S rediscounted these notes with a commercial bank. While the separate accounts of each company are correct, when the two sets of data are to be consolidated the intercompany transactions must be eliminated in the appropriate worksheet. In consolidating balance sheets as of June 30, Year 5, the following entry should be made:

Notes Receivable Discounted—P	40,000	
Notes Receivable—S		40,000

To eliminate the transfer of notes within the consolidation group.

Thus, a consolidated balance sheet as of June 30, Year 5, would indicate notes receivable amounting to $70,000 and contingent liabilities for notes discounted amounting to $40,000.

In a consolidated income statement for a period ending June 30, Year 5, any intercompany interest and discount should, of course, be eliminated.

9.3   INTERCOMPANY NOTES RECEIVABLE AND PAYABLE

EXAMPLE 2.   R Corp. owned 75 percent of the outstanding stock of T Corp.   Included in the balance sheets as of December 31, Year 6, were the following items:

	R Corp.	T Corp.
Notes Receivable		$30,000
Notes Receivable Discounted		$20,000
Notes Payable	$30,000	

An examination of the accounts of the two companies reveals that R had issued three notes in the amount of $10,000 each to T.   Subsequently, T had discounted two of these notes with a third party.   Thus, these two notes are held outside the group.   In a consolidated balance sheet, the amount of $20,000, which they represent, should be shown as a direct obligation of the group.   The intercompany aspect of the situation is recognized in the following elimination entry:

Notes Receivable Discounted—T	20,000	
Notes Receivable—T		20,000

To eliminate intercompany transactions.

The third note was never held outside of the consolidation group, so it should be entirely eliminated as follows:

Notes Payable—R	10,000	
Notes Receivable—T		10,000

To eliminate intercompany note receivable and note payable.

In a consolidated balance sheet, the remaining two notes payable in the amount of $20,000 should be shown as an obligation, even though the actual payee on the face of the notes may be the name of an affiliate.

In any consolidated income statements prepared for a period which includes a term of the notes, all intercompany interest and discount should be eliminated.

9.4   INTERCOMPANY BOND HOLDINGS

When a corporation purchases bonds it had once issued and retires them, the outstanding debt is reduced.   If the purchase price of the bonds retired is different from their carrying value, a gain or loss is recognized at the date of reacquisition.   In like fashion, when a corporation purchases bonds issued by an affiliate, the bonds are treated in consolidated statements as equivalent to retirement.

From a consolidated point of view, there is usually a net gain or loss on the acquisition, which may be measured by the difference between the cost to the company acquiring the bonds and the carrying value of the bonds on the issuer's books.   Any gain or loss, as such, will not appear on the books of either affiliate; it will appear only in consolidated workpapers and in statements prepared therefrom.

The corporation that issued the bonds continues to carry the bonds as an outstanding debt and pays interest to all bondholders, including the affiliate that holds some of these bonds.   The affiliate that had invested in these bonds collects interest on its investment.

The issuing corporation continues to amortize any discount or premium recorded upon original issue, and the investing corporation amortizes in its books any difference between the cost of the bonds and their par value.   Such net intercompany interest expense and income must be eliminated when preparing consolidated income statements.

9.5   BONDS OF AN AFFILIATE ACQUIRED AT DISCOUNT—YEAR OF ACQUISITION

EXAMPLE 3.   The B Corp. acquired 90 percent of the outstanding stock of S Corp. several years ago, and has maintained its investment account utilizing the equity method.   Thus, the parent recognizes 90 percent of the

(Example continued on p. 238.)

Equity Method

B Corp. and Subsidiary
Worksheet—Consolidated Income Statement
Year 6

	B Corp.		S Corp.		Eliminations		Consolidated	
	Dr.	Cr.	Dr.	Cr.	Dr.	Cr.	Dr.	Cr.
Sales		800,000		700,000				1,500,000
Cost of Goods Sold	490,000		425,000				915,000	
Interest Expense			20,000				20,000	
Other Expenses	266,000		215,000				481,000	
Income from Subsidiary		36,000			[b]36,000			
Gain from Acquisition of Intercompany Bonds						[a]3,000		3,000
	756,000	836,000	660,000	700,000				
Net Income—B	80,000				[c]38,700	[b]36,000	82,700	
Net Income—S			40,000		[a]3,000	[c]43,000		
	836,000	836,000	700,000	700,000				
Minority Interest						[c]4,300	4,300	
							1,503,000	1,503,000

[a] To record gain on acquisition of subsidiary bonds: $3,000 ($100,000 − $97,000).
[b] To eliminate income from subsidiary previously recorded by B.
[c] To allocate net income of S Corp. as adjusted ($40,000 + $3,000): 90% to parent and 10% to minority.

Equity Method

B Corp. and Subsidiary
Worksheet—Consolidated Balance Sheet
December 31, Year 6

	B Corp.		S Corp.		Eliminations		Consolidated	
	Dr.	Cr.	Dr.	Cr.	Dr.	Cr.	Dr.	Cr.
Current Assets	120,000		300,000				420,000	
Investment in S Corp.—Stock	270,000				[2]2,700	[3]272,700		
Investment in S Corp.—Bonds	97,000				[a]3,000	[1]100,000		
Other Assets—net	163,000		600,000				763,000	
Current Liabilities		110,000		100,000				210,000
Bonds Payable				500,000	[1]100,000			400,000
Capital Stock—B		250,000						250,000
Retained Earnings (1/1)—B		210,000						210,000
Net Income—B		80,000				[2]2,700		82,700
Capital Stock—S				200,000	[4]20,000 [3]180,000			
Retained Earnings (1/1)—S				60,000	[4]6,000 [3]54,000			
Net Income—S				40,000	[4]4,300 [3]38,700	[a]3,000		
	650,000	650,000	900,000	900,000				
Minority Interest						[4]30,300		30,300
							1,183,000	1,183,000

[1] To eliminate intercompany bonds.
[2] To add to investment in S Corp. stock, B's share of subsidiary's gain from bond acquisition.
[3] To eliminate 90% of shareholders' equity as of Dec. 31, Yr. 6.
[4] To classify 10% interest of minority shareholders, as of Dec. 31, Yr. 6.

Equity Method

B Corp. and Subsidiary
Consolidated Workpapers (3-tier)
Year 6

	Company		Adjustments & Eliminations		Consolidated
	B	S			
INCOME STATEMENT					
Revenue					
Sales	800,000	700,000			1,500,000
Income from Subsidiary	36,000		[3]38,700	[2]2,700	
Gain from Acquisition of Intercompany Bonds				[a]3,000	[a]3,000
Total Revenue	836,000	700,000			1,503,000
Costs and Expenses					
Cost of Goods Sold	490,000	425,000			915,000
Interest Expense		20,000			20,000
Other Expenses	266,000	215,000			481,000
Total Costs and Expenses	756,000	660,000			1,416,000
					87,000
Minority Interest in Income [10% of ($40,000 + $3,000)]			[4]4,300		4,300
Net Income	80,000	40,000			82,700
RETAINED EARNINGS					
Balance (1/1)—B	210,000				210,000
Balance (1/1)—S		60,000	{ [4]6,000 [3]54,000		
Net Income	80,000	40,000			82,700
Balance (12/31)	290,000	100,000			292,700
BALANCE SHEET					
Assets					
Current Assets	120,000	300,000			420,000
Investment in S Corp.—Stock	270,000		[2]2,700	[3]272,700	
Investment in S Corp.—Bonds	97,000		[a]3,000	[1]100,000	
Other Assets—net	163,000	600,000			763,000
Total Assets	650,000	900,000			1,183,000
Equities					
Current Liabilities	110,000	100,000			210,000
Bonds Payable		500,000	[1]100,000		400,000
Capital Stock—B	250,000				250,000
Retained Earnings—B	290,000				292,700
Capital Stock—S		200,000	{ [4]20,000 [3]180,000		
Retained Earnings—S		100,000			
Minority Interest				[4]30,300	30,300
Total Equities	650,000	900,000			1,183,000

subsidiary's reported net income as an addition to the parent's investment account and to its income accounts; the parent also records the receipt of dividends from its subsidiary as a reduction in its investment account.

Prior to the acquisition of control of S by B, S had issued $500,000 of bonds at par. The bonds bear interest at 4 percent per year, which is payable semi-annually on June 30 and December 31. The bonds mature on December 31, Year 10. On December 31, Year 6, the B Corp. purchased $100,000 par of these bonds in the market for $97,000. From a consolidated point of view, a debt of $100,000 has been settled with a payment of $97,000, giving rise to a gain of $3,000. However, this gain is not to be found in the accounts of either company; it must be introduced into the consolidated statements via the consolidation worksheets.

Condensed data from the income statements of the two companies for Year 6 have been entered in the first four columns of the accompanying worksheet to prepare a consolidated income statement for Year 6 (p. 236).

The $3,000 consolidated gain on acquisition of intercompany bonds is recorded in entry (a). In general journal form, the entry is as follows:

Net Income—S	3,000	
Gain from Acquisition of Intercompany Bonds		3,000

Entry (b) eliminates the income from subsidiary, which B had recognized in its accounts as a result of following the equity method. Entry (c) allocates the net income of S as adjusted in proportion to the holdings of its stockholders; 90 percent to the parent company, and 10 percent to the minority interests.

Condensed data from the balance sheets of the two corporations as of December 31, Year 6, are contained in the first four columns of the worksheet to prepare a consolidated balance sheet (p. 236). Entry (a) records the consolidated gain on the acquisition of intercompany bonds. Entry (2) adds 90 percent of this gain to the investment account and to the consolidated income. Entry (1) eliminates the intercompany bonds at par. Entry (3) eliminates the balance of the investment account against 90 percent of the shareholders' equity as of the end of the year. Entry (4) classifies the remaining 10 percent as the minority interest as of that date.

The foregoing worksheets indicate that the consolidated net income for Year 6 amounts to $82,700, which may be independently calculated as follows:

Net Income of B, as Reported	$80,000	
Less: Income from Subsidiary	36,000	
Net.Income, Own Operations		$44,000
Net Income of S, as Reported	$40,000	
Add: Gain from Acquisition of Intercompany Bonds	3,000	
Total	$43,000	
Less: Minority Interest	4,300	
Net Income of S—for Consolidation Purposes		38,700
Consolidated Net Income		$82,700

(*Note:* As an alternate approach, a three-tier worksheet is included in this problem.)

9.6 BONDS OF AFFILIATE ACQUIRED AT DISCOUNT—SUBSEQUENT YEAR

EXAMPLE 4. This illustration is based on a continuation of the previous example (Section 9.5) to the end of Year 7—the first full year in which the bonds of S will have been held by B.

The gain from acquisition of intercompany bonds (equivalent to the discount from the par of the bonds) was immediately recognized in the consolidated income of Year 6. In subsequent years, B amortizes this discount by debiting its investment in bonds account and crediting interest income. Assuming the straight-line method of amortization, the balance of investment in bonds will increase by $750 per year ($3,000 ÷ 4).

(*Example continued on p. 240.*)

Equity Method

B Corp. and Subsidiary
Worksheet—Consolidated Income Statement
Year 7

	B Corp.		S Corp.		Eliminations		Consolidated	
	Dr.	Cr.	Dr.	Cr.	Dr.	Cr.	Dr.	Cr.
Sales		790,000		695,000				1,485,000
Cost of Goods Sold	485,000		420,000				905,000	
Interest Expense			20,000			a4,000	16,000	
Other Expenses	260,000		205,000				465,000	
Income from Subsidiary		45,000			c45,000			
Interest Income		4,750				{ b750 / a4,000		
	745,000	839,750	645,000	695,000				
Net Income—B	94,750				d45,000	{ c45,000 / b750 }	94,000	
Net Income—S			50,000			d50,000		
	839,750	839,750	695,000	695,000				
Minority Interest					d5,000		5,000	
							1,485,000	1,485,000

a To eliminate intercompany bond interest.
b To eliminate annual amortization of discount on bonds purchased; entire discount recognized as income in year of purchase.
c To eliminate net income from subsidiary previously recorded by B.
d To allocate net income of S Corp.: 90% to parent and 10% to minority.

Equity Method

B Corp. and Subsidiary
Worksheet—Consolidated Balance Sheet
December 31, Year 7

	B Corp.		S Corp.		Eliminations		Consolidated	
	Dr.	Cr.	Dr.	Cr.	Dr.	Cr.	Dr.	Cr.
Current Assets	110,000		290,000				400,000	
Investment in S Corp.—Stock	297,000					3297,000		
Investment in S Corp.—Bonds	97,750				13,000	{ 2100,000 / b750 }		
Other Assets—net	230,000		630,000				860,000	
Current Liabilities		100,000		90,000				190,000
Bonds Payable				500,000	2100,000			400,000
Capital Stock—B		250,000						250,000
Retained Earnings (1/1)—B		290,000				12,700		292,700
Net Income—B		94,750			b750			94,000
Capital Stock—S				200,000	{ 420,000 / 3180,000 }			
Retained Earnings (1/1)—S				100,000	{ 410,000 / 390,000 }			
Dividends—S			20,000			{ 42,000 / 318,000 }		
Net Income—S				50,000	{ 45,000 / 345,000 }			
	734,750	734,750	940,000	940,000				
Minority Interest						{ 1300 / 433,000 }		33,300
							1,260,000	1,260,000

1 To record increase in consolidated retained earnings as result of recognition of gain on acquisition of intercompany bonds in Year 6: 90% to parent, 10% to minority.
2 To eliminate intercompany bonds.
3 To eliminate 90% of shareholders' equity as of Dec. 31, Yr. 7.
4 To classify remaining 10% interest of minority shareholders, as of Dec. 31, Yr. 7.

The interest expense account of S will amount to $20,000, of which $4,000 ($20,000 $\times$ $\frac{1}{5}$) is applicable to the bonds held by the parent company. B will record this $4,000 as interest income. In addition, B will recognize annual amortization of $750 per year. The entries in B's books in reference to interest income may be summarized as follows:

Cash	4,000	
Investment in S Corp.—Bonds	750	
Interest Income		4,750

In the accompanying worksheet to prepare a consolidated income statement for Year 7 (p. 239), entry (a) eliminates the reciprocal aspects of interest pertaining to $100,000 par of bonds, namely $4,000 (4% of $100,000). Entry (b) eliminates $750 of interest income recorded by B as a result of amortization of a portion of the discount on purchase of these bonds; it also reduces B's net income for consolidation purposes by the same amount. It should be recalled that the entire discount of $3,000 on acquisition of S's bonds had already been recognized in the consolidated net income of Year 6, the year of acquisition. Entry (c) eliminates the income of S, which had been previously recorded by B. Entry (d) allocates the net income of S in accordance with the holdings of the stockholders.

Condensed data from the balance sheets of the two corporations, as of December 31, Year 7, have been entered in the first four columns of the worksheet to prepare a consolidated balance sheet. The retained earnings of B as of the end of Year 6 had been increased by $2,700 as a result of recognition of 90 percent of the consolidated gain from intercompany acquisition of bonds in that year. Accordingly, entry (1) increases the retained earnings of B as of January 1, Year 7, by $2,700, and the minority interest is increased by $300. Entry (2) eliminates the par value of the intercompany bonds. Entry (3) eliminates the investment account balance against 90 percent of the subsidiary's equity, and entry (4) classifies the 10 percent interest of the minority shareholders.

9.7 INTERACTION OF INDIVIDUAL CORPORATE STATEMENTS WITH CONSOLIDATED STATEMENTS

From a consolidated point of view, any gain or loss from the acquisition of intercompany bonds should be recognized in the period in which the acquisition is made; since such a gain or loss does not normally appear in the books of either affiliated corporation, it generally becomes the subject of an adjustment in the worksheet to prepare consolidated statements.

In subsequent periods the amortization of bond discount or premium related to the intercompany bonds will be placed in the appropriate individual set of books and will then appear in the statements of the individual companies. Such entries in the accounts of the individual companies results in the booking of income or expense, which is equivalent to a portion of the gain or loss that had already been included in consolidated statements. To that extent, such income or expense must be eliminated in subsequent periods when preparing consolidated statements.

In the two preceding examples, the entire intercompany gain on reacquisition of bonds was included in the consolidated income and in the consolidated retained earnings of Year 6. In Year 7 (Example 4), it was therefore appropriate to increase the retained earnings as of January 1, Year 7, by $3,000. During Year 7, however, B Corp. augmented its income as a result of amortization of one-fourth of the discount on the intercompany bonds which had been acquired by an affiliate. Thus, as of January 1, Year 8, it will be necessary to increase the recorded retained earnings of B by $2,250 ($3,000 − $750) and in each subsequent year the necessary adjustment will decline by $750 until the bonds mature or are retired.

Several of the pertinent account balances and the changes therein, from the end of Year 6 through Year 10, are listed in the following table.

Date	Carrying Value of Bond Investment	Increase in Income from Amortization of Discount	Increase in Consolidated Retained Earnings	Consolidated Gain from Acquisition of Intercompany Bonds
Year 6				3,000
12/31, Yr. 6	97,000		3,000	
1/1, Yr. 7	97,000			
Year 7		750		
1/1, Yr. 8	97,750		2,250	
Year 8		750		
1/1, Yr. 9	98,500		1,500	
Year 9		750		
1/1, Yr. 10	99,250		750	
Year 10		750		
12/31, Yr. 10	100,000			

9.8 BONDS OF AFFILIATE ACQUIRED AT PAR—YEAR OF ACQUISITION

EXAMPLE 5. The R Corp. acquired 90 percent of the outstanding stock of T Corp. several years ago and has been utilizing the equity method in maintaining its investment account. Thus, the parent company recognizes 90 percent of the subsidiary's reported net income as an increment to the parent's investment in the subsidiary. The parent records the receipt of dividends from its subsidiary as a reduction in its investment account.

Prior to R's acquisition of control of T, it issued $500,000 of bonds at a discount that has been amortized following the straight-line method. The bonds bear interest at 4 percent per year payable on June 30 and December 31. The bonds mature on December 31, Year 10. As of December 31, Year 6, the unamortized discount amounted to $12,000. Thus, the carrying value of all of the bonds was $488,000 ($500,000 − $12,000).

On December 31, Year 6, the R Corp. purchased $100,000 of these bonds from a third party at par. From a consolidated point of view, a debt that the subsidiary had carried at $97,600 ($\frac{1}{5}$ of $488,000) has been retired by a payment of $100,000. The difference between these two amounts results in a consolidated loss of $2,400. However, this loss will not be visible in the ledger accounts of either company; it must be brought into the consolidated statements via the appropriate worksheets.

Condensed data from the income statements of the two companies for Year 6 have been entered in the first four columns of the accompanying worksheet to prepare a consolidated income statement for Year 6.

Entry (a) eliminates the income from subsidiary which had been previously recorded by R. The loss on prematurity retirement of T's bonded debt is recognized in entry (b), which in general journal form may be formulated as follows:

Loss from Acquisition of Intercompany Bonds	2,400	
Net Income—T		2,400

From a consolidated point of view, the net income of T now becomes $37,600 ($40,000 − $2,400), and it is this adjusted net income which is allocated to the shareholders in entry (c).

Condensed data from the balance sheets of the two corporations are contained in the first four columns of the worksheet to prepare a consolidated balance sheet as of December 31, Year 6. Entry (1) eliminates the intercompany bonds at par. Entry (2) eliminates that portion of the unamortized bond discount $2,400 ($\frac{1}{5}$ of $12,000), which is applicable to the bonds purchased by the parent company. This entry also has the effect of reducing the net income of T by $2,400. The purpose of entry (3) is to adjust R's net income and the equity value of the investment account by 90 percent of the reduction in T's net income $2,160 (90% of $2,400), which results from the previous entry. Entry (4) eliminates the adjusted balance of the investment account against 90 percent of the adjusted shareholders' equity of the subsidiary corporation, and entry (5) allocates the remaining 10 percent to the minority interests.

In both of the worksheets referred to above, the consolidated net income for Year 6 amounts to $77,840, which may be independently verified in the following schedule.

Net Income of R, as Reported	$80,000	
Less: Income from Subsidiary	36,000	
Net Income, Own Operations		$44,000
Net Income of T, as Reported	$40,000	
Less: Loss from Acquisition of Intercompany Bonds	2,400	
Net Income, as Adjusted for Purposes of Consolidation	$37,600	
Less: Minority Interest (10% of $37,600)	3,760	
Balance to Consolidated Entity		33,840
Consolidated Net Income		$77,840

Equity Method

R Corp. and Subsidiary
Worksheet—Consolidated Income Statement
Year 6

	R Corp.		T Corp.		Eliminations		Consolidated	
	Dr.	Cr.	Dr.	Cr.	Dr.	Cr.	Dr.	Cr.
Sales		800,000		700,000				1,500,000
Cost of Goods Sold	490,000		425,000				915,000	
Interest Expense			23,000				23,000	
Other Expenses	266,000		212,000				478,000	
Income from Subsidiary		36,000			[a]36,000			
	756,000	836,000	660,000	700,000				
Loss from Acquisition of Intercompany Bonds					[b]2,400		2,400	
Net Income—R	80,000				[c]33,840	[a]36,000	77,840	
Net Income—T			40,000			[c]37,600 [b]2,400		
	836,000	836,000	700,000	700,000				
Minority Interest					[c]3,760		3,760	
							1,500,000	1,500,000

[a] To eliminate income from subsidiary previously recorded by R.
[b] To record loss on acquisition of intercompany bonds: $2,400 ($100,000 − $97,600).
[c] To allocate net income of T Corp. as adjusted: 90% to parent and 10% to minority.

Equity Method

R Corp. and Subsidiary
Worksheet—Consolidated Balance Sheet
December 31, Year 6

	R Corp.		T Corp.		Eliminations		Consolidated	
	Dr.	Cr.	Dr.	Cr.	Dr.	Cr.	Dr.	Cr.
Current Assets	120,000		288,000				408,000	
Investment in T Corp.—Stock	270,000					[4]267,840 [3]2,160		
Investment in T Corp.—Bonds	100,000					[1]100,000		
Other Assets—net	160,000		600,000				760,000	
Current Liabilities		110,000		100,000				210,000
Bonds Payable				500,000	[1]100,000			400,000
Discount on Bonds			12,000			[2]2,400	9,600	
Capital Stock—R		250,000						250,000
Retained Earnings (1/1)—R		210,000						210,000
Net Income—R		80,000			[3]2,160			77,840
Capital Stock—T				200,000	[5]20,000 [4]180,000			
Retained Earnings (1/1)—T				60,000	[5]6,000 [4]54,000			
Net Income—T				40,000	[4]33,840 [2]2,400 [5]3,760			
	650,000	650,000	900,000	900,000				
Minority Interest						[5]29,760		29,760
							1,177,600	1,177,600

[1] To eliminate intercompany bonds.
[2] To write off portion of unamortized bond discount applicable to intercompany bonds.
[3] To reduce R's investment and net income equal to 90% of reduction in T's net income for Year 6: $2,160 (90% of $2,400).
[4] To eliminate 90% of shareholders' equity in T Corp., as adjusted, as of Dec. 31, Yr. 6.
[5] To classify 10% interest of minority stockholders as of Dec. 31, Yr. 6.

9.9 BONDS OF AFFILIATE ACQUIRED AT PAR—SUBSEQUENT YEAR

EXAMPLE 6. This illustration is based on a continuation of the previous example (Section 9.8) to the end of Year 7—the first full year in which the bonds of T will have been held by R. (The worksheets for this problem, including a three-tier worksheet, appear on p. 244 and p. 245.)

The loss from acquisition of intercompany bonds was immediately recognized in the consolidated income of Year 6. This loss was equal to that portion of the unamortized discount on T's books which was applicable to the bonds acquired by R. Nevertheless, T will continue to amortize all of its recorded bond discount to the date of maturity by debiting its interest expense account and crediting its unamortized bond discount account. Assuming the straight-line method of amortization, the total annual discount will be $3,000 per year ($12,000 ÷ 4 years). The amount applicable to the intercompany bonds will be one-fifth of that amount, or $600 per year.

The interest entries on R's books for Year 7 may be summarized as follows:

Interest Expense	23,000	
Cash		20,000
Bond Discount (Unamortized)		3,000

(Example continued on p. 246.)

Equity Method

R Corp. and Subsidiary
Worksheet—Consolidated Income Statement
Year 7

	R Corp.		T Corp.		Eliminations		Consolidated	
	Dr.	Cr.	Dr.	Cr.	Dr.	Cr.	Dr.	Cr.
Sales		790,000		695,000				1,485,000
Cost of Goods Sold	485,000		420,000				905,000	
Interest Expense			23,000			{^{c}600 ^{b}4,000}	18,400	
Other Expenses	260,000		202,000				462,000	
Income from Subsidiary		45,000			^{a}45,000			
Interest Income		4,000			^{b}4,000			
	745,000	839,000	645,000	695,000				
Net Income—R	94,000				^{d}45,540	^{a}45,000	94,540	
Net Income—T				50,000	^{c}600	^{d}50,600		
	839,000	839,000	695,000	695,000				
Minority Interest						^{d}5,060	5,060	
							1,485,000	1,485,000

^{a} To eliminate income from subsidiary previously recorded by R.
^{b} To eliminate intercompany bond interest.
^{c} To eliminate portion of T's annual amortization of bond discount applicable to $100,000 par.
^{d} To allocate net income of T, as adjusted: 90% to parent and 10% to minority.

Equity Method

R Corp. and Subsidiary
Worksheet—Consolidated Balance Sheet
December 31, Year 7

	R Corp.		T Corp.		Eliminations		Consolidated	
	Dr.	Cr.	Dr.	Cr.	Dr.	Cr.	Dr.	Cr.
Current Assets	107,000		281,000				388,000	
Investment in T Corp.—Stock	297,000				^{4}540	{^{5}295,380 ^{2}2,160}		
Investment in T Corp.—Bonds	100,000					^{4}100,000		
Other Assets—net	230,000		630,000				860,000	
Current Liabilities		100,000		90,000				190,000
Bonds Payable				500,000	^{4}100,000			400,000
Discount on Bonds			9,000		^{c}600	^{1}2,400	7,200	
Capital Stock—R		250,000						250,000
Retained Earnings (1/1)—R		290,000			^{2}2,160			287,840
Net Income—R		94,000				^{3}540		94,540
Capital Stock—T				200,000	{^{6}20,000 ^{5}180,000}			
Retained Earnings (1/1)—T				100,000	{^{5}87,840 ^{1}2,400 ^{6}9,760}			
Dividends—T			20,000			{^{6}2,000 ^{5}18,000}		
Net Income—T				50,000	{^{6}5,060 ^{5}45,540}	^{c}600		
	734,000	734,000	940,000	940,000				
Minority Interest						^{6}32,820		32,820
							1,255,200	1,255,200

^{1} To record decrease in consolidated retained earnings as result of recognition of loss on acquisition of intercompany bonds in Year 6.
^{2} To reduce R's investment and retained earnings account, as of Jan. 1, Yr. 7, for 90% of reduction in T's net income for Year 6: $2,160 (90% of $2,400).
^{3} To increase R's investment and net income, for 90% of increase in T's net income for Year 7: $540 (90% of $600).
^{4} To eliminate intercompany bonds.
^{5} To eliminate 90% of shareholders' equity in T Corp., as of Dec. 31, Yr. 7.
^{6} To classify 10% interest of minority shareholders.

R Corp. and Subsidiary
Consolidated Workpapers (3-tier)
Year 7

	Company		Adjustments & Eliminations		Consolidated
	R	T			
INCOME STATEMENT					
Revenue					
Sales	790,000	695,000			1,485,000
Income from Subsidiary	45,000		[5]45,540	[4]540	
Interest Income	4,000		[b]4,000		
Total Revenue	839,000	695,000			1,485,000
Costs and Expenses					
Cost of Goods Sold	485,000	420,000			905,000
Interest Expense		23,000		{ [c]600 [b]4,000 }	18,400
Other Expenses	260,000	202,000			462,000
Total Costs and Expenses	745,000	645,000			1,385,400
					99,600
Minority Interest in Income [10% of ($50,000 + $600)]			[6]5,060		5,060
Net Income	94,000	50,000			94,540
RETAINED EARNINGS					
Balance (1/1)—R	290,000		[2]2,160		287,840
Balance (1/1)—T		100,000	{ [5]87,840 [1]2,400 [6]9,760 }		
Net Income	94,000	50,000			94,540
Total	384,000	150,000			382,380
Less: Dividends—T		20,000		{ [6]2,000 [5]18,000 }	
Balance (12/31)	384,000	130,000			382,380
BALANCE SHEET					
Assets					
Current Assets	107,000	281,000			388,000
Investment in T Corp.—Stock	297,000		[3]540	{ [5]295,380 [2]2,160 }	
Investment in T Corp.—Bonds	100,000			[4]100,000	
Other Assets—net	230,000	630,000			860,000
Total Assets	734,000	911,000			1,248,000
Equities					
Current Liabilities	100,000	90,000			190,000
Bonds Payable		500,000	[4]100,000		400,000
Discount on Bonds		(9,000)	[c]600	[1]2,400	(7,200)
Capital Stock—R	250,000				250,000
Retained Earnings—R	384,000				382,380
Capital Stock—T		200,000	{ [6]20,000 [5]180,000 }		
Retained Earnings—T		130,000			
Minority Interest				[6]32,820	32,820
Total Equities	734,000	911,000			1,248,000

From a consolidated point of view, one-fifth of each of the foregoing items pertains to intercompany bonds and will therefore be eliminated in preparing consolidated statements. If a separate journal entry similar to the foregoing entry were to be constructed for the bonds held by the parent company, it might appear as follows:

Interest Expense	4,600	
Cash		4,000
Bond Discount (Unamortized)		600

In the accompanying worksheet to prepare a consolidated income statement for Year 7 (p. 244), entry (a) eliminates the income from subsidiary which the parent had already recorded in its books and which thus had already been included in its income for the year.

Each year, T will charge its interest expense account for $4,600 pertaining to the $100,000 par of intercompany bonds. Of this total, $4,000 represents interest expense on T's books and interest income on R's books, which are reciprocal and are eliminated in entry (b). The remaining $600 per year represents the booking by T of amortization pertaining to the intercompany bonds. Since this $600 had been included in the consolidated loss for Year 6, it is eliminated from Year 7 in entry (c) to avoid double counting. It should be recalled that the entire unamortized bond discount applicable to the intercompany bond acquisition had been recognized as a consolidated loss in Year 6. Entry (d) allocates the net income of T, as adjusted, to the parent company and to minority interests in proportion to their stockholdings.

Condensed data from the balance sheets of the two corporations as of December 31, Year 7 have been entered in the first four columns of the worksheet to prepare a consolidated balance sheet as of that date. The entire intercompany loss of $2,400 on reacquisition of $100,000 bonds was applied to reduce the income and retained earnings of T for consolidation purposes in Year 6, but did not appear in the books of either company; therefore entry (1) reduces the retained earnings of T as of January 1, Year 7, and the discount on bonds by $2,400, the amount of this loss.

When the accumulated retained earnings of T are considered to have diminished for consolidation purposes, the parent's investment account and the parent's retained earnings must be reduced by its appropriate share. Thus, in entry (2), R's accounts are reduced by $2,160 (90% of $2,400).

Consistent with the $600 increase in T's earnings in entry (c), R should increase its investment account and net income by $540 (90% of $600). This is accomplished in entry (3). The two foregoing entries may be compounded as follows:

Retained Earnings—R	2,160	
Investment in T—Stock		1,620
Net Income—R		540

Entry (4) eliminates the intercompany bonds at par. Entry (5) eliminates the adjusted balance of the investment in T Corp. stock against 90 percent of the shareholders' equity of T as of the end of Year 7. Entry (6) classifies the remaining 10 percent as the minority interest.

The worksheets for Example 6 indicate that the consolidated net income for Year 7 is $94,540, which may be independently calculated as follows:

Net Income of R, as reported	$94,000	
Less: Income from Subsidiary	45,000	
Net Income of R to Consolidated Entity		$49,000
Net Income of T, as reported	$50,000	
Add: Amortization of Discount on Intercompany Bonds	600	
Net Income of T, as Adjusted for Consolidation	$50,600	
Less: Minority Interest (10% of $50,600)	5,060	
Parent's Share of T's Income		45,540
Consolidated Net Income		$94,540

9.10 INTERCOMPANY BONDS: EXTENDED ILLUSTRATION—YEAR OF ACQUISITION

In Examples 3 and 4 we considered the issuance of bonds at par and a subsequent acquisition by an affiliate at a discount. In Examples 5 and 6 we considered the issuance of bonds at a discount and subsequent acquisition by an affiliate at par. We shall now consider the combination of original issuance at a discount and a later acquisition by an affiliate from a third party at a discount from par, which discount is unrelated to the original discount. In essence, Example 7 contains a synthesis of the main points covered in Examples 3 and 5, while Example 8 contains a synthesis of the chief points in Examples 4 and 6.

EXAMPLE 7. The P Corp., which owns 90 percent of the outstanding stock of U Corp., has been maintaining its investment on the equity method. The parent company recognizes 90 percent of the subsidiary's reported net income as an addition to the parent's investment account and to its income. The parent records the receipt of dividends from its subsidiary as a reduction in its investment account. The parent company also recognizes 90 percent of the subsidiary's reported net loss as a reduction in the investment account.

Prior to P's acquisition of control of U, it issued $500,000 par of bonds at a discount that has been amortized on the straight-line method. The bonds bear interest at 4 percent per annum, payable on June 30 and December 31. The bonds mature on December 31, Year 10. As of December 31, Year 6, when the unamortized discount amounted to $12,000, P purchased $100,000 par of these bonds for $97,000. A consolidated gain may be determined from data in the two sets of books as follows:

	All Bonds	Bonds Acquired by Affiliate
Bonds Payable	$500,000	$100,000
Less: Unamortized Discount	12,000	2,400
Carrying Values	$488,000	$ 97,600
Investment by P		97,000
Consolidated Gain		$ 600

The question may arise as to how the consolidated gain on constructive retirement of U's bonds should be allocated to the issuing and to the acquiring affiliate. This is particularly significant when one or both companies have minority interests. Many accountants hold that each affiliate played a part in the issuance and subsequent retirement of these bonds, and therefore the most appropriate allocation results when each party looks at the transaction as a constructive retirement at par. The parent company purchased $100,000 par of subsidiary bonds for $97,000, therefore a gain of $3,000 is attributable to P's action. On the other hand, the carrying value of these bonds on the books of S was $97,600. Since the acquisition is deemed to be equivalent to a retirement at par for consolidated purposes, a loss of $2,400 is attributable to U, the subsidiary. Thus, the consolidated gain of $600 is analyzed into two parts: a gain of $3,000 attributable to P Corp. and a loss of $2,400 attributable to U Corp. This approach will be followed in this and in the succeeding example.

Another school of thought holds that any gain or loss from the acquisition of intercompany bonds should normally be assigned entirely to the issuer, on the theory that any such action must have been taken primarily for the benefit of the issuer. This rationale will be illustrated in Examples 9 and 10.

Condensed data from the income statements of the two companies for Year 6 have been entered in the first four columns of the accompanying worksheet to prepare a consolidated income statement for Year 6 (p. 248). The $3,000 gain on acquisition of intercompany bonds is recorded in entry (a). As in Example 3, the gain is considered to have been earned by P, which purchased the bonds below par. On the other hand, entry (b) records the loss of $2,400, reducing the net income of the subsidiary U, which issued the bonds. This is computed as the difference between the par of the bonds and the carrying value on U's books ($100,000 − $97,600). Entry (c) eliminates the income from subsidiary, which P had previously recognized as a result of following the equity method. Entry (d) allocates the net income of U, as adjusted, to the parent and to the minority interests in proportion to their stockholdings.

Condensed data from the balance sheets of the two corporations are entered in the first four columns of the worksheet to prepare a consolidated balance sheet as of December 31, Year 6. Entry (1) eliminates the intercompany bonds at par. Entry (2) eliminates the portion of the unamortized bond discount applicable to the bonds purchased by P; this acquisition is treated as a constructive retirement. This is similar to entry (b) in this worksheet; however, now the loss of $2,400 ($\frac{1}{5}$ of $12,000) is expressed in terms of the portion of the unamortized bond discount balance, which is written off for consolidation purposes.

The object of entry (3) is to reduce P's net income and the equity value of the investment account by 90 percent of the reduction in the subsidiary net income that results from the previous entry; $2,160 (90% of $2,400). Entry (4) eliminates the adjusted balance of the investment account against 90 percent of the shareholders' equity of U, as adjusted. And entry (5) allocates the remaining 10 percent to the minority interests.

In both of the worksheets referred to above, the consolidated net income for Year 6 amounts to $80,840, which may be independently verified in the following schedule.

Net Income of P, as Reported	$80,000	
Less: Income from Subsidiary	36,000	
Net Income, Own Operations	$44,000	
Add: Gain from Acquisition of Intercompany Bonds	3,000	
Net Income of P to Consolidated Entity		$47,000
Net Income of U, as Reported	$40,000	
Less: Loss from Acquisition of Intercompany Bonds	2,400	
Net Income, as Adjusted, for Purposes of Consolidation	$37,600	
Less: Minority Interest (10% of $37,600)	3,760	
Balance to Consolidated Entity		33,840
Consolidated Net Income		$80,840

Equity Method

P Corp. and Subsidiary
Worksheet—Consolidated Income Statement
Year 6

	P Corp.		U Corp.		Eliminations		Consolidated	
	Dr.	Cr.	Dr.	Cr.	Dr.	Cr.	Dr.	Cr.
Sales		800,000		700,000				1,500,000
Cost of Goods Sold	490,000		425,000				915,000	
Interest Expense			23,000				23,000	
Other Expenses	266,000		212,000				478,000	
Income from Subsidiary		36,000			c36,000			
Gain/Loss from Acquisition of Intercompany Bonds					b2,400	a3,000		600
	756,000	836,000	660,000	700,000				
Net Income—P	80,000				d33,840 a3,000	c36,000	80,840	
Net Income—U			40,000			d37,600 b2,400		
	836,000	836,000	700,000	700,000				
Minority Interest					d3,760		3,760	
							1,500,600	1,500,600

[a] To record gain on acquisition of intercompany bonds: $3,000 ($100,000 − $97,000).
[b] To record loss on constructive retirement of intercompany bonds: $2,400 ($\frac{1}{5}$ of $12,000).
[c] To eliminate income from subsidiary previously recorded by P.
[d] To allocate net income of U Corp. as adjusted: 90% to parent and 10% to minority.

Equity Method

P Corp. and Subsidiary
Worksheet—Consolidated Balance Sheet
December 31, Year 6

	P Corp.		U Corp.		Eliminations		Consolidated	
	Dr.	Cr.	Dr.	Cr.	Dr.	Cr.	Dr.	Cr.
Current Assets	120,000		288,000				408,000	
Investment in U Corp.—Stock	270,000					[4]267,840 [3]2,160		
Investment in U Corp.—Bonds	97,000				[a]3,000	[1]100,000		
Other Assets—net	163,000		600,000				763,000	
Current Liabilities		110,000		100,000				210,000
Bonds Payable				500,000	[1]100,000			400,000
Discount on Bonds			12,000			[2]2,400	9,600	
Capital Stock—P		250,000						250,000
Retained Earnings (1/1)—P		210,000						210,000
Net Income—P		80,000			[3]2,160	[a]3,000		80,840
Capital Stock—U				200,000	[5]20,000 [4]180,000			
Retained Earnings (1/1)—U				60,000	[5]6,000 [4]54,000			
Net Income—U				40,000	[4]33,840 [2]2,400 [5]3,760			
	650,000	650,000	900,000	900,000				
Minority Interest						[5]29,760		29,760
							1,180,600	1,180,600

[1] To eliminate intercompany bonds.
[2] To write off portion of unamortized bond discount applicable to intercompany bonds.
[3] To reduce P's investment and net income by 90% of reduction in U's net income for Year 6: $2,160 (90% of $2,400).
[4] To eliminate 90% of shareholders' equity in U Corp., as of Dec. 31, Yr. 6.
[5] To classify 10% interest of minority shareholders, as of Dec. 31, Yr. 6.

9.11   INTERCOMPANY BONDS: EXTENDED ILLUSTRATION—SUBSEQUENT YEAR

EXAMPLE 8.   This illustration is based on a continuation of the previous example to the end of Year 7—the first full year in which the bonds of U will have been held by P. The net gain from acquisition of intercompany bonds, in the amount of $600, had been immediately recognized in the consolidated income of Year 6. Over the next four years, Years 7 through 10, P will amortize the investment discount by debiting its investment in bonds and crediting interest income for $3,000 at the rate of $750 per year. During the same four-year period, U will amortize the balance of the original bond discount at the rate of $3,000 per year, of which $600 is applicable to intercompany bonds.

The interest expense account of U will amount to $23,000, of which $4,600 ($\frac{1}{5}$ of $23,000) is applicable to the intercompany bonds. P's records should indicate $4,750 of interest income per year, or $150 per year more than U will record as expense in connection with the intercompany bonds. The entries in P's books in reference to interest income may be summarized as follows:

Cash	4,000	
Investment in U Corp.—Bonds	750	
Interest Income		4,750

Equity Method

P Corp. and Subsidiary
Worksheet—Consolidated Income Statement
Year 7

	P Corp.		U Corp.		Eliminations		Consolidated	
	Dr.	Cr.	Dr.	Cr.	Dr.	Cr.	Dr.	Cr.
Sales		790,000		695,000				1,485,000
Cost of Goods Sold	485,000		420,000				905,000	
Interest Expense			23,000			$\{$ [b]600 [a]4,000	18,400	
Other Expenses	260,000		202,000				462,000	
Income from Subsidiary		45,000			[d]45,000			
Interest Income		4,750			$\{$ [c]750 [a]4,000			
	745,000	839,750	645,000	695,000				
Net Income—P	94,750				[e]45,540	$\{$ [d]45,000 [c]750	94,540	
Net Income—U			50,000			[b]600 [e]50,600		
	839,750	839,750	695,000	695,000				
Minority Interest						[e]5,060	5,060	
							1,485,000	1,485,000

[a] To eliminate intercompany bond interest.
[b] To eliminate portion of U's annual amortization of discount on bonds applicable to $100,000 par.
[c] To eliminate annual amortization of investment discount on intercompany bonds.
[d] To eliminate income from subsidiary previously recorded by P.
[e] To allocate net income of U, as adjusted: 90% to parent and 10% to minority.

In the accompanying worksheet to prepare a consolidated income statement for Year 7, entry (a) eliminates the reciprocal aspects of interest ($4,000) pertaining to $100,000 par of bonds. The purpose of entry (b) is to eliminate that portion of the annual amortization of the balance of the original discount applicable to the intercompany bonds: $600. Entry (c) eliminates $750 of interest income recorded by P as a result of amortization of a portion of the discount on purchase of these bonds; it also reduces P's net income for consolidation purposes by the same amount. Entry (d) eliminates the income of U which had been previously recorded by P. Entry (e) allocates the net income of U, as adjusted, in accordance with stockholdings.

Condensed data from the balance sheets of the two corporations as of December 31, Year 7, have been entered in the first four columns of the worksheet to prepare a consolidated balance sheet as of that date. Since the entire intercompany loss of $2,400 on reacquisition of intercompany bonds was applied to reduce the income and retained earnings of U for consolidation purposes in Year 6, but did not appear in the books of either company, entry (1) reduces the retained earnings of U as of January 1, Year 7, and the discount on bonds by the amount of this loss, which is applicable to $100,000 par of U's bonds. When the accumulated retained earnings of U are considered to have diminished for consolidation purposes, then the parent's investment account and the parent's retained earnings must be reduced by its appropriate share. Thus, P's accounts are reduced by $2,160 (90% of $2,400), in entry (2).

The retained earnings as of the end of Year 6 had been increased by $3,000 in order to recognize the consolidated gain from intercompany acquisition of bonds in that year. Accordingly, entry (3) increases the retained earnings of P as of January 1, Year 7, by the same amount. Consistent with the increase in U's earnings by $600 in entry (c), P should increase its investment account and net income by $540 (90% of $600). This is accomplished in entry (4). Entry (5) eliminates the intercompany bonds at par. Entry (6) eliminates the adjusted balance of the investment in U Corp. stock against 90 percent of the shareholders' equity of U as of the end of Year 7. Entry (7) classifies the remaining 10 percent as the minority interest.

The worksheets indicate that the consolidated net income for Year 7 is $94,540, which may be independently calculated as follows:

Equity Method

P Corp. and Subsidiary
Worksheet—Consolidated Balance Sheet
December 31, Year 7

	P Corp.		U Corp.		Eliminations		Consolidated	
	Dr.	Cr.	Dr.	Cr.	Dr.	Cr.	Dr.	Cr.
Current Assets	110,000		281,000				391,000	
Investment in U Corp.—Stock	297,000				[4]540	{[6]295,380 [2]2,160		
Investment in U Corp.—Bonds	97,750				[3]3,000	{[5]100,000 [c]750		
Other Assets—net	230,000		630,000				860,000	
Current Liabilities		100,000		90,000				190,000
Bonds Payable				500,000	[5]100,000			400,000
Discount on Bonds			9,000		[b]600	[1]2,400	7,200	
Capital Stock—P		250,000						250,000
Retained Earnings (1/1)—P		290,000			[2]2,160	[3]3,000		290,840
Net Income—P		94,750			[c]750	[4]540		94,540
Capital Stock—U				200,000	{[7]20,000 [6]180,000			
Retained Earnings (1/1)—U				100,000	{[6]87,840 [1]2,400 [7]9,760			
Dividends—U			20,000			{[7]2,000 [6]18,000		
Net Income—U				50,000	{[7]5,060 [5]45,540}	[b]600		
	734,750	734,750	940,000	940,000				
Minority Interest						[7]32,820		32,820
							1,258,200	1,258,200

[1] To record decrease in consolidated retained earnings as of Dec. 31, Yr. 6: $2,400.
[2] To recognize reduction in equity in subsidiary equal to 90% of reduction in U's retained earnings.
[3] To record increase in consolidated retained earnings as of Dec. 31, Yr. 6: $3,000.
[4] To recognize increase in equity in subsidiary equal to 90% of increase in U's net income for Year 6: $540.
[5] To eliminate intercompany bonds, at par.
[6] To eliminate 90% of shareholders' equity in U Corp., as of Dec. 31, Yr. 7.
[7] To classify 10% interest of minority shareholders.

Net Income of P, as Reported		$94,750
Less: Income from Subsidiary	$45,000	
Add: Amortization of Discount on Intercompany Bonds	750	45,750
Net Income of P to Consolidated Entity		$49,000
Net Income of U, as Reported		$50,000
Add: Amortization of Discount on Intercompany Bonds		600
Net Income of U, as Adjusted for Consolidation Purposes		$50,600
Less: Minority Interest (10% of $50,600)		5,060
Parent's Share of U's Income		45,540
Consolidated Net Income		$94,540

9.12   INTERCOMPANY BONDS: EXTENDED ILLUSTRATION—ALTERNATE SOLUTION

Many accountants hold that any gain or loss from the acquisition of intercompany bonds should be assigned entirely to the issuer, on the theory that any such action would ordinarily have been taken primarily, if not exclusively, for the benefit of the issuer. This point of view will be illustrated in Examples 9 and 10. The underlying data for Example 9 is the same as that in Example 7, and the basic facts in Example 10 are the same as those in Example 8.

EXAMPLE 9. The F Corp., which owns 90 percent of the outstanding stock of Q Corp., has been maintaining its investment on the equity method. Condensed data from the income statements of the two companies for Year 6 have been entered in the first four columns of the accompanying worksheet to prepare a consolidated income statement for Year 6.

The $600 gain on acquisition of intercompany bonds is recorded in entry (a). The gain is considered to have been earned by Q, the company that issued the bonds. Entry (b) eliminates the income from subsidiary which F had previously recognized as a result of following the equity method. Entry (c) allocates the net income of Q, as adjusted, to the parent and to the minority interests in proportion to their stockholdings.

Condensed data from the balance sheets of the two corporations are entered in the first four columns of the worksheet to prepare a consolidated balance sheet as of December 31, Year 6. Entry (1) eliminates the intercompany bonds at par, against the cost of the bonds to F, and the portion of the unamortized bond discount applicable to the bonds purchased by F ($2,400); it also records the consolidated gain of $600, which is assigned to Q, the issuer of the bonds. The consolidated gain is similar to entry (a) in the income worksheet. The object of entry (2) is to reduce F's net income and the equity value of the investment account by 90 percent of the reduction in the subsidiary net income, which results from the previous entry. Entry (3) eliminates the adjusted balance of the investment account against 90 percent of the shareholders' equity of Q, as adjusted, and entry (4) allocates the remaining 10 percent to the minority interests.

In both of the worksheets referred to in this example, the consolidated net income for Year 6 amounts to $80,540, which may be independently verified in the schedule at the top of p. 253.

Equity Method				F Corp. and Subsidiary *Worksheet—Consolidated Income Statement* *Year 6*				
	F Corp.		Q Corp.		Eliminations		Consolidated	
	Dr.	Cr.	Dr.	Cr.	Dr.	Cr.	Dr.	Cr.
Sales		800,000		700,000				1,500,000
Cost of Goods Sold	490,000		425,000				915,000	
Interest Expense			23,000				23,000	
Other Expenses	266,000		212,000				478,000	
Income from Subsidiary		36,000			[b]36,000			
	756,000	836,000	660,000	700,000				
Gain from Acquisition of Intercompany Bonds						[a]600		600
Net Income—F	80,000				[c]36,540	[b]36,000	80,540	
Net Income—Q			40,000		[a]600	[c]40,600		
	836,000	836,000	700,000	700,000				
Minority Interest						[c]4,060	4,060	
							1,500,600	1,500,600

[a] To record gain on acquisition of intercompany bonds: $600 ($97,600 − $97,000).
[b] To eliminate income from subsidiary previously recorded by F.
[c] To allocate net income of Q Corp., as adjusted: 90% to parent and 10% to minority.

Net Income of F, as Reported	$80,000	
Less: Income from Subsidiary	36,000	
Net Income, Own Operations		$44,000
Net Income of Q as Reported	$40,000	
Add: Gain from Acquisition of Intercompany Bonds	600	
Net Income, as Adjusted, for Purposes of Consolidation	$40,600	
Less: Minority Interest (10% of $40,600)	4,060	
Balance to Consolidated Entity		36,540
Consolidated Net Income		$80,540

Equity Method

F Corp. and Subsidiary
Worksheet—Consolidated Balance Sheet
December 31, Year 6

	F Corp. Dr.	F Corp. Cr.	Q Corp. Dr.	Q Corp. Cr.	Eliminations Dr.	Eliminations Cr.	Consolidated Dr.	Consolidated Cr.
Current Assets	120,000		288,000				408,000	
Investment in Q Corp.—Stock	270,000				[2]540	[3]270,540		
Investment in Q Corp.—Bonds	97,000					[1]97,000		
Other Assets—net	163,000		600,000				763,000	
Current Liabilities		110,000		100,000				210,000
Bonds Payable				500,000	[1]100,000			400,000
Discount on Bonds			12,000			[1]2,400	9,600	
Capital Stock—F		250,000						250,000
Retained Earnings (1/1)—F		210,000						210,000
Net Income—F		80,000				[2]540		80,540
Capital Stock—Q				200,000	[4]20,000 [3]180,000			
Retained Earnings (1/1)—Q				60,000	[4]6,000 [3]54,000			
Net Income—Q				40,000	[4]4,060 [3]36,540	[1]600		
	650,000	650,000	900,000	900,000				
Minority Interest						[4]30,060		30,060
							1,180,600	1,180,600

[1] To eliminate investment in 20% of Q bonds against liability and related bond discount, and to record gain on constructive retirement: $600 ($97,600 − $97,000).

[2] To recognize increase in equity in subsidiary equal to 90% of increase in Q's net income for Year 6.

[3] To eliminate 90% of shareholders' equity in Q Corp., as of Dec. 31, Yr. 6.

[4] To classify 10% interest of minority shareholders as of Dec. 31, Yr. 6.

EXAMPLE 10. This illustration is based on a continuation of the previous example to the end of Year 7—the first full year in which the bonds of Q will have been held by F.

The net gain from acquisition of intercompany bonds, in the amount of $600, had been immediately recognized in the consolidated income of Year 6. However, over the next four years, Years 7 through 10, F will amortize the discount on investment in affiliate bonds by debiting its investment in bonds and crediting interest income for $3,000 at the rate of $750 per year. During the same four-year period, Q will amortize the balance of the original bond discount at the rate of $3,000 per year, of which $600 is applicable to intercompany bonds. The interest expense account of Q will amount to $23,000, of which $4,600 ($\frac{1}{5}$ of $23,000) is applicable to the $100,000 par of intercompany bonds. Pertaining to these bonds, F's records should indicate $4,750 of interest income per year, or $150 more per year than Q will record as expense in connection with these same bonds through the end of year 10. The entries in F's books for Year 7 in reference to interest income may be summarized as follows:

Cash	4,000	
Investment in Q Corp.—Bonds	750	
Interest Income		4,750

In the accompanying worksheet to prepare a consolidated income statement for Year 7, entry (a) eliminates the reciprocal aspects of interest pertaining to $100,000 par of bonds. Recall that the entire intercompany gain of $600 on acquisition of intercompany bonds was applied to increase the income and retained earnings of Q for consolidation purposes in Year 6, but did not appear in the books of either company. Thus, entry (a) confirms

Equity Method

F Corp. and Subsidiary
Worksheet—Consolidated Income Statement
Year 7

	F Corp.		Q Corp.		Eliminations		Consolidated	
	Dr.	Cr.	Dr.	Cr.	Dr.	Cr.	Dr.	Cr.
Sales		790,000		695,000				1,485,000
Cost of Goods Sold	485,000		420,000				905,000	
Interest Expense			23,000			[a]4,600	18,400	
Other Expenses	260,000		202,000				462,000	
Income from Subsidiary		45,000			[b]45,000			
Interest Income		4,750			[a]4,750			
	745,000	839,750	645,000	695,000				
Net Income—F	94,750				[c]44,865	[b]45,000	94,615	
Net Income—Q			50,000			$\left\{\begin{array}{l}\text{[c]49,850}\\ \text{[a]150}\end{array}\right.$		
	839,750	839,750	695,000	695,000				
Minority Interest					[c]4,985		4,985	
							1,485,000	1,485,000

[a] To eliminate F's interest income from Q Corp. bonds, against one-fifth of interest expense of Q and to confirm the booking of one-fourth of consolidated gain:

	Q Corp.	$\frac{1}{5}$ of Q Corp.	F Corp.
Interest Paid, at 4% per year	$20,000	$4,000	$4,000
Amortization of Original Discount	3,000	600	
Amortization of Discount on Reacquisition			750
		$4,600	$4,750

[b] To eliminate income from subsidiary previously recorded by F.
[c] To allocate net income of Q Corp. as adjusted: 90% to parent and 10% to minority.

the booking in Year 7 of one-fourth of the consolidated gain on acquisition of an affiliate's bonds—$150 per year ($600 ÷ 4 years).   In general journal form, the elimination entry is as follows:

Interest Income—F	4,750	
Interest Expense—Q		4,600
Net Income—Q		150

Entry (b) eliminates the income of Q which had been previously recorded by F, and entry (c) allocates the net income of Q in accordance with the holdings of the stockholders.

Condensed data from the balance sheets of the two corporations as of December 31, Year 7, have been entered in the first four columns of the worksheet to prepare a consolidated balance sheet as of that date.

To facilitate the elimination of intercompany debt and of related items as of the end of Year 7 the balances of selected accounts have been summarized in the schedule at the top of p. 256.

Equity Method

F Corp. and Subsidiary
Worksheet—Consolidated Balance Sheet
December 31, Year 7

	F Corp.		Q Corp.		Eliminations		Consolidated	
	Dr.	Cr.	Dr.	Cr.	Dr.	Cr.	Dr.	Cr.
Current Assets	110,000		281,000				391,000	
Investment in Q Corp.—Stock	297,000				[2]540	[4]297,405 [3]135		
Investment in Q Corp.—Bonds	97,750					[1]97,750		
Other Assets—net	230,000		630,000				860,000	
Current Liabilities		100,000		90,000				190,000
Bonds Payable				500,000	[1]100,000			400,000
Discount on Bonds			9,000			[1]1,800	7,200	
Capital Stock—F		250,000						250,000
Retained Earnings (1/1)—F		290,000				[2]540		290,540
Net Income—F		94,750			[2]135			94,615
Capital Stock—Q				200,000	[5]20,000 [4]180,000			
Retained Earnings (1/1)—Q				100,000	[5]10,060 [4]90,540	[1]600		
Net Income—Q				50,000	[5]4,985 [4]44,865 [1]150			
Dividends—Q			20,000			[5]2,000 [4]18,000		
	734,750	734,750	940,000	940,000				
Minority Interest						[5]33,045		33,045
							1,258,200	1,258,200

[1] To eliminate adjusted cost of bonds owned by F against one-fifth of carrying value of bonds payable by Q: $98,200 ($100,000 − $1,800), and to recognize increase in Q's retained earnings as of Dec. 31, Yr. 6 ($600).   Also, to eliminate excess of F's current interest income over one-fifth of Q's interest expense.

[2] To increase F's investment and retained earnings (as of 1/1) by 90% of Q's increase in net income in Year 6: $540 (90% of $600).

[3] To decrease F's investment and income by 90% of reduction in Q's net income in Year 7: $135 (90% of $150).

[4] To eliminate 90% of shareholders' equity in Q Corp. as adjusted as of Dec. 31, Yr. 7.

[5] To classify 10% interest of minority shareholders, as of Dec. 31, Yr. 7.

	Q Corp. Books		F Corp.	Add to Consolidated Retained Earnings
	Total	20%		
Par of Bonds	$500,000	$100,000	$100,000	
January 1, Year 7, Unamortized Discounts:				
Purchase Discount			3,000 ⎫	$600
Original Issue	12,000	2,400	⎭	
Carrying Values	$488,000	$ 97,600	$ 97,000	
Amortization of Discounts in Year 7:				
Purchase			750 ⎫	(150)
Original Issue	3,000	600	⎭	
December 31, Year 7 Carrying Values	$491,000	$ 98,200	$ 97,750	
Add to Consolidated Retained Earnings (net)				$450

Consistent with the foregoing schedule, entry (1) eliminates the intercompany bonded debt and the related unamortized discounts. The entry also recognizes that for consolidated purposes, the retained earnings of Q had been increased by the $600 gain on the intercompany acquisition of its bonds, and that $150 of the excess of interest income on F's books over the related interest expense on Q's books should now be deducted from consolidated retained earnings in Year 7. In general journal form, the entry would be as follows:

Bonds Payable—Q	100,000	
Net Income—Q	150	
Investment in Q Corp.—Bonds—F		97,750
Discount on Bonds—Q		1,800
Retained Earnings (1/1)—Q		600

When the retained earnings of Q is considered to have been increased, for consolidation purposes, the parent's investment account and its retained earnings (as of January 1) must be increased by the parent's appropriate share. Thus, in entry (2), F's accounts are increased by $540 (90 percent of $600). Consistent with the decrease in Q's net income of $150 in the foregoing entry, F's investment account and its income account should be decreased by $135 (90 percent of $150); this is accomplished in entry (3). Entry (4) eliminates the adjusted balance of the investment in Q Corp. stock against 90 percent of the shareholders' equity of Q as of the end of Year 7. Entry (5) classifies the remaining 10 percent as the minority interest.

The worksheets in this example indicate that the consolidated net income for Year 7 is $94,615, which may be independently calculated as follows:

Net Income of F, as Reported	$94,750	
Less: Income from Subsidiary	45,000	
Net Income of F to Consolidated Entity		$49,750
Net Income of Q, as Reported	$50,000	
Less: Amortization of Discount on Intercompany Bonds	150	
Net Income of Q, as Adjusted for Consolidation Purposes	$49,850	
Less: Minority Interest (10% of $49,850)	4,985	
Parent's Share of U's Income		44,865
Consolidated Net Income		$94,615

Summary

(1) The acquisition by an affiliate of the bonds of another affiliate is treated as a constructive _____ of the bonds.

(2) When the acquisition price of an affiliate's bonds is different from the carrying value on the issuers' books, a _____ gain or loss is to be recognized in the year of acquisition.

(3) A consolidated gain or loss on the acquisition of intercompany bonds will _____ be recognized in the subsidiary's books.

(4) In connection with intercompany bond holdings, the affiliates will continue to amortize premium and discount on their respective books. In preparing a consolidated income statement, these amortized amounts should be _____.

(5) In a consolidated balance sheet, the existence of intercompany bonds may be disclosed as _____ bonds.

(6) P Corp. owns 100 percent of the outstanding stock of S Corp. Subsequently P purchased 10 percent of S's bond for $9,700. On that date S had $100,000 par of bonds outstanding on which the unamortized discount was $1,000. The consolidated _____ on this transaction amounted to _____.

(7) R Corp. owns 100 percent of the capital stock of T Corp. T acquired 20 percent of R's outstanding bonds at a date when there were six years to maturity. The consolidated gain amounted to $12,000. Both corporations continue to amortize their respective premiums and discounts by the straight-line method. Each year $_____ of the gain will be confirmed in the accounts.

Answers: (1) retirement;   (2) consolidated;   (3) not;   (4) eliminated;   (5) treasury;   (6) gain, $200;
              (7) $2,000

Solved Problems

9.1   In each of the following cases, bonds of the parent company were acquired by a subsidiary.

	Parent's Books		Subsidiary's Purchase	
Case	Bonds Payable	Unamortized Premium (Discount)	Par Value of Bonds	Cost
I	100,000	4,000	25,000	24,000
II	200,000	(5,000)	40,000	38,000
III	300,000	(6,000)	60,000	57,000
IV	400,000	8,000	100,000	103,000

Required:

Determine the consolidated gain or loss from the acquisition of the affiliate's bonds.

SOLUTION

Case	Carrying Value of Bonds Payable	Percent Purchased	Carrying Value of Bonds Purchased	Acquisition Cost	Gain (Loss)
I	104,000	25%	26,000	24,000	2,000
II	195,000	20%	39,000	38,000	1,000
III	294,000	20%	58,800	57,000	1,800
IV	408,000	25%	102,000	103,000	(1,000)

9.2   The Rex Corporation acquired 80 percent of the outstanding capital stock of Aldo Corporation on August 12 of Year 1.

On January 1, Year 7, Aldo purchased $20,000 of Rex bonds for $19,640. The bonds bear interest at 4 percent and mature on January 1, Year 10. Condensed data from the trial balance as of December 31, Year 7, appear as follows:

	Rex Corp.	Aldo Corp.
Investment in Aldo: Stock	240,000	
Investment in Rex: Bonds		19,760
Bonds Payable: 4%—due January 1, Year 10	200,000	
Premium on Bonds	4,000	
Interest Expense	6,000	
Interest Income		920

Rex and Aldo intend to analyze any gain or loss on the purchase of intercompany bonds by assuming that actions of both affiliates are necessary to effectuate the constructive retirement. Thus, they will determine each company's gain or loss from the par value of the bonds so acquired.

Required:

(a)   Calculate the gain, or loss, on the acquisition of affiliates' bonds. Indicate what amount relates to each company.

(b) Write journal entries to eliminate the intercompany bonds, interest and related items
     as of:
     (i)   January 1, Year 7
     (ii)   December 31, Year 7
     (iii) December 31, Year 8

SOLUTION

(a)

	100%	20%
Bonds Payable—Rex	$200,000	
Unamortized Premium	6,000	
Carrying Value of Bonds	$206,000	$20,600
Cost of Investment by Aldo		19,640
Consolidated Gain		$ 960
Gain to parent corporation (issuer).		
Carrying Value		$20,600
Par		20,000
Gain to Rex		$600
Gain to subsidiary (investor).		
Par		$20,000
Investment		19,640
Gain to Aldo		360
Total Gain, as Above		$960

(b)

	(i) Jan. 1, Year 7		(ii) Dec. 31, Year 7		(iii) Dec. 31, Year 8	
	Dr.	Cr.	Dr.	Cr.	Dr.	Cr.
Bonds Payable—Rex	20,000					
Premium on Bonds—Rex	600					
Investment in Rex: Bonds—Aldo		19,640				
Gain on Acquisition of Intercompany Bonds:						
—Rex		600				
—Aldo		360				
Bonds Payable—Rex			20,000		20,000	
Premium on Bonds—Rex			400		200	
Interest Income—Aldo			920		920	
Investment in Rex: Bonds—Aldo ($19,760 + $120)				19,760		19,880
Interest Expense				600		600
Gain on Acquisition of Intercompany Bonds:						
—Rex				600		
—Aldo				360		
Retained Earnings (1/1):						
Rex ($600 − $200)						400
Aldo ($360 − $120)						240

9.3 This problem is based on the same data as in Problem 9.2. However, it should now be assumed that the acquisition of the affiliate's bonds was essentially for the benefit of the issuer, and therefore the entire gain or loss should be assigned to the issuer.

Required:

(a) Calculate the consolidated gain or loss on the acquisition of the affiliate's bonds.

(b) Write journal entries to eliminate the intercompany bonds, interest and related items as of:

    (i)   January 1, Year 7

    (ii) December 31, Year 7

    (iii) December 31, Year 8

SOLUTION

(a)

	100%	10%
Bonds Payable—Rex	$200,000	
Unamortized Premium	6,000	
Carrying Value of Bonds	$206,000	$20,600
Cost of Investment by Aldo		19,640
Consolidated Gain		$ 960

(b)

	(i) Jan. 1, Year 7		(ii) Dec. 31, Year 7		(iii) Dec. 31, Year 8	
	Dr.	Cr.	Dr.	Cr.	Dr.	Cr.
Bonds Payable—Rex	20,000					
Premium on Bonds—Rex	600					
Investment in Rex: Bonds—Aldo		19,640				
Gain on Acquisition of						
Intercompany Bonds—Rex		960				
Bonds Payable—Rex			20,000		20,000	
Premium on Bonds—Rex			400		200	
Interest Income—Aldo			920		920	
Investment in Rex: Bonds—Aldo				19,760		19,880
Interest Expense				600		600
Gain on Acquisition of						
Intercompany Bonds: Rex				960		
Retained Earnings (1/1)—Rex						640

9.4 The following data have been extracted from the trial balances of A Corp. and its subsidiary, B Corp., as of January 1, 19X6:

	A Corp.	B Corp.
Investment in B Corp.—Stock (at par)	80,000	
Bonds Payable—8%	200,000	
Unamortized Bond Premium	6,000	
Capital Stock—$10 par		100,000
Investment in A Corp.—Bonds (at cost)		49,100

The B Corp. purchased $50,000 par of A's bonds on January 1, 19X6. The bonds pay interest each January 1 and July 1; the principal matures on January 1, 19X9. Each corporation amortizes premiums and discounts utilizing the straight-line method. Both companies close their books at the end of the calendar year.

Any gain or loss on constructive retirement of bonds is assigned to the issuing corporation.

Required:

Write the journal entries to eliminate intercompany bond holdings and related matters as of:

(a) January 1, 19X6

(b) December 31, 19X6, 19X7, and 19X8.

SOLUTION

	19X6 Dr.	19X6 Cr.	19X7 Dr.	19X7 Cr.	19X8 Dr.	19X8 Cr.
(a) *January 1*						
Bonds Payable—8% (¼ of $200,000)	50,000					
Premium on Bonds Pay. (¼ of $6,000)	1,500					
Investment in A Corp.—Bonds		49,100				
Gain on Purchase of Intercompany Bonds ($1,500 + $900)		2,400				
(b) *December 31*						
Bonds Payable—8%	50,000		50,000		50,000	
Premium on Bonds Payable	1,000		500			
Interest Income ($4,000 + $300)	4,300		4,300		4,300	
Investment in A Corp.—Bonds		49,400		49,700		50,000
Interest Expense [¼ of ($16,000 − $2,000)]		3,500		3,500		3,500
Gain on Purchase of Intercompany Bonds		2,400				
Retained Earnings (1/1)—A				1,600		800

9.5 On January 1, 19X1, the Dart Corporation sold $1,000,000 of ten-year 6 percent bonds at 97. Interest is payable each January 1 and July 1.

On March 5, 19X4, the Phelps Corporation acquired 85 percent of the outstanding stock of the Dart Corporation at 69; on July 1, 19X4, the Phelps Corporation purchased bonds of Dart, with a par of $300,000, in the open market at a price of 92.

Any gain or loss on the constructive retirement of intercompany bonds is to be assigned to the issuer.

Required:

Write the elimination entries, in connection with the bonds, interest and related matters:

(a) As of July 1, 19X4.

(b) For the year ended December 31, 19X4.

(c) For the year ended December 31, 19X5.

SOLUTION*

	(a) July 1, 19X4 Dr.	(a) Cr.	(b) Dec. 31, 19X4 Dr.	(b) Cr.	(c) Dec. 31, 19X5 Dr.	(c) Cr.
Income Worksheet						
Interest Income:						
[($18,000 + $3,692)6/12]			10,846			
($18,000 + $3,692)					21,692	
Net Income—Dart	18,150		16,754			2,792
Interest Expense:						
($9,000 + $450)				9,450		
($18,000 + $900)						18,900
Gain on Reacquisition						
of Bonds		18,150		18,150		
Balance Sheet Worksheet						
Bonds Payable	300,000		300,000		300,000	
Discount on Bonds:						
($19,500 × 0.30)		5,850				
($18,000 × 0.30)				5,400		
($15,000 × 0.30)						4,500
Investment in Bonds		276,000				
($276,000 + $1,846)				277,846		
($276,000 + $1,846 + $3,692)						281,538
Net Income—Dart		18,150		16,754	2,792	
Retained Earnings (1/1)—Dart						16,754

* Explanatory notes appear at the top of p. 263, and an alternate solution appears below.

ALTERNATE SOLUTION

	(a) July 1, 19X4 Dr.	(a) Cr.	(b) Dec. 31, 19X4 Dr.	(b) Cr.	(c) Dec. 31, 19X5 Dr.	(c) Cr.
Bonds Payable	300,000		300,000			
Interest Income						
[($18,000 + $3,692)6/12]			10,846			
Discount on Bonds						
($19,500 × 0.30)		5,850				
($18,000 × 0.30)				5,400		
Investment in Bonds—Dart		276,000		277,846		
Gain on Reacquisition						
of Bonds		18,150		18,150		
Interest Expense						
($9,000 + $450)				9,450		
Bonds Payable					300,000	
Interest Income						
($18,000 + $3,692)					21,692	
Discount on Bonds						
($15,000 × 0.30)						4,500
Interest Expense						
($18,000 + $900)						18,900
Investment in Bonds						
($276,000 + $1,846 + $3,692)						281,538
Retained Earnings (1/1)—Dart						
($18,150 − $1,396)						16,754

Notes for solution and alternate solution on p. 262:

Discount on Original Issue by Dart	$ 30,000
Annual Amortization ($300,000 ÷ 10 years)	3,000
Amortized to July 1, 19X4 ($3,000 × 3.5 years)	10,500
Unamortized Discount, July 1, 19X4	19,500
Carrying Value of Dart Bonds, as of July 1, 19X4 ($1,000,000 − $19,500)	$980,500
Carrying Value of Intercompany Bonds ($980,500 × 30%)	$294,150
Cost of Intercompany Bonds to Phelps	276,000
Gain on Constructive Retirement of Bonds with Par of $300,000	$ 18,150
Discount on Investment by Phelps	$ 24,000
Annual Amortization to maturity ($24,000 ÷ 6.5 years)	3,692
Semiannual Amortization to Maturity	$ 1,846

9.6   On January 1, Year 4, the Pad Corp. purchased 100 percent of the capital stock of Quad Corp., paying $40,000 above the book value of Quad. The excess was paid because land owned by Quad was deemed to have appreciated in value. At that date, Quad had a $500,000 ten-year bond issue outstanding on which interest is payable at 8 percent per annum on January 1 and July 1. The bonds had been issued by Quad on July 1, Year 3, at a premium of $8,000.

The Pad Corp. purchased Quad bonds with a par of $100,000 on January 1, Year 8, at 95 plus $50 purchasing commission. Both companies amortize premium and discounts utilizing the straight-line method.

Required:

(*a*)   Compute the gain or loss on reacquisition of bonds and determine the amount that will be booked annually.

(*b*)   Complete the worksheet to consolidate the income statements of the two companies for Year 9.

(*c*)   Complete the worksheet to consolidate the balance sheets of the two companies as of December 31, Year 9.

SOLUTION

(*a*)

	100%	*20%*
Bonds Payable—Quad	$500,000	
Unamortized Premium [$8,000—(4.5)($800)]	4,400	
Carrying Value of Bonds January 1, Year 8	$504,400	$100,880
Cost of Investment by Pad ($95,000 + $50)		95,050
Gain on Reacquisition of Bonds		$ 5,830

Amount of gain to be booked annually, until maturity:

$5,830 ÷ 5.5 years = $1,060 per annum

(b)

Pad Corp. and Subsidiary
Worksheet—Consolidated Income Statement
Year 9

	Pad Corp.		Quad Corp.		Eliminations		Consolidated	
	Dr.	Cr.	Dr.	Cr.	Dr.	Cr.	Dr.	Cr.
Sales		896,000		935,000				
Cost of Goods Sold	625,000		708,000					
Interest Expense			39,200					
Other Expenses	210,900		117,800					
Income from Subsidiary		70,000						
Interest Income		8,900						
	835,900	974,900	865,000	935,000				
Net Income—Pad	139,000							
Net Income—Quad			70,000					
	974,900	974,900	935,000	935,000				

(c)

Pad Corp. and Subsidiary
Worksheet—Consolidated Balance Sheet
Year 9

	Pad Corp.		Quad Corp.		Eliminations		Consolidated	
	Dr.	Cr.	Dr.	Cr.	Dr.	Cr.	Dr.	Cr.
Cash	22,100		19,600					
Accounts Receivable	27,300		30,000					
Interest Receivable	2,000							
Inventory	86,000		67,000					
Depreciable Assets—net	148,000		610,000					
Land			50,000					
Investments:								
Quad Corp—Stock	222,600							
Quad Corp—Bonds	96,850							
Vouchers Payable		83,400		91,200				
Bonds Payable				500,000				
Premium on Bonds Payable				2,800				
Capital Stock—Pad		250,000						
Retained Earnings (1/1)—Pad		132,450						
Net Income—Pad		139,000						
Capital Stock—Quad				100,000				
Retained Earnings (1/1)—Quad				12,600				
Net Income—Quad				70,000				
	604,850	604,850	776,600	776,600				

(b)

Pad Corp. and Subsidiary
Worksheet—Consolidated Income Statement
Year 9

	Pad Corp.		Quad Corp.		Eliminations		Consolidated	
	Dr.	Cr.	Dr.	Cr.	Dr.	Cr.	Dr.	Cr.
Sales		896,000		935,000				1,831,000
Cost of Goods Sold	625,000		708,000				1,333,000	
Interest Expense			39,200			[a]7,840	31,360	
Other Expenses	210,900		117,800				328,700	
Income from Subsidiary		70,000			[b]70,000			
Interest Income		8,900			[a]8,900			
	835,900	974,900	865,000	935,000				
Net Income—Pad	139,000				[c]68,940	[b]70,000	137,940	
Net Income—Quad			70,000			[c]68,940		
						[a]1,060		
	974,900	974,900	935,000	935,000			1,831,000	1,831,000

[a] To eliminate Pad's interest income against 20% of interest expense of Q and to confirm the booking of 1/5.5 of consolidated gain of $5,830:

	Q Corp.	20% of Q Corp.	P Corp.	
Interest Paid at 8% per Year	$40,000	$8,000	$8,000	
Amortization of Premium	(800)	(160)		
Amortization of Discount			900	
Portion of Consolidated Gain Booked	$7,840	$8,900		$1,060

[b] To eliminate income from subsidiary, previously recorded by P.
[c] To recognize net income of Q, as adjusted.

(c)

Pad Corp. and Subsidiary
Worksheet—Consolidated Balance Sheet
Year 9

	Pad Corp.		Quad Corp.		Eliminations		Consolidated	
	Dr.	Cr.	Dr.	Cr.	Dr.	Cr.	Dr.	Cr.
Cash	22,100		19,600				41,700	
Accounts Receivable	27,300		30,000				57,300	
Interest Receivable	2,000					[5]2,000		
Inventory	86,000		67,000				153,000	
Depreciable Assets—net	148,000		610,000				758,000	
Land			50,000		[4]40,000		90,000	
Investments:								
Quad Corp—Stock	222,600				[2]4,770	[6]186,310		
						[4]40,000		
						[3]1,060		
Quad Corp—Bonds	96,850					[1]96,850		
Vouchers Payable		83,400		91,200	[5]2,000			172,600
Bonds Payable				500,000	[1]100,000			400,000
Premium on Bonds Payable				2,800	[1]560			2,240
Capital Stock—Pad		250,000						250,000
Retained Earnings (1/1)—Pad		132,450				[2]4,770		137,220
Net Income—Pad		139,000			[3]1,060			137,940
Capital Stock—Quad				100,000	[6]100,000			
Retained Earnings (1/1)—Quad				12,600	[6]17,370	[1]4,770		
Net Income—Quad				70,000	[6]68,940			
					[1]1,060			
	604,850	604,850	776,600	776,600			1,100,000	1,100,000

[1] To eliminate adjusted cost of bonds owned by P against 20% of carrying value of bonds payable by Q: $100,560 (20% of $502,800), and to recognize increase in Q's retained earnings as of Dec. 31, Yr. 8: $4,770 ($5,830 − $1,060). Also, to eliminate excess of P's current interest income over 20% of Q's current interest expense: $1,060 ($8,900 − $7,840).
[2] To increase P's investment and retained earnings (as of 1/1) by increase in Q's retained earnings as of Jan. 1, Yr. 9.
[3] To decrease P's investment and income by reduction in Q's net income for Year 9.
[4] To recognize appreciation in land as of date of acquisition of control.
[5] To eliminate intercompany interest receivable and payable.
[6] To eliminate investment, as adjusted, against shareholders' equity of Q.

Chapter 10

Consolidated Statements—
Multilevel Affiliations

10.1 INDIRECT HOLDINGS

Suppose Corporation A holds a majority interest in the common stock of Corporation B, and Corporation B holds a controlling interest in Corporation C. In such a case, A may be described as a major parent, B as a minor parent, and C as a second-level subsidiary. The entire intercompany relationship is frequently referred to as a grandfather or grandson relationship. Each of these companies other than the parent may have a minority interest, and at each level the majority interest may be affected by minority interests in lower-level subsidiaries.

In the case of complicated relationships, it may be most practical to make successive consolidations, commencing with the lowest father-son relationship, then consolidating this result with the next higher parent, and so on up the line of control. For example, in the relationship just referred to, Corporations C and B may be consolidated first, then that result can be consolidated with Corporation A. The resultant statements may be described as A and subsidiaries. This chapter, however, will be devoted to some techniques and practices of managing multilevel relationships in one worksheet.

10.2 PARENT CORPORATION BECOMES
THE SUBSIDIARY OF ANOTHER CORPORATION

EXAMPLE 1. P Corp. purchased 90 percent of the outstanding stock of S Corp. on January 1, Year 1, for $135,000, which represented 90 percent of S's book value as of that date. Condensed data from the respective balance sheets at the end of Year 1 are presented below.

	P Corp.		S Corp.	
Current Assets	$103,000		$ 56,000	
Investment in S—Stock	144,000			
Other Assets—net	190,000		135,000	
Liabilities		$155,000		$ 31,000
Capital Stock—P		200,000		
Retained Earnings (1/1)—P		60,000		
Net Income—P		37,000		
Dividends—P	15,000			
Capital Stock—S				100,000
Retained Earnings—S				50,000
Net Income—S				20,000
Dividends—S			10,000	
	$452,000	$452,000	$201,000	$201,000

An elimination entry to consolidate* these data as of December 31, Year 1, follows:

---

* See Example 4 in Chapter 6 (Section 6.6) for a complete worksheet.

Capital Stock—S	100,000	
Retained Earnings (1/1)—S	50,000	
Net Income—S	20,000	
Dividends—S		10,000
Investment in S—Stock		144,000
Minority Interest in S Corp.		16,000

To eliminate shareholders' equity of S Corp.

One year later, on January 1, Year 2, the G Corporation purchased 80 percent of the outstanding capital stock of P Corp., paying $225,600. The results of operations for Year 2 are condensed as follows:

	G Corp.	P Corp.	S Corp.
Sales	$129,000	$118,000	$115,000
Cost of Goods Sold	79,000	76,000	72,000
Gross Profit	$ 50,000	$ 42,000	$ 43,000
Selling Expenses	$ 18,000	$ 12,500	$ 10,000
General Expenses	12,000	10,000	8,000
Total Expenses	$ 30,000	$ 22,500	$ 18,000
Income from Operations	$ 20,000	$ 19,500	$ 25,000
Income from Subsidiary	33,600	22,500	
Net Income	$ 53,600	$ 42,000	$ 25,000

The schedule of retained earnings for Year 2 is as follows:

	G Corp.	P Corp.	S Corp.
Balance, January 1	$40,000	$ 82,000	$60,000
Add: Net Income	53,600	42,000	25,000
Total	$93,600	$124,000	$85,000
Less: Dividends	20,000	15,000	10,000
Balance, December 31	$73,600	$109,000	$75,000

The investment account on P's books at the end of Year 2 may be summarized as follows:

Investment in S Corp.—Stock

	Dr.	Cr.	Balance
1/1, Yr. 1: Cost	135,000		135,000
Year 1: Dividend		9,000	126,000
12/31, Yr. 1: 90% of Net Income	18,000		144,000
Year 2: Dividend		9,000	135,000
12/31, Yr. 2: 90% of Net Income	22,500		157,500

The investment account on G's books for Year 2 is summarized as follows:

Investment in P Corp.—Stock

	Dr.	Cr.	Balance
1/1, Yr. 2: Cost	225,600		225,600
Year 2: Dividend		12,000	213,600
12/31, Yr. 2: 80% of Net Income	33,600		247,200

In consolidating the income statements of the three companies, the earnings of S Corp. must first be allocated to P Corp. and to the minority shareholders in S Corp. in the ratio of 90:10. Then the earnings of P Corp. should be allocated to G Corp. and to the minority shareholders in P Corp. in the ratio of 80:20.

The reported net income of S Corp. for Year 2 is $25,000; an allocation of 90 percent to its parent company amounts to $22,500, which leaves $2,500 (10 percent of $25,000) for the minority shareholders in S. The $22,500 is only temporarily allocated to P, as 20 percent of this amount, or $4,500, should be allocated to the minority stockholders in P, and 80 percent of $22,500, or $18,000, becomes part of the consolidated net income. The schedule that follows summarizes these calculations and indicates an abbreviated method of making such allocations.

The reported net income of P Corp., $42,000, is first reduced by the subsidiary income of $22,500 in order to avoid double counting the income of S. The balance of $19,500 is then allocated 80 percent to the parent company and 20 percent to the minority interest in P.

Once the net income of each affiliate from its own operations has been calculated, a more direct determination of the allocation may be prepared, as illustrated in the following schedule:

Corp.	Net Income Own Operations	Allocation	Net Income Consolidated	Minority Income P Corp.	Minority Income S Corp.
S	$25,000				
		10%			$2,500
		20% × 90% = 18		$4,500	
		80% × 90% = 72	$18,000		
		100%			
P	19,500				
		20%		3,900	
		80%	15,600		
		100%			
G	20,000	100%	20,000		
Totals	$64,500		$53,600	$8,400	$2,500

The income statements of the three corporations for Year 2 are presented in the first six columns of the accompanying worksheet to consolidate the income statements for that year. Entries (a) and (b) remove the income from subsidiaries in order to avoid double counting of this income. The next two entries are based on the allocations in the schedule above. Entry (c) allocates the net income of S Corp. among G (72%), P (18%), and the minority interest in S (10%). Entry (d) allocates P's net income, from its own operations, between G (80%) and the minority interests (20%).

The balance sheets of the three corporations as of December 31 of Year 2 are presented in the first six columns of the accompanying worksheet to consolidate the balance sheets as of that date. Entry (1) eliminates the balance in the investment in S Corp. account against 90 percent of the shareholders' equity of S Corp., and entry (2) classifies the remaining 10 percent as the minority interest.

Entry (3) eliminates the investment in P Corp. against 80 percent of the shareholders' equity in P Corp. as of December 31, Year 2, and entry (4) classifies the remaining 20 percent as the minority interest.

Notes for worksheets on p. 269:

[a] To eliminate income from subsidiary P previously recorded by G.
[b] To eliminate income from subsidiary S previously recorded by P.
[c] To allocate net income of S among G (72%), P (19%), and minority (10%).
[d] To allocate net income of P from its own operations, between G (80%) and minority (20%).

[1] To eliminate 90% of shareholders' equity in S as of Dec. 31, Yr. 2.
[2] To classify 10% interest in S as minority interest.
[3] To eliminate 80% of shareholders' equity in P as of Dec. 31, Yr. 2.
[4] To classify 20% interest in P as minority interest.

G Corp. and Subsidiaries
Worksheet—Consolidated Income Statement
Year 2

	G Corp.		P Corp.		S Corp.		Eliminations		Consolidated	
	Dr.	Cr.	Dr.	Cr.	Dr.	Cr.	Dr.	Cr.	Dr.	Cr.
Sales		129,000		118,000		115,000				362,000
Cost of Goods Sold	79,000		76,000		72,000				227,000	
Selling Expenses	18,000		12,500		10,000				40,500	
General Expenses	12,000		10,000		8,000				30,000	
Income from Subsidiary P		33,600					a33,600			
Income from Subsidiary S				22,500			b22,500			
	109,000	162,600	98,500	140,500	90,000	115,000				
Net Income—G	53,600						{d15,600 c18,000}	a33,600	53,600	
Net Income—P			42,000					{d19,500 b22,500}		
Net Income—S					25,000			c25,000		
	162,600	162,600	140,500	140,500	115,000	115,000				
Minority Interest in S							c2,500		2,500	
Minority Interest in P							{d3,900 c4,500}		8,400	
									362,000	362,000

G Corp. and Subsidiaries
Worksheet—Consolidated Balance Sheet
December 31, Year 2

	G Corp.		P Corp.		S Corp.		Eliminations		Consolidated	
	Dr.	Cr.	Dr.	Cr.	Dr.	Cr.	Dr.	Cr.	Dr.	Cr.
Current Assets	40,400		106,500		90,000				236,900	
Investment in S Corp.—Stock			157,500					1157,500		
Investment in P Corp.—Stock	247,200							3247,200		
Other Assets—net	146,000		180,000		125,000				451,000	
Liabilities		110,000		135,000		40,000				285,000
Capital Stock—G		250,000								250,000
Retained Earnings (1/1)—G		40,000								40,000
Net Income—G		53,600								53,600
Dividends—G	20,000								20,000	
Capital Stock—P				200,000			{440,000 3160,000}			
Retained Earnings (1/1)—P				82,000			{416,400 365,600}			
Net Income—P				42,000			{48,400 333,600}			
Dividends—P			15,000					{43,000 312,000}		
Capital Stock—S						100,000	{210,000 190,000}			
Retained Earnings (1/1)—S						60,000	{26,000 154,000}			
Net Income—S						25,000	{22,500 122,500}			
Dividends—S					10,000			{21,000 19,000}		
	453,600	453,600	459,000	459,000	225,000	225,000				
Minority Interest in S								217,500		17,500
Minority Interest in P								461,800		61,800
									707,900	707,900

The amounts necessary to eliminate the controlling interests and to show the minority interests are summarized in the following two schedules.

S Corp.	Total	Controlling Interest (90%)	Minority (10%)
Capital Stock	$100,000	$ 90,000	$10,000
Retained Earnings, Jan. 1	60,000	54,000	6,000
Net Income, Year 2	25,000	22,500	2,500
Dividends	(10,000)	(9,000)	(1,000)
Totals	$175,000	$157,500	$17,500

P Corp.	Total	Controlling Interest (80%)	Minority (20%)
Capital Stock	$200,000	$160,000	$40,000
Retained Earnings, Jan. 1	82,000	65,600	16,400
Net Income, Year 2	42,000	33,600	8,400
Dividends	(15,000)	(12,000)	(3,000)
Totals	$309,000	$247,200	$61,800

10.3 INTERCOMPANY TRANSACTIONS BETWEEN MULTILEVEL CORPORATIONS —SALES AND PURCHASES

EXAMPLE 2. This example is based on the same data as in Example 1; however, the following information has been added: During Year 2, P Corp. sold $50,000 of goods to G Corp., and $10,000 of these goods remain in G's inventory at the end of the year. The unrealized gross profit contained in this merchandise amounts to $3,500.

The investment accounts in the books of P and G will be identical with those in Example 1. Also, the individual income statements for Year 2 and the balance sheets at the end of Year 2 will be the same as those in the previous example. However, adjustments for the above-mentioned intercompany transactions will have to be made when preparing consolidated statements. (*Note*: As an alternate approach, a three-tier worksheet is included in this example on p. 273.)

The income statements of the three corporations for Year 2 are presented in the first six columns of the accompanying worksheet to consolidate the income statements for that year (p. 272). Entries (a) and (b) remove any income from subsidiaries in order to avoid double counting of this income. Entry (c) eliminates intercompany sales and purchases, and entry (d) eliminates the unrealized gross profit in goods sold by P that remain in G's inventory at end of Year 2.

Entry (e) allocates the net income of S Corp. among G (72 percent), P (18 percent), and the minority interest in S (10 percent). Entry (f) allocates P's net income, as adjusted, between G (80 percent) and the minority interests (20 percent). The calculation of the foregoing percentages and the allocation of income is summarized in the following schedule:

	Consolidated Net Income	Minority Income P Corp.	Minority Income S Corp.
S Corp. Reported Net Income	$25,000		
80% of 90% =	72%	$18,000	
20% of 90% =	18%		$4,500	
Minority =	10%			$2,500
	100%			
P Corp. Reported Net Income	$42,000		
Less: Subsidiary Income	22,500		
P's Own Operations	$19,500		
Less: Unrealized Gross Profit in Ending Inventory	3,500		
Balance	$16,000		
Control by P	80%	12,800	
Minority	20%		3,200	
	100%			
G Corp., Reported Net Income	$53,600		
Less: Subsidiary Income	33,600		
G's Own Operations		20,000		
Totals		$50,800	$7,700	$2,500

The balance sheets of the three corporations as of December 31, Year 2, are presented in the first six columns of the accompanying worksheet to consolidate the balance sheets as of that date. Entry (d) recognizes the unrealized profit in merchandise held by G and reduces P's net income by the same $3,500. Consistent with the reduction in P's net income for Year 2, the net income of G is reduced by $2,800 (90% of $3,500), and the investment in P is reduced by the same amount. This is accomplished in entry (1).

Entry (2) eliminates the balance in the investment in S Corp. account against 90 percent of the shareholders' equity of S Corp. Entry (3) classifies the remaining 10 percent as the minority interest.

Entry (4) eliminates the investment in P Corp. against 80 percent of the shareholders' equity in P Corp. as of December 31, Year 2. Entry (5) classifies the remaining 20 percent as the minority interest.

The amounts necessary to eliminate controlling interests and to set the minority interests are as follows:

S. Corp.	Total	Controlling (90%)	Minority (10%)
Capital Stock	$100,000	$ 90,000	$10,000
Retained Earnings, Jan. 1	60,000	54,000	6,000
Net Income, Year 2	25,000	22,500	2,500
Dividends	(10,000)	(9,000)	(1,000)
Totals	$175,000	$157,500	$17,500

P. Corp.	Total	Controlling (80%)	Minority (20%)
Capital Stock	$200,000	$160,000	$40,000
Retained Earnings, Jan. 1	82,000	65,600	16,400
Net Income, Year 2, as Adjusted ($42,000 − $3,500)	38,500	30,800	7,700
Dividends	(15,000)	(12,000)	(3,000)
Totals	$305,500	$244,400	$61,100

Equity Method

G Corp. and Subsidiaries
Worksheet—Consolidated Income Statement
Year 2

	G Corp.		P Corp.		S Corp.		Eliminations		Consolidated	
	Dr.	Cr.	Dr.	Cr.	Dr.	Cr.	Dr.	Cr.	Dr.	Cr.
Sales		129,000		118,000		115,000	c50,000			312,000
Cost of Goods Sold	79,000		76,000		72,000		d3,500	c50,000	180,500	
Selling Expenses	18,000		12,500		10,000				40,500	
General Expenses	12,000		10,000		8,000				30,000	
Income from Subsidiary P		33,600					a33,600			
Income from Subsidiary S				22,500			b22,500			
	109,000	162,600	98,500	140,500	90,000	115,000				
Net Income—G	53,600						{f12,800 / e18,000}	a33,600	50,800	
Net Income—P			42,000					{d3,500 / b22,500 / f16,000}		
Net Income—S					25,000			e25,000		
	162,600	162,600	140,500	140,500	115,000	115,000				
Minority Interest in S								e2,500	2,500	
Minority Interest in P								{f3,200 / e4,500}	7,700	
									312,000	312,000

Equity Method

G Corp. and Subsidiaries
Worksheet—Consolidated Balance Sheet
December 31, Year 2

	G Corp.		P Corp.		S Corp.		Eliminations		Consolidated	
	Dr.	Cr.	Dr.	Cr.	Dr.	Cr.	Dr.	Cr.	Dr.	Cr.
Current Assets	40,400		106,500		90,000			d3,500	233,400	
Investment in S Corp.—Stock			157,500					2157,500		
Investment in P Corp.—Stock	247,200							{4244,400 / 12,800}		
Other Assets—net	146,000		180,000		125,000				451,000	
Liabilities		110,000		135,000		40,000				285,000
Capital Stock—G		250,000								250,000
Retained Earnings (1/1)—G		40,000								40,000
Net Income—G		53,600					12,800			50,800
Dividends—G	20,000								20,000	
Capital Stock—P				200,000			{540,000 / 4160,000}			
Retained Earnings (1/1)—P				82,000			{516,400 / 465,600}			
Net Income—P				42,000			{57,700 / 430,800 / d3,500}			
Dividends—P			15,000					{53,000 / 412,000}		
Capital Stock—S						100,000	{310,000 / 290,000}			
Retained Earnings (1/1)—S						60,000	{36,000 / 254,000}			
Net Income—S						25,000	{32,500 / 222,500}			
Dividends—S					10,000			{31,000 / 29,000}		
	453,600	453,600	459,000	459,000	225,000	225,000				
Minority Interest in S								317,500		17,500
Minority Interest in P								561,100		61,100
									704,400	704,400

G Corp. and Subsidiaries
Consolidated Workpapers (3-tier)
Year 2

	Company			Adjustments & Eliminations		Consolidated
	G	P	S			
INCOME STATEMENT						
Revenue						
Sales	129,000	118,000	115,000	ᶜ50,000		312,000
Income from Subsidiary—P	33,600			{ ⁴30,800 ¹2,800		
Income from Subsidiary—S		22,500		²22,500		
Total Revenue	162,600	140,500	115,000			312,000
Costs and Expenses						
Cost of Goods Sold	79,000	76,000	72,000	ᵈ3,500	ᶜ50,000	180,500
Selling Expenses	18,000	12,500	10,000			40,500
General Expenses	12,000	10,000	8,000			30,000
Total Costs and Expenses	109,000	98,500	90,000			251,000
						61,000
Minority Interest in Income of S (10% of $25,000)				³2,500 ⎫		10,200
Minority Interest in Income of P [20% of ($42,000 − $3,500)]				⁵7,700 ⎭		
Net Income	53,600	42,000	25,000			50,800
RETAINED EARNINGS						
Balance (1/1)—G	40,000					40,000
Balance (1/1)—P		82,000		{ ⁵16,400 ⁴65,600		
Balance (1/1)—S			60,000	{ ³6,000 ²54,000		
Net Income	53,600	42,000	25,000			50,800
Total	93,600	124,000	85,000			90,800
Less: Dividends—G	20,000					20,000
Dividends—P		15,000		{ ⁵3,000 ⁴12,000		
Dividends—S			10,000	{ ³1,000 ²9,000		
Balance (12/31)	73,600	109,000	75,000			70,800
BALANCE SHEET						
Assets						
Current Assets	40,400	106,500	90,000		ᵈ3,500	233,400
Investment in P Corp.	247,200				{ ⁴244,400 ¹2,800	
Investment in S Corp.		157,500			²157,500	
Other Assets—net	146,000	180,000	125,000			451,000
Total Assets	433,600	444,000	215,000			684,400
Equities						
Liabilities	110,000	135,000	40,000			285,000
Capital Stock—G	250,000					250,000
Retained Earnings—G	73,600					70,800
Capital Stock—P		200,000		{ ⁵40,000 ⁴160,000		
Retained Earnings—P	*	109,000				
Capital Stock—S			100,000	{ ³10,000 ²90,000		
Retained Earnings—S			75,000			
Minority Interest in S					³17,500	17,500
Minority Interest in P					⁵61,100	61,100
Total Equities	433,600	444,000	215,000			684,400

ᵃ To eliminate income from P previously recorded by G.

ᵇ To eliminate income from S previously recorded by P.

ᶜ To eliminate intercompany sales and purchases.

ᵈ To eliminate unrealized gross profit in inventory of G at end of Year 2; goods sold by P.

ᵉ To allocate net income of S among G (72%), P (18%), and minority (10%).

ᶠ To allocate net income of P, as adjusted, between G (80%) and minority (20%).

¹ To reduce G's investment in P, and G's net income, by 80% of P's unrealized profit; $2,800 (80% of $3,500).

² To eliminate 90% of shareholders' equity of S as of Dec. 31, Yr. 2.

³ To classify 10% interest in S as minority interest.

⁴ To eliminate 80% of shareholders' equity of P as of Dec. 31, Yr. 2.

⁵ To classify 20% interest in P as minority interest.

10.4 SUBSIDIARY CORPORATION BECOMES THE PARENT OF ANOTHER CORPORATION

EXAMPLE 3. R Corp. purchased 90 percent of the outstanding stock of S Corp. on January 1, Year 1, for $252,000, which represented 90 percent of S's book value as of that date. Condensed data from the respective balance sheets at the end of Year 1 are presented here:

	R Corp.		S Corp.	
Current Assets	$ 96,000		$ 85,000	
Investment in S—Stock	261,000			
Other Assets—net	190,000		235,000	
Liabilities		$215,000		$ 30,000
Capital Stock—R		250,000		
Retained Earnings (1/1)—R		60,000		
Net Income—R		37,000		
Dividends—R	15,000			
Capital Stock—S				200,000
Retained Earnings—S				80,000
Net Income—S				20,000
Dividends—S			10,000	
	$562,000	$562,000	$330,000	$330,000

The elimination entries, in general journal form, to consolidate these data as of December 31, Year 1 are as follows:

Capital Stock—S	180,000	
Retained Earnings (1/1)—S	72,000	
Net Income—S	18,000	
Dividends—S		9,000
Investment in S—Stock		261,000

To eliminate 90% of shareholders' equity of S Corp. against investment account.

Capital Stock—S	20,000	
Retained Earnings (1/1)—S	8,000	
Net Income—S	2,000	
Dividends—S		1,000
Minority Interest in S Corp.		29,000

To classify 10% of shareholders' equity of S Corp. as minority interest.

One year later, on January 1, Year 2, S Corp. purchased 80 percent of the outstanding capital stock of T Corp., paying $143,000. T Corp. had outstanding capital stock of $100,000 and retained earnings of $60,000. The recorded net assets of T were considered to be proper, except that T owned rights to a fully amortized patent which R and S considered to have an additional six years of economic life from the beginning of Year 2, the date of acquisition of control. The value of T's patent is calculated as follows.

Amount Paid by S for 80% Interest in T	$143,000	
Indicated Value of 100% ($143,000 ÷ 0.80)		$178,750
Book Value of T Corp., Jan. 1, Year 2:		
Capital Stock	$100,000	
Retained Earnings	60,000	
Total		160,000
Value of Patent		$ 18,750

The results of operations for Year 2, are condensed as follows:

	R Corp.	S Corp.	T Corp.
Sales	$130,000	$118,000	$115,000
Cost of Goods Sold	80,000	76,000	72,000
Gross Profit	$ 50,000	$ 42,000	$ 43,000
Selling Expenses	$ 18,000	$ 12,500	$ 10,000
General Expenses	12,000	10,000	8,000
Total Expenses	$ 30,000	$ 22,500	$ 18,000
Income from Operations	$ 20,000	$ 19,500	$ 25,000
Income from Subsidiary	35,550	20,000	
Net Income	$ 55,550	$ 39,500	$ 25,000

The schedule of retained earnings for Year 2 is as follows:

	R Corp.	S Corp.	T Corp.
Balance, Jan. 1	$ 82,000	$ 90,000	$60,000
Add: Net Income	55,550	39,500	25,000
Total	$137,550	$129,500	$85,000
Less: Dividends	20,000	15,000	10,000
Balance, Dec. 31	$117,550	$114,500	$75,000

The consolidated net income and minority interests for Year 2 may be independently calculated as follows:

	Consolidated Net Income	Minority Income S Corp.	T Corp.
T Corp., Reported Net Income	$25,000		
Less: Amortization of Patent ($\frac{1}{6}$ of $18,750)	3,125		
Net Income for Consolidation Purposes	$21,875		
90% of 80% = 72%	$15,750		
10% of 80% = 8		$1,750	
Minority—T = 20			$4,375
100%			
S Corp., Reported Net Income	$39,500		
Less: Subsidiary Income	20,000		
Net Income from S's Own Operations	$19,500		
Control by R 90%	17,550		
Minority—S 10		1,950	
100%			
R Corp., Reported Net Income	$55,550		
Less: Subsidiary Income	35,550		
Net Income from R's Own Operations	20,000		
Totals	$53,300	$3,700	$4,375

The investment account on R's books at the end of Year 2 may be summarized as follows:

Investment in S Corp.—Stock

	Dr.	Cr.	Balance
1/1, Yr. 1: Cost	252,000		252,000
Year 1: Dividend		9,000	243,000
12/31, Yr. 1: 90% of Net Income	18,000		261,000
Year 2: Dividend		13,500	247,500
12/31, Yr. 2: 90% of Net Income	35,550		283,050

Investment in T Corp.—Stock

	Dr.	Cr.	Balance
1/1, Yr. 2: Cost	143,000		143,000
Year 2: Dividend		8,000	135,000
12/31, Yr. 2: 80% of Net Income	20,000		155,000

In consolidating the income statements of the three companies, the earnings of T Corp. (adjusted for amortization of patent) must first be allocated to S Corp. and to the minority shareholders in the ratio of 80:20. Then the earnings of S Corp. should be allocated to R Corp. and to its minority shareholders in the ratio of 90:10. A more direct allocation is made based on the foregoing schedule, which shows the direct percentage of equity in each element of income.

The income statements of the three corporations for Year 2 are presented in the first six columns of the accompanying worksheet to consolidate the income statements for that year. Entries (a) and (b) remove the

Equity Method

R Corp. and Subsidiaries
Worksheet—Consolidated Income Statement
Year 2

	R Corp.		S Corp.		T Corp.		Eliminations		Consolidated	
	Dr.	Cr.	Dr.	Cr.	Dr.	Cr.	Dr.	Cr.	Dr.	Cr.
Sales		130,000		118,000		115,000				363,000
Cost of Goods Sold	80,000		76,000		72,000				228,000	
Selling Expenses	18,000		12,500		10,000				40,500	
General Expenses	12,000		10,000		8,000				30,000	
Income from Subsidiary S		35,550					a35,550			
Income from Subsidiary T				20,000			b20,000			
Amortization of Patent							c3,125		3,125	
	110,000	165,550	98,500	138,000	90,000	115,000				
Net Income—R	55,550						{e17,550 / d15,750}	a35,550	53,300	
Net Income—S			39,500					{e19,500 / b20,000}		
Net Income—T					25,000			{d21,875 / c3,125}		
	165,550	165,550	138,000	138,000	115,000	115,000				
Minority Interest in S							{e1,950 / d1,750}		3,700	
Minority Interest in T							d4,375		4,375	
									363,000	363,000

[a] To eliminate income from S previously recorded by R.
[b] To eliminate income from T previously recorded by S.
[c] To record amortization of patent for Year 2: $3,125 ($\frac{1}{6}$ of $18,750).
[d] To allocate net income of T, as adjusted, among R (72%), S (8%), and minority (20%).
[e] To allocate net income of S between R (90%) and minority (10%).

income from subsidiaries in order to avoid double counting of that income. Entry (c) records amortization of value of the patent assigned to T, $3,125 ($\frac{1}{6}$ of $18,750$).

Entry (d) allocates the net income of T Corp., as adjusted, among R (72 percent), S (8 percent), and the minority interest in T (20 percent). Entry (e) allocates S's net income between R (90 percent) and the minority interests (10 percent).

The balance sheets of the three corporations as of December 31, Year 2, are presented in the first six columns of the accompanying worksheet to consolidate the balance sheets as of that date. Entry (1) recognizes the entire value of the patent, $18,750$, which had been determined at the date of acquisition of 80 percent of the stock of T Corp. Entry (c) is similar to the same lettered entry in the worksheet to consolidate the income statements for

Equity Method

R Corp. and Subsidiaries
Worksheet—Consolidated Balance Sheet
December 31, Year 2

	R Corp. Dr.	R Corp. Cr.	S Corp. Dr.	S Corp. Cr.	T Corp. Dr.	T Corp. Cr.	Eliminations Dr.	Eliminations Cr.	Consolidated Dr.	Consolidated Cr.
Current Assets	104,550		108,500		90,000				303,050	
Investment in T Corp.—Stock			155,000					[4]152,500 [2]2,500		
Investment in S Corp.—Stock	283,050							[6]280,800 [3]2,250		
Other Assets—net	146,000		180,500		125,000				451,500	
Liabilities		166,050		129,500		40,000				335,550
Capital Stock—R		250,000								250,000
Retained Earnings (1/1)—R		82,000								82,000
Net Income—R		55,550						[3]2,250		53,300
Dividends—R	20,000								20,000	
Capital Stock—S				200,000			[7]20,000 [6]180,000			
Retained Earnings (1/1)—S				90,000			[7]9,000 [6]81,000			
Net Income—S				39,500			[7]3,700 [6]33,300 [2]2,500			
Dividends—S			15,000					[7]1,500 [6]13,500		
Capital Stock—T						100,000	[5]20,000 [4]80,000			
Retained Earnings (1/1)—T						60,000	[5]12,000 [4]48,000			
Net Income—T						25,000	[4]17,500 [c]3,125 [5]4,375			
Dividends—T					10,000			[5]2,000 [4]8,000		
	553,600	553,600	459,000	459,000	225,000	225,000				
Appraisal Capital—T							[5]3,750 [4]15,000	[1]18,750		
Patent							[1]18,750	[c]3,125	15,625	
Minority Interest in T								[5]38,125		38,125
Minority Interest in S								[7]31,200		31,200
									790,175	790,175

[1] To record value of T's patent based on cost of 80% of outstanding stock of T.

[2] To adjust S's investment and net income for 80% of reduction in T's net income for Year 2: $2,500 (80% of $3,125).

[3] To adjust R's investment and net income for 80% of reduction in S's net income for Year 2: $2,250 (90% of $2,500).

[4] To eliminate 80% of shareholders' equity in T as of Dec. 31, Yr. 2.

[5] To classify 20% of shareholders' equity in T as minority interest.

[6] To eliminate 90% of shareholders' equity in S as of Dec. 31, Yr. 2.

[7] To classify 10% of shareholders' equity in S as minority interest.

Year 2, and it performs the same function. The purpose of entry (2) is to reduce the investment in T by $2,500, 80 percent of the $3,125 reduction made to the net income of T in the consolidation workpapers. Consistent with the foregoing adjustment of S's equity, it is necessary to reduce R's net income and its investment in S by $2,250 (90 percent of $2,500); this is accomplished in entry (3).

Entry (4) eliminates the balance in the investment in T Corp. account against 80 percent of the shareholders' equity of T Corp., and entry (5) classifies the remaining 20 percent as the minority interest. Entry (6) eliminates the investment in S Corp. against 90 percent of the shareholders' equity in S Corp. as of December 31, Year 2. Entry (7) classifies the remaining 10 percent as the minority interest.

10.5 CONNECTING AFFILIATES

EXAMPLE 4. P Corp. owns 80 percent of F Corp. and 70 percent of T Corp. In addition, F owns 10 percent of T. In such a case, F's interest in T is described as a connecting affiliate; it may not properly be described as a minor parent since it does not own a controlling interest in T.

The relationship described above may be diagrammed as in Fig. 10-1.

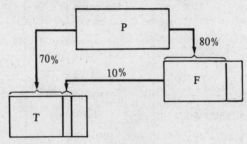

Fig. 10-1

The results of operations for Year 5 are condensed as follows:

	P Corp.	F Corp.	T Corp.
Sales	$285,000	$242,000	$88,000
Cost of Goods Sold	180,000	160,000	29,000
Gross Profit	$105,000	$ 82,000	$59,000
Selling Expenses	$ 10,000	$ 11,000	$10,000
General Expenses	15,000	11,000	9,000
Total Expenses	$ 25,000	$ 22,000	$19,000
Income from Operations	$ 80,000	$ 60,000	$40,000
Income from Subsidiaries:			
F Corp.	51,200		
T Corp.	28,000	4,000	
Net Income	$159,200	$ 64,000	$40,000

The schedule of retained earnings for Year 5 is as follows:

	P Corp.	F Corp.	T Corp.
Balance, Jan. 1	$ 40,000	$ 82,000	$ 60,000
Add: Net Income	159,200	64,000	40,000
Total	$199,200	$146,000	$100,000
Less: Dividends	50,000	20,000	10,000
Balance, Dec. 31	$149,200	$126,000	$ 90,000

The investment accounts on P's books at the end of Year 5 are summarized as follows:

Investment in F Corp.—Stock

	Dr.	Cr.	Balance
1/1, Yr. 5: Balance	135,000		135,000
Year 5: Dividend		16,000	119,000
12/31, Yr. 5: 80% of Net Income	51,200		170,200

Investment in T Corp.—Stock

	Dr.	Cr.	Balance
1/1, Yr. 5: Balance	100,000		100,000
Year 5: Dividend		7,000	93,000
12/31, Yr. 5: 70% of Net Income	28,000		121,000

The investment account on F's books for Year 5 is summarized as follows:

Investment in T Corp.—Stock

	Dr.	Cr.	Balance
1/1, Yr. 5: Cost	14,286		14,286
Year 5: Dividend		1,000	13,286
12/31, Yr. 5: 10% of Net Income	4,000		17,286

The income statements of the three corporations for Year 5 are presented in the first six columns of the accompanying worksheet to consolidate the income statements for that Year (p. 280). Entries (a) and (b) remove the income from subsidiaries in order to avoid double counting of this income.

The consolidated net income and minority interests in income for Year 5 may be independently calculated as follows:

		Consolidated Net Income	Minority Income F Corp.	Minority Income T Corp.
T Corp. Reported Net Income	$40,000			
Control by P—Directly	70%	$ 28,000		
Through Co. F (80% × 10%)	8	3,200		
Minority in F (20% × 10%)	2		$ 800	
Minority in T	20			$8,000
	100%			
F Corp. Reported Net Income	$64,000			
Less: Subsidiary Income	4,000			
F's Own Operations	$60,000			
Control by P	80%	48,000		
Minority	20		12,000	
	100%			
P Corp. Reported Net Income	$159,200			
Less: Subsidiary Income	79,200			
P's Own Operations		80,000		
Totals		$159,200	$12,800	$8,000

The next two entries are based on the allocations in the foregoing schedule. Entry (c) allocates the net income of T Corp. among P (78%), F (2%), and the minority interest in T (20%). Entry (d) allocates F's net income as adjusted, between P (80%) and the minority interests (20%).

The balance sheets of the three corporations as of December 31, Year 5, are presented in the first six columns of the accompanying worksheet to consolidate the balance sheets as of that date. Entry (1) eliminates the balance of P's investment in T Corp. account against 70 percent of the shareholders' equity of F Corp. Entry (2) eliminates F's investment account against 10 percent of the shareholders' equity of F Corp. Entry (3) classifies the remaining 20 percent as the minority interest.

Entry (4) eliminates the investment in F Corp. against 80 percent of the shareholders' equity in F Corp. as of December 31, Year 5. Entry (5) classifies the remaining 20 percent as the minority interest.

(Example continued on p. 282.)

Equity Method

P Corp. and Subsidiaries
Worksheet—Consolidated Income Statement
Year 5

	P Corp.		F Corp.		T Corp.		Eliminations		Consolidated	
	Dr.	Cr.	Dr.	Cr.	Dr.	Cr.	Dr.	Cr.	Dr.	Cr.
Sales		285,000		242,000		88,000				615,000
Cost of Goods Sold	180,000		160,000		29,000				369,000	
Selling Expenses	10,000		11,000		10,000				31,000	
General Expenses	15,000		11,000		9,000				35,000	
Income from Subsidiary F		51,200					[a]51,200			
Income from Subsidiary T		28,000		4,000			[b]32,000			
	205,000	364,200	182,000	246,000	48,000	88,000				
Net Income—P	159,200						[d]48,000 [c]31,200	[b]28,000 [a]51,200	159,200	
Net Income—F				64,000				[d]60,000 [b]4,000		
Net Income—T					40,000			[c]40,000		
	364,200	364,200	246,000	246,000	88,000	88,000				
Minority Interest in F								[d]12,000 [c]800	12,800	
Minority Interest in T								[c]8,000	8,000	
									615,000	615,000

[a] To eliminate income from F previously recorded by P.
[b] To eliminate income from T previously recorded by P and F.
[c] To allocate net income of T among P (78%), F (2%), and minority (20%).
[d] To allocate net income of F, as adjusted, between P (80%) and minority (20%).

Equity Method

P Corp. and Subsidiaries
Worksheet—Consolidated Balance Sheet
December 31, Year 5

	P Corp.		F Corp.		T Corp.		Eliminations		Consolidated	
	Dr.	Cr.	Dr.	Cr.	Dr.	Cr.	Dr.	Cr.	Dr.	Cr.
Current Assets	68,000		94,714		69,000				231,714	
Investment in F Corp.—Stock	170,200							[4]170,200		
Investment in T Corp.—Stock	121,000							[1]121,000		
Investment in T Corp.—Stock			17,286					[2]17,286		
Other Assets—net	200,000		227,000		260,000				687,000	
Liabilities		110,000		126,250		156,143				392,393
Capital Stock—P		300,000								300,000
Retained Earnings (1/1)—P		40,000								40,000
Net Income—P		159,200								159,200
Dividends—P	50,000								50,000	
Capital Stock—F				200,000			{ [5]40,000 [4]160,000			
Retained Earnings (1/1)—F			31,250					{ [5]6,250 [4]25,000		
Net Income—F				64,000			{ [5]12,800 [4]51,200			
Dividends—F			20,000					{ [5]4,000 [4]16,000		
Capital Stock—T						100,000	{ [2]10,000 [1]70,000 [3]20,000			
Retained Earnings (1/1)—T						42,857	{ [2]4,286 [1]30,000 [3]8,571			
Net Income—T						40,000	{ [2]4,000 [1]28,000 [3]8,000			
Dividends—T					10,000			{ [2]1,000 [1]7,000 [3]2,000		
	609,200	609,200	390,250	390,250	339,000	339,000				
Minority Interest in T								[3]34,571		34,571
Minority Interest in F								[5]42,550		42,550
									968,714	968,714

[1] To eliminate 70% of shareholders' equity of T as of end of Year 6.
[2] To eliminate 10% of shareholders' equity of T as of end of Year 6.
[3] To classify 20% of shareholders' equity of T as minority interest.
[4] To eliminate 80% of shareholders' equity of F as of end of Year 7.
[5] To classify 20% of shareholders' equity of F as minority interest.

A summary of the amounts necessary to eliminate the controlling interests and to show the minority interests as of the end of Year 5 are contained in the following two schedules.

T Corp.	Total	P (70%)	F (10%)	Minority (20%)
Capital Stock	$100,000	$ 70,000	$10,000	$20,000
Retained Earnings, Jan. 1	42,857	30,000	4,286	8,571
Net Income, Year 5	40,000	28,000	4,000	8,000
Dividends	(10,000)	(7,000)	(1,000)	(2,000)
Totals	$172,857	$121,000	$17,286	$34,571

The controlling columns P and F are headed "Controlling Interests".

F Corp.	Total	Controlling (80%)	Minority (20%)
Capital Stock	$200,000	$160,000	$40,000
Retained Earnings, Jan. 1	(31,250)	(25,000)	(6,250)
Net Income, Year 5	64,000	51,200	12,800
Dividends	(20,000)	(16,000)	(4,000)
Totals	$212,750	$170,200	$42,550

10.6 CONNECTING AFFILIATES—SUBSEQUENT YEAR

EXAMPLE 5. This example is a continuation of Example 4 into the next year, Year 6. During Year 6, P made sales of $50,000 to T. At the end of Year 6, T had $22,000 of these goods in its inventory, on which P had recorded a gross profit of $10,000. At the end of Year 6, T still owed $15,000 to P.

The investment accounts on P's books at the end of Year 6 are summarized as follows:

Investment in F Corp.—Stock

	Dr.	Cr.	Balance
1/1, Yr. 5: Balance	135,000		135,000
Year 5: Dividend		16,000	119,000
12/31, Yr. 5: 80% of Net Income	51,200		170,200
Year 6: Dividend		16,000	154,200
12/31, Yr. 6: 80% of Net Income	52,000		206,200

Investment in T Corp.—Stock

	Dr.	Cr.	Balance
1/1, Yr. 5: Balance	100,000		100,000
Year 5: Dividend		7,000	93,000
12/31, Yr. 5: 70% of Net Income	28,000		121,000
12/31, Yr. 6: 70% of Net Income	24,500		145,500

The investment account on F's books for Years 5 and 6 is summarized as follows:

Investment in T Corp.—Stock

	Dr.	Cr.	Balance
1/1, Yr. 5: Cost	14,286		14,286
Year 5: Dividend		1,000	13,286
12/31, Yr. 5: 10% of Net Income	4,000		17,286
12/31, Yr. 6: 10% of Net Income	3,500		20,786

The results of operations of the three corporations for Year 6 are presented in the first six columns of the accompanying worksheet to consolidate the income statements for that year (p. 284). Entry (a) eliminates intercompany purchases and sales. Entry (b) eliminates the unrealized gross profit in the merchandise inventory of T at the end of Year 6. Entries (c) and (d) remove the income from subsidiaries in order to avoid double counting of this income.

The next two entries are based on the calculations in the schedule that follows. Entry (e) allocates the net income of T Corp. among P (78%), F (2%), and the minority interest in T (20%). Entry (f) allocates F's net income as adjusted between P (80%) and the minority interests (20%).

The balance sheets of the three corporations as of December 31, Year 6, are presented in the first six columns of the accompanying worksheet to consolidate the balance sheets as of that date (p. 285). Entry (1) eliminates the intercompany receivables and payables. Entry (2) eliminates the balance of P's investment in T Corp. account against 70 percent of the shareholders' equity of F Corp. Entry (3) eliminates F's investment account against 10 percent of the shareholders' equity of F Corp. Entry (4) classifies the remaining 20 percent as the minority interest.

Entry (5) eliminates the investment by P Corp. in F Corp. against 80 percent of the shareholders' equity in F, as of December 31, Year 6. Entry (6) classifies the remaining 20 percent as the minority interest.

The consolidated net income and minority interests in income for Year 6 may be independently calculated as follows:

		Consolidated Net Income	Minority Income F Corp.	Minority Income T Corp.
T Corp. Reported Net Income	$35,000			
Control by P				
—Directly	70%	$ 24,500		
—Through F (80% × 10%)	8	2,800		
Minority in F (20% × 10%)	2		$ 700	
Minority in T	20			$7,000
	100%			
F Corp. Reported Net Income	$65,000			
Less: Subsidiary Income	3,500			
F's Own Operations	$61,500			
Control by P	80%	49,200		
Minority in F	20		12,300	
	100%			
P Corp. Reported Net Income	$159,500			
Less: Subsidiary Income	76,500			
	$ 83,000			
Less: Unrealized Profit on Intercompany Sale	10,000			
P's Income for Consolidation	$ 73,000			
	100%	73,000		
Totals		$149,500	$13,000	$7,000

Equity Method

P Corp. and Subsidiary
Worksheet—Consolidated Income Statement
Year 6

	P Corp.		F Corp.		T Corp.		Eliminations		Consolidated	
	Dr.	Cr.	Dr.	Cr.	Dr.	Cr.	Dr.	Cr.	Dr.	Cr.
Sales		300,000		250,500		90,000	[a]50,000			590,500
Cost of Goods Sold	190,000		165,000		34,000		[b]10,000	[a]50,000	349,000	
Selling Expenses	11,000		12,000		11,000				34,000	
General Expenses	16,000		12,000		10,000				38,000	
Income from Subsidiary F		52,000					[c]52,000			
Income from Subsidiary T		24,500		3,500			[d]28,000			
	217,000	376,500	189,000	254,000	55,000	90,000				
Net Income—P	159,500						{ [f]49,200 [e]27,300 }	{ [d]24,500 [c]52,000 [b]10,000 }	149,500	
Net Income—F			65,000					{ [f]61,500 [d]3,500 }		
Net Income—T					35,000			[e]35,000		
	376,500	376,500	254,000	254,000	90,000	90,000				
Minority Interest in F								{ [f]12,300 [e]700 }	13,000	
Minority Interest in T								[e]7,000	7,000	
									590,500	590,500

[a] To eliminate intercompany purchases and sales.
[b] To eliminate unrealized gross profit in final inventory of T.
[c] To eliminate income from F, previously recorded by P.
[d] To eliminate income from T, previously recorded by P and F.
[e] To allocate net income of T among P (78%), F (2%), and minority (20%).
[f] To allocate net income of F between P (80%) and minority (20%).

A summary of the amounts necessary to eliminate the controlling interests and to show the minority interests as of the end of Year 6 are contained in the following two schedules.

T Corp.	Total	Controlling Interests P (70%)	F (10%)	Minority (20%)
Capital Stock	$100,000	$ 70,000	$10,000	$20,000
Retained Earnings, Jan. 1	72,867	51,000	7,286	14,571
Net Income, Year 6	35,000	24,500	3,500	7,000
Totals	$207,857	$145,500	$20,786	$41,571

F Corp.	Total	Controlling Interest (80%)	Minority (20%)
Capital Stock	$200,000	$160,000	$40,000
Retained Earnings, Jan. 1	12,750	10,200	2,550
Net Income, Year 6	65,000	52,000	13,000
Dividends	(20,000)	(16,000)	(4,000)
Totals	$257,750	$206,200	$51,550

Equity Method

P Corp. and Subsidiary
Worksheet—Consolidated Balance Sheet
December 31, Year 6

	P Corp.		F Corp.		T Corp.		Eliminations		Consolidated	
	Dr.	Cr.	Dr.	Cr.	Dr.	Cr.	Dr.	Cr.	Dr.	Cr.
Current Assets	149,000		138,000		70,000			[1]15,000 [b]10,000	332,000	
Investment in F Corp.—Stock	206,200							[5]206,200		
Investment in T Corp.—Stock	145,500							[2]145,500		
Investment in T Corp.—Stock			20,786					[3]20,786		
Other Assets—net	200,000		227,000		195,857				622,857	
Liabilities		117,000		128,036		58,000	[1]15,000			288,036
Capital Stock—P		300,000								300,000
Retained Earnings (1/1)—P		149,200								149,200
Net Income—P		159,500					[b]10,000			149,500
Dividends—P	25,000								25,000	
Capital Stock—F				200,000			[6]40,000 [5]160,000			
Retained Earnings (1/1)—F				12,750			[6]2,550 [5]10,200			
Net Income—F				65,000			[6]13,000 [5]52,000			
Dividends—F			20,000					[6]4,000 [5]16,000		
Capital Stock—T						100,000	[4]20,000 [3]10,000 [2]70,000			
Retained Earnings (1/1)—T						72,857	[4]14,571 [3]7,286 [2]51,000			
Net Income—T						35,000	[4]7,000 [3]3,500 [2]24,500			
	725,700	725,700	405,786	405,786	265,857	265,857				
Minority Interest in F								[4]41,571		41,571
Minority Interest in T								[6]51,550		51,550
									979,857	979,857

[1] To eliminate intercompany receivables and payables.
[2] To eliminate 70% of shareholders' equity of T as of end of Year 6.
[3] To eliminate 10% of shareholders' equity of T as of end of Year 6.
[4] To classify 20% of shareholders' equity of T as minority interest.
[5] To eliminate 80% of shareholders' equity of F as of end of Year 6.
[6] To classify 20% of shareholders' equity of F as minority interest.

Summary

(1) G Corp. holds a majority interest in the common stock of P Corp. P Corp. holds a majority interest in S Corp. G Corp. may be described as a _____ parent, and P Corp. may be described as a _____ parent.

(2) X Corp. owns 70 percent of the outstanding stock of Y Corp. and Y Corp. owns 60 percent of the outstanding stock of Z Corp. The maximum number of corporations whose statements may be consolidated is _____.

(3) A Corp. owns 70 percent of the stock of B Corp., and B Corp. owns 30 percent of the stock of D Corp. A Corp. also owns 70 percent of the stock of E Corp. The maximum number of corporations whose statements may be consolidated is _____.

(4) A Corp. owns 70 percent of the stock of B Corp., and B Corp. owns 30 percent of D Corp. A Corp. also owns 70 percent of the stock of C Corp., and C owns 30 percent of the stock of D Corp. The maximum number of corporations whose statements may be consolidated is _____.

(5) A Corp., sold $100,000 of merchandise to B Corp. In the same year B Corp. resold one-third of these goods to C Corp. for $50,000. In a consolidated income statement, the amount of sales to be eliminated is $_____.

Answers: (1) major, minor; (2) three (X, Y, and Z); (3) three (A, B, and E); (4) four (A, B, C, and D); (5) $150,000

Solved Problems

10.1 G Corp. owns 90 percent of the stock of H Corp., which in turn owns 75 percent of the stock of J Corp. During the current year, J Corp. shows net income of $100,000.

Required:

Complete the following statements concerning the allocation of net income.

(a) $_____ to the controlling interests.

(b) $_____ to the minority interest in J Corp.

(c) $_____ to the minority interest in H Corp.

SOLUTION

(a) To the controlling interests, (0.90×0.75)	or	67.5%	$ 67,500
(b) To minority in J, (0.25)	or	25.0%	25,000
(c) To minority in H, (0.10×0.75)	or	7.5%	7,500
		100.0%	$100,000

10.2 A Corp. owns 70 percent of the stock of B Corp. and B Corp. owns 15 percent of the stock of E Corp. A Corp. also owns 80 percent of the stock of C Corp.; C Corp. owns 60 percent of the stock of D Corp.

The following table shows the intercompany sales during 19X6 and the inventory of merchandise that remained on hand at the end of the year. Each company earns a gross profit (gross margin) of 35 percent on sales of merchandise.

Required:

In each case, determine the amount of sales to be eliminated in a consolidated income statement and the amount of gross profit to be eliminated.

	Intercompany		Inventory	Eliminations	
Case	Sales	Amount	at Year End	Sales	Gross Profit
I	A to B	$ 50,000	$10,000	_____	_____
II	A to C	100,000	20,000	_____	_____
III	B to A	50,000	10,000	_____	_____
IV	B to C	100,000	20,000	_____	_____
V	B to D	100,000	20,000	_____	_____
VI	A to E	100,000	20,000	_____	_____

SOLUTION

Case	Intercompany Sales	Amount	Inventory at Year End	Eliminations Sales	Eliminations Gross Profit
I	A to B	$ 50,000	$10,000	$ 50,000	$3,500
II	A to C	100,000	20,000	100,000	7,000
III	B to A	50,000	10,000	50,000	3,500
IV	B to C	100,000	20,000	100,000	7,000
V	B to D	100,000	20,000	100,000	7,000
VI	A to E	100,000	20,000	–0–*	–0–*

*Insufficient stock to exercise control

10.3 The P Corp. purchased 90 percent of the outstanding stock of the S Corp. on January 1, Year 1, for $110,000. The S Corp. purchased 80 percent of the stock of T Corp. on June 15, Year 2, for $97,000. Accounts for investments in stock are maintained on the equity method.

Selected data from books of S Corp. and its subsidiary T Corp. for Year 6 indicate individual results from each company's own operations, as follows:

	Dr.	Cr.
Income Summary—S		20,000
Income Summary—T		40,000
Dividends Declared—S	10,000	
Dividends Declared—T	15,000	

Required:

Write journal entries on the books of:

(a) S Corp. to recognize its share of T's income and dividends in Year 6.
(b) P Corp. to recognize its share of S's income and dividends in Year 6.

SOLUTION

(a) *Books of S Corp.*

| Investment in T Corp. | 32,000 | |
| Income from Subsidiary | | 32,000 |

To record 80% of net income of T Corp. (80% of $40,000).

| Dividends Receivable | 12,000 | |
| Investment in T Corp. | | 12,000 |

To record 80% of dividend declared by T Corp. (80% × $15,000).

(b) *Books of P Corp.*

| Investment in S Corp. | 46,800 | |
| Income from Subsidiary | | 46,800 |

To record 90% of net income of S Corp. [90% × ($20,000 + $32,000)].

| Dividends Receivable | 13,500 | |
| Investment in T Corp. | | 13,500 |

To record 90% of dividend declared by S Corp. (90% × $15,000).

10.4 A Corp. owns 90 percent of B Corp. and 80 percent of C Corp. B Corp. owns 80 percent of D Corp., and C Corp. owns 90 percent of E Corp. In 19X6 each corporation reported its individual net income or loss as follows:

	A Corp.	B. Corp.	C Corp.	D Corp.	E Corp.
Net Income	$100,000	$40,000	$44,000	$28,000	
Net Loss					$16,000

Required:

Determine the consolidated net income and the minority interest in the net income or loss of each corporation.

SOLUTION

	A Corp.	B Corp.	C Corp.	D Corp.	E Corp.
Net Income (Loss) per Books	$100,000	$40,000	$44,000	$28,000	($16,000)
C's Share of E (0.90)			(14,400)		14,400
B's Share of D (0.80)		22,400		(22,400)	
Subtotals	$100,000	$62,400	$29,600		
A's Share of C (0.80)	23,680		(23,680)		
A's Share of B (0.90)	56,160	(56,160)			
Consolidated Net Income	$179,840				
Minority Interests:					
in B Corp.		$ 6,240			
in C Corp.			$ 5,920		
in D Corp.				$ 5,600	
in E Corp.					($ 1,600)

10.5 The B Corp. acquired an 80 percent interest in C Corp. in Year 1, the date that C was organized.

The A Corp. purchased its 70 percent interest in B Corp. at the end of Year 4. The net assets of B were deemed to have been properly stated at that date, but A paid $32,200 in excess of the book value of B because of the intangible benefits expected from the affiliation. The board of directors of A decided that this intangible asset should be amortized in the consolidated statements over a ten-year period, utilizing the straight-line method.

On January 1, Year 5, A sold to C, for $130,000, a machine which had a book value to A of $60,000. The machine had an estimated useful life of ten years from the date of purchase.

During Year 6, C sold $150,000 of merchandise to B. The intercompany profit at December 31, Year 5, in B's inventory was $12,000; at December 31, Year 6, it amounted to $35,000.

Companies A and B maintain their investment accounts on the equity basis.

Required:

    (a) Complete the worksheet to consolidate the income statements of the three corporations for Year 6.

    (b) Complete the worksheet to consolidate the balance sheets of the three corporations as of December 31, Year 6.

    (c) Prepare an independent calculation of consolidated net income and minority interests in net income for Year 6.

(a)

A Corp. and Subsidiaries
Worksheet—Consolidated Income Statement
Year 6

	A Corp.		B Corp.		C Corp.		Eliminations		Consolidated	
	Dr.	Cr.	Dr.	Cr.	Dr.	Cr.	Dr.	Cr.	Dr.	Cr.
Sales		400,000		350,000		250,000				
Cost of Goods Sold	210,080		190,000		160,000					
Selling Expenses	25,300		46,500		11,800					
General Expenses	27,200		30,500		16,200					
Depreciation	40,000		20,000		15,000					
Income from Subsidiary B		70,420								
Income from Subsidiary C				37,600						
	302,580	470,420	287,000	387,600	203,000	250,000				
Net Income—A	167,840									
Net Income—B			100,600							
Net Income—C					47,000					
	470,420	470,420	387,600	387,600	250,000	250,000				

(b)

A Corp. and Subsidiaries
Worksheet—Consolidated Balance Sheet
December 31, Year 6

	A Corp.		B Corp.		C Corp.		Eliminations		Consolidated	
	Dr.	Cr.	Dr.	Cr.	Dr.	Cr.	Dr.	Cr.	Dr.	Cr.
Merchandise Inventory	99,900		137,000		132,000					
Machinery and Equipment	313,500		150,000		130,000					
Accum'd. Depreciation		43,710		98,000		30,000				
Investment in B Corp.—Stock	396,620									
Investment in C Corp.—Stock			295,200							
Other Assets	145,750		98,000		169,000					
Liabilities		80,000		61,600		32,000				
Capital Stock—A		325,000								
Retained Earnings (1/1)—A		381,720								
Net Income—A		167,840								
Dividends—A	42,500									
Capital Stock—B				300,000						
Retained Earnings—B				150,000						
Net Income—B				100,600						
Dividends—B			30,000							
Capital Stock—C						200,000				
Retained Earnings (1/1)—C						142,000				
Net Income—C						47,000				
Dividends—C					20,000					
	998,270	998,270	710,200	710,200	451,000	451,000				

SOLUTION

(a) *See p. 292.*

(b) *See p. 293.*

(c) *Calculation of consolidated net income and minority interests, Year 6*

	Consolidated Net Income	Minority Interest	
		B Corp.	C Corp.
C Corp., Reported Net Income	$ 47,000		
Add: Intercompany Profit Deferred from Prior Year	12,000		
	$ 59,000		
Less: Intercompany Profit Not Recognized in Year 6	35,000		
Net Income of C, for Consolidation Purposes	$ 24,000		
70% of 80% = 56%		$ 13,440	
30% of 80% = 24			$ 5,760
Minority = 20			$4,800
	100%		
B Corp., Reported Net Income	$100,600		
Less: Subsidiary Income	37,600		
Net Income from Own Operations	$ 63,000		
Control by A 70%		44,100	
Minority 30		18,900	
	100%		
A Corp., Reported Net Income	$167,840		
Less:-Subsidiary Income	70,420		
Net Income from Own Operations	$ 97,420		
Add: Portion of Excess Depreciation Based on Intercompany Profit	7,000		
	$104,420		
Less: Amortization of Excess of Cost over Book Value	3,220		
Net Income of A, for Consolidation Purposes	101,200		
Totals	$158,740	$24,660	$4,800

(a)

A Corp. and Subsidiaries
Worksheet—Consolidated Income Statement
Year 6

	A Corp.		B Corp.		C Corp.		Eliminations		Consolidated	
	Dr.	Cr.	Dr.	Cr.	Dr.	Cr.	Dr.	Cr.	Dr.	Cr.
Sales		400,000		350,000		250,000	[c]150,000			850,000
Cost of Goods Sold	210,080		190,000		160,000		[b]35,000	[c]150,000 [a]12,000	433,080	
Selling Expenses	25,300		46,500		11,800				83,600	
General Expenses	27,200		30,500		16,200				73,900	
Depreciation	40,000		20,000		15,000			[d]7,000	68,000	
Income from Subsidiary B		70,420					[e]70,420			
Income from Subsidiary C				37,600			[f]37,600			
	302,580	470,420	287,000	387,600	203,000	250,000				
Net Income—A	167,840						[i]44,100 [h]13,440 [d]7,000	[g]3,220 [e]70,420	158,740	
Net Income—B			100,600					[i]63,000 [f]37,600		
Net Income—C					47,000		[a]12,000	[h]24,000 [b]35,000		
	470,420	470,420	387,600	387,600	250,000	250,000				
Amortization—Excess of Cost Over Value of Interest							[g]3,220		3,220	
Minority Interest in C							[h]4,800		4,800	
Minority Interest in B							[i]18,900 [b]5,760		24,660	
									850,000	850,000

[a] To eliminate unrealized gross profit in inventory of B as of Jan. 1, Yr. 6.
[b] To eliminate unrealized gross profit in inventory of B as of Dec. 31, Yr. 6.
[c] To eliminate intercompany sales and purchases.
[d] To eliminate excess depreciation in Year 6: $7,000; 10% of ($130,000 − $60,000).
[e] To eliminate income from subsidiary B previously recorded by A.
[f] To eliminate income from subsidiary C previously recorded by B.
[g] To amortize intangible asset; 10% of $32,200.
[h] To allocate net income of C among A (56%), B (24%), and minority (20%).
[i] To allocate net income of B between A (70%), and minority (30%).

[1] To record excess of cost of investment in B over book value of 70% interest: $32,200.
[2] To recognize amortization of foregoing intangible in Year 5: $3,220 ($\frac{1}{10}$ of $32,200).
[3] To eliminate gain on intercompany sale of equipment by A to C in Year 5: $70,000 ($130,000 − $60,000).
[4] To reflect the realization in Year 5 of $\frac{1}{10}$ of intercompany gain on equipment.
[5] To reduce B's retained earnings as of Jan. 1, Yr. 6, and increase B's net income in Year 6 for unrealized gross profit in intercompany merchandise at Jan. 1, Yr. 6: $9,600 (80% of $12,000).
[6] To reduce A's retained earnings as of Jan. 1, Yr. 6, and to increase A's net income in Year 6 for unrealized gross profit in intercompany merchandise at Jan. 1, Yr. 6: $6,720 (70% of $9,600).
[7] To reduce B's investment in C and B's net income, for 80% of unrealized gross profit in intercompany merchandise at Dec. 31, Yr. 6: $28,000 (80% of $35,000).
[8] To reduce A's investment in B, and A's net income for Year 6 for unrealized gross profit of $19,600: (70% of 28,000).
[9] To eliminate 80% of shareholders' equity in C as of Dec. 31, Yr. 6.
[10] To classify 20% of shareholders' equity in C as minority interest.
[11] To eliminate 70% of shareholders' equity in B as of Dec. 31, Yr. 6.
[12] To classify 30% of shareholders' equity in B as minority interest.

(b)

A Corp. and Subsidiaries*
Worksheet—Consolidated Balance Sheet
December 31, Year 6

	A Corp. Dr.	A Corp. Cr.	B Corp. Dr.	B Corp. Cr.	C Corp. Dr.	C Corp. Cr.	Eliminations Dr.	Eliminations Cr.	Consolidated Dr.	Consolidated Cr.
Merchandise Inventory	99,900		137,000		132,000			[b]35,000	333,900	
Machinery and Equipment	313,500		150,000		130,000			[3]70,000	523,500	
Accum'd. Depreciation		43,710		98,000		30,000	{[4]7,000 / [d]7,000}			157,710
Investment in B Corp.—Stock	396,620							{[8]19,600 / [10]344,820 / [1]32,200}		
Investment in C Corp.—Stock			295,200					{[9]267,200 / [7]28,000}		
Other Assets	145,750		98,000		169,000				412,750	
Liabilities		80,000		61,600		32,000				173,600
Capital Stock—A		325,000								325,000
Retained Earnings (1/1)—A		381,720					{[6]6,720 / [3]70,000 / [2]3,220}	[4]7,000		308,780
Net Income—A		167,840					{[8]19,600 / [g]3,220}	{[6]6,720 / [d]7,000}		158,740
Dividends—A	42,500								42,500	
Capital Stock—B				300,000			{[12]90,000 / [11]210,000}			
Retained Earnings—B				150,000			{[11]98,280 / [5]9,600 / [12]42,120}			
Net Income—B				100,600			{[12]24,660 / [11]57,540 / [7]28,000}	[5]9,600		
Dividends—B			30,000					{[12]9,000 / [11]21,000}		
Capital Stock—C						200,000	{[10]40,000 / [9]160,000}			
Retained Earnings (1/1)—C						142,000	{[9]104,000 / [a]12,000 / [10]26,000}			
Net Income—C						47,000	{[10]4,800 / [9]19,200 / [b]35,000}	[a]12,000		
Dividends—C					20,000			{[10]4,000 / [9]16,000}		
	998,270	998,270	710,200	710,200	451,000	451,000				
Excess of Cost Over Fair Value of Interest in Subsidiary							[1]32,200	{[2]3,220 / [g]3,220}	25,760	
Minority Interest in C								[10]66,800		66,800
Minority Interest in B								[12]147,780		147,780
									1,338,410	1,338,410

* The notes for this worksheet are on p. 292.

Chapter 11

Consolidated Statements—
The Pooling of Interests Method

11.1 THE POOLING OF INTERESTS METHOD OF ACCOUNTING

In some business combinations of two or more corporate interests, the stockholders and managements frequently continue their respective interests and activities in the new corporate setup. When the affiliation comes about through an exchange of common stock, it may be that neither of the combining corporations could logically be considered to have acquired the other one. If the combination of two or more corporations involves an exchange of voting stock, the common stock shareholders of the combining corporations would maintain their relative positions as owners of the combined corporation. For such situations, the *pooling of interests method of accounting* has evolved for the combination.

The pooling of interests method is intended to present, as a single entity, common stock interests which were previously independent and the combined rights and risks represented by those interests. In effect the previously independent interests exchange voting common stock in a ratio that determines their respective interests in a new and combined economic entity.

When the pooling of interests method of accounting is appropriate, the assets and liabilities of the combining companies are carried forward at their respective book amounts. Thus, there is no need to ascertain fair values of the respective assets or to make a determination of goodwill, and the fair market value of the stock issued in such a combination is disregarded. In other words, when a combination is deemed to be a pooling of interests, a new basis of accountability does not arise.

The Accounting Principles Board (APB) specified twelve criteria that must be met in order for a business combination to be treated as a pooling of interests.[1] A business combination that meets all of the criteria specified in APB No. 16 (see the appendix to this chapter, p. 303) must be accounted for as a pooling of interests; all others must be accounted for as purchases.

The combining of existing common stock interests by the exchange of voting common stock is the essence of a business combination to be accounted for by the pooling of interests method. Typically, the separate stockholder interests lose their identities when one corporation issues only voting common stock, with rights identical to those of the majority of its outstanding voting common stock, in exchange for substantially "all" of the voting common stock of another company. Substantially, "all" of the voting common stock has been held to mean 90 percent or more of the latter's common stock. Thus, when there is a minority interest, it will generally not exceed 10 percent.[2]

It is not essential that only one corporation remain after the pooling of interests. If all other conditions are met, one of the corporations may become a subsidiary of the other. When a parent-subsidiary relationship is deemed to be a pooling of interests, the shareholder equities of the affiliated corporations are combined, as are the various assets and liabilities. Thus, the retained earnings or deficits of the separate companies are generally combined and recognized as the retained earnings of

---

[1] Accounting Principles Board, Opinion No. 16, "Business Combinations." New York, American Institute of Certified Public Accountants, August 1970.

[2] APB 16 provided for certain exceptions which existed as of October 31, 1970. While APB 16 provided that these exceptions would expire in five years, the Financial Accounting Standards Board (in Statement No. 10) eliminated this expiration date.

the combined corporation or of the consolidated group.   This is so regardless of when the earnings or losses occurred.

When a combination of two corporations is deemed to be a pooling of interests, the income statements of the combination integrate the continuing operations of the two corporations.   Thus, costs incurred to effect such a combination must be treated as expenses in determining the net income of the period in which the combination occurred.

A single method should be used for the entire combination; it is no longer permissible to treat an affiliation as part purchase and part pooling of interests.

11.2 CONSOLIDATION ACCOUNTED FOR AS A POOLING OF INTERESTS

EXAMPLE 1.   The C Corporation was organized on January 1, 19X7 to combine the A Corporation and the B Corporation.   The condensed balance sheets of A Corporation and B Corporation were as follows:

	A Corp.	B Corp.
Assets	$155,000	$345,000
Liabilities	$ 5,000	$ 15,000
Capital Stock—$10 par	100,000	250,000
Amount Paid-in in Excess of Par	20,000	30,000
Retained Earnings	30,000	50,000
Totals	$155,000	$345,000
Net Assets	$150,000	$330,000

The C Corporation issues one share of its $25 par common stock for each $40 of net assets received from A Corporation and B Corporation.   Journal entries on the books of C are as follows:

Assets	155,000	
Liabilities		5,000
Capital Stock—$25 par		93,750
Amount Paid-in in Excess of Par		26,250
Retained Earnings[3]		30,000

To record issuance of 3,750 shares for assets and liabilities of A Corp.

Assets	345,000	
Liabilities		15,000
Capital Stock—$25 par		206,250
Amount Paid-in in Excess of Par		73,750
Retained Earnings		50,000

To record issuance of 8,250 shares for assets and liabilities of B Corp.

After the former interests of A Corporation and of B Corporation are consolidated into the new C Corporation, the total shareholders' equity of the new corporation will be $480,000.   This is equal to the sum of the combined shareholders' equity of the two former entities.

EXAMPLE 2.   Assume the same preacquisition balance sheets for A Corporation and for B Corporation as in Example 1.   However, the C Corporation issues one share of its $25 par common stock for each $30 of net assets

---

[3] Some accountants prefer to open a new account, such as "Retained Earnings of Pooled Affiliate."

received from A Corporation and from B Corporation.   Journal entries on the books of C Corporation are as follows:

Assets	155,000	
Liabilities		5,000
Capital Stock—$25 par		125,000
Retained Earnings		25,000

To record the issuance of 5,000 shares for assets and liabilities of A Corp.

Assets	345,000	
Liabilities		15,000
Capital Stock—$25 par		275,000
Amount Paid-in in Excess of Par		5,000
Retained Earnings		50,000

To record the issuance of 11,000 shares for assets and liabilities of B Corp.

It should be observed that the total shareholders' equity of C Corporation will be $480,000, the same amount as in the previous example.   This result comes about because in both examples the combination was a pooling of interests; thus, the assets and liabilities were recorded at their prior book values.

11.3   MERGER ACCOUNTED FOR AS A POOLING OF INTERESTS

EXAMPLE 3.   The preacquisition balance sheets for A Corporation and B Corporation are the same as in Example 1.   However, in this case it has been agreed that B Corporation will merge into A Corporation.   A Corporation is to issue 12,000 additional shares of its $10 par common stock in exchange for the assets and liabilities of B Corporation.   B Corporation will then distribute the shares of A Corporation to the shareholders of B Corporation, and B Corporation will be dissolved.   The journal entry on A Corporation books is as follows:

Assets	345,000	
Liabilities		15,000
Capital Stock—$10 par		120,000
Amount Paid-in in Excess of Par		160,000
Retained Earnings		50,000

To record the issuance of 12,000 shares for the assets and liabilities of B.

The condensed balance sheets of A Corporation before and after the merger are as follows:

	Before	After
Assets	$155,000	$500,000
Liabilities	$ 5,000	$ 20,000
Capital Stock—$10 Par	100,000	220,000
Amount Paid-in in Excess of Par	20,000	180,000
Retained Earnings	30,000	80,000
Totals	$155,000	$500,000

The total shareholders' equity of A Corporation after the merger will amount to $480,000, the same as in the preceding two examples.   In all three examples, the combination was deemed to be a pooling of interests. Thus, the assets and liabilities were brought forward at the previous book values.

11.4 ACQUISITION ACCOUNTED FOR AS A POOLING OF INTERESTS

When an affiliation is deemed to be a pooling of interests, one corporation may emerge as a subsidiary of another corporation. In recording an investment in common stock of another corporation, which is treated as a pooling of interests, no attempt is made to measure any difference between the market value of the shares given up and the value of the underlying subsidiary assets. The parent corporation's investment account should be debited for an amount equal to the parent's share of the stockholders' equity of the subsidiary corporation. There is *never* any revaluation of the subsidiary's assets or liabilities, thus there is no differential between cost and book value to be accounted for. The parent's common stock account will be credited for an amount equal to the par (or stated) value of the parent's stock multiplied by the number of shares issued. The credit to retained earnings is based on the balance in the subsidiary's books; the maximum amount will be the subsidiary's balance multiplied by the percent of the parent's ownership. The remainder of the entry is an adjustment to the parent's paid-in capital.

EXAMPLE 4. The shareholders' equity accounts of P Corporation and of S Corporation are as follows:

	P Corp.	S Corp.
Common Stock—$10 par	$120,000	$ 80,000
Amount Paid-in in Excess of Par	12,000	10,000
Retained Earnings	88,000	60,000
Totals	$220,000	$150,000

The shareholders of S Corporation exchange all of their shares for 6,000 newly issued shares of P Corporation. The journal entry on the books of P Corporation is as follows:

Investment in Subsidiary	150,000	
Common Stock—$10 par		60,000
Amount Paid-in in Excess of Par		30,000
Retained Earnings		60,000

To record the issuance of 6,000 shares for the stock of S Corp.

The total shareholders' equity of S Corporation amounts to $150,000. Since the par value of the common stock of P Corp. is $60,000 and the retained earnings of S Corp. is $60,000, the paid-in capital of P Corp. is increased by $30,000. Thus the consolidated shareholders' equity will be increased by $150,000, the exact amount of the shareholders' equity of S Corp.

If a worksheet to consolidate the balance sheets of P Corporation and S Corporation were to be prepared as of the date of combination, the elimination entry would be as follows:

Common Stock—S	80,000	
Amount Paid-in in Excess of Par—S	10,000	
Retained Earnings—S	60,000	
Investment in Subsidiary		150,000

To eliminate investment against shareholders' equity of subsidiary.

EXAMPLE 5. The shareholders' equity of P Corporation and of S Corporation are the same as in the previous example. However, P Corporation issues 10,000 newly issued shares for the outstanding shares of S Corporation. The journal entry on the books of P Corporation is as follows:

Investment in Subsidiary	150,000	
Amount Paid-in in Excess of Par	10,000	
Common Stock—$10 par		100,000
Retained Earnings		60,000

To record the issuance of 10,000 shares of P's stock for the stock of S Corporation.

The sum of the par value of P's common stock issued and S's retained earnings is $160,000. Since this exceeds the net assets of S Corp., it is necessary to diminish the paid-in capital of the parent by $10,000. However, it should be recognized that the net increase in the consolidated shareholders' equity is still $150,000 ($100,000 + $60,000 − $10,000).

When preparing a worksheet to consolidate the balance sheets of P Corporation and S Corporation as of the date of acquisition, the elimination entry would be exactly the same as that in the previous example.

EXAMPLE 6.   The shareholders' equity of P Corporation and of S Corporation are the same as in Example 4. Assume, however, that P Corporation issues 12,000 shares of its common stock for the outstanding shares of S Corporation.   The journal entry on the books of P Corporation is as follows:

Investment in Subsidiary	150,000	
Amount Paid-in in Excess of Par	12,000	
Common Stock—$10 par		120,000
Retained Earnings ($60,000 − $18,000)		42,000

To record the issuance of 12,000 shares of P's stock for the stock of S Corporation.

The sum of the par value of the newly issued common stock of P Corporation ($120,000) and the retained earnings of S Corporation ($60,000) would be $180,000.   This sum exceeds the total shareholders' equity of S Corporation by $30,000.   If the paid-in capital of P Corporation amounted to $30,000, the entry could be completed by debiting the paid-in capital of P Corporation for this amount.   Since the paid-in capital of P Corporation is only $12,000, this represents the maximum debit to the paid-in capital of P Corporation.   Thus, the remaining $18,000 will reduce the credit to retained earnings.   It should be observed that the net increase in consolidated shareholders' equity as a result of the foregoing entry is again $150,000 ($120,000 + $42,000 − $12,000).

When preparing a worksheet to consolidate the balance sheets of P Corporation and S Corporation as of the date of combination, the elimination entry would be the same as that in the previous two examples.

11.5   CONSOLIDATION WORKPAPERS: YEAR OF ACQUISITION

EXAMPLE 7.   R Corporation and T Corporation had the following condensed balance sheets as of January 1, 19X1

	R Corp.	T Corp.
Current Assets	$ 80,000	$ 50,000
Equipment—net	120,000	120,000
	$200,000	$170,000
Liabilities	$ 10,000	$ 10,000
Capital Stock—$10 par	100,000	120,000
Paid-in in Capital in Excess of Par	10,000	
Retained Earnings	80,000	40,000
	$200,000	$170,000
Net Assets	$190,000	$160,000

On January 2 the R Corporation issued 7,000 shares of its common stock in exchange for all of the outstanding stock of T Corporation in a transaction which is deemed to be a pooling of interests. The journal entry on the books of the acquiring firm should be as follows:

Investment in Subsidiary	160,000	
Common Stock—$10 par		70,000
Paid-in Capital in Excess of Par		50,000
Retained Earnings		40,000

To record the investment in T Corp. at the book value of its underlying net assets; the transaction is deemed to be a pooling of interests.

After the above entry has been posted to the ledger of the parent corporation, the resultant balance sheet data appear in the first two columns of the accompanying worksheet.

In order to consolidate the two balance sheets, the following elimination entry is entered in the worksheet:

Capital Stock—T	120,000	
Retained Earnings—T	40,000	
Investment in Subsidiary		160,000

A comparison of the respective shareholders' equity of R Corp. and T Corp. before affiliation and of the consolidated shareholders' equity after consolidation will demonstrate that while components have changed, the totals are equal in amount.

	Equity Before Consolidation			Consolidated Shareholders' Equity
	R Corp.	T Corp.	Total	
Capital Stock	$100,000	$120,000	$220,000	$170,000
Paid-in Capital	10,000		10,000	60,000
Retained Earnings	80,000	40,000	120,000	120,000
Totals	$190,000	$160,000	$350,000	$350,000

R Corp. and Subsidiary
Worksheet—Consolidated Balance Sheet
January 2, Year 1

	R Corp.		T Corp.		Eliminations		Consolidated	
	Dr.	Cr.	Dr.	Cr.	Dr.	Cr.	Dr.	Cr.
Current Assets	80,000		50,000				130,000	
Investment in T Corp.	160,000					[1]160,000		
Equipment—net	120,000		120,000				240,000	
Liabilities		10,000		10,000				20,000
Capital Stock: $10 par—R		170,000						170,000
Paid-in Capital in Excess of Par—R		60,000						60,000
Retained Earnings—R		120,000						120,000
Capital Stock: $10 par—T				120,000	[1]120,000			
Retained Earnings—T				40,000	[1]40,000			
	360,000	360,000	170,000	170,000			370,000	370,000

[1] To eliminate investment account against shareholders' equity of T Corp.

EXAMPLE 8. Assume the same January 1, 19X1 balance sheets as in the previous example. However, on January 2 the R Corporation issued 14,000 shares of its common stock in exchange for all of the outstanding stock of T Corporation in a transaction which is interpreted to be a pooling of interests. The journal entry on the books of the acquiring firm should be as follows:

Investment in Subsidiary	160,000	
Paid-in Capital in Excess of Par	10,000	
Common Stock—$10 Par		140,000
Retained Earnings		30,000

To record the investment in T Corp. at book value of its underlying net assets. The transaction is interpreted to be a pooling of interests.

The sum of the par value of the newly issued common stock of R Corp. ($140,000) plus the retained earnings of T Corp. ($40,000) would be $180,000. This amount exceeds the total shareholders' equity of T Corp. by $20,000. The paid-in capital of R Corp. ($10,000) is eliminated and the retained earnings of the pooled subsidiary is reduced by $10,000. Thus, the net increase in the consolidated shareholders' equity is $160,000 ($140,000 + $30,000 − $10,000).

The condensed balance sheet data, after the investment has been recorded, appear in the first two columns of the accompanying worksheet. The elimination entry is the same as in Example 7.

R Corp. and Subsidiary
Worksheet—Consolidated Balance Sheet
January 2, Year 1

	R Corp.		T Corp.		Eliminations		Consolidated	
	Dr.	Cr.	Dr.	Cr.	Dr.	Cr.	Dr.	Cr.
Current Assets	80,000		50,000				130,000	
Investment in T Corp.	160,000					[1]160,000		
Equipment—net	120,000		120,000				240,000	
Liabilities		10,000		10,000				20,000
Capital Stock: $10 par—R		240,000						240,000
Retained Earnings—R		110,000						110,000
Capital Stock: $10 par—T				120,000	[1]120,000			
Retained Earnings—T				40,000	[1]40,000			
	360,000	360,000	170,000	170,000			370,000	370,000

[1] To eliminate investment account against shareholders' equity of T Corp.

EXAMPLE 9. Example 9 is based on the same preacquisition balance sheets as in Example 7. However, on January 2 the R Corp. issued 7,000 shares of its common stock in exchange for 90 percent of the outstanding stock of T Corp. The journal entry on the books of the parent company follows:

Investment in Subsidiary (90% of $160,000)	144,000	
Common Stock—$10 par (7,000 × $10)		70,000
Paid-in Capital in Excess of Par		38,000
Retained Earnings (90% of $40,000)		36,000

To record the investment in T Corp. at 90% of the book value of its underlying net assets. The transaction is deemed to be a pooling of interests.

After the foregoing entry has been entered in the books of the parent corporation, the resultant balance sheet data appear in the first two columns of the accompanying worksheet.

Worksheet entry (1) eliminates the investment account against 90 percent of the shareholders' equity of T Corporation. Entry (2) classifies the remaining 10 percent of the shareholders' equity as the minority interest.

R Corp. and Subsidiary
Worksheet—Consolidated Balance Sheet
January 2, Year 1

	R Corp.		T Corp.		Eliminations		Consolidated	
	Dr.	Cr.	Dr.	Cr.	Dr.	Cr.	Dr.	Cr.
Current Assets	80,000		50,000				130,000	
Investment in T Corp.	144,000					[1]144,000		
Equipment—net	120,000		120,000				240,000	
Liabilities		10,000		10,000				20,000
Capital Stock: $10 par—R		170,000						170,000
Paid-in Capital in Excess of Par—R		48,000						48,000
Retained Earnings—R		116,000						116,000
Capital Stock: $10 par—T				120,000	{[2]12,000 {[1]108,000			
Retained Earnings—T				40,000	{[2]4,000 {[1]36,000			
	344,000	344,000	170,000	170,000				
Minority Interest						[2]16,000		16,000
							370,000	370,000

[1] To eliminate investment account against 90% of the shareholders' equity of T Corp.
[2] To classify 10% interest in T Corp. as minority interest.

EXAMPLE 10. The condensed balance sheets of P Corp. and of S Corp. on January 1, Year 1, before the acquisition by P Corp. of the stock of S. Corp., are as follows:

	P Corp.	S Corp.
Current Assets	$200,000	$ 55,000
Depreciable Assets	250,000	130,000
Accumulated Depreciation	(50,000)	(30,000)
Land		25,000
Total Assets	$400,000	$180,000
Liabilities	$140,000	$ 30,000
Capital Stock—$10 par	200,000	100,000
Retained Earnings	60,000	50,000
	$400,000	$180,000

The combination complied with all criteria for pooling of interests.

Assume that P Corp. issued 15,750 shares of its $10 par common stock for 90 percent of the capital stock of S Corp., and that the former stockholders of S Corp. are now participating in the management of the combination.

The journal entry on the books of P Corp. on January 1, Year 1 for the investment in S Corp. follows:

Investment in Subsidiary	135,000	
Retained Earnings	22,500	
Capital Stock—$10 par		157,500

To record the acquisition of 90% of the common stock of S Corp. in exchange of $10 common. Transaction is a pooling of interests.

The investment account is debited for 90 percent of the shareholders' equity of S Corp., $135,000 (90% of $150,000). Since the par value of the stock issued by P Corp. exceeds the investment by $22,500, this amount is charged to the retained earnings carried forward. The effect is to capitalize a portion of the preaffiliation retained earnings. This can be demonstrated by comparing the shareholders' equity of P Corp. and of S Corp. before affiliation with the consolidated shareholders' equity.

	Before Affiliation			Consolidated Shareholders' Equity
	P Corp.	*S Corp.*	*Total*	
Capital Stock	$200,000	$100,000	$300,000	$357,500
Retained Earnings	60,000	50,000	110,000	37,500
Minority Interest				15,000
Totals	$260,000	$150,000	$410,000	$410,000

The balance sheets of the two corporations after affiliation have been placed in the first four columns of the accompanying worksheet to prepare a consolidated balance sheet as of January 1, Year 1. Entry (1) eliminates the investment account against 90 percent of the capital stock and retained earnings of S Corp. Entry (2) classifies 10 percent of the shareholders' equity of S Corp. as the minority interest.

P Corp. and Subsidiary
Worksheet—Consolidated Balance Sheet
January 1, Year 1

	P Corp.		S Corp.		Eliminations		Consolidated	
	Dr.	Cr.	Dr.	Cr.	Dr.	Cr.	Dr.	Cr.
Current Assets	200,000		55,000				255,000	
Investment in S Corp.	135,000					[1]135,000		
Depreciable Assets	250,000		130,000				380,000	
Accumulated Depreciation		50,000		30,000				80,000
Land			25,000				25,000	
Liabilities		140,000		30,000				170,000
Capital Stock—P		357,500						357,500
Retained Earnings—P		37,500						37,500
Capital Stock—S				100,000	{[1]90,000 {[2]10,000			
Retained Earnings—S				50,000	{[1]45,000 {[2]5,000			
	585,000	585,000	210,000	210,000				
Minority Interest						[2]15,000		15,000
							660,000	660,000

[1] To eliminate investment account against 90% of the shareholders' equity of S Corp.
[2] To classify 10% interest in S Corp. as minority interest.

11.6 CONSOLIDATION WORKPAPERS: SUBSEQUENT YEARS

A parent corporation should use the equity method for investments in subsidiaries acquired in transactions that meet the criteria for pooling of interests. The cost method is not in harmony with the pooling of interests concept.

When the equity method is followed, the investment account balance will increase or decrease in proportion to the changes in the subsidiary's shareholders' equity. Thus, in years subsequent to the year of combination, the consolidation workpapers will be handled in the same manner as the workpapers for a purchased subsidiary. For example, the worksheet entries to eliminate unrealized profit on intercompany sales would be the same regardless of whether the combination had originally been treated as a purchase or as a pooling of interests.

Appendix

CONDITIONS WHICH REQUIRE POOLING OF INTERESTS ACCOUNTING

Attributes of the Combining Companies

(a) Each of the combining companies is autonomous, and has not been a subsidiary or division of another corporation within two years before plan is initiated.

(b) Each of the combining companies is independent of the other combining companies.

Manner of Combining of Interests

The separate stockholder interests lose their identities and all share mutually in the combined risks and rights.

(a) The combination is effected in a single transaction or is completed, in accordance with a specific plan, within one year after the plan is initiated.

(b) A corporation offers and issues only common stock (with rights identical to those of the majority of its outstanding voting common stock) in exchange for substantially all of the voting common stock interest of another corporation.

(c) None of the combining companies changes the equity interest of the voting common stock in contemplation of effecting the combination either within two years before the plan of combination is initiated or between the date the combination is initiated and consummated.

(d) Each of the combining companies reacquires shares of voting common stock only for purposes other than business combinations accounted for as pooling of interests.

(e) The ratio of the interest of an individual common stockholder to those of other common stockholders in a combining company remains the same as a result of the exchange of stock to effect the combination.

(f) The voting rights, to which the common stock ownership interests in the resulting combined corporation are entitled, are exercisable by the stockholders.

(g) The combination is resolved at the date the plan is consummated, and no provisions of the plan relating to the issue of securities or other considerations are pending.

Absence of Planned Transactions

(a) The combined corporation does not agree to retire or reacquire all or part of the common stock issued to effect the combination.

(b) The combined corporation does not enter into other financial arrangements for the benefit of the former stockholders of a combining company, which in effect negates the exchange of equity securities.

(*c*) The combined corporation does not intend or plan to dispose of a significant part of the assets of the combining companies within two years after the combination other than disposals in the ordinary course of business of the formerly separate companies to eliminate duplicate facilities or excess capacity.

Summary

(1) According to APB No. 16, a business combination which meets twelve specified conditions _____ the use of the pooling of interests method of accounting; any other business combination must be accounted for as a _____.

(2) Both the pooling of interests and the purchase methods are acceptable, but not as _____.

(3) A pooling of interests involves the _____ of ownership interests of two or more corporations by an exchange of _____ securities.

(4) A concept underlying the pooling of interests is that neither corporation acquires _____ or obtains _____.

(5) Pooling of interests always involves a combination which results from the _____ of common stock.

(6) When there is a pooling of interests, a new basis of accountability is not _____.

(7) In the case of pooling of interests, the consolidated retained earnings after combination may be _____, but never _____ than the sum of the retained earnings of the corporations immediately prior to the combination.

(8) An essential feature of a business combination which is to be accounted for by the pooling of interests method is the combination of voting _____ stock interests by the exchange of voting _____ stock.

(9) When a transaction is interpreted as a pooling of interests, the _____ principle does not apply at the acquisition date.

(10) The P Corporation acquired 90 percent of the stock of S Corporation in a transaction deemed to be a pooling of interests. In the balance sheet, the minority interest is equal to _____ percent of the _____ _____ of the subsidiary.

(11) When a combination is interpreted as a pooling of interests, if the values of the net assets can be objectively ascertained such values should be _____.

(12) When accounting for a business combination, if the pooling of interests method is appropriate, the parent's investment account should be debited with the _____ value of the parent's interest in the shareholders' equity of the _____. However, if the purchase method is appropriate, the parent's investment account is debited with the _____ value of the consideration received, or given, whichever is more _____ determinable.

(13) If a combination is deemed to be a pooling of interests, one of the corporations may become a _____ of the other.

(14) The DP Corporation owns 25 percent of the common stock of GM Corporation. DP exchanges all of its GM stock for 90 percent of the outstanding common stock of the EQ Corporation. The combination of DP and EQ must be treated as a _____.

(15) A combination is deemed to be a pooling of interests. When consolidating the statements of the parent and its subsidiary, the parent's share of the subsidiary's retained earnings is generally _____ with the parent's _____.

Answers: (1) requires, purchase; (2) alternatives; (3) combination, equity (voting common); (4) assets, capital; (5) exchange; (6) permitted; (7) less, more; (8) common, common; (9) cost; (10) 10, shareholders' equity; (11) ignored; (12) book, subsidiary, fair, objectively; (13) subsidiary; (14) purchase; (15) combined, retained earnings

Solved Problems

11.1 The shareholders' equity of Pixley Corp. and Sharps Corp. at the date of their combination are as follows:

	Pixley Corp.	Sharps Corp.
Common Stock—$10 par	$100,000	$80,000
Contributed Capital	15,000	10,000
Retained Earnings	85,000	60,000

The shareholders of Sharps Corp. exchanged all of their shares for newly issued shares of Pixley common stock as follows:

Case I	6,000 shares
Case II	8,000 shares
Case III	10,000 shares
Case IV	12,000 shares

The combination is classified as a pooling of interests.

Required:

For each of the above cases:

(*a*) Write the journal entry (entries) on the books of Pixley Corp. to record the issuance of shares.

(*b*) Write the worksheet elimination entry as of the date of the combination.

(*c*) Calculate the consolidated retained earnings after the combination.

SOLUTION

(*a*) *Journal entries on the books of Pixley Corp.*

Case I	Investment in Sharps	150,000	
	Common Stock—$10 par		60,000
	Retained Earnings		60,000
	Other Contributed Capital		30,000
Case II	Investment in Sharps	150,000	
	Common Stock—$10 par		80,000
	Retained Earnings		60,000
	Other Contributed Capital		10,000
Case III	Investment in Sharps	150,000	
	Contributed Capital	10,000	
	Common Stock—$10 par		100,000
	Retained Earnings		60,000

Case IV	Investment in Sharps	150,000	
	Contributed Capital	15,000	
	Common Stock—$10 par		120,000
	Retained Earnings		
	($60,000 − $15,000)		45,000

(*b*) *Worksheet elimination entry* (same for all four cases).

Capital Stock—$10 par	80,000	
Contributed Capital	10,000	
Retained Earnings [Sharps]	60,000	
Investment in Sharps		150,000

(*c*) *Consolidated retained earnings.*

	Pixley Corp.	Sharps Corp.	Total
Case I	$85,000	$60,000	$145,000
Case II	85,000	60,000	145,000
Case III	85,000	60,000	145,000
Case IV	85,000	45,000	130,000

11.2 The shareholders' equity accounts of Pixley Corp. and of Sharps Corp. at the date of their combination are the same as in Problem 11.1. However, the stockholders of Sharps Corp. exchange only 90 percent of their shares for newly issued shares of Pixley common stock, as follows:

Case I	5,400 shares
Case II	7,200 shares
Case III	9,000 shares
Case IV	10,800 shares

The combination is classified as a pooling of interests.

Required:

For each of the above cases:

(*a*) Write the journal entry (entries) on the books of Pixley Corp. to record the issuance of shares.

(*b*) Write the worksheet elimination entry as of the date of the combination.

(*c*) Calculate the consolidated retained earnings after the combination.

SOLUTION

(*a*) *Journal entries on the books of Pixley Corp.*

Case I	Investment in Sharps	135,000	
	Common Stock—$10 par		54,000
	Retained Earnings		54,000
	Other Contributed Capital		27,000

Case II	Investment in Sharps	135,000	
	Common Stock—$10 par		72,000
	Retained Earnings		54,000
	Other Contributed Capital		9,000

Case III	Investment in Sharps	135,000	
	Contributed Capital	9,000	
	Common Stock—$10 par		90,000
	Retained Earnings		54,000

Case IV	Investment in Sharps	135,000	
	Contributed Capital	13,500	
	Common Stock—$10 par		108,000
	Retained Earnings		40,500
	($54,000 − $13,500)		

(b) *Worksheet elimination entry* (same for all four cases).

Capital Stock—$10 par	72,000	
Contributed Capital	9,000	
Retained Earnings [Sharps]	54,000	
Investment in Sharps		135,000

(c) *Consolidated retained earnings.*

	Pixley Corp.	Sharps Corp.	Total
Case I	$85,000	$54,000	$139,000
Case II	85,000	54,000	139,000
Case III	85,000	54,000	139,000
Case IV	85,000	40,500	125,500

11.3 The Long Corp. and the Song Corp. have agreed to affiliate. The final balances of the two corporations as of December 31, 19X1, are as follows:

	Long Corp.		Song Corp.	
	Dr.	Cr.	Dr.	Cr.
Cash	$ 18,800		$ 24,900	
Accounts Receivable	31,700		37,800	
Inventories	98,000		64,700	
Plant and Equipment	494,700		328,000	
Accounts Payable		$ 31,700		$ 16,900
Accrued Expenses		26,500		28,500
Notes Payable		90,000		
Capital Stock—$10 par		300,000		300,000
Paid-in Capital				25,000
Retained Earnings		195,000		85,000
	$643,200	$643,200	$455,400	$455,400

On January 2, 19X2, Long issued 35,000 shares of its common stock in exchange for all of the common stock of Song Corp. The common stock of Long had a fair market value of $16 per share.

The acquisition of Song's stock was properly recorded in the following entry on Long's books:

Investment in Subsidiary	410,000	
Capital Stock—$10 par		350,000
Retained Earnings		60,000

Required:

Complete the worksheet to consolidate the balance sheets as of January 2, 19X2.

Long Corp. and Subsidiary
Worksheet—Consolidated Balance Sheet
January 1, 19X2

	Long Corp.		Song Corp.		Eliminations		Consolidated	
	Dr.	Cr.	Dr.	Cr.	Dr.	Cr.	Dr.	Cr.
Cash	18,800		24,900					
Accounts Receivable	31,700		37,800					
Inventories	98,700		64,700					
Investment in Song	410,000							
Plant and Equipment	494,000		328,000					
Accounts Payable		31,700		16,900				
Accrued Expenses		26,500		28,500				
Notes Payable		90,000						
Capital Stock—Parent		650,000						
Capital Stock—Subsidiary				300,000				
Paid-in Capital in Excess of Par				25,000				
Retained Earnings—Parent		255,000						
Retained Earnings—Subsidiary				85,000				
	1,053,200	1,053,200	455,400	455,400				

SOLUTION

Long Corp. and Subsidiary
Worksheet—Consolidated Balance Sheet
January 1, 19X2

	Long Corp.		Song Corp.		Eliminations		Consolidated	
	Dr.	Cr.	Dr.	Cr.	Dr.	Cr.	Dr.	Cr.
Cash	18,800		24,900				43,700	
Accounts Receivable	31,700		37,800				69,500	
Inventories	98,700		64,700				163,400	
Investment in Song	410,000					¹410,000		
Plant and Equipment	494,000		328,000				822,000	
Accounts Payable		31,700		16,900				48,600
Accrued Expenses		26,500		28,500				55,000
Notes Payable		90,000						90,000
Capital Stock—Parent		650,000						650,000
Capital Stock—Subsidiary				300,000	¹300,000			
Paid-in Capital in Excess of Par				25,000	¹25,000			
Retained Earnings—Parent		255,000						255,000
Retained Earnings—Subsidiary				85,000	¹85,000			
	1,053,200	1,053,200	455,400	455,400			1,098,600	1,098,600

¹ To eliminate investment against shareholders' equity of Song.

11.4 The Puff Corporation and the Snuff Corporation agreed to an affiliation as of July 1, 19X3. Partial trial balances of the two corporations, as of December 31, 19X3, were as follows:

	Puff Corp.	Snuff Corp.
DEBITS		
Accounts Receivable	$ 29,200	$ 14,000
Inventory	25,300	15,950
Land	15,000	
Building	42,700	
Furniture and Equipment	39,800	25,600
Cost of Goods Sold	123,000	70,750
Operating Expenses	64,000	15,000
Expenses of Business Combination	2,250	
Dividends	10,000	
CREDITS		
Accumulated Depreciation	$ 37,250	$ 5,900
Accounts Payable	10,200	3,450
Accrued Expenses	7,100	2,100
Capital Stock—$10 par	75,000	30,000
Additional Paid-in Capital		5,000
Retained Earnings, Jan. 1, 19X3	32,450	13,950
Sales	205,000	92,200

On July 1, 19X3, the Puff Corporation distributed 2,750 shares of its newly issued common stock in exchange for all of the common stock of Snuff Corp.

The Puff Corporation properly recorded the transaction as follows:

Investment in Snuff	48,950	
Capital Stock—$10 par		27,500
Additional Paid-in Capital		7,500
Retained Earnings of Pooled Subsidiary		13,950

Assume that there were no intercompany transactions during 19X3, and that the parent company maintains its investment account on the equity method.

Required:

(a) Prepare a statement of consolidated net income for the year ended December 31, 19X3.

(b) Prepare a schedule of consolidated retained earnings for the year ended December 31, 19X3.

(c) Prepare the elimination entry (entries) to consolidate the financial statements for the year 19X3.

SOLUTION

(a)

Puff Corporation and Subsidiary
Income Statement
Year Ended December 31, 19X3

Sales ($205,000 + $92,200)		$297,200
Cost of Goods Sold ($123,000 + $70,750)		193,750
Gross Profit		$103,450
Operating Expenses ($64,000 + $15,000)		79,000
Operating Income		$ 24,450
Expenses of Business Combination		2,250
Net Income		$ 22,200

(b) *Retained earnings.*

January 1 ($32,450 + $13,950)	$46,400
Add: Net Income	22,200
	$68,600
Less: Dividends	10,000
December 31	$58,600

(c) *Elimination entries.*

Income from Subsidiary	6,450*	
Retained Earnings (1/1)—S	13,950	
Additional Paid-in Capital	5,000	
Capital Stock—S	30,000	
Investment in Snuff ($48,950 + $6,450)		55,400

---

* $92,200 − $70,750 − $15,000 = $6,450

11.5 Forest Corporation acquired control of Tach Corporation by issuing 2,000 shares of Forest common stock in exchange for all of the outstanding common stock of Tach Corporation. The trial balance of Tach Corporation follows:

	Dr.	Cr.
Cash	$15,000	
Accounts Receivable	25,000	
Merchandise Inventory	12,000	
Plant and Equipment	45,000	
Accumulated Depreciation		$20,000
Vouchers Payable		23,000
Capital Stock—$10 par		20,000
Retained Earnings		34,000
	$97,000	$97,000

The par value of the capital stock of both corporations is $10 per share. The fair market value of the Forest stock is $40 per share. Tach's merchandise has a fair value of $18,000; all other assets are worth book value.

Required:

  (a) Write the journal entry (entries) to record the acquisition of Tach stock if:
   (1) Tach is merged into Forest and the transaction is deemed to be a purchase.
   (2) Tach is merged into Forest and the transaction is deemed to be a pooling of interests.

  (b) Write the journal entry to record the acquisition of Tach if Forest issues 1,800 shares for 90 percent of the shares of Tach and the combination is treated as a pooling of interests.

SOLUTION

  (a) *Acquisition of 100 percent of Tach stock.*

	(1) Purchase Method		(2) Pooling of Interests	
Cash	15,000		15,000	
Accounts Receivable	25,000		25,000	
Merchandise Inventory	18,000		12,000	
Plant and Equipment	25,000		45,000	
Goodwill*	20,000			
Accumulated Depreciation				20,000
Vouchers Payable		23,000		23,000
Capital Stock—$10 par		20,000		20,000
Amount Paid-in in Excess of Par		60,000		
Retained Earnings				34,000

---

* Calculation of Goodwill:

Market Value of Forest stock:	
2,000 shares × $40 per share	$80,000
Less: Fair Value of Other Assets—net	$60,000
Goodwill	$20,000

(b) *Combination treated as a pooling of interests.*

Investment in Tach (90% × $54,000)	48,600	
Capital Stock—$10 par (1,800 shares)		18,000
Retained Earnings (90% × $34,000)		30,600

11.6 The balance sheets of Parr Corp. and Toon Corp. as of the close of business on December 30, 19X1, are as follows:

ASSETS	Parr Corp.	Toon Corp.
Cash	$ 32,560	$ 34,000
Accounts Receivable	79,030	85,220
Merchandise Inventory	134,700	112,220
Machinery and Equipment	357,820	109,288
Accumulated Depreciation	(43,360)	(45,952)
Prepaid Expenses	4,210	3,394
Total Assets	$564,960	$298,170

EQUITIES		
Vouchers Payable	$ 86,040	$ 48,420
Mortgage Payable	100,200	
Capital Stock—$10 par	160,000	180,000
Retained Earnings	218,720	69,750
	$564,960	$298,170

On December 31, 19X1, the Parr Corp. issued 10,000 shares of its common stock in exchange for 90 percent of the common stock of Toon Corp. The transaction meets all criteria for the pooling of interests method of accounting.

Required:

(a) Write the journal entry (entries) on the books of Parr Corp. for acquisition of stock in Toon Corp.

(b) Prepare a worksheet to consolidate the balance sheets of Parr and Toon as of the close of business, December 31, 19X1.

SOLUTION

(a) *Journal entry on the books of Parr Corp.*

Investment in Toon (90% × $249,750)	224,775	
Capital Stock—$10 par (10,000 shares)		100,000
Retained Earnings (90% × $69,750)		62,775
Paid-in Capital		62,000

To record the acquisition of 16,200 shares of Toon Corp. common stock. The transaction meets the criteria for pooling of interests.

(b)

Parr Corp. and Subsidiary
Worksheet—Consolidated Balance Sheet
December 31, 19X1

	Parr Corp. Dr.	Parr Corp. Cr.	Toon Corp. Dr.	Toon Corp. Cr.	Eliminations Dr.	Eliminations Cr.	Consolidated Dr.	Consolidated Cr.
Cash	32,560		34,000				66,560	
Accounts Receivable	79,030		85,220				164,250	
Merchandise Inventory	134,700		112,220				246,920	
Machinery and Equipment	357,820		109,288				467,108	
Accumulated Depreciation		43,360		45,952				89,312
Prepaid Expenses	4,210		3,394				7,604	
Investment in Toon	224,775					[1]224,775		
Vouchers Payable		86,040		48,420				134,460
Mortgage Payable		100,200						100,200
Capital Stock—$10 Par		260,000						260,000
Retained Earnings		281,495						281,495
Paid-in Capital		62,000						62,000
Capital Stock—$10 Par				180,000	$\begin{cases} [2]18,000 \\ [1]162,000 \end{cases}$			
Retained Earnings				69,750	$\begin{cases} [2]6,975 \\ [1]62,775 \end{cases}$			
	833,095	833,095	344,122	344,122				
Minority Interest						[2]24,975		24,975
							952,442	952,442

11.7 The Aido Corporation became affiliated with the Ronald Corporation on December 31, 19X9. This combination complied with all the criteria for pooling of interests. The condensed income statements of the individual corporations prior to the affiliation, for 19X9, follow:

	Ronald Corp.	Aido Corp.
REVENUE		
Sales	$840,000	$361,000
Interest Income	16,000	
Rent Income	3,000	40,000
Total Revenue	$859,000	$401,000
COSTS AND EXPENSES		
Cost of Goods Sold	$480,000	$270,000
Selling and Administrative Expenses	280,000	110,000
Interest Expense	61,000	22,000
Loss on Reacquisition of Bonds	42,000	
Total Costs and Expenses	$863,000	$402,000
Net Loss	$ 4,000	$ 1,000

In June 19X9, Ronald purchased merchandise from Aido for $215,000. All of these goods were resold during the next three months for a total of $268,000.

During the year 19X9 Aido had borrowed funds from Ronald for which Ronald received $16,000 of interest. Ronald rented office space from Aido for $40,000. During 19X9, Ronald paid $34,000 rent and accrued the balance.

Required:

Complete the following worksheet to combine the income statements of Ronald Corporation and Aido Corporation following the affiliation.

Ronald Corporation
Worksheet—Combined Income Statement
Year 19X9

	Ronald Corp. Dr.	Ronald Corp. Cr.	Aido Corp. Dr.	Aido Corp. Cr.	Eliminations Dr.	Eliminations Cr.	Consolidated Dr.	Consolidated Cr.
Sales		840,000		361,000				
Interest		16,000						
Rent Income		3,000		40,000				
Cost of Goods Sold	480,000		270,000					
Selling and Administrative Expenses	280,000		110,000					
Interest Expense	61,000		22,000					
Loss on Reacquisition of Bonds	42,000							
Net Loss		4,000		1,000				
	863,000	863,000	402,000	402,000				

SOLUTION

Ronald Corporation
Worksheet—Combined Income Statement
Year 19X9

	Ronald Corp. Dr.	Ronald Corp. Cr.	Aido Corp. Dr.	Aido Corp. Cr.	Eliminations Dr.	Eliminations Cr.	Consolidated Dr.	Consolidated Cr.
Sales		840,000		361,000	[1]215,000			986,000
Interest		16,000			[2]16,000			
Rent Income		3,000		40,000	[3]40,000			3,000
Cost of Goods Sold	480,000		270,000			[1]215,000	535,000	
Selling and Administrative Expenses	280,000		110,000			[3]40,000	350,000	
Interest Expense	61,000		22,000			[2]16,000	67,000	
Loss on Reacquisition of Bonds	42,000						42,000	
Net Loss		4,000		1,000				5,000
	863,000	863,000	402,000	402,000			994,000	994,000

[1] To eliminate intercompany sales.
[2] To eliminate intercompany interest.
[3] To eliminate intercompany rent.

Chapter 12

Consolidated Statements—
Miscellaneous Topics

12.1 PIECEMEAL PURCHASE OF INVESTMENT

In previous chapters it was always assumed that one corporation achieved control of another corporation by means of a single acquisition. In this section it will be assumed that acquisition of majority control is accomplished by more than one purchase.

An important question arises in a situation that requires the purchase of several blocks of another corporation's stock to achieve majority control: At what point should the difference between the cost of an investment and the fair value of the net assets of the underlying equity of the investee be recognized? In general, it is not necessary to wait until more than 50 percent of the investee's stock has been purchased. In 1971, the Accounting Principles Board extended the requirement that the equity method be utilized for most investments in the common stock of other companies amounting to 20 percent or more of the investee's outstanding voting stock. The rationale is that an investment of 20 percent or more (in the absence of evidence to the contrary) should lead to a presumption of control by the investor.[1] Thus, the equity method is recommended for such investments.

EXAMPLE 1. Assume that S Corp. had 10,000 shares of $10 par capital stock outstanding during a period of time in which P Corp. purchased stock of S as follows:

Date	S Corp.—Net Assets	Shares Acquired by P Corp.	Book Value of Stock Acquired	Cost	Excess of Cost over Book Value
1/1, Yr. 1	$200,000	2,000	$ 40,000	$ 45,000	$ 5,000
1/1, Yr. 2	240,000	1,000	24,000	30,000	6,000
1/1, Yr. 3	270,000	4,000	108,000	140,000	32,000

The outstanding capital stock of S amounted to a constant of $100,000 throughout this entire period. The retained earnings of S Corp. is summarized in the following account.

Retained Earnings

Date		Dr.	Cr.	Balance
1/1, Yr. 1:	Balance			100,000
10/1, Yr. 1:	Dividends	10,000		90,000
12/31, Yr. 1:	Net Income		50,000	140,000
10/1, Yr. 2:	Dividends	10,000		130,000
12/31, Yr. 2:	Net Income		40,000	170,000
10/1, Yr. 3:	Dividends	20,000		150,000
12/31, Yr. 3:	Net Income		60,000	210,000

---

[1] Accounting Principles Board, Opinion No. 18, "The Equity Method of Accounting for Investments in Common Stock." New York, American Institute of Certified Public Accountants, March, 1971.

Clearly, consolidated statements would not be permissible before control exceeded 50 percent. Nevertheless, in statements on and after January 1, Year 1, any difference between the cost of a block of stock and the fair value of those shares should be analyzed. For purposes of this illustration, it will be assumed that the net assets of S Corp. have been properly recorded and that the excess of cost over book value of S's assets implies the existence of goodwill, which will be amortized by the investor over a period of 40 years.

The P Corp. would make the following entries, in general journal form, pertaining to its investment in S Corp.

Year 1

Jan. 1

Investment in S Corp.	45,000	
Cash		45,000

To record purchase of 20% of voting stock of S Corp.

Oct. 1

Cash	2,000	
Investment in S Corp.		2,000

To record dividend received from S Corp.

Dec. 31

Investment in S Corp.	10,000	
Income from Investment		10,000

To record 20% of net income reported by S Corp.

Income from Investment	125	
Investment in S Corp.		125

To amortize $1/40$ of implied goodwill re 20% interest:
$5,000 ÷ 40 yrs. = $125 per year.

Year 2

Jan. 1

Investment in S Corp.	30,000	
Cash		30,000

To record purchase of 10% of voting stock of S Corp.

Oct. 1

Cash	3,000	
Investment in S Corp.		3,000

To record dividend received from S Corp.

Dec. 31

Investment in S Corp.	12,000	
Income from Investment		12,000

To record 30% of net income reported by S Corp.

Income from Investment	275	
Investment in S Corp.		275

To amortize $1/40$ of implied goodwill:
re 20%: $5,000 ÷ 40 = $125
re 10%: $6,000 ÷ 40 = 150
Total $275

Year 3

Jan. 1

| Investment in S Corp. | 140,000 | |
| Cash | | 140,000 |

To record purchase of 40% of voting stock of S Corp.

Oct. 1

| Cash | 14,000 | |
| Investment in S Corp. | | 14,000 |

To record dividend received from S Corp.

Dec. 31

| Investment in S Corp. | 42,000 | |
| Income from Investment | | 42,000 |

To record 70% of net income reported by S Corp.

| Income from Investment | 1,075 | |
| Investment in S Corp. | | 1,075 |

To amortize ¹/₄₀ of implied goodwill:
  re 20%: $ 5,000 ÷ 40 = $ 125
  re 10%: $ 6,000 ÷ 40 =   150
  re 40%: $32,000 ÷ 40 =   800
     Total $1,075

The investment account on the books of P Corp., in accordance with the equity method, would appear as follows:

Investment in S Corp.—Stock

Date	Dr.	Cr.	Balance
1/1, Yr. 1: Cost	45,000		45,000
10/1: Dividend		2,000	43,000
12/31: Income (20%)	10,000		53,000
12/31: Amortization		125	52,875
1/1, Yr. 2: Cost	30,000		82,875
10/1: Dividend		3,000	79,875
12/31: Income (30%)	12,000		91,875
12/31: Amortization		275	91,600
1/1, Yr. 3: Cost	140,000		231,600
10/1: Dividend		14,000	217,600
12/31: Income (70%)	42,000		259,600
12/31: Amortization		1,075	258,525

During Years 1 and 2 the percentage of the investment by P Corp. in the stock of S Corp. was not sufficient for consolidation. Therefore, the balance of the investment account should have been included in the balance sheet of P under an appropriate category such as investments or long-term assets. As of the end of Year 1 and Year 2, the balances are $52,875 and $91,600, respectively. In Year 3, however, a parent-subsidiary relationship exists, since the percentage of stock owned by P in S is over 50 percent. Assuming that an economic affiliation also exists, the balance sheets of the two corporations should be consolidated on and after January 1, Year 3. In the process of consolidation, the investment account will, of course, be eliminated.

The income statements of P Corp. for Years 1 and 2 should include its adjusted income from its investment in S Corp. For Years 1 and 2, these amounts are $9,875 and $11,725, respectively. However, since S Corp. became a subsidiary of P Corp. in Year 3, any income from P's investment in S, which P's books will show, should be eliminated when the two income statements are consolidated.

12.2   CHANGES IN PARENT COMPANY'S OWNERSHIP INTEREST IN SUBSIDIARY

Subsequent to the date of the original business combination, a parent company may increase its ownership interest in a subsidiary by purchasing stock from minority stockholders or directly from the subsidiary. A parent company may also sell some of its subsidiary holdings, thus decreasing its controlling interest. (A similar result would come about if the subsidiary were to sell additional stock to the public.)

Assume the same set of facts as in Example 1. On January 1, Year 4, the P Corp. purchased an additional 1,000 shares of common stock from the minority interests for $41,000. If the book value of this 10 percent lot of S Corp. shares amounted to $31,000 on that date, an implied additional $10,000 goodwill should be recognized and amortized over a maximum period of 40 years, commencing January 1, Year 4.

If a parent company sells a portion of its holdings in a subsidiary and still retains an interest amounting to over 50 percent in the latter company, then the parent-subsidiary relationship is maintained and consolidated statements should be continued. The cost of the block of stock sold should be ascertained on the first-in, first-out, or some other appropriate, basis. The gain or loss on disposal of the stock should be reported as a sale of a noncurrent asset.

12.3   SUBSIDIARY ISSUES ADDITIONAL SHARES TO THE PUBLIC

Stock Issued at Book Value

EXAMPLE 2.   The P Corporation owned 90 percent of the stock of S Corporation. As of December 31, Year 4, the pertinent accounts of S Corporation are summarized in the following schedule:

	Total	Controlling Interest (90%)	Minority Interest (10%)
Capital Stock	$100,000	$ 90,000	$10,000
Retained Earnings	50,000	45,000	5,000
Total Book Value	$150,000	$135,000	$15,000

On January 2, Year 6, the S Corporation sold 2,000 shares to the public at book value, $15 per share. There would be no change in the dollar amount of the parent's interest in S Corp., although the percentage would be reduced; this may be seen in the following comparison:

	Before	After
Capital Stock—S	$100,000	$120,000
Paid-in Capital—S		10,000
Retained Earnings—S	50,000	50,000
Totals	$150,000	$180,000
Parent's Interest:		
Before Sale (90%)	$135,000	
After Sale (75%)		$135,000

Stock Issued at More Than Book Value

EXAMPLE 3. Assume the same facts as in Example 2, except that S Corporation sold 2,000 shares of newly issued stock to outsiders for $19 per share. There will then be an increase in the shareholders' equity of S Corporation; there will also be a concurrent increase in the book value of the controlling interest. This is observed in the following schedule, which compares the before and after results:

	Before	After
Capital Stock—S	$100,000	$120,000
Paid-in Capital—S		18,000
Retained Earnings—S	50,000	50,000
Totals	$150,000	$188,000
Parent's Interest:		
Before Sale (90%)	$135,000	
After Sale (75%)		$141,000

The increase in the parent's equity in its subsidiary, amounting to $6,000, should be recognized in the parent's books by means of a journal entry such as the following:

Investment in Stock—S	6,000	
Paid-in Capital		6,000

To recognize increase in equity in S Corp. stock as a result of subsidiary issuing shares to outsiders at more than book value.

The increase in the capital of P Corporation is basically the result of a reduction in a portion of the minority interest. Since it arises from a transaction which involved the raising of capital, it is generally credited to a paid-in capital account or to a contributed capital account. This point of view, however, is not unanimous; there is a significant school of accounting thought which favors recognition of a nonoperating gain by the parent.

Stock Issued at Less Than Book Value

It is possible that a subsidiary may sell newly issued stock to outsiders at a price less than the book value per share before the sale. In such a case, a decrease in the parent's equity should be recognized. The journal entry on the parent's books would be the reverse of the type which has been described in the foregoing paragraphs.

12.4 CONTROL ACHIEVED DURING FISCAL YEAR

In various illustrations up to this point, it has generally been assumed that a controlling interest in a subsidiary had been acquired at the beginning of a fiscal year. This is not always the case; frequently the controlling interest is acquired at some other date.

When control of a subsidiary is acquired during a fiscal year it is necessary to prepare interim statements for the subsidiary as of or up to the date of acquisition of control. This is necessary to ascertain the difference between the book value of the interest acquired and the cost thereof, and may be used to determine the price to be paid for the stock in the first place.

The portion of the net income of the subsidiary assigned to the minority interest is based on its percentage as of the end of the year. However, the portion representing the controlling interest from the beginning of the fiscal year to the date of control is generally treated as if it had been purchased, whereas that portion of the net income for the balance of the fiscal year should be included in consolidated income.

When a controlling interest in a subsidiary has been acquired during a fiscal year, there are two possible approaches to preparing the first consolidated income statement. One is to consolidate for a fraction of a year; that is, include only the portion of the subsidiary's revenue and expenses for the latter part of the year, and from that deduct the minority interest for the latter part of the year.

The alternative is to consolidate the two income statements for the entire year, and from this deduct the following:

(a) the minority interest for the entire year computed in the usual way, and

(b) the subsidiary's net income prior to acquisition of control by the parent multiplied by the parent's fractional control.

The latter procedure is generally utilized because it gives a better picture of the earning power of the consolidated companies. It also facilitates comparisons with later years.

EXAMPLE 4. The P Corporation purchased 90 percent of the outstanding stock of T Corporation, for which P Corporation paid $162,000 on April 1 of Year 1. All of the recorded assets were considered to be worth their book values, and the recorded liabilities properly reflected the obligations of T Corporation. However, in addition to the recorded assets, T Corporation owned the rights to a fully amortized patent. P Corporation estimated the patent to be worth $25,000 and to have an additional four years of economic life from April 1 of Year 1.

As illustrated in Chapter 6, such a patent should be recognized in the consolidated balance sheet, and amortization of the amount applicable to the patent should be included in the consolidated income statement. The T Corporation shows $20,000 of net income for the entire Year 1. It is assumed that this income was earned at the rate of $5,000 per calendar quarter.

In the accompanying worksheet to prepare a consolidated income statement for the first year of operations of the two corporations (p. 322), entry (a) eliminates the income from subsidiary, which the parent had already recorded on the parent's books, $13,500 (90% of $15,000) and thus had been included in its income. Entry (b) records the amortization of patent expense for nine months, $4,688 [($\frac{1}{4}$ of $25,000) $\times$ $\frac{9}{12}$], and thus reduces the subsidiary's net income for consolidation purposes to $15,312 for Year 1.

Entry (c) segregates P's share of the net income of the subsidiary earned prior to the acquisition, $4,500 (90 percent of $5,000). Entry (d) allocates the balance of the adjusted net income of T, $10,812 ($15,312 − $4,500), as indicated in the following entry:

Net Income—P		
(90% of $10,312)	9,281	
Minority Interest in T		
(10% of $10,312) + (10% of $5,000)	1,531	
Net Income		10,812

The investment account on the parent company's books appears as follows:

Investment in T Corp.—Stock

Date	Dr.	Cr.	Balance
1/1, Yr. 1: Cost	162,000		162,000
Year 1: Dividend		9,000	153,000
12/31, Yr. 1: Net Income	13,500		166,500

The balance sheets of P Corp. and of T Corp. at the end of Year 1 are condensed in the first four columns of the accompanying worksheet to prepare a consolidated balance sheet as of that date. Entry (b) is similar to the same lettered entry in the worksheet to consolidate the income statements for Year 1, and performs the same function. Entry (1) recognizes the patent, at the value of $25,000, which was determined as of the date of acquisition of 90 percent of the stock of T Corp. The combined effect of entries (1) and (b) is that the amortized value of the patent, for consolidation purposes at the end of the first year, is $20,312 ($25,000 − $4,688).

The purpose of entry (2) is to reduce the parent company's investment account by $4,219 (90% of the $4,688 reduction made in the net income of T Corp. as a result of the amortization of the patent). The patent and its amortization will normally appear only in the consolidated workpapers and in the consolidated statements.

Entry (3) eliminates the adjusted cost of the investment in T Corp. against 90 percent of the shareholders' equity of T Corp. as of the end of Year 1. Entry (4) classifies the remaining 10 percent as the minority interest.

The minority interest in T Corp. as of December 31, Year 1, totals $18,031, which may be verified from the following table:

	Total	Minority
Capital Stock	$100,000	$10,000
Retained Earnings, January 1	50,000	5,000
Appraisal Capital	25,000	2,500
Net Income—Year 1 (as adjusted)	15,312	1,531
Dividends	(10,000)	(1,000)
Totals	$180,312	$18,031

(*Note*: As an alternate approach, a three-tier worksheet is included in this example on p. 323.)

The amount of consolidated net income for Year 1 may also be calculated from an analysis of each corporation's contribution to the consolidated net income as follows:

P Corp. Reported Net Income	$32,500	
Less: Income from Subsidiary	13,500	
Income from Own Operations		$19,000
T Corp. Reported Net Income	$20,000	
Less: Amortization of Patent	4,688	
Adjusted Net Income	$15,312	
Less: Minority Interest in Income	1,531	
Income Available for Controlling Interest	$13,781	
Less: Net Income of T Corp., Earned Prior to Purchase of Control (90% of $5,000)	4,500	
Net Income for Consolidation		9,281
Consolidated Net Income		$28,281

12.5 SUBSIDIARY HAVING BOTH COMMON AND PREFERRED STOCK

When a subsidiary has both common and preferred stock outstanding, the first problem is the allocation of the subsidiary's retained earnings at the date or dates of purchase. Thereafter, the chief problem is the allocation of the subsidiary's net income or loss between the two classes of stock. The rule in both cases is to assign to the preferred stock an amount equal to the book value, or a higher amount when appropriate, of the preferred shares; the remainder is assigned to the common stock as the residual class.

Typically, preferred stock has a fixed cumulative dividend and does not have the right to vote; generally, only common stock has the voting power. If the foregoing is assumed, then two questions arise: (1) How much equity is to be assigned to the preferred stock at the date of acquisition of control (this is vital when dividends are in arrears)? (2) How shall the net income, or loss, of the subsidiary be allocated to consolidated net income and to minority interests?

Preferred stock may have a par value, a liquidation value, and a call price. Usually, the last will be the highest of the three. In any event, for consolidation purposes it is generally the highest of these values which is to be assigned to the preferred stock. If dividends are in arrears, such amount

(Text continued on p. 324.)

P Corp. and Subsidiary
Worksheet—Consolidated Income Statement
Year 1

	P Corp.		T Corp.		Eliminations		Consolidated	
	Dr.	Cr.	Dr.	Cr.	Dr.	Cr.	Dr.	Cr.
Sales		120,000		116,000				236,000
Cost of Goods Sold	70,000		75,000				145,000	
Selling Expenses	16,000		12,000				28,000	
General Expenses	15,000		9,000				24,000	
Income from Subsidiary		13,500			a13,500			
	101,000	133,500	96,000	116,000				
Net Income—P	32,500				d9,281	a13,500	28,281	
Net Income—T			20,000			d10,812		
						c4,500		
						b4,688		
	133,500	133,500	116,000	116,000				
Amortization of Patent					b4,688		4,688	
Preacquisition Earnings of Subsidiary Purchased by P					c4,500		4,500	
Minority Interest					d1,531		1,531	
							236,000	236,000

[a] To eliminate income of T Corp. previously recorded by P.
[b] To amortize patent for 9 months (Apr. 1–Dec. 31): $4,688 (25% of $25,000 × 9/12).
[c] To segregate net income earned by subsidiary prior to control by P: $4,500 (90% of $5,000).
[d] To allocate balance of net income of T as adjusted: parent—90% of $10,312 (9 months); minority—10% of $15,312 (12 months).

P Corp. and Subsidiary
Worksheet—Consolidated Balance Sheet
December 31, Year 1

	P Corp.		T Corp.		Eliminations		Consolidated	
	Dr.	Cr.	Dr.	Cr.	Dr.	Cr.	Dr.	Cr.
Current Assets	80,000		85,000				165,000	
Investment in T Stock	166,500					3 162,281		
						2 4,219		
Depreciable Assets—net	190,000		90,000				280,000	
Land			25,000				25,000	
Liabilities		159,000		40,000				199,000
Capital Stock—P		200,000						200,000
Retained Earnings (1/1)—P		60,000						60,000
Net Income—P		32,500			2 4,219			28,281
Dividends—P	15,000						15,000	
Capital Stock—T				100,000	4 10,000			
					3 90,000			
Retained Earnings (1/1)—T				50,000	4 5,000			
					3 45,000			
Net Income—T				20,000	3 13,781			
					b 4,688			
					4 1,531			
Dividends—T			10,000			4 1,000		
						3 9,000		
	451,500	451,500	210,000	210,000				
Patent					1 25,000	b 4,688	20,312	
Appraisal Capital—T					4 2,500	1 25,000		
					3 22,500			
Minority Interest in T						4 18,031		18,031
							505,312	505,312

[1] To record value of patent owned by subsidiary.
[2] To adjust P's investment and net income for 90% of reduction in T's net income for Year 1: $4,219 (90% of $4,688).
[3] To eliminate 90% of shareholders' equity in T as of Dec. 31, Yr. 1.
[4] To classify 10% interest of minority shareholders.

P Corp. and Subsidiary
Consolidated Workpapers (3-tier)
Year 1

	Company		Adjustments & Eliminations		Consolidated
	P	T			
INCOME STATEMENT					
Revenue					
Sales	120,000	116,000			236,000
Income from Subsidiary	13,500		$\{$ [3]9,281 [2]4,219		
Total Revenue	133,500	116,000			236,000
Costs and Expenses					
Cost of Goods Sold	70,000	75,000			145,000
Selling Expenses	16,000	12,000			28,000
General Expenses	15,000	9,000			24,000
Amortization of Patent			[b]4,688		4,688
Total Costs and Expenses	101,000	96,000			201,688
					34,312
Preacquisition Earnings of Subsidiary Purchased by P			[3]4,500 $\}$		6,031
Minority Interest in Income [10% of ($20,000 − $4,688)]			[4]1,531		
Net Income	32,500	20,000			28,281
RETAINED EARNINGS					
Balance (1/1)—P	60,000				60,000
Balance (1/1)—T		50,000	$\{$ [4]5,000 [3]45,000		
Net Income	32,500	20,000			28,281
Total	92,500	70,000			88,281
Less: Dividends—P	15,000				15,000
Dividends—T		10,000		$\{$ [4]1,000 [3]9,000	
Balance (12/31)	77,500	60,000			73,281
BALANCE SHEET					
Assets					
Current Assets	80,000	85,000			165,000
Investment in T Corp.	166,500			$\{$ [3]162,281 [2]4,219	
Depreciable Assets—net	190,000	90,000			280,000
Land		25,000			25,000
Patent			[1]25,000	[b]4,688	20,312
Total Assets	436,500	200,000			490,312
Equities					
Liabilities	159,000	40,000			199,000
Capital Stock—P	200,000				200,000
Retained Earnings—P	77,500				73,281
Capital Stock—T		100,000	$\{$ [4]10,000 [3]90,000		
Retained Earnings—T		60,000			
Appraisal Capital—T			[4]2,500 $\}$ [3]22,500	[1]25,000	
Minority Interest				[4]18,031	18,031
Total Equities	436,500	200,000			490,312

should be added to the previous value in order to obtain the book value of the preferred stock for consolidation purposes. This is done even if the subsidiary corporation has a deficit in its retained earnings account; the convention is to assume that the company's operations will ultimately be profitable. After the book value of the preferred stock has been calculated, the balance of the net assets is assigned to the common stockholders as the owners of the residual equity.

EXAMPLE 5. S Corporation had outstanding $100,000 par value of common stock and $100,000 par value of 6 percent preferred stock. Each share of $100 par value preferred stock is cumulative, nonvoting, and callable at 110. On December 31, Year 1, P Corporation purchased 90 percent of the common stock of S Corporation and 30 percent of its preferred stock for a total of $168,000. On that date S Corporation had accumulated retained earnings of $60,000; there were no dividends in arrears.

The entry, in general journal form, which P Corporation would make upon its acquisition of S Corporation stock follows:

Investment in S Corp.—Pfd.	33,000	
Investment in S Corp.—Comm.	135,000	
Cash		168,000

To record investment in preferred stock at call price (3,000 × $110); balance assigned to investment in common stock.

The allocation of the total shareholders' equity in S Corp., as of the date of acquisition, is included in the following schedule.

	Total	Controlling Interest	Minority Interest
Preferred Stock—par	$100,000	$ 30,000	$70,000
Call premium (10%)	10,000	3,000	7,000
Total to Preferred	$110,000	$ 33,000	$77,000
Common Stock—par	$100,000	$ 90,000	$10,000
Retained Earnings—balance ($60,000 − $10,000)	50,000		
Controlling Interest (90%)		45,000	
Minority (10%)			5,000
Total to Common	$150,000	$135,000	$15,000
Totals	$260,000	$168,000	$92,000

The accompanying worksheet to prepare a consolidated balance sheet as of December 31, Year 1, reflects the foregoing allocation among the preferred and common shareholders and the minority interests in S Corp.

P Corp. and Subsidiary
Worksheet—Consolidated Balance Sheet
December 31, Year 1

	P Corp.		S Corp.		Eliminations		Consolidated	
	Dr.	Cr.	Dr.	Cr.	Dr.	Cr.	Dr.	Cr.
Current Assets	80,000		70,000				150,000	
Investment in S Corp.—Pfd.	33,000					[1]33,000		
Investment in S Corp.—Comm.	135,000					[3]135,000		
Other Assets—net	252,000		240,000				492,000	
Liabilities		100,000		50,000				150,000
Capital Stock—P		200,000						200,000
Retained Earnings—P		200,000						200,000
Capital Stock: Pfd.—S				100,000	[2]70,000 [1]30,000			
Capital Stock: Comm.—S				100,000	[4]10,000 [3]90,000			
Retained Earnings—S				60,000	[2]7,000 [1]3,000 [3]45,000 [4]5,000			
	500,000	500,000	310,000	310,000				
Minority Interest						[4]15,000 [2]77,000		92,000
							642,000	642,000

[1] To eliminate investment in preferred stock against 30% of preferred stock of S, based on call price of $110 per share.
[2] To classify 70% interest of minority shareholders in preferred stock of S, based on call price of $110 per share.
[3] To eliminate 90% of S's capital stock, common, and balance of retained earnings as of Dec. 31, Yr. 1.
[4] To classify 10% interest of minority shareholders, as of Dec. 31, Yr. 1.

EXAMPLE 6.   Example 6 is a continuation of the previous example into Year 3.   A summary of the retained earnings accounts for both corporations follows:

	P Corp.	S Corp.
Retained Earnings, 1/1, Yr. 2	$200,000	$60,000
Net Income, Year 2	59,200	20,000
	$259,200	$80,000
Less: Dividends, Year 2:		
Preferred		(6,000)
Common	(25,000)	(10,000)
Retained Earnings, 12/31, Yr. 2	$234,200	$64,000
Net Income, Year 3	33,400	20,000
	$267,600	$84,000
Less: Dividends, Year 3:		
Preferred	–0–	–0–
Common	(15,000)	–0–
Retained Earnings, 12/31, Yr. 3	$252,600	$84,000

In Year 3 the S Corporation omitted the preferred dividend; thus it is in arrears to the extent of $6,000. However, regardless of whether the preferred dividend has been paid, there will be no effect on the net income of the parent company and of the minority interests. When allocating the net income for Year 3, $6,000 (an amount equivalent to the preferred dividend) is first assigned to the preferred stock; the balance is then allocated to the common. This may be observed in the investment accounts below; and also in the accompanying consolidation worksheets.

The investment accounts on P's books are summarized as follows:

Investment in S Corp. Stock—Preferred

Date	Dr.	Cr.	Balance
12/31, Yr. 2: Cost	33,000		33,000
10/31, Yr. 2: Dividend Received		1,800	31,200
12/31, Yr. 2: Net Income	1,800		33,000
10/31, Yr. 3: Dividend Accrued		1,800	31,200
12/31, Yr. 3: Net Income	1,800		33,000

Investment in S Corp. Stock—Common

Date	Dr.	Cr.	Balance
12/31, Yr. 2: Cost	135,000		135,000
10/31, Yr. 2: Dividend Received		9,000	126,000
12/31, Yr. 2: Net Income	12,600		138,600
12/31, Yr. 3: Net Income	12,600		151,200

Equity Method

P Corp. and Subsidiary
Worksheet—Consolidated Income Statement
Year 3

	P Corp. Dr.	P Corp. Cr.	S Corp. Dr.	S Corp. Cr.	Eliminations Dr.	Eliminations Cr.	Consolidated Dr.	Consolidated Cr.
Sales		120,000		116,000				236,000
Cost of Goods Sold	70,000		75,000				145,000	
Selling Expenses	16,000		12,000				28,000	
General Expenses	15,000		9,000				24,000	
Income from Subsidiary		14,400			[a]14,400			
	101,000	134,400	96,000	116,000				
Net Income—P	33,400				[b]14,400	[a]14,400	33,400	
Net Income—S			20,000			[b]20,000		
	134,400	134,400	116,000	116,000				
Minority Interest					[b]5,600		5,600	
							236,000	236,000

[a] To eliminate income from subsidiary previously recorded by P.
[b] To allocate net income of subsidiary as follows:

	Total	Control	Minority
Preferred	$ 6,000	$ 1,800 (30%)	$4,200 (70%)
Common	14,000	12,600 (90%)	1,400 (10%)
	$20,000	$14,400	$5,600

Equity Method

P Corp. and Subsidiary
Worksheet—Consolidated Balance Sheet
December 31, Year 3

	P Corp.		S Corp.		Eliminations		Consolidated	
	Dr.	Cr.	Dr.	Cr.	Dr.	Cr.	Dr.	Cr.
Current Assets	103,000		95,000				198,000	
Investment in S Corp.—Pfd.	33,000					[1]33,000		
Investment in S Corp.—Comm.	151,200					[3]151,200		
Dividend Receivable from S Corp.	1,800					[2]1,800		
Other Assets—net	263,000		220,000				483,000	
Liabilities		99,400		31,000				130,400
Capital Stock—P		200,000						200,000
Retained Earnings (1/1)—P		234,200						234,200
Net Income—P		33,400						33,400
Dividends—P	15,000						15,000	
Capital Stock: Pfd.—S				100,000	[1]100,000			
Capital Stock: Comm.—S				100,000	[4]10,000 [3]90,000			
Retained Earnings (1/1)—S				64,000	[2]6,000 [1]10,000 [3]43,200 [4]4,800			
Net Income–S				20,000	[4]2,000 [3]18,000			
	567,000	567,000	315,000	315,000				
Minority Interests						[2]4,200 [1]77,000 [4]16,800		98,000
							696,000	696,000

[1] To allocate equity of preferred shareholders at liquidation value: $110,000 ($110 × 1,000 shares).

[2] To allocate portion of S's retained earnings for dividend omitted in Year. 2.

[3] To eliminate 90% of capital stock, common, and balance of retained earnings: $151,200 [90% of ($100,000 + $48,000 + $20,000)].

[4] To classify 10% interest of minority shareholders' in capital stock, common, and retained earnings.

12.6 STOCK DIVIDEND BY A SUBSIDIARY

A pro-rata distribution of a corporation's stock to a stockholder of the same class results in a larger number of shares outstanding, but each stockholder will have the same proportionate interest in the corporation as before the stock distribution. The assets and liabilities of a subsidiary corporation which declares and distributes a stock dividend remain unchanged; the total of the shareholder equity accounts is also unaffected. However, within the shareholders' equity section there will be a decrease in the amount of retained earnings along with a concurrent increase in its capital stock accounts.

Since the degree of control of a parent will remain unchanged after the receipt of a stock dividend in the same class of stock, the amount of the investment will remain unchanged, although it will be represented by an increased number of shares. When an investment account is maintained on the equity method, such stock dividends may be ignored, since the investment account will automatically include the parent's share of the undistributed earnings of the subsidiary from the date of acquisition of control.

If the parent company maintains its investment in a subsidiary on the cost basis, the growth in the retained earnings of the subsidiary may be obscured. The simplest approach to this difficulty is to reverse the stock dividend in the consolidation worksheet. Thereafter, one may proceed as if the stock dividend had not occurred.

12.7　TREASURY STOCK HELD BY A SUBSIDIARY

If any corporation holds treasury stock, such stock is not considered outstanding; it may not be voted nor may it receive normal distributions of the issuing corporation. However, treasury stock is invariably adjusted for stock splits and for stock dividends. In the event that another corporation acquires control of a corporation which holds treasury stock, the percentage of control is measured by comparing the investor's holdings with the outstanding stock of the investee corporation. Thus, treasury stock is treated, for consolidation purposes, as if it had been constructively retired.

EXAMPLE 7. Assume that P Corporation purchased 7,000 shares of the common stock of T Corporation on January 1, Year 1, for $145,000. The condensed balance sheets of the two corporations appear in the first four columns of the accompanying worksheet to prepare a consolidated balance sheet as of the date of acquisition of control. The assets and liabilities of T Corporation are properly recorded, and the book amounts represent the fair value of the individual items. Any excess paid by P Corporation is deemed to be due to the value of the advantages of affiliation of the two companies. The treasury stock on the books of T Corporation represents the cost of 1,000 shares of common stock (par value, $10 per share) which T acquired in a previous year and which was recorded at cost.

The first elimination entry (1) recognizes the constructive retirement of the treasury stock held by T Corporation. The worksheet entry follows:

Capital Stock—$10 par—T	10,000	
Retained Earnings (1/1)—T	5,000	
Treasury Stock		15,000

To record the constructive retirement of 1,000 shares of treasury stock. Excess of cost above par is treated as a dividend.

After giving effect to entry (1) the resultant shareholders' equity of T Corporation is as follows:

Capital Stock—$10 par	$100,000
Retained Earnings	50,000
Total	$150,000

Since 70 percent of the book value amounts to $105,000, the excess of $40,000 ($145,000 − $105,000) is to be treated as excess of cost over fair value of interest in subsidiary, and should be amortized over a reasonable period of time.

Entry (2) segregates the excess of cost of investment in subsidiary over 70 percent of the book value of T. Entry (3) eliminates the balance of the investment account against 70 percent of the shareholders' equity in T Corporation as adjusted. Entry (4) classifies the remaining 30 percent as the interest of the minority shareholders.

P Corp. and Subsidiary
Worksheet—Consolidated Balance Sheet
January 1, Year 1

	P Corp.		T Corp.		Eliminations		Consolidated	
	Dr.	Cr.	Dr.	Cr.	Dr.	Cr.	Dr.	Cr.
Current Assets	120,000		105,000				225,000	
Investment in T Corp.	145,000					[3]105,000 [2]40,000		
Depreciable Assets—net	205,000		90,000				295,000	
Liabilities		110,000		45,000				155,000
Capital Stock—$100 par—P		200,000						200,000
Retained Earnings (1/1)—P		160,000						160,000
Treasury Stock			15,000			[1]15,000		
Capital Stock—$10 par—T				110,000	[4]30,000 [3]70,000 [1]10,000			
Retained Earnings (1/1)—T				55,000	[3]35,000 [1]5,000 [4]15,000			
	470,000	470,000	210,000	210,000				
Excess of Cost over Fair Value of Interest in Subsidiary					[2]40,000		40,000	
Minority Interest in T						[4]45,000		45,000
							560,000	560,000

[1] To recognize the constructive retirement of T's treasury stock.
[2] To record excess of cost of investment over the book value of 70% of T Corp.
[3] To eliminate 70% of subsidiary capital stock and retained earnings, as adjusted.
[4] To classify 30% interest of minority stockholders.

12.8 PARENT COMPANY STOCK OWNED BY SUBSIDIARY

When two corporations are affiliated and each one owns stock in the other, a reciprocal affiliation is said to exist. For example, assume that A Corporation owns 90 percent of B Corporation and B Corporation owns 10 percent of A Corporation. Such an affiliation is often referred to as a father-son reciprocal affiliation. Many accountants favor the apportionment of net income to the various interests by means of simultaneous algebraic equations, or by formulas which take into consideration the interdependency of the reciprocal holdings.

Present theory and practice, however, favor a treasury stock approach in such a reciprocal type of relationship. Thus, any stock of the parent corporation which is owned by a subsidiary is treated as if the parent had reacquired its own stock; the entire cost of the subsidiary's investment in a parent's stock is deducted in the consolidated shareholders' equity section of the balance sheet. In calculating the minority interest in the subsidiary, one ignores any income that the subsidiary might have recorded as having been received from the parent.

EXAMPLE 8. The P Corporation purchased 80 percent of the outstanding stock of S Corporation on January 1, Year 1, for $96,000. At that date, the shareholders' equity sections of the respective balance sheets were as follows:

	P Corp.	S Corp.
Capital Stock	$200,000	$100,000
Retained Earnings	120,000	20,000
Totals	$320,000	$120,000

The assets of S Corporation, include 10 percent of the outstanding shares of P Corporation, which S Corporation had acquired several years earlier at a cost of $32,000.

The results of operations of the two corporations for Year 1 are included in the first four columns of the accompanying worksheet to consolidate the income statements for Year 1. Entry (a) eliminates the dividend income recorded by S Corporation as a result of its holding 10 percent of the stock of P Corporation. Although S Corporation maintains its investment account on the cost basis, P Corporation maintains its investment account on the equity basis. Thus, P Corporation had recorded 80 percent of the net income reported by S Corporation. Since the latter figure includes an intercompany dividend of $2,000, which has been eliminated in the foregoing entry, it is now consistent to eliminate $1,600 (80 percent of $2,000), which P Corporation had included in its investment income; this is accomplished in entry (b). Entry (c) allocates the adjusted net income of S Corporation, $68,000 ($70,000 − $2,000), between the parent, $54,400 (80 percent of $68,000), and the minority interest of $13,600 (20 percent of $68,000).

The balance sheets of P Corporation and S Corporation at the end of Year 1 are condensed in the first four columns of the accompanying worksheet to prepare a consolidated balance sheet as of that date. Entry (a) is the same as the lettered entry (a) in the worksheet to consolidate the income statements for Year 1 and performs the same function. Entry (1) is similar to entry (b) in the worksheet to consolidate the income statements for Year 1. However, the credit is now to the investment account, which is maintained on the equity basis. Entry (2) eliminates the adjusted investment account against 80 percent of the shareholders' equity of S Corporation, as of the end of Year 1. Entry (3) classifies the remaining 20 percent as the minority interest.

A consolidated balance sheet of P Corporation and its subsidiary as of the end of Year 1 has been prepared from the last two columns of the consolidation worksheet. Notice that the investment of S Corporation in 10 percent of the stock of P Corporation has been extended to these columns; however, it is classified as treasury stock in the balance sheet.

Equity Method

P Corp. and Subsidiary
Worksheet—Consolidated Income Statement
Year 1

	P Corp.		S Corp.		Eliminations		Consolidated	
	Dr.	Cr.	Dr.	Cr.	Dr.	Cr.	Dr.	Cr.
Sales		250,000		300,000				550,000
Cost of Goods Sold	140,000		190,000				330,000	
Selling Expenses	32,000		24,000				56,000	
General Expenses	30,000		18,000				48,000	
Dividend Income				2,000	ª2,000			
Income from Subsidiary		56,000			$\left\{\begin{array}{l}{}^c54,400\\{}^b1,600\end{array}\right.$			
	202,000	306,000	232,000	302,000				
Net Income—P	104,000					ᵇ1,600	102,400	
Net Income—S			70,000			$\left\{\begin{array}{l}{}^c68,000\\{}^a2,000\end{array}\right.$		
	306,000	306,000	302,000	302,000				
Minority Interest					ᶜ13,600		13,600	
							550,000	550,000

ª To eliminate intercompany dividend received by subsidiary, $2,000.
ᵇ To reduce parent's income by 80% of reduction in subsidiary's income, $1,600 (80% of $2,000).
ᶜ To allocate adjusted net income of subsidiary, $68,000 ($70,000 − $2,000), 80% to parent and 20% to minority interest.

Equity Method

P Corp. and Subsidiary
Worksheet—Consolidated Balance Sheet
December 31, Year 1

	P Corp.		S Corp.		Eliminations		Consolidated	
	Dr.	Cr.	Dr.	Cr.	Dr.	Cr.	Dr.	Cr.
Current Assets	109,000		258,000				367,000	
Investment in S Corp.	152,000					[2]150,400 [1]1,600		
Investment in P Corp.			32,000				32,000	
Depreciable Assets—net	243,000		50,000				293,000	
Liabilities		100,000		150,000				250,000
Capital Stock—P		200,000						200,000
Retained Earnings (1/1)—P		120,000						120,000
Net Income—P		104,000			[1]1,600			102,400
Dividends—P	20,000					[a]2,000	18,000	
Capital Stock—S				100,000	[3]20,000 [2]80,000			
Retained Earnings (1/1)—S				20,000	[3]4,000 [2]16,000			
Net Income—S				70,000	[2]54,400 [a]2,000 [3]13,600			
	524,000	524,000	340,000	340,000				
Minority Interest						[3]37,600		37,600
							710,000	710,000

[1] To reduce parent's income by 80% of reduction in subsidiary's income.
[2] To eliminate investment account, as adjusted, against 80% of shareholders' equity of subsidiary, as of Dec. 31, Yr. 1.
[3] To classify 20% interest of minority shareholders as of Dec. 31, Yr. 1.

P Corp. and Subsidiary
Consolidated Balance Sheet
December 31, Year 1

ASSETS

Current Assets	$367,000	
Depreciable Assets—net	293,000	
Total Assets		$660,000

LIABILITIES AND SHAREHOLDERS' EQUITY

Liabilities		$250,000
Minority Interest		37,600
Capital Stock, $100 par	$200,000	
Retained Earnings (See schedule on p. 332.)	204,400	
Total	$404,400	
Less: Treasury Stock (200 Shares at Cost)	32,000	372,400
Total Liabilities and Shareholders' Equity		$660,000

A supporting schedule of consolidated retained earnings for Year 1 follows:

Retained Earnings, January 1	$120,000
Add: Consolidated Net Income Year 1	102,400
Total	$222,400
Less: Dividends	18,000
Retained Earnings, December 31	$204,400

Summary

(1) The equity method should generally be used when accounting for investments in common stock which equal or exceed _____ percent of the investee's outstanding common stock.

(2) When a subsidiary sells common stock to the public at less than book value, the investment account on the parent's books should be _____.

(3) When a subsidiary corporation has both preferred and common stock outstanding, the generally accepted convention is to assume that the subsidiary operations will ultimately be _____.

(4) After the book value of a subsidiary's preferred stock has been calculated, the balance of the shareholders' equity is assigned to the _____ stockholders, as they are the owners of the residual equity.

(5) After a parent corporation receives a stock dividend from a subsidiary, the dollar amount of the investment account should be _____.

(6) Under the treasury stock approach, the cost of a subsidiary's investment in the stock of its parent should be _____ in the consolidated balance sheet.

Answers: (1) 20; (2) reduced (decreased); (3) profitable; (4) common; (5) unchanged; (6) deducted

Solved Problems

12.1 The Bradley Corporation owns an 85 percent interest in the Summit Corporation, which had been acquired as follows:

Date	Percent	Cost ($)
Jan. 1, 19X1	25	66,000
Jan. 1, 19X2	10	32,000
Jan. 1, 19X3	50	150,000

During these years, the Summit Corporation has had common stock outstanding with a par value of $200,000. A summary of its retained earnings account for the period follows.

Date	Dr.	Cr.	Balance
Balance, Jan. 1, 19X1			40,000
Net Income, 19X1		50,000	90,000
Dividends, Dec. 15, 19X1	24,000		66,000
Net Income, 19X2		28,000	94,000
Dividends, Dec. 16, 19X2	20,000		74,000
Net Income, 19X3		36,000	110,000
Dividends, Dec. 17, 19X3	30,000		80,000

Required:

Prepare a schedule which will clearly show the difference between the cost of the parent's investment and the book value of its interest at the date of each acquisition.

SOLUTION

Date	Shareholders' Equity— Summit			Acquired by Bradley		Cost of Investment	Excess of Cost Over Book Value
	Capital Stock	Retained Earnings	Total	Percent	Book Value		
1/1, Yr. 1	200,000	40,000	240,000	25	60,000	66,000	6,000
1/1, Yr. 2	200,000	66,000	266,000	10	26,600	32,000	5,400
1/1, Yr. 3	200,000	74,000	274,000	50	137,000	150,000	13,000

12.2 The Dubb Corporation has 10,000 shares of $10 par value common stock outstanding. The Lynn Company purchased 8,000 of these shares for $185,600 on January 1, 19X6, and 880 shares on December 1, 19X6 for $32,100.

The retained earnings account of Dubb Corporation for 19X6 and 19X7 is summarized as follows:

Date	Dr.	Cr.	Balance
Jan. 1, 19X6: Balance			132,000
Nov. 10, 19X6: Dividends	10,000		122,000
Dec. 31, 19X6: Net Income		18,000	140,000
Oct. 31, 19X7: Dividends	10,000		130,000
Dec. 31, 19X7: Net Income		20,000	150,000

The Lynn Company sold 1,000 shares of the Dubb stock on January 1, 19X8 for $20,000.

Required:

(a) Compute the carrying value of the shares sold, using the first-in, first-out method.

(b) Determine the amount of gain or loss on the sale.

SOLUTION

(a)   1. *Carrying value of first 8,000 shares*

Cost, 1/1, X6	$185,600
Parent's Share of Increase in Subsidiary's Equity 80% of ($150,000 − $132,000)	14,400
Carrying Value, 1/1, X8	$200,000

2. *Carrying value of first 1,000 shares (1/8 of $200,000)* $ 25,000

(b)

Sale Price on Jan. 1, 19X8	$ 20,000
Carrying Value	25,000
Loss	$ 5,000

12.3 The Prindle Corporation organized the Soun Corporation on February 27, 19X6. Prindle held all of the stock of Soun until June 30, 19X9, when it sold 10 percent to employees for $10,000.
    Selected financial data for the two corporations for the Year 19X9 are summarized in the following table.

	Prindle Corp.	Soun Corp.
Sales	$500,000	$300,000
Cost of Goods Sold	380,000	200,000
Selling and Administrative Expenses	93,000	80,000
Income from Subsidiary	19,000	
Gain/Loss on Sale of Investment	?	
Investment in Subsidiary	76,500	
Other Assets	145,000	110,000
Liabilities	40,000	30,000
Capital Stock—$100 par	74,000	20,000
Amount Paid-in in Excess of Par	26,000	5,000
Retained Earnings, January 1	30,000	35,000

Both corporations earned income uniformly throughout the year. There were no intercompany transactions during the year.

Required:

(a) Determine the gain or loss on the sale of Soun stock, June 30, 19X9.

(b) Prepare a statement of consolidated income for 19X9.

(c) Prepare a schedule of minority interests as of December 31, 19X9.

SOLUTION

(*a*) 1. *Basis of investment in subsidiary as of June 30, 19X9*

Capital Stock	$20,000
Amount Paid-in in Excess of Par	5,000
Retained Earnings, January 1	35,000
Total Shareholders' Equity, January 1	$60,000
Net Income for First Half of Year 6/12 ($300,000 − $200,000 − $80,000)	10,000
Investment Account, June 30	$70,000
Basis of Stock Sold (10% of $70,000)	$ 7,000

2. *Sale of stock, June 30, 19X9*

Sales Price	$10,000
Basis of Stock Sold	7,000
Gain	$ 3,000

(*b*)

Prindle Corp. and Subsidiary
Income Statement
Year Ended December 31, 19X9

Sales ($500,000 + $300,000)	$800,000
Cost of Goods Sold ($380,000 + $200,000)	580,000
Gross Margin	$220,000
Less: Expenses ($93,000 + $80,000)	173,000
Net Income from Operations	$ 47,000
Add: Gain on Sale of Investment	3,000
Total	$ 50,000
Less: Minority Interest (10% of $20,000)	2,000
Net Income	$ 48,000

(*c*)

	Total	Parent (90%)	Minority (10%)
Capital Stock	$20,000	$18,000	$2,000
Amount Paid-in in Excess of Par	5,000	4,500	500
Retained Earnings, January 1	35,000	31,500	3,500
Net Income, 19X9:			
January–June	10,000	9,000	1,000
July–December	10,000	9,000	1,000
Totals	$80,000	$72,000	$8,000

12.4 The Held Corporation had acquired 75 percent of the outstanding common stock of Ross Corporation on March 29, 19X4. The Ross Corporation was authorized to issue 10,000 shares of common stock with a par value of $100 per share. As of the close of business on December 30, 19X8, the Ross Corporation had undivided profits of $60,000. It had issued 2,000 shares of its capital stock, which had been sold at an average price of $150 each.

In order to increase its working capital, on December 31, 19X8, the Ross Corporation sold 500 shares of its unissued stock to outsiders for a total of $100,000. This was the only transaction on December 31.

Required:

Prepare the journal entries which should be made on December 31, 19X8, as a result of the stock issued by Ross Corporation:

    (*a*) On the books of Ross.

    (*b*) On the books of Held.

SOLUTION

(*a*) *Books of Ross Corp.*

Cash	100,000	
Capital Stock—$100 par		50,000
Amount Paid-in in Excess of Par		50,000

To record issuance of 500 shares of common stock for $100,000.

(*b*) *Books of Held Corp.*

Investment in Ross Corp.	6,000	
Paid-in Capital		6,000

To record increase in equity in subsidiary as a result of Ross Corp. having sold shares above book value.

Stockholders' Equity in Ross Corp. determined as follows:

	Before	After
Capital Stock—$100 par	$200,000	$250,000
Paid-in Capital in Excess of Par	100,000	150,000
Retained Earnings	60,000	60,000
Totals	$360,000	$460,000
Shares Outstanding	2,000	2,500
Parent's percentage	75%	60%*
Parent's equity	$270,000	$276,000

$$* \ \frac{1{,}500 \ sh.}{2{,}500 \ sh.} = 60\%$$

12.5 P Company purchased a 70 percent interest in S Company on March 1, 19X1 for $38,500. On January 1, 19X1, S Company had capital stock of $20,000 and retained earnings of $25,000. The companies' operating data for 19X1 are as follows:

	P Company	S Company
Sales	$500,000	$300,000
Income from Subsidiary	35,000	
	$535,000	$300,000
Cost of Goods Sold	$360,000	$190,000
Rent Expense	40,000	18,000
Other Expenses	45,000	32,000
	$445,000	$240,000
Net Income	$ 90,000	$ 60,000

It is assumed that S Company's net income is earned uniformly throughout the year. Neither company paid any dividends in 19X1.

Required:

(a) Determine the book value of S Company as of March 1, 19X1.

(b) Write the journal entries to consolidate the foregoing income statements for the year 19X1. Include the minority interest.

SOLUTION

(a) *Book value of S Company as of March 1, 19X1.*

	100%	70%
Capital Stock	$20,000	
Retained Earnings, Jan. 1	25,000	
Net Income—January and February (2/12 × $60,000)	10,000	
Book Value	$55,000	$38,500
Cost of Investment		38,500
Differential		–0–

(b) *Consolidation entries (for worksheet).*

Income from Subsidiary	35,000	
Net Income—P		35,000

To eliminate net income of subsidiary previously recorded by P.

Net Income—P	35,000	
Portion of Subsidiary Net Income Earned Prior to Acquisition of Control (70% of $10,000)	7,000	
Minority Interest (30% of $60,000)	18,000	
Net Income—S		60,000

To allocate net income of S Company.

12.6 S Corporation had outstanding $200,000 par value of common stock and $100,000 par value of 6 percent preferred stock. Each share of $100 par value preferred stock is cumulative, nonvoting, and entitled to a premium of 8 percent upon liquidation. On January 1, Year 1, P

Corporation purchased 80 percent of the common stock and 20 percent of the preferred stock of S Corporation for $235,600. On that date S Corporation had accumulated retained earnings of $80,000, and dividends were in arrears for one year.

Required:

(a) Prepare a schedule to show the allocation of the shareholders' equity in S Corporation between the parent and the minority interests.

(b) Write the journal entry on the books of P Corporation for the investment in S Corporation.

(c) Prepare worksheet elimination entries to consolidate the two balance sheets as of December 31.

SOLUTION

(a)

	Total	Controlling Interest	Minority Interests
Preferred Stock—par	$100,000	$ 20,000	$ 80,000
Dividend in Arrears	6,000	1,200	4,800
Liquidation Premium	8,000	1,600	6,400
Total to Preferred	$114,000	$ 22,800	$ 91,200
Common Stock—par	$200,000	$160,000	$ 40,000
Retained Earnings—Balance ($80,000 − $6,000 − $8,000)	66,000		
Controlling Interest (80%)		52,800	
Minority (20%)			13,200
Total to Common	$266,000	$212,800	$ 53,200
Totals	$380,000	$235,600	$144,400

(b)

Investment in S Corp.—Pfd.	22,800	
Investment in S Corp.—Comm.	212,800	
Cash		235,600

To record investment in preferred stock per foregoing schedule.

(c)

Capital Stock: Pfd.—S	100,000	
Retained Earnings—S	14,000	
Investment in S Corp.—Pfd.		22,800
Minority Interests		91,200

To eliminate investment in preferred stock and to set up minority interest in preferred.

Capital Stock: Comm.—S	200,000	
Retained Earnings—S	66,000	
Investment in S Corp.—Comm.		212,800
Minority Interests		53,200

To eliminate investment in common stock and to set up minority interest in common.

12.7 The financial statements of Carr Corporation and its subsidiary are summarized in the worksheets accompanying this problem.

Carr Corporation acquired 85 percent of the outstanding stock of Toon Corporation on March 1, 19X5. The price paid by Carr was $149,600. The investment account is maintained on the equity method.

Both corporations pay dividends at the end of each calendar quarter.

Required:

(*a*) Complete the worksheet to consolidate the income statements for the year.

(*b*) Complete the worksheet to consolidate the balance sheets at the end of the year.

(*a*)

Carr Corp. and Subsidiary
Worksheet—Consolidated Income Statement
Year 19X5

	Carr Corp.		Toon Corp.		Eliminations		Consolidated	
	Dr.	Cr.	Dr.	Cr.	Dr.	Cr.	Dr.	Cr.
Sales		500,500		300,000				
Cost of Goods Sold	380,000		200,000					
Selling Expenses	25,000		18,000					
General Expenses	55,000		46,000					
Income from Subsidiary		25,500						
	460,000	526,000	264,000	300,000				
Net Income—Carr	66,000							
Net Income—Toon			36,000					
	526,000	526,000	300,000	300,000				

(*b*)

Carr Corp. and Subsidiary
Worksheet—Consolidated Balance Sheet
December 31, 19X5

	Carr Corp.		Toon Corp.		Eliminations		Consolidated	
	Dr.	Cr.	Dr.	Cr.	Dr.	Cr.	Dr.	Cr.
Current Assets	180,000		90,000					
Investment in Toon	170,000							
Equipment	161,000		140,000					
Accumulated Depreciation		15,000		10,000				
Liabilities		40,000		20,000				
Capital Stock—Carr		250,000						
Retained Earnings (1/1)—Carr		160,000						
Net Income—Carr		66,000						
Dividends—Carr	20,000							
Capital Stock—Toon				120,000				
Retained Earnings (1/1)—Toon				56,000				
Net Income—Toon				36,000				
Dividends—Toon			12,000					
	531,000	531,000	242,000	242,000				

SOLUTION

(a)

Carr Corp. and Subsidiary
Worksheet—Consolidated Income Statement
Year 19X5

	Carr Corp.		Toon Corp.		Eliminations		Consolidated	
	Dr.	Cr.	Dr.	Cr.	Dr.	Cr.	Dr.	Cr.
Sales		500,500		300,000				800,500
Cost of Goods Sold	380,000		200,000				580,000	
Selling Expenses	25,000		18,000				43,000	
General Expenses	55,000		46,000				101,000	
Income from Subsidiary		25,500			a25,500			
	460,000	526,000	264,000	300,000				
Net Income—Carr	66,000				c25,500	a25,500	66,000	
Net Income—Toon			36,000			{ c30,900 b5,100		
	526,000	526,000	300,000	300,000				
Income Earned by Subsidiary Prior to Acquisition of Control						b5,100	5,100	
Minority Interest						c5,400	5,400	
							800,500	800,500

a To eliminate income of subsidiary previously recorded by parent.
b To segregate net income earned by subsidiary prior to control by parent (85% of $6,000).
c To allocate balance of net income of subsidiary:
    Parent—85% of $30,000 (9 months)
    Minority—15% of $36,000 (12 months)

(b)

Carr Corp. and Subsidiary
Worksheet—Consolidated Balance Sheet
December 31, 19X5

	Carr Corp.		Toon Corp.		Eliminations		Consolidated	
	Dr.	Cr.	Dr.	Cr.	Dr.	Cr.	Dr.	Cr.
Current Assets	180,000		90,000				270,000	
Investment in Toon	170,000					1170,000		
Equipment	161,000		140,000				301,000	
Accumulated Depreciation		15,000		10,000				25,000
Liabilities		40,000		20,000				60,000
Capital Stock—Carr		250,000						250,000
Retained Earnings (1/1)—Carr		160,000						160,000
Net Income—Carr		66,000						66,000
Dividends—Carr	20,000						20,000	
Capital Stock—Toon				120,000	{ 218,000 1102,000			
Retained Earnings (1/1)—Toon				56,000	{ 28,400 147,600			
Net Income—Toon				36,000	{ 25,400 130,600			
Dividends—Toon			12,000			{ 21,800 110,200		
	531,000	531,000	242,000	242,000				
Minority Interest						230,000		30,000
							591,000	591,000

1 To eliminate 85% of shareholders' equity in subsidiary as of Dec. 31, 19X5.
2 To classify 15% interest of minority shareholders.

Examination II

Chapters 4–12

1 On March 1, 19X1, the Philo Corporation purchased 80 percent of the outstanding stock of Deak Corporation for $135,000. At the date of acquisition the subsidiary had retained earnings of $30,000. The investment account has been maintained on the *cost* basis.

A summary of retained earnings of the two corporations for 19X6 and 19X7 follows:

	Philo	*Deak*
Balance, January 1, 19X6	$ 64,000	$ 73,000
Add: Net Income, 19X6	26,000	17,000
	$ 90,000	$ 90,000
Less: Dividends, 19X6	20,000	10,000
Balance, December 31, 19X6	$ 70,000	$ 80,000
Add: Net Income, 19X7	30,000	20,000
	$100,000	$100,000
Less: Dividends, 19X7	10,000	10,000
Balance, December 31, 19X7	$ 90,000	$ 90,000

Required:

Write journal entry (entries) necessary to convert the investment account from the cost to the equity basis as of December 31, 19X7.

2 The Grande Corporation owns 80 percent of the common stock of the Pier Corporation, which in turn owns 70 percent of the common stock of Searle Corporation.

The operating income from own operations of each corporation during 19X8 was as follows:

Grande	$100,000
Pier	60,000
Searle	40,000

Required:

Prepare a chart showing how the income of the three corporations should be apportioned to consolidated net income and to the minority interests.

3 The Eagle Corporation has outstanding 10,000 shares of its $10 par common stock. On January 1, 19X6, the Turquoise Company purchased 9,000 of these shares for $208,000, and 780 shares on December 1, 19X6 for $31,800. The investment account is kept on the equity basis.

The retained earnings account of Eagle for 19X6 and 19X7 is summarized as follows:

Date	*Dr.*	*Cr.*	*Balance*
Jan. 1, 19X6—Balance			140,000
Nov. 10, 19X6—Dividends	10,000		130,000
Dec. 31, 19X6—Net Income		18,000	148,000
Oct. 31, 19X7—Dividends	10,000		138,000
Dec. 31, 19X7—Net Income		20,000	158,000

The Turquoise Company sold 1,000 shares of the Eagle stock on January 1, 19X8 for $28,000.

Required:

(a) Compute the carrying value of the shares sold, using the first-in, first-out method.

(b) Determine the amount of gain or loss on the sale.

4 The Pert Corporation purchased 80 percent of the capital stock of Set Inc. on January 1, 19X7 for $102,000. All of the assets of Set were worth book value except for the inventory, which was valued in excess of book amount. All of these goods were sold in 19X7. The notes payable of Set include a $5,000 non-interest-bearing note payable to Pert.

The financial statements of Pert Corporation and its subsidiary for the year ended December 31, 19X7 are summarized in the worksheets that appear on pp. 343 and 344.

Required:

(a) Complete the worksheet to consolidate the income statements for the year 19X7.

(b) Complete the worksheet to consolidate the balance sheets at the end of 19X7.

(c) Complete the three-tier consolidated workpapers for the year 19X7.

5 The P Corporation acquired 75 percent of the outstanding stock of the T Corporation on June 9, Year 1.

On December 31, Year 3, P Corporation purchased in the open market $50,000 par of T's 8 percent bonds, which mature on December 31, 19X7. P paid $46,000 for these bonds. The bond issue, which has a total maturity value of $500,000, had been issued several years earlier at a discount. As of December 31, Year 3, the unamortized discount amounted to $16,000.

Required:

In connection with the bonds and related items, prepare adjusting and elimination journal entries to consolidate the statements of the two corporations for the year ended December 31, Year 4.

6 R Corporation acquired 90 percent of the outstanding stock of T Corporation on January 2, Year 1 in a transaction which qualified as a pooling of interests. On that date the R Corporation issued 7,000 shares of its common stock in exchange for 10,800 shares of T Corporation common stock. The retained earnings of T amounted to $40,000.

The condensed statements of the two corporations for Year 5 and as of December 31, Year 5 are as follows:

	R Corp.	T Corp.
Income Statements		
Sales	$500,000	$300,000
Cost of Goods Sold	350,000	200,000
Gross Margin	$150,000	$100,000
Less: Operating Expenses	95,000	60,000
Income from Operations	$ 55,000	$ 40,000
Add: Income from Subsidiary	36,000	
Net Income	$ 91,000	$ 40,000

(Problem continued on p. 345.)

Pert Corp. and Subsidiary
Worksheet—Consolidated Income Statement
Year 19X7

	Pert Corp.		Set Inc.		Eliminations		Consolidated	
	Dr.	Cr.	Dr.	Cr.	Dr.	Cr.	Dr.	Cr.
Merchandise Inventory (1/1)	56,000		22,000					
Sales		410,600		242,000				
Dividend Income		8,000						
Interest Income		1,000						
Purchases	300,000		160,000					
Freight In	22,000		6,400					
Selling Expenses	24,400		17,200					
Administrative Expenses	30,200		16,400					
Merchandise Inventory (12/31)		82,000		36,000				
	432,600	501,600	222,000	278,000				
Net Income—Pert	69,000							
Net Income—Set			56,000					
	501,600	501,600	278,000	278,000				

Pert Corp. and Subsidiary
Worksheet—Consolidated Balance Sheet
December 31, 19X7

	Pert Corp.		Set Inc.		Eliminations		Consolidated	
	Dr.	Cr.	Dr.	Cr.	Dr.	Cr.	Dr.	Cr.
Cash	55,000		25,000					
Notes Receivable	11,000		4,000					
Investment in Set, Inc.	102,000							
Merchandise Inventory	82,000		36,000					
Other Assets	117,000		161,000					
Vouchers Payable		32,000		24,000				
Notes Payable		15,000		5,000				
Other Liabilities		5,000		27,000				
Capital Stock, $10 par—P		150,000						
Retained Earnings—P		112,000						
Net Income—P		69,000						
Dividends—P	16,000							
Capital Stock, $10 par—S				100,000				
Retained Earnings—S				24,000				
Net Income—S				56,000				
Dividends—S			10,000					
	383,000	383,000	236,000	236,000				

Pert Corp. and Subsidiary
Consolidated Workpapers (3-tier)
Year 19X7

	Company		Adjustments & Eliminations	Consolidated
	Pert	Set		
INCOME STATEMENT				
Credits				
Sales	410,600	242,000		
Dividend Income	8,000			
Interest Income	1,000			
Merchandise Inventory (12/31)	82,000	36,000		
Total Credits	501,600	278,000		
Debits				
Merchandise Inventory (1/1)	56,000	22,000		
Purchases	300,000	160,000		
Freight In	22,000	6,400		
Selling Expenses	24,400	17,200		
Administrative Expenses	30,200	16,400		
Total Debits	432,600	222,000		
Minority Interest in Income				
Net Income	69,000	56,000		
RETAINED EARNINGS				
Balance (1/1)—P	112,000			
Balance (1/1)—S		24,000		
Net Income	69,000	56,000		
Total	181,000	80,000		
Less: Dividends—P	16,000			
Dividends—S		10,000		
Balance (12/31)	165,000	70,000		
BALANCE SHEET				
Assets				
Cash	55,000	25,000		
Notes Receivable	11,000	4,000		
Investment in Set, Inc.	102,000			
Merchandise Inventory	82,000	36,000		
Other Assets	117,000	161,000		
Total Assets	367,000	226,000		
Equities				
Vouchers Payable	32,000	24,000		
Notes Payable	15,000	5,000		
Other Liabilities	5,000	27,000		
Capital Stock—P	150,000			
Retained Earnings—P	165,000			
Capital Stock—S		100,000		
Retained Earnings—S		70,000		
Minority Interest				
Total Equities	367,000	226,000		

Retained Earnings

Balance, January 1	$300,000	$100,000
Add: Net Income	91,000	40,000
Total	$391,000	$140,000
Less: Dividends	51,000	30,000
Balance, December 31	$340,000	$110,000

Balance Sheet

ASSETS

Current Assets	$120,000	$110,000
Investment in Subsidiary	207,000	
Other Assets—net	433,000	790,000
Total	$760,000	$900,000

EQUITIES

Current Liabilities	$202,000	$170,000
Bonds Payable		500,000
Capital Stock—$10 par	170,000	120,000
Paid-in Capital	48,000	
Retained Earnings	340,000	110,000
Total	$760,000	$900,000

Required:

Write the adjustment and elimination entries necessary to consolidate the statements. (Show the minority interests as of the end of the year.)

7 The Faber Corporation purchased 80 percent of the outstanding common stock of Singlex Corporation on June 7, 19X2 for $121.50 per share, and on July 7, 19X4 Faber purchased 10 percent of the outstanding preferred stock of Singlex for $311 per share.

On December 31, 19X8 the shareholders' equity accounts of Singlex Corp. contained the following balances:

Preferred Stock, 6% cumulative: $100 par (nonparticipating)*	$ 500,000
Amount Paid-in in Excess of Par	200,000
Common Stock, Without Par Value	500,000
Retained Earnings	160,000
Total	$1,360,000

* Dividends are in arrears for 19X7 and 19X8.

Required:

Complete the following schedule. Show clearly how each element of the subsidiary's shareholders' equity is allocated between the parent and the minority interest.

	Amount	Parent's Portion		Minority Interest	
	Amount	Percent	Amount	Percent	Amount
Preferred Stock	$_____	_____	$_____	_____	$_____
Paid-in Capital	_____	_____	_____	_____	_____
Common Stock	_____	_____	_____	_____	_____
Retained Earnings:					
—to Preferred	_____	_____	_____	_____	_____
—to Common	_____	_____	_____	_____	_____
Totals	$_____		$_____		$_____

8 The Paper Corporation purchased a 90 percent interest in Standard Corporation on January 18, 19X1 at book value. During 19X2 Standard sold a tract of land to Paper at a profit of $4,000.

On December 31, 19X3 Paper sold a machine to Standard at a profit of $15,000. This machine is being depreciated over a period of ten years.

The inventory of Paper on January 1, 19X7 included merchandise purchased from Standard during the previous year on which Standard had recorded a gross profit of $5,000.

During 19X7 Standard sold goods to Paper for $90,000, of which $20,000 remained in the inventory of Paper at December 31, 19X7. It is estimated that Standard made a gross profit of $8,000 on these goods.

The Paper Corporation adjusts its investment account by increasing it for 90 percent of the reported earnings of the subsidiary and reducing it by the amount of dividends received from the subsidiary.

Statements of the two corporations, in condensed form, are as follows:

Paper Corporation and Subsidiary
Income Statements
Year Ended December 31, 19X7

	Parent		Subsidiary	
Sales	$511,000		$225,000	
Cost of Goods Sold	346,000	$165,000	139,100	$85,900
Operating Expenses		130,800		50,200
Operating Income		$ 34,200		$35,700
Subsidiary Income		32,130		
Net Income		$ 66,330		$35,700

Retained Earnings

Balance, Jan. 1	$143,310		$ 27,900	
Net Income	66,330	$209,640	35,700	$63,600
Dividends:		30,000		12,000
Balance, Dec. 31		$179,640		$51,600

Balance Sheets

Cash	$ 32,000	$ 29,100
Accounts Receivable	68,400	25,000
Inventory	72,400	40,200
Investment In Subsidiary	109,440	
Land	30,000	
Plant and Equipment	176,400	48,200
	$488,640	$142,500

Accumulated Depreciation	$ 41,400	$ 10,700
Accounts Payable	59,000	6,400
Accrued Liabilities	8,600	3,800
Capital Stock: $100 par—P	200,000	
$10 par—S		70,000
Retained Earnings: P	179,640	
S		51,600
	$488,640	$142,500

Required:

(a) Write the adjustment and elimination entries necessary to consolidate the foregoing statements.

(b) Prepare a schedule of the minority interests as of December 31, 19X7.

Answers to Examination II

1

Deak	100%	80%
Retained Earnings, Dec. 31, 19X7	$90,000	$72,000
Retained Earnings, Mar. 1, 19X1	30,000	24,000
Increase	$60,000	$48,000

Journal Entry on Books of Parent

Investment in Subsidiary	48,000	
Retained Earnings		48,000

2

	Consolidated Net Income	Minority Interest in Pier	Minority Interest in Searle
Grande:			
100% of $100,000	$100,000		
Pier:			
80% of $60,000	48,000		
20% of $60,000		$12,000	
Searle:			
80% of (70% of $40,000)	22,400		
20% of (70% of 40,000)		5,600	
30% of $40,000			$12,000
Totals	$170,400	$17,600	$12,000

3 (a)

Cost		$208,000.00
Increase in Retained Earnings of Eagle ($158,000 − $140,000)	$18,000.00	
Eagle's share (90% of $18,000)		16,200.00
Carrying Value of:		
9,000 shares		$224,200.00
1,000 shares		$ 24,911.11

(b)

Gain ($28,000.00 − $24,911.11)		$ 3,088.89

Pert Corp. and Subsidiary
Worksheet—Consolidated Income Statement
Year 19X7

	Pert Corp.		Set Corp.		Eliminations		Consolidated	
	Dr.	Cr.	Dr.	Cr.	Dr.	Cr.	Dr.	Cr.
Merchandise Inventory (1/1)	56,000		22,000		b3,500		81,500	
Sales		410,600		242,000				652,600
Dividend Income		8,000			a8,000			
Interest Income		1,000						1,000
Purchases	300,000		160,000				460,000	
Freight In	22,000		6,400				28,400	
Selling Expenses	24,400		17,200				41,600	
Administrative Expenses	30,200		16,400				46,600	
Merchandise Inventory (12/31)		82,000		36,000				118,000
	432,600	501,600	222,000	278,000				
Net Income—Pert	69,000				c42,000	a8,000	103,000	
Net Income—Set			56,000			{c52,500 / b3,500}		
	501,600	501,600	278,000	278,000				
Minority Interest					c10,500		10,500	
							771,600	771,600

a To eliminate intercompany dividend.
b To eliminate excess of fair value of Jan. 1 inventory over the book value.
c To eliminate net income of Set Corp., as adjusted.

Pert Corp. and Subsidiary
Worksheet—Consolidated Balance Sheet
December 31, 19X7

	Pert Corp.		Set Inc.		Eliminations		Consolidated	
	Dr.	Cr.	Dr.	Cr.	Dr.	Cr.	Dr.	Cr.
Cash	55,000		25,000				80,000	
Notes Receivable	11,000		4,000			1 5,000	10,000	
Investment in Set, Inc.	102,000					{2 99,200 / b2,800}		
Merchandise Inventory	82,000		36,000				118,000	
Other Assets	117,000		161,000				278,000	
Vouchers Payable		32,000		24,000				56,000
Notes Payable		15,000		5,000	1 5,000			15,000
Other Liabilities		5,000		27,000				32,000
Capital Stock, $10 par—P		150,000						150,000
Retained Earnings—P		112,000						112,000
Net Income—P		69,000			a8,000	c42,000		103,000
Dividends—P	16,000						16,000	
Capital Stock, $10 par—S				100,000	{3 20,000 / 2 80,000}			
Retained Earnings—S				24,000	{3 4,800 / 2 19,200}			
Net Income—S				56,000		{c52,500 / b3,500}		
Dividends—S			10,000			a10,000		
	383,000	383,000	236,000	236,000				
Minority Interest					a2,000	{c10,500 / b700 / 3 24,800}		34,000
							502,000	502,000

1 To eliminate intercompany note.
2 To eliminate 80% of subsidiary's capital stock and retained earnings as of Jan. 1, Yr. 1.
3 To classify the 20% interest of the minority stockholders as of Jan. 1, Yr. 1.

4 (a)

(b)

Pert Corp. and Subsidiary
Consolidated Workpapers (3-tier)
Year 19X7

	Company		Adjustments		Consolidated
	Pert	Set	& Eliminations		
INCOME STATEMENT					
Credits					
Sales	410,600	242,000			652,600
Dividend Income	8,000		[a]8,000		
Interest Income	1,000				1,000
Merchandise Inventory (12/31)	82,000	36,000			118,000
Total Credits	501,600	278,000			771,600
Debits					
Merchandise Inventory (1/1)	56,000	22,000	[b]3,500		81,500
Purchases	300,000	160,000			460,000
Freight In	22,000	6,400			28,400
Selling Expenses	24,400	17,200			41,600
Administrative Expenses	30,200	16,400			46,600
Total Debits	432,600	222,000			658,100
					113,500
Minority Interest in Income (20% of $52,500)			[c]10,500		10,500
Net Income	69,000	56,000			103,000
RETAINED EARNINGS					
Balance (1/1)—P	112,000				112,000
Balance (1/1)—S		24,000	{[3]4,800 [2]19,200		
Net Income	69,000	56,000			103,000
Total	181,000	80,000			215,000
Less: Dividends—P	16,000				16,000
Dividends—S		10,000		[a]10,000	
Balance (12/31)	165,000	70,000			199,000
BALANCE SHEET					
Assets					
Cash	55,000	25,000			80,000
Notes Receivable	11,000	4,000		[1]5,000	10,000
Investment in Set, Inc.	102,000			{[2]99,200 [b]2,800	
Merchandise Inventory	82,000	36,000			118,000
Other Assets	117,000	161,000			278,000
Total Assets	367,000	226,000			486,000
Equities					
Vouchers Payable	32,000	24,000			56,000
Notes Payable	15,000	5,000	5,000		15,000
Other Liabilities	5,000	27,000			32,000
Capital Stock—P	150,000				150,000
Retained Earnings—P	165,000				199,000
Capital Stock—S		100,000	{[3]20,000 [2]80,000		
Retained Earnings—S		70,000			
Minority Interest			[a]2,000	{[c]10,500 [b]700 [3]24,800}	34,000
Total Equities	367,000	226,000			486,000

5

	$500,000 Par		$50,000 Par	
	Dr.	Cr.	Dr.	Cr.
Balances—Dec. 31, 19X3				
Bonds Payable		$500,000		$50,000
Unamortized Bond Discount	$16,000		$ 1,600	
Investment in Bonds			46,000	
Loss to Issuer (Subsidiary)			1,600	
Gain to Investor (Parent)				4,000
Balances—Dec. 31, 19X4				
Bonds Payable		500,000		50,000
Unamortized Bond Discount	12,000		1,200	
Interest Expense ($40,000 + $4,000)	44,000		4,400	
Investment in Bonds			47,000	
Interest Income				5,000

Consolidating Journal Entries
December 31, 19X4

To consolidate income statements:

Interest Income	4,000	
Interest Expense		4,000
Interest Income	1,000	
Net Income—P		1,000
Net Income—T	400	
Interest Expense		400

To consolidate balance sheets:

	Dr.	Cr.
Retained Earnings (Jan. 1)—T	1,600	
Net Income—T		400
Unamortized Bond Discount		1,200
Investment in Bonds	3,000	
Net Income—P	1,000	
Retained Earnings (Jan. 1)—P		4,000
Bonds Payable	50,000	
Investment in Bonds		50,000

Alternate Solution to Problem 5

Retained Earnings (Jan. 1)—T	1,600	
Interest Expense		400
Unamortized Bond Discount		1,200
Investment in Bonds	3,000	
Interest Income	1,000	
Retained Earnings (Jan. 1)—P		4,000
Interest Income	4,000	
Interest Expense		4,000
Bonds Payable	50,000	
Investment in Bonds		50,000

6 *To consolidate income statements:*

Income from Subsidiary	36,000	
Net Income—R		36,000
Minority Interest	4,000	
Net Income—R	36,000	
Net Income—T		40,000

(*Note:* The two foregoing entries may be compounded.)

To consolidate balance sheets:

Capital Stock—T	108,000	
Retained Earnings (Jan. 1)—T	90,000	
Net Income—T	36,000	
Dividends		27,000
Investment in Subsidiary		207,000
Capital Stock—T	12,000	
Retained Earnings (Jan. 1)—T	10,000	
Net Income—T	4,000	
Dividends		3,000
Minority Interests		23,000

7

	Amount	Parent's Portion		Minority Interest	
		Percent	Amount	Percent	Amount
Preferred Stock	$ 500,000	10	$ 50,000	90	$450,000
Paid-in Capital	200,000	80	160,000	20	40,000
Common Stock	500,000	80	400,000	20	100,000
Retained Earnings:					
—to Preferred	60,000*	10	6,000	90	54,000
—to Common	100,000	80	80,000	20	20,000
Totals	$1,360,000		$696,000		$664,000

*Dividends in arrears for two years: 6% ($500,000) × (2) = $60,000

8 (a)   1. *Journal entries to consolidate income statements:*

Sales	90,000	
Cost of Goods Sold		90,000
Net Income—S	5,000	
Cost of Goods Sold		5,000
Cost of Goods Sold	8,000	
Net Income—S		8,000
Net Income—P	1,500	
Operating Expenses (Depreciation)		1,500
Subsidiary Income	32,130	
Net Income—P		32,130
Net Income—P	29,430	
Minority Interest	3,270	
Net Income—S		32,700

2. *Journal entries to consolidate balance sheets.*

Retained Earnings (Jan. 1)—S	4,000	
Land		4,000

To cancel intercompany gain in Year 19X2.

Retained Earnings (Jan. 1)—P	3,600	
Investment in Subsidiary		3,600

To cancel parent's share of reported gain.

Retained Earnings (Jan. 1)—P	15,000	
Plant and Equipment		15,000

To reduce equipment to cost.

Accumulated Depreciation	6,000	
Retained Earnings (Jan. 1)—P		4,500
Net Income—P		1,500

To eliminate excess depreciation for current year and recognize portion of gain to seller.

(*Note:* The foregoing two entries are frequently combined)

Retained Earnings (Jan. 1)—S	5,000	
Net Income—S		5,000

To eliminate unrealized gross profit in inventory at January 1.

| Retained Earnings (1/1)—P | 4,500 | |
| Net Income—P | | 4,500 |

To cancel parent's share of unrealized gross profit in inventory at Jan. 1.

| Net Income—S | 8,000 | |
| Inventory | | 8,000 |

To eliminate unrealized gross profit in inventory at December 31.

| Net Income—P | 7,200 | |
| Investment in Subsidiary | | 7,200 |

To cancel parent's share of reported gain.

Capital Stock: .90 ($70,000)	63,000	
Retained Earnings (Jan. 1)—S:		
.90($27,900 − $5,000 − $4,000)	17,010	
Net Income—S:		
.90($35,700 + $5,000 − $8,000)	29,430	
Dividends: .90($12,000)		10,800
Investment in Subsidiary:		
($109,440 − $3,600 − $7,200)		98,640

To eliminate 90 percent of shareholders' equity, as adjusted, against balance of investment.

Capital Stock—S	7,000	
Retained Earnings (Jan. 1)—S	1,890	
Net Income—S	3,270	
Dividends		1,200
Minority Interest		10,960

(b) *Schedule of controlling and minority interests:*

	Balances per Books	Balances as Adjusted	90%	10%
Capital Stock	$ 70,000	$ 70,000	$ 63,000	$ 7,000
Retained Earnings (1/1)	27,900	18,900	17,010	1,890
Net Income	35,700	32,700	29,430	3,270
Totals	$133,600	$121,600	$109,440	$12,160
Less: Dividends	12,000	12,000	10,800	1,200
Totals	$121,600	$109,600	$ 98,640	$10,960

Alternative solution to Part (a):

| Retained Earnings (1/1)—S | 4,000 | |
| Land | | 4,000 |

To cancel intercompany gain in 19X2.

Retained Earnings (1/1)—P	3,600	
Investment in Subsidiary		3,600

To cancel parent's share of reported gain on land.

Retained Earnings (1/1)—P	15,000	
Equipment		15,000

To reduce equipment to cost.

Accumulated Depreciation (4 × $1,500)	6,000	
Retained Earnings (1/1)—P		4,500
(3 × $1,500)		
Operating Expenses		1,500

To eliminate excess depreciation expense and to recognize portion of gain by seller.

Retained Earnings (1/1)—S	5,000	
Cost of Goods Sold		5,000

To eliminate unrealized gross profit in inventory at Jan. 1.

Retained Earnings (1/1)—P	4,500	
Investment in Subsidiary		4,500

To cancel parent's share of unrealized gross profit.

Sales	90,000	
Cost of Goods Sold		90,000

To eliminate intercompany sales and purchases.

Cost of Goods Sold	8,000	
Inventory		8,000

Subsidiary Income: .90($35,700)	32,130	
Retained Earnings (1/1)—S:		
.90($27,900 − $4,000 − $5,000)	17,010	
Capital Stock—S: .90($70,000)	63,000	
Dividends—S: .90($12,000)		10,800
Investment in Subsidiary:		
($109,440 − $3,600 − $4,500)		101,340

To eliminate 90 percent of shareholders' equity, as adjusted, against balance of investment.

Capital Stock—S	7,000	
Retained Earnings (1/1)—S	1,890	
Minority Interest in Income	3,270	
Dividends		1,200
Minority Interest		10,960

To classify 10% of shareholders' equity as minority interest.

Part III

Foreign Transactions and Operations

In October 1975 the Financial Accounting Standards Board (FASB) issued its Statement No. 8, concerning the treatment of foreign transactions and the translation of foreign currency statements. It prescribed, for the first time, precise rules for reporting the results of transactions and operations involving foreign currencies.

In August 1980 the Board released an exposure draft which, if adopted, would make substantial changes in the present rules for translation of foreign currency statements. For example, the draft would require the use of current exchange rates for all translations. Only minor changes are proposed for exchange differences arising from transactions involving foreign currency.

The most important proposed change from current (1981) rules is that adjustments from translation of foreign currency statements would be reported as a separate component of shareholders' equity. However, if the investment in the foreign subsidiary becomes permanently impaired, any necessary write-downs would then be recognized in the income statement.

Hearings held by the FASB in December 1980 indicated that there was much controversy over the proposed changes. While the exposure draft seems to eliminate much of the criticism of Statement No. 8, the draft raises many new issues which are themselves the subject of debate.

Chapters 13 and 14 have been written based on the rules in effect at the time of writing (August 1981).

Publisher's Note: An Appendix to Chapter 14 (p. 377) describes the most recent FASB pronouncement as of December 1981.

Chapter 13

Foreign Currency Transactions

13.1 INTRODUCTION

In recent years the activities of many businesses have become international. Involvement in foreign operations is often accomplished by establishment of a foreign branch. However, the most common procedure is to invest in a foreign corporation which frequently will become a subsidiary of the domestic corporation. FASB Statement No. 8[1] applies to all American companies which engage in foreign currency transactions or foreign operations. Foreign currency transactions include:

1. buying or selling goods and services whose prices are denominated in a foreign currency

2. borrowing or lending funds denominated in a foreign currency

3. being a party to an unperformed foreign exchange contract

4. for other reasons, incurring liabilities or acquiring assets denominated in a foreign currency.

A company is also considered to be engaged in foreign operations when it conducts activities through a subsidiary corporation, an investee company, or a branch whose accounts are measured in a foreign currency.

Statement No. 8 also applies to a foreign entity which reports in its local currency in conformity with American generally accepted accounting principles. By way of illustration, a French subsidiary of an American parent should translate the foreign currency financial statements of its Italian subsidiary in accordance with Statement No. 8. The translation of foreign statements and foreign trial balances into domestic currency will be covered in the next chapter.

13.2 EXCHANGE RATES

In the United States and in most other countries, a foreign currency is generally regarded as a commodity. The relative values of two currencies will usually be expressed as a price called the rate of exchange.

Cash balances can normally be spent only in the country of origin. Thus, transactions between firms in different countries generally require one of the firms to purchase (or sell) the currency of another country. In a free money market, the price of one country's currency will fluctuate in terms of the currency of the other country. These fluctuations introduce a new variable into the calculation of income, which will undoubtedly result in a gain or loss to the company which utilizes the currency of another country.

Rates of exchange may be expressed directly or indirectly. Direct quotations are stated in terms of the domestic currency; this is the practice in the United States at the present time. For example, Netherlands guilders may be quoted at US$0.464. This means that it would require .464 U.S. dollars to purchase 1 guilder. When using indirect quotations, one unit of domestic currency is expressed in terms of the number of foreign units required to purchase 1 U.S. dollar. Thus, the U.S. dollar would be quoted in the Netherlands at 2.155 guilders (US$1.00 ÷ 0.464).

---

[1] Statement of Financial Accounting Standards Board, No. 8, October 1975. This was slightly amended by FASB Statement No. 20, issued in December 1977.

A major problem in accounting for foreign operations arises because of fluctuations in exchange rates. If the purchased currency is to be delivered immediately, the exchange rate is referred to as a spot rate. However, if there is to be future delivery of an exchanged currency, the rate is referred to as a forward, or future, exchange rate.

A forward rate expresses the exchange rate which is currently agreed upon for future delivery or receipt of foreign currency at a fixed date. In the United States there are forward (futures) markets for the currencies of about a half-dozen major trading countries. At the present time, bank transfers of foreign currencies for forward delivery are generally quoted in terms of 30-day, 90-day, and 180-day futures. Other forward rates may be negotiated with a bank's foreign exchange desk or with a foreign exchange broker. The International Monetary Market (of the Chicago Mercantile Exchange) uses only standardized contracts, with maturity dates being the third Wednesday of each March, June, September, and December.

The company which agrees to accept a foreign currency will be exposed to the risk of fluctuations in exchange rates between the date of the sale and the date of collection. The futures or forward market is often utilized to minimize this risk. This operation is generally described as hedging or covering. The true hedging operation is not designed to seek a profit from trading on the futures market. Rather, its goal is to protect the gain which is expected from the company's commercial activities.

13.3　FOREIGN PURCHASES AND SALES: RISK NOT HEDGED

Assume that an American importer purchases goods amounting to US$10,000 from West Germany. If the billing is in U.S. dollars and the term of payment is 30 days, the importer will pay US$10,000 at the date of settlement. The importer cannot possibly have any gain or loss as a result of fluctuations in the price of the West German mark (DM). Any fluctuation in the exchange rate will affect only the number of West German marks the exporter will receive.

On the other hand, if the American importer is billed in West German marks, fluctuations in exchange rates will affect the number of marks which the importer will have to pay on settlement date, unless the importer minimizes his risk by purchasing marks for future delivery or by executing some other hedging operation.

Assume that a Chicago exporter sells merchandise to a West German importer. If the American company bills the buyer in dollars, the exporter will not have any gain or loss due to fluctuations of the United States dollar vis-à-vis the West German mark. However, if the Chicago exporter sells merchandise to a West German importer and the billing is in marks, the American exporter is exposed to the risk of a decline in the value of the mark between the billing date and the date of settlement.

Prior to the promulgation of Statement No. 8, treatment of exchange gains and losses varied considerably. Now, foreign exchange gains and losses are generally recognized whenever a settlement occurs or whenever interim statements are prepared. The FASB statement requires that: "At each balance sheet date, recorded dollar balances representing cash and amounts owed by or to the enterprise that are denominated in foreign currency shall be adjusted to reflect the current rate." In other words, such exchange gains and losses should be included in the determination of income for the period in which there is a change in the foreign currency exchange rate.

EXAMPLE 1. The following transactions took place during year 19X1. On May 31 the General Corporation sold merchandise to the Oaxaca Company for 200,000 Mexican pesos (Mex$) due in 90 days.

The spot rates for one peso were as follows:

	May 31	US$0.044
	June 30	US$0.042
	Aug. 29	US$0.041

Assume that the General Corporation operates on the calendar year. The journal entries on its books would be as follows:

May 31, 19X1

Accounts Receivable		
(Mex$200,000 × US$0.044)	8,800	
Sales		8,800

August 29, 19X1

Cash		
(Mex$200,000 × US$0.041)	8,200	
Exchange Loss	600	
Accounts Receivable		8,800

The foregoing treatment is frequently referred to as the *dual transaction* method. Thus, the sale in May and the collection in August are handled as two separate transactions.

EXAMPLE 2. Assume the same data as in the previous example except that the General Corporation operates on a June 30 fiscal year.

The journal entries on May 31 would be the same as in Example 1. However, the entries for June 30 and for August 29 would be as follows:

June 30, 19X1

Exchange Loss	400	
Accounts Receivable		400

To accrue loss due to decline of peso:
Mex$200,000 × (US$0.044 − US$0.042)

August 29, 19X1

Cash		
(Mex$200,000 × US$0.041)	8,200	
Exchange Loss	200	
Accounts Receivable		
(US$8,800 − US$400)		8,400

The total exchange loss is US$600. However, US$400 is now applicable to the first fiscal year, and US$200 is applicable to the second fiscal year.

13.4   FOREIGN PURCHASES AND SALES: RISK HEDGED

A domestic exporter often sells merchandise for which it is to receive payment in foreign currency. If the exporter does not wish to accept the risk of possible future reductions in the value of the foreign currency relative to the U.S. dollar, it should hedge the transaction.

In the previous examples, hedging could have been accomplished by selling 200,000 pesos for future delivery. Thus, the American exporter can make certain how many dollars it will receive. There usually would be a small cost equivalent to the difference between the spot rate on May 31, and the 90-day forward rate on that date. Assume that the cost amounted to $100. The exporter then knows that it will receive US$8,800 from the foreign exchange dealer at maturity, less the hedging cost of US$100. The exporter can then concentrate on its merchandising and manufacturing operations and is insulated from a decline of the peso. Of course, the exporter does not profit if the peso rises relative to the U.S. dollar.

EXAMPLE 3. The following transactions took place during the year 19X1. On May 31, 19X1, when the peso was quoted at US$0.044, the General Corporation sold merchandise to the Taxco Company for Mex$200,000; the terms of sale were 90 days. In order to cover its exposed net asset position, the General Corporation sold Mex$200,000 for delivery in 90 days at US$0.044.

On August 29, 19X1, the General Corporation received a draft for Mex$200,000, which was immediately turned over to the foreign exchange desk of the West National Bank in settlement of the forward contract. At the latter date, the spot rate for Mexican pesos was US$0.041.

The journal entries for these transactions on the books of General Corporation, which operates on a calendar year, are as follows:

Mar 31, 19X1

Accounts Receivable		
(Mex$200,000 × US$0.044)	8,800	
Sales		8,800
Due from West National Bank		
(Mex$200,000 × US$0.044)	8,800	
Liability for Mexican Pesos Sold		8,800

August 29, 19X1

Foreign Currency (Mexican Pesos)		
(Mex$200,000 × US$0.041)	8,200	
Exchange Loss	600	
Accounts Receivable		8,800
Cash	8,800	
Due from West National Bank		8,800
Liability for Mexican Pesos Sold	8,800	
Exchange Gain		600
Foreign Currency (Mexican Pesos)		
(Mex$200,000 × US$0.041)		8,200

The exchange loss is the result of the decline in the Mexican peso from US$0.044 to US$0.041. The exchange gain is the result of the American company settling a liability of US$8,800 with foreign currency which had a value of US$8,200. Note that in this example the exchange gain and loss cancel each other. In actual practice, however, there would usually be a small net loss as a result of such currency transactions due to commissions and service charges which the General Corporation would undoubtedly have to pay. Also, the future (forward) rate at any one point in time frequently differs from the spot rate at that same point in time due to the various factors which influence the expectations of currency traders and brokers.

EXAMPLE 4. On May 31, 19X1, the Kirk Corp. of the United States purchased merchandise from the Rotorua Company of New Zealand. The purchase amounted to NZ$100,000, payable August 29, 19X1. On May 31, the Kirk Corp. covered (hedged) its obligation in full. The following selected foreign exchange rates were in effect during the 90-day period:

Date	Spot Rate	90-Day Forward Rate
May 31	NZ$1 = US$1.020	NZ$1 = US$1.022
June 30	NZ$1 = US$1.025	NZ$1 = US$1.027
Aug. 29	NZ$1 = US$1.032	NZ$1 = US$1.035

Since there is a hedge of a foreign currency commitment, exchange gains and losses are calculated by using the current spot rates, although the cost of currency for future delivery is determined by using an appropriate forward rate.

The following journal entries summarize the transactions on the books of the American importer, which operates on a June 30 fiscal year:

May 31, 19X1		
Merchandise	102,000	
Vouchers Payable		
(NZ$100,000 × US$1.020)		102,000
Foreign Money Due from F.E. Desk	102,000	
Deferred Contract Expense	200	
Liability to F.E. Desk		
(NZ$100,000 × US$1.022)		102,200
June 30, 19X1		
Exchange Loss	500	
Vouchers Payable		
[NZ$100,000 (US$1.025 − US$1.020)]		500
Forward Contract Expense	67	
Deferred Contract Expense		
(30/90 of US$200)		67
Foreign Money Due from F.E. Desk	500	
Exchange Gain		
[NZ$100,000(US$1.025 − US$1.020)]		500
August 29, 19X1		
Liability to F.E. Desk	102,200	
Investment in Foreign Money (NZ$)		
(NZ$100,000 × US$1.032)	103,200	
Foreign Money Due from F.E. Desk		102,500
Cash		102,200
Exchange Gain		700

To record settlement of forward contract.

Forward Contract Expense	133	
Deferred Contract Expense		
(60/90 of US$200)		133
Vouchers Payable	102,500	
Exchange Loss	700	
Investment in Foreign Money (NZ$)		103,200

To record payment to creditor.

If the American importer had not hedged its exposed liability position, the exchange loss would have amounted to US$1,200 [NZ$100,000 × (US$1.032 − US$1.020)]. As a result of covering the exposed position, there was no net exchange gain or loss. However, there was the expense of the forward contract, which amounted to US$200.

13.5 SPECULATION IN FOREIGN EXCHANGE

EXAMPLE 5.   Assume that an American company without any identifiable foreign currency commitment or an exposed foreign currency position decided to speculate in the Canadian dollar. On December 1, 19X1, the American company purchased Can$100,000 for delivery in 90 days. On this date the spot price for Canadian dollars is US$0.90 and the price for 90-day forward contracts is US$0.87. The 60-day forward rate on December 31, the end of the seller's year, is US$0.86; on March 1, 19X2 the spot rate is US$0.84.

December 1, 19X1

Receivable for Currency Purchased		
(Can$100,000 × US$0.87)	87,000	
Due to Exchange Broker		87,000

December 31, 19X1

Exchange Loss		
[Can$100,000(US$0.87 − US$0.86)]	1,000	
Receivable for Currency Purchased		1,000

March 1, 19X2

Due to Exchange Broker	87,000	
Cash		87,000
Foreign Currency		
(Can$100,000 × US$0.84)	84,000	
Exchange Loss		
[Can$100,000(US$0.86 − US$0.84)]	2,000	
Receivable for Currency Purchased		
(US$87,000 − US$1,000)		86,000

A future contract entered into for speculative purposes is valued at the current rate (current rate for forward contract; not the spot rate) for the remaining life of the contract. Thus, on December 31, 19X1, the forward rate for a 60-day delivery was appropriate because the original contract matures on March 1, 19X2. This procedure results in an exchange loss of US$1,000 that is recognized in 19X1 income. The final settlement on March 1, 19X2 produces an additional exchange loss of US$2,000.

In this example the speculative nature of the transaction was readily identifiable. However, any amount of a forward contract which exceeds the exposed net asset or net liability position of an entity should be treated as a speculation. This rule also applies to the amount of foreign currency on forward contracts in excess of identifiable foreign currency commitments.

If an exporter sells merchandise which is to be paid for in a foreign currency and the exporter does not hedge the transaction, this action is regarded as a financial decision to speculate in the price of the foreign currency. Thus, any resulting exchange gain or loss should be classified in the income statement as a financial item.

13.6 HEDGE OF IDENTIFIABLE FOREIGN CURRENCY COMMITMENT

A forward contract shall be considered a hedge of an identifiable foreign currency commitment if it meets the three criteria established in FASB Statement No. 8 (paragraph 27, as modified by FASB Statement No. 20), namely:

(*a*) The life of the forward contract extends from foreign currency commitment date to the anticipated transaction date, or to a later date.

(*b*) The forward contract is denominated in the same currency as the commitment.

(*c*) The foreign currency commitment is firm and uncancelable.

The FASB has decided that the United States dollar basis of such a foreign currency commitment should be established at the transaction date. By rejecting the commitment date the FASB implicitly endorsed a *one-transaction* view for such future commitments in foreign currency from the date of commitment to the date of the transaction. The Board stated that the effects of rate changes between the commitment date and transaction date are not to be separately identified and accounted for as exchange gains or losses. Instead, they are to be included in the dollar basis of the transaction. (However, losses on a forward contract should not be deferred, if such deferral would lead to recognizing losses in later periods.)

EXAMPLE 6. Assume that on January 1, 19X1 an American importer contracts with a customer to sell for US$400,000 equipment that will be manufactured by a West German firm. Delivery is to be in 18 months. On January 1, 19X1, the spot rate for German marks (DM) is US$0.40 and the cost to the American importer is DM800,000. Since DM800,000 is equivalent to US$320,000, the contract sales price of US$400,000 promises a gross margin to the seller of US$80,000 (at spot rates). In order to ensure this potential margin, the American importer enters into a forward commitment to purchase DM800,000 in 18 months from Rico & Clay, foreign exchange brokers, at the forward rate of US$0.42. (There is a premium on West German marks because the consensus of market opinion is that West German currency will advance relative to U.S. currency.) Assume further that the following spot rates for West German marks exist at subsequent dates:

June 30, 19X1	US$0.44
Dec. 31, 19X1	US$0.46
June 30, 19X2	US$0.53

The following journal entries summarize the transactions on the books of the American importer:

January 1, 19X1

Forward Currency Purchased (DM800,000 × $0.40)	320,000	
Premium on Futures Contract	8,000	
Due to Exchange Broker (DM800,000 × $0.42)		328,000

December 31, 19X1

Forward Currency Purchased	48,000	
Deferred Exchange Gain		
[DM800,000($0.46 − $0.40)]		48,000

June 30, 19X2

Forward Currency Purchased	56,000	
Deferred Exchange Gain		
[DM800,000($0.53 − $0.46)]		56,000
Due to Exchange Broker	328,000	
Cash in Bank		328,000
Merchandise Inventory	424,000	
Vouchers Payable		
(DM800,000 × $0.53)		424,000
Foreign Currency (DM)	424,000	
Forward Currency Purchased		
($320,000 + $48,000 + $56,000)		424,000
Vouchers Payable	424,000	
Foreign Currency (DM)		424,000

Deferred Exchange Gain ($48,000 + $56,000)	104,000	
Premium on Futures Contract		8,000
Merchandise Inventory		96,000
Accounts Receivable	400,000	
Sales		400,000
Cost of Goods Sold	328,000	
Merchandise Inventory		
($424,000 − $96,000)		328,000

The foreign currency receivable (foreign currency purchased) is adjusted at each balance sheet date to reflect the current spot rate. The calculated exchange gains and the premium on the futures contract were deferred to the date of the transaction; they are then recognized as adjustments to the recorded acquisition cost of the merchandise. An alternative treatment of discount or premium on such a futures contract is to amortize the cost against operations over the contract life.

In summary, the importer paid a total of $328,000 to acquire equipment for which the customer was invoiced $400,000. The importer has achieved a gross margin of $72,000, which equals the desired margin of $80,000 less the premium on the future contract of $8,000. If the importer had not obtained a forward currency commitment, its cost on June 30, 19X2 would have been $424,000, and thus it would have sustained a loss of $24,000.

13.7 MULTIPLE EXCHANGE RATES

When exchange rates reflect the normal influence of supply and demand of currency as an economic good, the rates are frequently described as free exchange rates. However, in some countries exchange rates are established by government edict; these are referred to as official rates. Some countries even have more than one official rate. Each rate then applies to a different type, or class, of financial and economic activity. For example, one rate may apply to the importation of raw materials, while another, less favorable, rate may apply to the importation of finished goods. In some situations the official exchange rates may have limited practical use, because black markets are prevalent or only limited sums are permitted to be transferred out of the country.

If transactions are denominated in a foreign currency that has multiple exchange rates, the following rules should be observed:

1. At the transaction date, the transaction should be translated and recorded at the rate at which that particular type of transaction could be then settled.

2. At a subsequent balance sheet date on which the amount owing remains unsettled, the receivable, or payable, should be translated at the rate at which it then could be settled.

Normally, the applicable rate will remain unchanged between the transaction date and the settlement date. When more than one "official" exchange rate is in effect, a major problem is to decide which rate is appropriate. The accountant should select the rate which is most realistic and appropriate in the circumstances.

Summary

(1) In the United States, the Portuguese escudo is generally regarded as a _____.

(2) In the United Kingdom, 1 British pound will purchase 2.2 U.S. dollars. The direct quotation for the pound in the United States would be _____.

(3) An American exporter sells merchandise for which it is to receive foreign currency. To avoid the risk of fluctuations in the value of the foreign currency, the importer should _____ the transaction.

(4) An American corporation imported merchandise from Canada in 19X1 for Can$10,000 when the spot rate was US$0.90. The corporation issued financial statements on December 31, 19X1, when the current rate was US$0.93. It paid for the merchandise on March 1, 19X2, when the spot rate was US$0.95. The _____ to be included in the American corporation's income statement for 19X1 is US$_____. For 19X2, the _____ to be included in income is US$_____.

(5) The dual transaction method should be utilized for all transactions involving foreign currency except the _____.

(6) When a business entity has hedged an identifiable foreign currency contract, exchange gains and losses are calculated by using the _____ rate.

(7) If an American exporter sells merchandise for which it is to be paid in a foreign currency and does not hedge the transaction, the exporter is deemed to have decided to _____ in a foreign currency.

(8) When an American company without any identifiable foreign currency commitment or an exposed foreign currency position contracts to sell 100,000 Swiss francs for delivery in six months, the transaction is deemed to be a _____.

(9) At any balance sheet date, a contract entered into as a speculation is valued at the current rate for a _____ contract, which would _____ on the delivery date.

(10) Financial Accounting Standards Board Statement No. 8 recognizes three stages to a transaction. At the transaction date, amounts are recorded in _____ on the books of the U.S. entity. Unrealized gains and losses must be recognized at the _____ date. _____ gains and losses are recognized on the settlement date.

Answers: (1) commodity;   (2) $2.20;   (3) hedge (cover);   (4) loss, $300; loss, $200;   (5) hedge of an identifiable foreign currency commitment;   (6) current spot; (7) speculate;   (8) speculation;   (9) forward, expire;   (10) dollars, balance sheet, Realized

Solved Problems

13.1 The Apelle Corporation purchased electronic parts from the Kyoto Corporation of Japan on June 15, 19X1. The price was 10,000,000 yen (¥), due in 30 days. The Apelle Corporation closes its books on June 30.

The spot rates for one yen were as follows:

June 15	US$0.00425
June 30	US$0.00430
July 15	US$0.00427

Required:

Write the journal entries to record the purchase in June and the payment in July. Also, prepare the journal entry to adjust the accounts at June 30.

SOLUTION

> *June 15, 19X1*
>
> | | | |
> |---|---|---|
> | Purchases | 42,500 | |
> | ($¥10,000,000 \times \$0.00425$) | | |
> | Accounts Payable (yen) | | 42,500 |

> *June 30, 19X1*
>
> | | | |
> |---|---|---|
> | Exchange Loss | 500 | |
> | Accounts Payable (yen) | | |
> | $¥10,000,000$ ($\$0.00430 - \$0.00425$) | | 500 |

> *July 15, 19X1*
>
> | | | |
> |---|---|---|
> | Accounts Payable (yen) | 43,000 | |
> | Cash ($¥10,000,000 \times \$0.00427$) | | 42,700 |
> | Exchange Gain | | 300 |

13.2 On June 1, 19X1, the Andrus Corporation sold goods to the Basel Company of Switzerland for 100,000 Swiss francs (SwF) due on July 30. On the same day, Andrus sold 100,000 Swiss francs for delivery in 60 days in order to hedge its exposed net asset position.

The Andrus Corporation operates on a June 30 fiscal year. The receivable from Basel was collected on July 30 and turned over to the foreign exchange department of the Lincoln National Bank.

Selected foreign exchange rate for the Swiss franc were as follows:

	June 1	*June 30*	*July 30*
Spot Rate	US$0.600	US$0.605	US$0.608
30-Day Forward	US$0.595	US$0.598	US$0.600
60-Day Forward	US$0.592	US$0.596	US$0.598

Required:

Write the journal entries for the foregoing events from June 1 through July 31.

SOLUTION

> *June 1, 19X1*
>
> | | | |
> |---|---|---|
> | Accounts Receivable (SwF100,000 $\times$ $0.60) | 60,000 | |
> | Sales | | 60,000 |
> | | | |
> | Due from F. E. Dept. (SwF100,000 $\times$ $0.592) | 59,200 | |
> | Discount on Forward Contract | 800 | |
> | Liability to F. E. Dept. | | 60,000 |

> *June 30, 19X1*
>
> | | | |
> |---|---|---|
> | Accounts Receivable | 500 | |
> | Exchange Gain | | |
> | [SwF100,000 ($\$0.605 - \$0.600$)] | | 500 |
> | Exchange Loss | 500 | |
> | Liability to F. E. Dept. | | 500 |

June 30, 19X1 (continued)

| Amortization of Discount on Forward Contract | 400 | |
| Discount on Forward Contract (30/60 × $800) | | 400 |

July 30, 19X1

Cash (SwF100,000 × $0.608)	60,800	
Accounts Receivable		60,500
Exchange Gain		300

Liability to F. E. Dept.	60,500	
Exchange Loss	300	
Cash		60,800

| Amortization of Discount on Forward Contract | 400 | |
| Discount on Forward Contract | | 400 |

| Cash | 59,200 | |
| Due from F. E. Dept. | | 59,200 |

13.3 During the year 19X1, the Barglen Corporation of the United States entered into three transactions which involved foreign exchange, as follows:

July 7: Purchased merchandise from the Mikimoto Corporation of Japan for 10,000,000 yen when the exchange rate was US$0.00423. This was paid on August 6, when the exchange rate was US$0.00420.

August 25: Sold merchandise to the Geneva Corporation of Switzerland for 200,000 Swiss francs when the exchange rate was US$0.601. The receivable was collected on September 24, when the exchange rate was US$0.599.

November 12: Sold merchandise to Sheffield Ltd. of Great Britain for 100,000 U.K. pounds when the exchange rate was US$2.200. This receivable was collected on January 10, when the rate was US$2.215.

December 31: Current exchange rates were as follows:

Japanese yen	US$0.00428
Swiss francs	US$0.60110
U.K. pounds	US$2.21500

Required:

Prepare a schedule of the exchange gains and losses for the year 19X1.

SOLUTION

August 6, 19X1

Liability (¥10,000,000 × $0.00423)	$ 42,300
Payment (¥10,000,000 × $0.00420)	42,000
Gain	$ 300

September 24, 19X1

Receivable (SwF200,000 × $0.601)	$120,200	
Collection (SwF200,000 × $0.599)	$119,800	
Loss		(400)

December 31, 19X1

Receivable (£100,000 × $2.200)	$220,000	
Current Value (£100,000 × $2.215)	221,500	
Gain		1,500
Net Exchange Gain		$1,400

13.4 The Rover Corporation is located in the United States. It engaged in the following transactions on July 1, 19X1. The Rover Corporation closes its books on July 31.

(*a*) Sold 100,000 Austrian schillings for delivery in 90 days when the forward rate for schillings was US$0.0777 and the spot rate was US$0.0780. The Rover Corporation had no other involvement in Austrian currency.

(*b*) Purchased merchandise from the Taj Corporation of India for 100,000 rupees when the exchange rate was US$0.1200. At the same time 100,000 rupees were purchased for delivery in 60 days at a forward rate of US$0.1222.

(*c*) Sold 150,000 Netherlands guilders for delivery in 120 days in order to hedge an identifiable future commitment to deliver machinery to a Dutch company at a selling price of 150,000 guilders. The spot rate for guilders on July 1 was US$0.5020 and the forward rate for 120 days was US$0.5000.

Selected foreign exchange rates at July 31, 19X1 are as follows:

	Current Rate	Forward Rates		
		30 days	*60 days*	*90 days*
Austrian schilling (S)	US$0.0772	US$0.0774	US$0.0773	US$0.0771
Indian rupee (Rs)	US$0.1220	US$0.1210	US$0.1212	US$0.1215
Netherlands guilder (f.)	US$0.5030	US$0.5020	US$0.5010	US$0.5010

Required:

For each of the above transactions, determine the exchange gain or loss which should be included in the income statement for the year ended July 31, 19X1.

SOLUTION

July 31, 19X1

(*a*) This transaction is a speculation.

Forward Sale (S100,000 × $0.0777)	$7,770	
60-Day Forward Rate (S100,000 × $0.0773)	7,730	
Gain		$40

(b) This transaction is hedged—a purchase of merchandise payable in foreign currency.

Accounts Payable:		
July 1 (Rs100,000 × $0.1200)	$12,000	
July 31 (Rs100,000 × $0.1220)	12,200	
Loss		$(200)
Receivable from Foreign Exchange Broker:		
July 1 (Rs100,000 × $0.1200)	12,000	
July 31 (Rs100,000 × $0.1220)	12,200	
Gain		200
Amortization of Discount on Forward Rate:		
30/60($12,222 − $12,000)		(111)

(c) This transaction is a hedge of an identifiable currency commitment. No gain or loss is recognized until the sale is consummated. A deferred exchange loss of $150 should appear in the balance sheet only:

$$f.150,000(\$0.5030 - \$0.5020) = \$150$$

13.5 The following unadjusted accounts have been extracted from the ledgers of the Detroit Corporation as of June 30, 19X1:

	Dr.	Cr.
Account Receivable: Basel (billing in Swiss francs)	$98,000	
Due from Foreign Exchange Bank (from sale of 200,000 Swiss francs for delivery in 90 days from May 31)	97,100	
Discount on Forward Contract (re: hedge of receivable from Basel)	900	
Due from Foreign Exchange Bank (from purchase of 34,480,000 Italian lira for receipt in 90 days from May 1)	43,100	
Premium on Forward Contract (re: hedge of payable to Turin)	1,200	
Due from Foreign Exchange Bank (hedge of 35,000 Australian dollars; purchase commitment from Sydney Corp. of Melbourne for 60 days from May 31)	38,500	
Premium on Forward Contract (re: hedge of Australian dollars)	800	
Liability to Foreign Exchange Bank (re: hedge of Swiss francs)		$98,000
Account Payable: Turin (billing in Italian lira)		43,300
Liability to Foreign Exchange Bank (re: hedge of Italian lira)		44,000
Liability to Foreign Exchange Bank (re: hedge of Australian dollars)		39,300

Current exchange rates at June 30 were as follows:

	Spot Rate	Forward Rates		
		30 days	*60 days*	*90 days*
Swiss francs(SwF)	US$0.49800	US$0.50000	US$0.51000	US$0.51200
Italian lira(Lit)	US$0.00127	US$0.00130	US$0.00130	US$0.00133
Australian dollars($A)	US$1.11000	US$1.11300	US$1.12000	US$1.12300

Required:

Write the journal entries to adjust the accounts as of June 30.

SOLUTION

(*a*)   Swiss francs (SwF):

Accounts Receivable: Basel	1,600	
Exchange Gain		
[(SwF200,000 × $0.4980) − $98,000]		1,600
Exchange Loss	1,600	
Liability to Foreign Exchange Bank		1,600
Amortization of Discount on Forward Contract (SwF)	300	
Exchange Gain (30/90 × $900)		300

(*b*)   Italian lira (Lit):

Due from Foreign Exchange Bank (Lit)	490	
Exchange Gain		
[(Lit34,480,000 × $0.00127) − $43,300]		490
Exchange Loss	490	
Accounts Payable: Turin		490
Amortization of Premium on Forward Contract (Lit)	800	
Exchange Gain (60/90 × $1,200)		800

(*c*)   Australian dollars ($A):

Due from Foreign Exchange Bank ($A)	350	
Deferred Exchange Gain		
[$A35,000(US$1.11 − US$1.10)]		350

Note: No amortization of the premium on the hedge of an identifiable purchase commitment is required. However, under optional provisions of FASB Statement No. 8, 30/60 of $800 could be amortized.

Chapter 14

Translation of Foreign Statements

14.1 INTRODUCTION

The purpose of this chapter is to explain how statements originally prepared in a foreign currency should be translated into U.S. dollars. Foreign statements that are to be included by consolidation, combination, or the equity method in an American firm's financial statements should first be prepared in conformity with generally accepted United States accounting principles. Thereafter, translation (conversion) of foreign amounts will change the unit of measurement without changing the accounting principles.

For several decades the AICPA favored the *current-noncurrent* concept for the translation of foreign balance sheets. Under this approach, current assets and current liabilities would be translated into dollars by using the current rate at the balance sheet date, while long-term assets, long-term liabilities, and capital stock would be translated at the prevailing rate at the time the asset or capital stock was acquired or the liability incurred.

Gradually a more realistic division of the balance sheet accounts for purposes of translation prevailed. By 1960 most multinational companies were using a *monetary-nonmonetary* approach, which may be summarized as follows:

(*a*) Cash, accounts receivable, and any nonmonetary assets are converted at the current rate of exchange.

(*b*) Inventories, fixed assets, and other nonmonetary assets are converted by using the rate of exchange in effect when such assets were acquired.

(*c*) All liabilities are converted at the current rate of exchange.

(*d*) Capital stock is converted at the rate of exchange in effect when the stock was issued or acquired by the U.S. company.

14.2 TRANSLATION OF FOREIGN CURRENCY STATEMENTS

In FASB Statement No. 8 (October 1975), the Financial Accounting Standards Board decided that the *temporal* method of translating assets and liabilities expressed in foreign currency would be most appropriate. This method generally converts assets and liabilities carried at past, current, or future prices in a manner which retains the accounting principles used in the foreign statements. As a practical matter, such results are usually similar to the monetary-nonmonetary method. However, this is due to the nature of present-day generally accepted accounting principles; if other accounting principles were in place, results might be significantly different.

In reference to assets and liabilities, the Statement says:

(*a*) Accounts carried at prices in past exchanges (past prices) shall be translated at historical rates.

(*b*) Accounts carried at prices in current purchase or sale exchanges (current prices) or future exchanges (future prices) shall be translated at the current rate.

Exchange rates used to translate the most commonly found assets and liabilities are presented on page 20 of FASB Statement No. 8.

Revenue and expense transactions should be translated in a manner which will produce the same dollar amounts that would have been produced had the transactions been translated at rates in effect when the transactions occurred. As a practical matter, suitably weighted average rates may be used for all revenue and expense categories except those that relate to assets and liabilities, which are translated at historical rates. Thus, depreciation expense is converted by using the same rate utilized for the related long-lived asset, and bad debt expense is converted by using the current rate at the end of the accounting period.

Accounts for shareholders' equity are generally converted by using the rates that were in existence when the events were originally recorded. Thus, capital stock and paid-in capital accounts are converted at the relevant historical rates. Retained earnings are generally converted by observing the following steps:

(a) Bring forward the U.S. dollar balance of retained earnings at the end of the previous fiscal period.

(b) Add the converted net income for the current period.

(c) Deduct dividends declared at their converted amounts.

If there is a minority interest, it is calculated from the stockholders' equity in the translated statement. Reciprocal accounts are converted (translated) to the dollar balances of related accounts in the home office, or parent corporation, ledger. Financial statements of a foreign operation in a country where multiple exchange rates are in effect should be translated at the rate or rates applicable to dividend remittances.

14.3 TRANSLATION OF FOREIGN BRANCH TRIAL BALANCE

A branch normally sends a copy of its trial balance to the home office. The branch also sends transcripts of those accounts which are reciprocal to related accounts in the home office ledger, summaries of its inventory, and other significant data. Translation of the foreign branch trial balance typically takes place in the home office.

EXAMPLE 1. The Topper Corporation of Trenton, New Jersey, established a branch in Bonn, Germany, on July 18, 19X1. The company and its branch operate on a calendar year. The branch submitted the following trial balance as of December 31, 19X1.

	Dr.	Cr.
Cash	DM 15,000	
Accounts Receivable	250,000	
Inventory	135,000	
Cost of Goods Sold	410,000	
Operating Expenses	100,000	
Home Office Control		DM310,000
Sales		600,000
	DM910,000	DM910,000

When goods were shipped by the home office to the branch, the exchange rate for one West German mark was US$0.40; at the end of the calendar year the rate was US$0.46. An appropriate weighted average for the year was US$0.44. As of December 31, the branch office account on the home office books showed a debit balance of $130,900.

The worksheet for the translation of the foreign trial balance includes a column which indicates the exchange rates utilized. Cash and accounts receivable are translated at the current rate as of December 31. The inventory on hand and the cost of goods sold are converted by using the rate in effect when the goods were shipped to the branch. The corporation uses the first-in, first-out (FIFO) method for costing sales.

The balance of the home office control account is converted by using the U.S. dollar amount in the reciprocal account on the home office books. Sales and operating expenses are converted by using a suitably weighted average exchange rate.

Since the various items in the branch trial balance are converted at different exchange rates, the debits and credits in the translated trial balance will rarely be equal. The difference between these two columns is treated as an exchange gain or loss in the entity's statements. For internal purposes, many firms identify this as a translation gain or loss.

Topper Corporation, Bonn Branch
Translation of Foreign Trial Balance
December 31, 19X1

	Trial Balance, West German Marks (DM)		Exchange Rate		Trial Balance United States Dollars (US$)	
	Dr.	Cr.	Code	Rate	Dr.	Cr.
Cash	15,000		C	0.46	6,900	
Accounts Receivable	250,000		C	0.46	115,000	
Inventory	135,000		B	0.40	54,000	
Cost of Goods Sold	410,000		B	0.40	164,000	
Operating Expenses	100,000		A	0.44	44,000	
Home Office Control		310,000	R	—		130,900
Sales		600,000	A	0.44		264,000
	910,000	910,000			383,900	394,900
Exchange Loss					11,000	
					394,900	394,900

Code: A—Weighted average.
     B—Rate when goods were shipped to branch.
     C—Current rate at end of year.
     R—Reciprocal amount.

EXAMPLE 2. During 19X2 the Topper Corporation changed its method of billing the Bonn branch. Instead of billing at cost, as in 19X1, the home office billed the Bonn branch at 120 percent of cost during year 19X2. It was also decided to keep separate accounts for remittances from the branch to the home office.

The trial balance submitted by the Bonn branch as of December 31, 19X2, was as follows:

	Dr.	Cr.
Cash	DM 40,000	
Accounts Receivable	220,000	
Inventory	120,000	
Remittances to Home Office	320,000	
Cost of Goods Sold	600,000	
Operating Expenses	200,000	
Home Office Control		DM 650,000
Sales		850,000
	DM1,500,000	DM1,500,000

As of December 31, 19X2 the general ledger of the home office showed the following balances (in dollars) pertaining to the Bonn branch.

Shipments to Bonn Branch	$275,000
Remittances from Bonn Branch	156,000
Bonn Branch Control	308,000

During year 19X2 the West German mark rose from US$0.46 to US$0.50. The inventory at December 31, 19X2, had been acquired during the fourth quarter of the year, during which time the mark rose gradually from US$0.49 to US$0.50. Since the corporation uses FIFO, the inventory can be costed at US$0.495, the average for the fourth quarter. This works out to $59,400 (DM120,000 × $0.495).

The cost of goods sold in 19X2 is translated as follows:

Inventory, Jan. 1	DM 135,000	$ 54,000
Shipments, 19X2	585,000	275,000
	DM 720,000	329,000
Inventory, Dec. 31	120,000	59,400
Cost of Goods Sold	DM 600,000	$269,600

Cash and accounts receivable are translated by utilizing the current rate at the end of the year. Sales and operating expenses are converted at US$0.48, the average rate for the year.

Remittances to home office and home office control are translated by utilizing the balances of the reciprocal accounts on the home office books.

Topper Corporation, Bonn Branch
Translation of Foreign Trial Balance
December 31, 19X2

	Trial Balance, West German Marks (DM)		Exchange Rate		Trial Balance, United States Dollars (US$)	
	Dr.	Cr.	Code	Rate	Dr.	Cr.
Cash	40,000		C	.50	20,000	
Accounts Receivable	220,000		C	.50	110,000	
Inventory	120,000		D	.495	59,400	
Remittances to Home Office	320,000		R	—	156,000	
Cost of Goods Sold	600,000		E	—	269,600	
Operating Expenses	200,000		A	.48	96,000	
Home Office Control		650,000	R	—		308,000
Sales		850,000	A	.48		408,000
	1,500,000	1,500,000			711,000	716,000
Exchange Loss					5,000	
					716,000	716,000

Code: A—Weighted average.
      C—Current rate at end of year.
      D—Average for fourth quarter.
      E—See text.
      F—Reciprocal amount.

EXAMPLE 3. The Norton Corporation of Philadelphia has been operating a branch in London for several years. The trial balance of the London branch for the year ended December 31, 19X3, is included in the first two columns of the following worksheet.

Current assets other than inventories are translated at the spot (current) rate in effect at the end of the year. Equipment is translated at the rate in effect when the equipment was purchased. Thus, accumulated depreciation and depreciation expense are also translated at the same historical rate.

The following accounts are converted by using dollar balances in the related reciprocal accounts: home office control, remittance to home office, and shipments from home office.

Norton Company, London Branch
Worksheet for Translation of Trial Balance
December 31, 19X3

	Trial Balance, £		Exchange Rate		Trial Balance, US$	
	Dr.	Cr.	Code	Rate	Dr.	Cr.
Cash	2,500		C	2.00	5,000	
Accounts Receivable	2,000		C	2.00	4,000	
Equipment	10,000		H	2.40	24,000	
Accumulated Depreciation		3,000	H	2.40		7,200
Accounts Payable		4,500	C	2.00		9,000
Home Office Control		21,000	R			40,000
Remittance to Home Office	27,000		R		53,000	
Sales		80,000	A	1.95		156,000
Shipments from Home Office	44,000		R		87,000	
Purchases	11,000		A	1.95	21,450	
Inventory, January 1	1,000		B	1.90	1,900	
Inventory, December 31:						
From Home Office	1,900	1,900	H	1.98	3,762	3,762
From Great Britain	1,100	1,100	H	1.99	2,189	2,189
Depreciation	1,000		H	2.40	2,400	
Other Expenses	10,000		A	1.95	19,500	
	111,500	111,500			224,201	218,151
Exchange Gain						6,050
					224,201	224,201

Code: A—Weighted average exchange rate for current year.
        B—Translated dollar amount of inventory at end of previous fiscal year.
        C—Rate of exchange at end of current year.
        H—Historical rate of exchange at date of purchase.
        R—Balance of respective reciprocal account in home office ledger.

Merchandise inventory at the beginning of the year is converted by utilizing the dollar balance which resulted from conversion at the end of the previous year. Merchandise inventories at the end of the current year are translated according to their source. Thus, goods which were obtained from the home office are converted back to their cost in U.S. dollars (plus applicable freight, etc.), while merchandise acquired in Great Britain is converted by using the U.S. dollar rate in effect at the date of acquisition.

Cash, accounts receivable, and accounts payable are translated by using the current rate at the balance sheet date. Allowance for doubtful accounts and doubtful account expense would be translated at the same rate used for accounts receivable.

Revenue and expenses (other than depreciation and doubtful accounts) are translated at weighted average rates for the year.

The difference between the translated debits and credits is computed and labelled as exchange gain. This translation gain is to be included in the income statement under the caption of exchange gain or loss.

After the trial balance of the foreign branch has been translated into U.S. dollars, statements may be prepared therefrom. Such statements should then be combined with home office statements in a manner similar to the combination of home office statements with domestic branches.

14.4 TRANSLATION OF FOREIGN SUBSIDIARY TRIAL BALANCE

The translation of a foreign subsidiary's assets, liabilities, and reciprocal accounts is based on the same general principles that apply to translation of any foreign currency trial balance. However, the translation of certain subsidiary accounts will depend on whether the acquisition had been classified as a *purchase* or as a *pooling of interests*.

When a business combination with a foreign operation is accounted for by the *purchase method*, the assets and liabilities of the foreign operation at the date of acquisition should be adjusted to fair value in local currency and then translated at the rate in effect at the date of acquisition. Thus, an excess of the U.S. dollar cost of acquisition over the translated net assets should be accounted for as goodwill and/or an excess of acquired net assets over cost (see "Accounting Principles Bulletin" No. 16, August 1970).

When a business combination is accounted for by the *pooling-of-interests method*, the assets and liabilities of the foreign operation should be translated as if the foreign operation had always been a subsidiary of the American firm. Thus, assets and liabilities which are translated at historical rates should be translated at the rates in effect at the date the foreign operation recognized the specific event or transaction.

EXAMPLE 4. The United Corporation owns 90 percent of the Marker Corporation, which is located in the country of Dealand. The Marker Corporation keeps its records in its domestic currency, called the Ducat (D). The trial balance of the Marker Corporation as of December 31, 19X2, is included in the first two columns of the following worksheet.

It is first necessary to convert the foreign trial balance to U.S. dollars before the resultant statements can be consolidated with those of its parent.

Cash and accounts receivable are translated at the current rate of US$0.40 as of the trial balance date. The allowance for bad debts and bad debt expense are also translated at the same current rate.

The Marker Corporation utilizes the last-in, first-out (LIFO) method. A comparison of the balance of the merchandise inventory at the end of the year with that at the beginning of the year indicates an increase in inventory of D10,000, which is priced at the exchange rate of US$0.48, the rate in effect during its acquisition. The inventory at December 31, 19X1 had been converted to $23,500. Thus, the total inventory at December 31, 19X2 amounts to $28,300 ($23,500 + $4,800).

Amounts due to or from the parent company are converted to the dollar amount in the reciprocal account on the parent's books.

Equipment is translated by using the rate of exchange at the date of purchase or acquisition. By the same token, the related accumulated depreciation and depreciation expense are also translated at the same historical rate. Prepaid expenses are translated at the appropriate historical rates. Current liabilities, such as vouchers payable, are converted at the current rate.

The subsidiary's capital stock is translated at the exchange rate in effect on the date of acquisition of control. The retained earnings balance at January 1 is converted by using the U.S. dollar translation at the end of the previous year.

Sales and other expenses are translated by using a suitably weighted average for the current year.

From a theoretical point of view, the goods sold should be costed at the current acquisitions in the year 19X2. Since this is rarely feasible, the cost of goods sold is generally translated at a weighted average exchange rate for the current year. The difference between the debits and credits in the translated trial balance is treated as an exchange loss for the year.

Marker Corp.
Worksheet for Translation of Trial Balance
December 31, 19X2

	Trial Balance, D		Exchange Rate		Trial Balance, US$	
	Dr.	Cr.	Code	Rate	Dr.	Cr.
Cash	80,000		C	.40	32,000	
Accounts Receivable	54,000		C	.40	21,600	
Allowance for Bad Debts		2,000	C	.40		800
Inventory (LIFO)	60,000		I		28,300	
Due from Parent	40,000		R		19,800	
Equipment	240,000		H	.60	144,000	
Accumulated Depreciation		48,000	H	.60		28,800
Prepaid Expenses	6,000		H		2,980	
Vouchers Payable		46,000	C	.40		18,400
Common Stock		200,000				121,000
Retained Earnings (Jan. 1)		100,000	E			46,480
Sales		580,000	A	.46		266,800
Cost of Goods Sold	380,000		A	.46	174,800	
Depreciation Expense	24,000		H	.60	14,400	
Bad Debt Expense	2,000		C	.40	800	
Other Expenses	90,000		A	.46	41,400	
	976,000	976,000			480,080	482,280
Exchange Loss					2,200	
					482,280	482,280

Code: A—Weighted average exchange rate for current year.
C—Rate of exchange at end of current year.
E—Translated dollar amount of retained earnings at end of previous fiscal year.
H—Historical rate of exchange at date of purchase or acquisition.
I—LIFO inventory at end of previous year: $23,500
    Increment at acquisition cost: 4,800
        Total $28,300
R—Balance of the reciprocal account on the parent company's books.

14.5 APPLYING THE LOWER-OF-COST-OR-MARKET RULE
IN TRANSLATED FINANCIAL STATEMENTS

Foreign currency statements which are to be translated should follow accounting principles generally accepted in the United States. One of these principles is that inventory should generally be stated at cost or market, whichever is lower (LCM). To ensure that inventory in translated statements is properly stated, the LCM rule must be applied in U.S. dollars. Thus, translated historical cost should be compared with translated market. Any inventory write-downs which are the result of applying the LCM rule are *not* exchange losses.

EXAMPLE 5. A foreign subsidiary of a U.S. corporation purchases one unit of inventory for 1,000 ducats (D) at a date when 1 ducat equals US$1.20.

At the balance sheet date of the foreign subsidiary, the current rate is one ducat equals US$1.00. Assume that the current replacement cost is D1,120 and that the net realizable value is D1,260. The net realizable value reduced by an allowance for normal profit margin is D1,100.

Since current replacement cost measured in U.S. dollars ($1,120) is less than the translated historical cost ($1,200), an inventory write-down of $80 is required in the translated statement.

EXAMPLE 6. Assume the same data as given in the preceding example except that the current replacement cost at the foreign subsidiary's balance sheet date is D1,240.

Since market measured in U.S. dollars ($1,240) is greater than translated historical cost ($1,200), an inventory write-down is not required.

EXAMPLE 7. This example is based on the same data as Example 5 except that the foreign currency selling prices have increased so that the net realizable value is D1,440 and the net realizable value reduced by an allowance for an approximately normal profit margin is D1,280.

Replacement cost measured in dollars ($1,120) is less than net realizable value reduced by an allowance for a normal profit margin ($1,280). The translated market is $1,280. Since the translated market exceeds the translated historical cost of $1,200, an inventory write-down is not required in the dollar financial statements.

Appendix

On December 7, 1981, the FASB adopted its Statement No. 52, which makes major changes in the way that most companies will translate foreign statements into United States dollars. It will become mandatory in 1983, and will be optional for financial statements commencing in 1981.

The new Statement distinguishes between transaction gains and losses and translation adjustments. Translation gains and losses will be reported as a separate component of stockholders' equity; transaction gains and losses will continue to be reported in the income statement.

Under the revised rules, all assets and liabilities are to be translated into United States dollars at *current* exchange rates. However, a corporation's foreign exchange gains and losses from balance sheet translations will not be reflected in earnings, as they have been up to now. Instead, they will be placed in a special category in the stockholders' equity section of the balance sheet.

In general, the FASB has replaced the temporal method of FASB Statement No. 8 with a *functional-currency/current-rate* concept. The functional currency of each operation will become the measurement unit for that entity. The functional currency of an entity is defined as the primary currency of the economic environment in which the entity operates and in which it is expected to generate its cash flows. An entity's functional currency is presumed to be a matter that is determinable from the facts. If the operations of a foreign entity are contained within a single country, its functional currency would be the currency of that country. However, if a foreign entity's operations are economically linked to the parent's operations, the entity's functional currency will be that of its parent. In complex situations, the determination of an entity's functional currency may depend upon management's evaluation of the various economic circumstances pertaining to the operations of the entity.

The temporal method (FASB Statement No. 8) continues to apply to the translation of statements of foreign subsidiaries where the functional currency is the United States dollar and for subsidiaries operating in countries that have experienced hyperinflation in recent years. Thus, if cumulative inflation has been in excess of 100 percent over a three-year period, the temporal method in FASB Statement No. 8 is to be continued.

The new Statement also permits any foreign currency transaction that was intended as a hedge to be accounted for as such.

Summary

(1) When translating foreign company balances to a domestic currency, one objective is to convert the amounts without changing the accounting _____ involved.

(2) Exchange gains and losses _____ translation gains and losses.

(3) The aggregate exchange gains and losses for a fiscal period should be _____ in the company's financial statements.

(4) Monetary assets and liabilities in foreign currency statements are generally translated at _____ exchange rates. Nonmonetary assets and liabilities are generally translated at _____ exchange rates.

(5) The goal in translating revenue and expense balances is to approximate the results which would have been achieved if each transaction had been _____ at the time it had occurred.

(6) A suitably weighted average of foreign exchange rates is generally used to translate revenue and expenses other than _____ and _____.

(7) Cost of goods sold is generally translated at an appropriate _____ rate for the goods sold.

(8) The dollar amount of retained earnings of a foreign subsidiary is included in a translated trial balance at the _____ amount as of the beginning of the period.

(9) After a foreign trial balance has been translated to domestic currency, a balancing amount is supplied in order that the debits and credits in the converted trial balance will be equal. This is labelled as an _____ or _____.

Answers: (1) principle; (2) include; (3) disclosed; (4) current, historical; (5) translated (converted); (6) depreciation, bad debts (sometimes also cost of goods sold); (7) historical; (8) translated; (9) exchange gain, loss

Solved Problems

14.1 The Tivoli Company operates a branch in Stockholm. The following trial balance in Swedish krona (SKr) was obtained from the branch as of December 31, 19X5.

	Dr.	Cr.
Cash	SKr 5,500	
Accounts Receivable	40,000	
Inventory	10,000	
Remittances to Home Office	100,000	
Sales		SKr150,000
Shipments from Home Office	78,000	
Expenses	8,500	
Home Office		92,000
	SKr242,000	SKr242,000

Required:

Assuming that the exchange rate for the krona was US$0.24 throughout the year, write summary journal entries to record the following on the home office books: (a) cash remittances from branch; (b) merchandise shipments to the branch.

SOLUTION

(a)	Cash	24,000	
	Remittances from Branch		
	(SKr100,000 × $0.24)		24,000
(b)	Branch	18,720	
	Shipments to Branch		
	(SKr78,000 × $0.24)		18,720

14.2 The Jaffin Corporation operates a branch in The Hague, Holland. The branch's December 31, 19X3, trial balance, in guilders (f.), follows:

Jaffin Corporation, The Hague Branch
Trial Balance
December 31, 19X3

	Dr.	Cr.
Cash	f. 15,400	
Accounts Receivable	113,200	
Allowance for Bad Debts		f. 1,650
Remittances to Home Office	75,950	
Merchandise Inventory: Jan. 1	26,800	
Dec. 31	34,850	34,850
Fixtures and Equipment	20,000	
Accumulated Depreciation		4,000
Accounts Payable		48,100
Home Office		123,000
Sales		420,000
Shipments from Home Office	238,330	
Purchases	60,700	
Administrative Expenses	28,500	
Selling Expenses	14,870	
Depreciation Expense	2,000	
Bad Debts	1,000	
	f.631,600	f.631,600

The following balances appeared on the home office records as of December 31, 19X3:

Shipments to Branch	$119,000
Remittances from Branch	37,800
Branch Office—The Hague	61,000

The following exchange rates prevailed during the year:

January 1	US$0.490
December 31	US$0.500
Weighted Average	US$0.494
Merchandise Inventory	
January 1	US$0.478
December 31	US$0.496
Date of Acquisition of Fixtures and Equipment	US$0.480

Required:

Translate the trial balance of the branch into U.S. dollars.

SOLUTION

Jaffin Corporation, The Hague Branch
Translation of Foreign Trial Balance
December 31, 19X3

	Trial Balance, f.		Exchange Rate		Trial Balance, US$	
	Dr.	Cr.	Code	Rate	Dr.	Cr.
Cash	15,400		C	0.500	7,700	
Accounts Receivable	113,200		C	0.500	56,600	
Allowance for Bad Debts		1,650	C	0.500		825
Remittances to Home Office	75,950		R		37,800	
Merchandise Inventory						
January 1	26,800		I–1	0.478	12,810	
December 31	34,850	34,850	I–2	0.496	17,286	17,286
Fixtures and Equipment	20,000		H	0.480	9,600	
Accumulated Depreciation		4,000	H	0.480		1,920
Accounts Payable		48,100	C	0.500		24,050
Home Office		123,000	R			61,000
Sales		420,000	A	0.494		207,480
Shipments from Home Office	238,330		R		119,000	
Purchases	60,700		A	0.494	29,986	
Administrative Expenses	28,500		A	0.494	14,079	
Selling Expenses	14,870		A	0.494	7,346	
Depreciation Expense	2,000		H	0.480	960	
Bad Debts	1,000		C	0.500	500	
	631,600	631,600			313,667	312,561
Exchange Gain						1,106
					313,667	313,667

Code: A—Appropriate weighted average.
           C—Current rate at balance sheet date.
           H—Rate on date of acquisition of equipment.
           I—Rate on dates of acquisition of inventory.
           R—Reciprocal account on home office books.

14.3 The Trading Corporation operates a branch in Transylvania. The December 31, 19X4 trial balance of the branch in Sylvan dollars (SD) is presented below:

The Trading Corporation, Transylvania Branch
Trial Balance
December 31, 19X4

	Dr.	Cr.
Cash	SD 4,600	
Accounts Receivable	25,100	
Allowance for uncollectibles		SD 1,020
Remittances to Home Office	32,000	
Merchandise Inventory Jan. 1, 19X4	33,700	
Fixtures and Equipment	40,400	
Accumulated Depreciation— Fixtures and Equipment		8,080
Notes Payable		20,000
Accounts Payable		7,260
Remittances from Home Office		9,000
Home Office		46,400
Sales		236,760
Shipments from Home Office	77,020	
Purchases	43,400	
Administrative Expenses	37,000	
Selling Expenses	29,700	
Depreciation Expense	4,400	
Interest Expense	1,200	
	SD328,520	SD328,520

Additional information:

1. *Exchange rates—United States dollars per Sylvan dollar:*

December 31, 19X3	US$0.36
December 31, 19X4	US$0.40
19X4 average	US$0.38
When Fixtures and Equipment Were Acquired	US$0.35

2. *Balances on home office records—December 31, 19X4:*

Branch	US$18,300
Shipments to Branch	30,200
Remittances to Branch	3,600
Remittances from Branch	12,500

The dollar-origin cost of merchandise inventory as of December 31, 19X3, was US$12,000. The dollar-origin cost of merchandise inventory as of December 31, 19X4, was US$14,000.

Required:

Convert the branch trial balance into U.S. dollars.

SOLUTION   *The Trading Corporation, Transylvania Branch*
                        Translation of Foreign Trial Balance
                        December 31, 19X4

	Trial Balance, SD		Exchange Rate		Trial Balance, US$	
	Dr.	Cr.	Code	Rate	Dr.	Cr.
Cash	4,600		C	0.40	1,840	
Accounts Receivable	25,100		C	0.40	10,040	
Allowance for Uncollectibles		1,020	C	0.40		408
Remittances to Home Office	32,000		R		12,500	
Merchandise Inventory						
January 1	33,700		I		12,000	
Fixtures and Equipment	40,400		H	0.35	14,140	
Accumulated Depreciation		8,080	H	0.35		2,828
Notes Payable		20,000	C	0.40		8,000
Accounts Payable		7,260	C	0.40		2,904
Remittances from Home Office		9,000	R			3,600
Home Office		46,400	R			18,300
Sales		236,760	A	0.38		89,969
Shipments from Home Office	77,020		R		30,200	
Purchases	43,400		A	0.38	16,492	
Administrative Expenses	37,000		A	0.38	14,060	
Selling Expenses	29,700		A	0.38	11,286	
Depreciation Expense	4,400		H	0.35	1,540	
Interest Expense	1,200		A	0.38	456	
	328,520	328,520			124,554	126,009
Translation Loss					1,455	
					126,009	126,009

Code: A—Appropriate weighted average.
          C—Current rate at balance sheet date.
          H—Rate on date of acquisition of equipment.
          I—Dollar-origin cost of merchandise.
          R—Reciprocal account on home office books.

14.4   The Gramercy Corporation opened a branch in Mexico City on January 2, 19X8. The branch receives all of its merchandise from the home office and deposits all sales proceeds in an account against which the home office draws from time to time. An imprest fund for branch expenses was established by the home office sending a draft of $1,000 to the branch. This fund is reimbursed by the home office as required.

The branch submits the following trial balance as of December 31, 19X8:

Gramercy Corporation, Mexico City Branch
Trial Balance
December 31, 19X8

	Dr.	Cr.
Imprest Cash Fund	Mex$ 22,727	
Accounts Receivable	253,750	
Sales		Mex$1,173,830
Shipments from Home Office	997,250	
Expenses	232,273	
Home Office		332,170
	Mex$1,506,000	Mex$1,506,000

The trial balance of the home office follows:

	Dr.	Cr.
Cash	$ 11,720	
Accounts Receivable	43,500	
Inventory	24,000	
Equipment—Home Office	18,000	
Equipment—Branch	5,020	
Accumulated Depreciation		$ 4,300
Accounts Payable		8,220
Shipments to Branch		41,200
Remittances from Branch		38,100
Remittances to Branch	10,200	
Sales		180,000
Cost of Goods Sold	156,100	
Expenses	21,100	
Capital Stock		50,000
Retained Earnings		8,560
Branch	40,740	
	$330,380	$330,380

The merchandise inventories at December 31, 19X8, were: branch, Mex$26,000; home office, $24,000. Shipments to the branch are made at cost.

The following rates of exchange prevailed during the year:

Jan. 3	US$0.0440
Dec. 31	US$0.0420
Merchandise Inventory, Dec. 31	US$0.0425
Date of Acquisition of Equipment	US$0.0432

Required:

(a) Determine the average exchange rate for year.

(b) Convert the Mexico City branch trial balance to U.S. dollars.

(c) Prepare worksheets to combine the income statements and balance sheets of the branch and home office.

SOLUTION

(a) *Computation of average exchange rate.*

Shipments to Branch		Mex$ 997,250	US$41,200
Remittances to Branch:			
Imprest Fund	Mex$ 22,727		
Expenses	232,273	255,000	10,200
Remittances from Branch:			
Sales	Mex$1,173,830		
Less: Accounts Receivable	253,750	920,080	38,100
		Mex$2,172,330	US$89,500

Average exchange rate:　　　US$89,500 ÷ Mex$2,172,330 = US$0.0412

(b)

The Gramercy Corporation, Mexico City Branch
Translation of Trial Balance
December 31, 19X8

	Trial Balance, Mex$		Exchange Rate		Trial Balance, US$	
	Dr.	Cr.	Code	Rate	Dr.	Cr.
Imprest Cash Fund	22,727		C	0.0420	955	
Accounts Receivable	253,750		C	0.0420	10,658	
Merchandise	26,000	26,000	I	0.0425	1,105	1,105
Sales		1,173,830	A	0.0412		48,362
Shipments from Home Office	997,250		R		41,200	
Expenses	232,273		Q		9,200	
Home Office		332,170	R			12,840*
	1,532,000	1,532,000			63,118	62,307
Exchange Gain						811
					63,118	63,118

Code:　A—Weighted average.
　　　　C—Current rate.
　　　　I—Merchandise inventory.
　　　　Q—Remittances to branch, $10,200 less $1,000.
　　　　R—Reciprocal(s) account on home office books.

*Combination of three accounts on home office books:

Remittances to Branch	US$10,200
Branch	40,740
	US$50,940
Less: Remittances from Branch	38,100
	US$12,840

(c)

Gramercy Company & Mexico City Branch
Worksheet to Combine Income Statements
Year Ended December 31, 19X8

	Home Office		Branch		Eliminations		Combined Statement	
	Dr.	Cr.	Dr.	Cr.	Dr.	Cr.		
Sales		180,000		48,362				228,362
Cost of Goods Sold	156,100						156,100	
Shipments to Branch		41,200			[a]41,200			
Shipments from Home Office			41,200			[a]41,200		
Inventory, Dec. 31				1,105				1,105
Expenses	21,100		9,200				30,300	
Exchange Gain				811				811
	177,200	221,200	50,400	50,278			186,400	230,278
Net Income	44,000			122			43,878	
	221,200	221,200	50,400	50,400			230,278	230,278

[a] To eliminate intracompany shipments.

Gramercy Company & Mexico City Branch
Worksheet to Combine Balance Sheets
December 31, 19X8

	Home Office		Branch		Eliminations		Combined Statement	
	Dr.	Cr.	Dr.	Cr.	Dr.	Cr.		
Cash	11,720		955				12,675	
Accounts Receivable	43,500		10,658				54,158	
Inventory	24,000		1,105				25,105	
Branch	40,740							
Remittances from Branch		38,100				[1]12,840		
Remittances to Branch	10,200							
Equipment—Home Office	18,000						23,020	
Equipment—Branch	5,020							
Accumulated Depreciation		4,300						4,300
Accounts Payable		8,220						8,220
Home Office				12,840	[1]12,840			
Capital Stock		50,000						50,000
Retained Earnings, Jan. 1		8,560						8,560
Net Income		44,000	122					43,878
	153,180	153,180	12,840	12,840			114,958	114,958

[1] To eliminate reciprocal balances.

386   FOREIGN TRANSACTIONS AND OPERATIONS   [PART III

14.5 On March 29, 19X2, the Corde Corporation formed a foreign subsidiary in Norway which operates on a calendar year. Selected items from two balance sheets in Norwegian krone (NKr) follow:

	December 31	
	19X3	*19X2*
Accounts Receivable (net of allowance for bad debts)	80,000	70,000
Inventories (at cost)	90,000	140,000
Equipment	340,000	280,000
Accumulated Depreciation	62,000	28,000
Bonds Payable	850,000	900,000
Common Stock, NKr100 par (100,000 shares authorized)	400,000	400,000

Additional information is as follows:

1. Exchange rates:

March 29, 19X2–August 15, 19X2	US$0.200
August 16, 19X2–November 30, 19X2	US$0.202
December 1, 19X2–May 31, 19X3	US$0.205
June 1, 19X3–December 31, 19X3	US$0.207
Weighted average rate for 19X2	US$0.201
Weighted average rate for 19X3	US$0.206

2. The first-in, first-out method is used for inventories.

3. An analysis of inventories is as follows:

	19X3	*19X2*
Inventory, January 1	NKr140,000	–0–
Purchases:		
May 19X3 and May 19X2	300,000	NKr400,000
November 19X3	150,000	–0–
Available for Sale	NKr590,000	NKr400,000
Inventory, December 31	90,000	140,000
Cost of Goods Sold	NKr500,000	NKr260,000

4. The foreign subsidiary purchased equipment as follows:

April 5, 19X2	NKr280,000
February 20, 19X3	60,000

5. On May 1, 19X3, the subsidiary sold 9 percent debentures with a par value of NKr 900,000. The bonds mature in ten years and interest is paid semiannually on May 1 and November 1.

Required:

Convert the selected balance sheet items into U.S. dollars at December 31, 19X3 and 19X2.

SOLUTION

	NKr	Exchange Rate	Date	US$
December 31, 19X2				
Accounts Receivable	70,000	0.205	12/31, 19X2	14,350
Inventories	140,000	0.200	May 1972	28,000
Equipment	280,000	0.200	4/5, 19X2	56,000
Accumulated Depreciation	28,000	0.200	4/5, 19X2	5,600
Bonds Payable	900,000	0.205	12/31, 19X2	184,500
Common Stock	400,000	0.200	4/5, 19X2	80,000
December 31, 19X3				
Accounts Receivable	80,000	0.207	12/31, 19X3	16,560
Inventories	90,000	0.207	Nov. 19X3	18,630
Equipment	280,000	0.200	4/5, 19X2	56,000
Equipment	60,000	0.205	2/20, 19X3	12,300
Accumulated Depreciation	56,000	0.200	4/5, 19X2	11,200
Accumulated Depreciation	6,000	0.205	2/20, 19X3	1,230
Bonds Payable	850,000	0.207	12/31, 19X3	175,950
Common Stock	400,000	0.200	4/5, 19X2	80,000

14.6 The Clinton Corporation invested $155,000 to acquire 90 percent of the stock of the Spring Corporation, located in the Philippines. Clinton purchased its investment on January 3, 19X4, when the stockholders' equity of the subsidiary consisted of the following: capital stock, 400,000 pesos (₱), retained earnings, ₱80,000.

The condensed trial balance of Spring in pesos, as of December 31, 19X4, was as follows:

	Dr.	Cr.
Cash	₱167,000	
Accounts Receivable	194,000	
Merchandise Inventory	170,000	
Equipment	340,000	
Accumulated Depreciation		₱103,000
Vouchers Payable		112,000
Other Current Liabilities		56,000
Capital Stock		400,000
Retained Earnings		200,000
	₱871,000	₱871,000

Merchandise was acquired during the fourth quarter of 19X4. The equipment, which has a ten-year life, was acquired on two different dates, as follows: May 1, 19X1, ₱240,000; July 1, 19X3, ₱100,000.

Exchange rates for selected dates are as follows:

May 1, 19X1	US$0.141
Jan. 1, 19X3	US$0.140
July 1, 19X3	US$0.146
Jan. 1, 19X4	US$0.150
July 1, 19X4	US$0.154
Oct. 1, 19X4	US$0.156
Dec. 31, 19X4	US$0.158

Required:

Translate the December 31, 19X4, trial balance of the Philippine branch into U.S. dollars.

SOLUTION

	Trial Balance, ₱ Dr.	Trial Balance, ₱ Cr.	Exchange Rate Code	Exchange Rate Rate	Trial Balance, US$ Dr.	Trial Balance, US$ Cr.
Cash	167,000		C	0.158	26,386	
Accounts Receivable	194,000		C	0.158	30,652	
Merchandise	170,000		A	0.157	26,690	
Equipment:						
May 1, 19X1	240,000		H	0.140	33,600	
July 1, 19X3	100,000		J	0.146	14,600	
Accumulated Depreciation		88,000*	H	0.140		12,320
		15,000*	J	0.146		2,190
Vouchers Payable		112,000	C	0.158		17,696
Other Current Liabilities		56,000	C	0.158		8,848
Capital Stock		400,000	H	0.140		56,000
					131,928	97,054
Retained Earnings		200,000	S			34,874
	871,000	871,000			131,928	131,928

Code: A—Appropriate weighted average.
  C—Current rate at balance sheet date.
  H—Rate on date of acquisition of investment by parent.
  J—Rate on date of acquisition of equipment.
  S—Amount necessary to balance converted trial balance. (*Note*: This is the best that can be done with the limited data.)

*Cost of Equipment	₱240,000	₱100,000

Accumulated Depreciation:		
19X1	₱16,000	
19X2	24,000	
19X3	24,000	₱ 5,000
19X4	24,000	10,000
Totals	₱88,000	₱15,000

Examination III

Chapters 13 and 14

1   On November 1, 19X2 the Lowe Corporation, a United States company, purchased 100,000 Swiss francs (SwF) for delivery in 90 days. Exchange rates for the Swiss franc on selected dates in the years 19X2 and 19X3 were as follows:

Rate	Nov. 1, 19X2	Dec. 31, 19X2	Jan. 30, 19X3
Spot	US$0.475	US$0.4775	US$0.480
Forward:			
30-day futures	US$0.480	US$0.484	US$0.483
90-day futures	US$0.485	US$0.490	US$0.486
180-day futures	US$0.510	US$0.4795	US$0.487

Required:

Write all necessary journal entries for a forward exchange contract on the books of Lowe Corporation from November 1, 19X2 to January 30, 19X3 under each of the following assumptions:

(a) The forward contract is a speculation in foreign currency.

(b) The forward contract is a hedge against an exposed net liability position of the Lowe Corporation's Geneva branch.

(c) The forward contract is a hedge of an identifiable foreign currency commitment as defined in FASB Statement No. 8.

2   The Chadwick Corporation, located in San Francisco, established a branch in Acapulco, Mexico on July 1, 19X1. Merchandise is shipped from the home office and all receipts are deposited in a Mexican bank account that can be drawn against only by the home office. All fixed assets are carried on the home office books.

The branch makes disbursements from an imprest fund that is reimbursed by the home office as needed. The transactions during July 19X1 are as follows:

(a) The home office forwarded US$10,000 to the branch for a working fund. The peso was worth US$0.040.

(b) Merchandise that cost the home office US$4,000 was shipped and billed to the branch at US$5,000. The peso was worth US$0.042.

(c) The branch purchased merchandise locally for Mex$45,000. The exchange rate was US$0.043.

(d) Rent of 2,000 pesos for July was paid by the branch. The exchange rate was US$0.040.

(e) Fixed assets were purchased by the branch for Mex$100,000, which was paid for by a 60-day note. The exchange rate was US$0.045.

(f) The branch sold merchandise on open account for Mex$35,000 pesos; the cost was Mex$21,000. The exchange rate was US$0.044.

(g) The branch collected Mex$25,000 from customers. This was immediately transferred to a United States bank by the home office. The exchange rate was US$0.040.

(h) Operating expenses paid by the branch amounted to Mex$15,000. The exchange rate was US$0.041.

(*i*) The imprest fund at the branch was reduced by Mex$125,000. The exchange rate was US$0.044.

(*j*) At the end of the month the home office informed the branch that the operating expenses paid by the home office amounted to US$2,000.   The exchange rate was US$0.0445.

Required:

Write the necessary journal entries for the month on the home office and branch books.

3   The Gabriel Corporation owns 83 percent of a foreign subsidiary which has plant and equipment that cost 3,600,000 zaps (local currency units) as of December 31, 19X8. Of this amount, 2,400,000 zaps were acquired in 19X6, when the rate of exchange was 1.6 zaps to $1, and 1,200,000 zaps were acquired in 19X7, when the rate of exchange was 1.8 zaps to $1. The rate of exchange in 19X8 was 1.92 zaps to $1.

Required:

If the foreign subsidiary calculates depreciation over a ten-year period using the straight-line method with no salvage value, how much depreciation expense should be charged in the income statement for 19X8?

(*a*) $180,000

(*b*) $187,500

(*c*) $200,000

(*d*) $216,667

4   The Hill Corporation has a subsidiary in Luxembourg. Selected balance sheets accounts of the subsidiary, which have been translated into U.S. dollars, are as follows:

	Translated at Current Rates	Translated at Historical Rates
Inventories Carried at Cost	$260,000	$264,000
Inventories Carried at Net Realizable Value	160,000	168,000
Marketable Equity Securities Carried at Cost	200,000	220,000
Marketable Equity Securities Carried at Current Market Price	240,000	250,000
	$860,000	$902,000

Required:

The proper amount to be included in the parent company's balance sheet is:

(*a*) $860,000

(*b*) $872,000

(*c*) $884,000

(*d*) $902,000

5   The Johnson Corporation owns 100 percent of the common stock of a foreign subsidiary. For the year 19X8, its net income was 6,000,000 ducats, which are appropriately translated into $1,000,000. On September 2, 19X8, when the rate of exchange was 5.7 ducats to $1, the foreign subsidiary paid a dividend to Johnson of 2,400,000 ducats. The dividend represented the net income of the foreign subsidiary for the first 6 months of 19X8. The weighted average of exchange rates during this 6-month period was 5.8 ducats to $1. The rate of exchange as of December 31, 19X8 was 5.9 ducats to $1.

Required:

The rate of exchange which should be used to translate the dividend to be utilized in year-end statements is:

(*a*) 5.7 ducats to $1

(*b*) 5.8 ducats to $1

(*c*) 5.9 ducats to $1

(*d*) 6.0 ducats to $1

6 On January 2, 19X7, the Orange Corporation of New York established a branch in Rotterdam by cabling US$10,000, which was immediately converted to guilders (f.) at the exchange rate of US$0.40. By December 31, the guilder had risen to US$0.43. On that date, the branch office account on the home office books showed a debit balance of US$39,875.

After the end of the year, the home office received a trial balance from the foreign branch, as of December 31, 19X7. This trial balance was expressed in Dutch guilders, and part of it is reproduced below.

	Trial Balance, f.		Translation to US$	
	Dr.	*Cr.*	*Rate*	*Amount*
Cash in Bank of Hague	90,000			
Accounts Receivable	197,000			
Merchandise Inventory (a)	80,400			
Equipment (b)	200,000			
Vouchers Payable		50,000		
Notes Payable (due 19X9)		300,000		
Home Office Control		99,600		
Sales		600,000		
Depreciation of Equipment	20,000			
Selling Expenses	45,000			

Additional data:

(*a*) Inventory on hand represents one-half of the latest shipment from the United States when the guilder was quoted at US$0.42.

(*b*) Equipment was purchased in The Netherlands when the guilder was equal to US$0.40.

Required:

Indicate the proper exchange rate to be used in translating the foreign currency amount *or* write in the appropriate United States dollar balance. (It is not necessary to do both.)

7 The Hennessy Corporation of Hempstead, New York operates a branch in Beaulieu, France. The trial balance of the branch at December 31, 19X2 in French francs (F) is included in the worksheet accompanying this problem.

The home office records showed the following balances at December 31, 19X2:

Remittances from Branch	$21,640
Shipments to Branch	$48,875
Branch office—Beaulieu	$59,100

Selected exchange rates for one French franc were as follows:

January 1	US$0.190
December 31	US$0.200
Weighted average	US$0.196

Inventories:

January 1	US$0.187
December 31	US$0.198

Plants assets:

	Rate	Francs
June 30, 19X1	US$0.180	60,000
September 15, 19X2	US$0.196	40,000

Required:

Complete the worksheet to convert the branch trial balance to U.S. dollars. (Depreciation is calculated on the straight-line method using estimated lives of five years.)

Hennessy Corporation, Beaulieu Branch
Trial Balance
December 31, 19X2

	Trial Balance, F		Exchange Rate		Trial Balance, US$	
	Dr.	Cr.	Code	Rate	Dr.	Cr.
Cash in Bank	39,000					
Accounts Receivable	180,000					
Allowance for Doubtful Accounts		3,000				
Remittances to Home Office	110,000					
Inventories—January 1	68,000					
Inventories—December 31	82,000	82,000				
Plant and Equipment	100,000					
Accumulated Depreciation		20,000				
Vouchers Payable		70,000				
Home Office		300,000				
Sales		540,000				
Shipments from Home Office	250,000					
Purchases	110,000					
Depreciation Expense	16,000					
Selling Expenses	25,000					
Administrative Expenses	35,000					
	1,015,000	1,015,000				
Exchange Gain or Loss						
Totals						

Answers to Examination III

1   (*a*) *Speculation.*

November 1, 19X2

Receivable for Currency Purchased		
(SwF100,000 × $0.485)	48,500	
Due to Exchange Broker		48,500

December 31, 19X2

Exchange Loss	100	
Receivable for Currency Purchased		
[SwF100,000($0.485 − $0.484)]		100

January 30, 19X3

Due to Exchange Broker	48,500	
Cash in Bank		48,500

Foreign Currency		
(SwF100,000 × $0.480)	48,000	
Exchange Loss		
[SwF100,000($0.484 − $0.480)]	400	
Receivable for Currency Purchased		
($48,500 − $100)		48,400

(*b*) *Hedge against exposed net liability position.*

November 1, 19X2

Foreign Money Due from F. E. Broker	47,500	
Deferred Contract Expense	1,000	
Liability to F. E. Broker		48,500

December 31, 19X2

Forward Contract Expense	667	
Deferred Contract Expense		
(60/90 × $1,000)		667

Foreign Money Due from F. E. Broker	250	
Exchange Gain		
SwF100,000 ($0.4775 − $0.4750)		250

January 30, 19X3

Forward Contract Expense	333	
Deferred Contract Expense		
(30/90 × $1,000)		333

Liability to F. E. Broker	48,500	
Cash in Bank		48,500

Foreign Currency		
(SwF100,000 × $0.48)	48,000	
Exchange Gain		250
Foreign Money Due from F. E. Broker		47,750

(c) *Hedge of an identifiable foreign currency commitment.*

November 1, 19X2

Forward Currency Purchased		
(SwF100,000 × $0.475)	47,500	
Premium on Futures Contract	1,000	
Due to F. E. Broker		
(SwF100,000 × $0.485)		48,500

December 31, 19X2

Forward Currency Purchased	250	
Deferred Exchange Gain		
[SwF100,000($0.4775 − $0.4750)]		250

January 30, 19X2

Forward Currency Purchased	250	
Deferred Exchange Gain		
[SwF100,000($0.4800 − $0.4775)]		250

Due to F. E. Broker	48,500	
Cash in Bank		48,500

Foreign Currency	48,000	
Foreign Currency Purchased		
($47,500 + $250 + $250)		48,000

Vouchers Payable	48,000	
Foreign Currency		48,000

Merchandise:		
($48,500 − $500 + $1,000)	49,000	
Deferred Exchange Gain	500	
Premium on Futures Contract		1,000
Vouchers Payable		48,500

2

The Chadwick Corporation
Journal Entries
July 19X1

Home Office Books—Dollars			Branch Office Books—Pesos		
(a)	Investment in Branch	10,000	Cash	250,000	
	Cash	10,000	Home Office (US$10,000 ÷ 0.04)		250,000
(b)	Investment in Branch	5,000	Inventories	119,048	
	Inventories	4,000	Home Office		
	Inventory Mark-up	1,000	(US$5,000 ÷ 0.042)		119,048
(c)			Purchases	45,000	
			Accounts Payable		45,000
(d)			Rent Expense	2,000	
			Cash		2,000
(e)	Fixed Assets	4,500	Home Office	100,000	
	Acapulco Branch (Mex$100,000 × 0.045)	4,500	Notes Payable		100,000
(f)			Accounts Receivable	35,000	
			Sales		35,000
			Cost of Goods Sold	21,000	
			Inventories		21,000
(g)	Cash	1,000	Home Office	25,000	
	Investment in Branch (Mex$25,000 × 0.04)	1,000	Accounts Receivable		25,000
(h)			Operating Expenses	15,000	
			Cash		15,000
			Home Office	125,000	
(i)	Cash	5,500			
	Investment in Branch		Cash		125,000
	(Mex$125,000 × 0.044)	5,500			
			Operating Expenses	44,944	
(j)	Investment in Branch	2,000	Home Office		
	Operating Expenses	2,000	(US$2,000 ÷ 0.0445)		44,944

3 (d)

4 (c)

5 (a)

6

	Trial Balance, f.		Translation to US$	
	Dr.	Cr.	Rate	Amount
Cash in Bank of Hague	90,000		0.430	
Accounts Receivable	197,000		0.430	
Merchandise Inventory	80,400		0.420	
Equipment	200,000		0.400	
Vouchers Payable		50,000	0.430	
Notes Payable (due 19X9)		300,000	0.430	
Home Office Control		99,600		39,875
Sales		600,000	0.415*	
Depreciation of Equipment	20,000		0.400	
Selling Expenses	45,000		0.415*	

*Average

7

Hennessy Corporation, Beaulieu Branch
Translation of Foreign Trial Balance
December 31, 19X2

	Trial Balance, F		Exchange Rate		Trial Balance, US$	
	Dr.	Cr.	Code	Rate	Dr.	Cr.
Cash in Bank	39,000		C	0.200	7,800	
Accounts Receivable	180,000		C	0.200	36,000	
Allowance for Doubtful Accounts		3,000	C	0.200		600
Remittances to Home Office	110,000		R		21,640	
Inventories—January 1	68,000		B	0.187	12,716	
Inventories—December 31	82,000	82,000	B	0.198	16,236	16,236
Plant and Equipment	60,000		H	0.180	10,800	
	40,000		H	0.196	7,840	
Accumulated Depreciation		18,000	H	0.180		3,240
		2,000	H	0.196		392
Vouchers Payable		70,000	C	0.200		14,000
Home Office		300,000	R			59,100
Sales		540,000	A	0.196		105,840
Shipments from Home Office	250,000		R		48,875	
Purchases	110,000		A	0.196	21,560	
Depreciation Expense	16,000		H	*	2,552	
Selling Expenses	25,000		A	0.196	4,900	
Administrative Expenses	35,000		A	0.196	6,860	
	1,015,000	1,015,000			197,779	199,408
Exchange Loss					1,629	
Totals					199,408	199,408

Code: A—Average rate.   H—Historical rate.   *(12,000 × 0.18) + (2,000 × 0.196)
          B—Rate when inventory was acquired.   R—Reciprocal amount.
          C—Current rate (end of year).

Index

Index

Catalog

If you are interested in a list of SCHAUM'S
OUTLINE SERIES send your name
and address, requesting your free catalog, to:

SCHAUM'S OUTLINE SERIES, Dept. C
McGRAW-HILL BOOK COMPANY
1221 Avenue of Americas
New York, N.Y. 10020